The New
Wider World
Foundation Edition
Second Edition

David Waugh and Tony Bushell

Nelson Thornes

First published in 2001 by:
Nelson Thornes Ltd
Delta Place
27 Bath Road
CHELTENHAM
GL53 7TH
United Kingdom

This edition published in 2005.

08 09 / 10 9 8 7 6 5 4

A catalogue record for this book is available from the British Library

ISBN 978-0-7487-9460-7

Page make-up by Hardlines and eMC Design
Illustrations by Hardlines, Richard Morris, Angela Lumley and Oxford Designers and Illustrators

Printed and bound in China by Midas Printing International Ltd

Acknowledgements

With thanks to the following for permission to reproduce photographs and other copyright material in this book:

Ace Pictures: 47B, 84B. Aerials Only Gallery: 46A. Airphotos: 31B, 55C. Tom Kidd/Alamy: 44B, Justin Kase/Alamy: 45D, Vicky Skeet/Alamy: 51Biii. Nick Gregory/Apex: 237C. Associated Press: 222A. BBC Education: 73D, 128A, 129E. Penni Bickle: 42A, 91D, 116A, 142Ai, 192A. Tony Bushell: 5C, 145D. CairnGorm Mountain Ltd: 251Biv. Caroline Malatesta: 224A. Corbis: 47D, Chinch Gryniewick/Ecoscene/Corbis: 50A, Picimpact/Corbis: 139, Beawiharta/Reuters/Corbis: 225C, Howard Davies/Corbis: 251Bii. James Davis: 27C, 137C, 141D, 142Aii, 253D, 257C. Eye Ubiquitous: 21B, 57C, 76D, 85D, 101C, 119Dii, 141C, 170B, 172B, 245B, 246A. Chris Fairclough Colour Library: 134C, 204B. Frank Lane Picture Agency: 81C bl, 107C. Geophoto: 56A, 87D, 135E, 202C, 203D. Geoscience Features: 81C br, 81C tr, 87D, 200A, 200B, 200C, 202A, 218A, 249B, 255C. Getty Images: 237E, Graeme Robertson/Getty Images: 237D. Holt Studios: 91C. Hutchison Library: 68B, 101D, 129D, 263C. Image Bank: 31C. Intermediate Technology: 125F, 126B all. Jon Arnold Images/Alamy: 138. Len Grant/Pictures of Manchester: 44A, 51B. London Aerial: 117B. MetroCentre, Newcastle: 62. Martin Mayer/Network: 45C. NHPA: 167C, 167D. Aidan O'Rourke: 119Di. Oxfam: 154B. Oxford Scientific Films: 92B. Photoair: 32, 33C. Photolibrary, Wales: 57Cii. Rex Features: 25C, 123D, 220B. Robert Harding Picture Library: 81C tl, 136A, 189D, 252A. Chris Rowley: 13C. Sheffield Local History: 41C. Still Pictures: 14A, 15C, 58A, 69D, 70B, 71E, 76A, 76B, 76C, 80A, 80B, 99Dii, 100A, 100B, 104B, 105C, 109C, 124D, 155D, 174B, 179D, 188A, 196A, 197B, 209D, 263B, Joerg Boething/Still Pictures: 150A, David Woodall/WW1/Still Pictures: 54B. Telegraph colour Library: 190C, 191D. Tony Stone: 108A. TopFoto: 71D, 86B, 120A. Trip Photography: 5B, 42B, 55D, 60B, 71D, 88C, 92A, 132C, 155E, 193B, 204C, 233C, 241B, 241C, 257D. David Waugh: 12A, 32A, 103F, 195B, 201D, 243C. www.walkingbritain: 251B. www.buyimage.co.uk: 53C. www.virtualbrum.co.uk: 51Bii.

The maps in Figures 37C and 250A are reproduced by permission of Ordnance Survey on behalf of HMSO. © Crown copyright 2005. All rights reserved. Ordnance Survey Licence number 100017284.

Every effort has been made to contact copyright holders. The publishers apologise to anyone whose rights have been inadvertently overlooked, and will be happy to rectify any errors or omissions.

CONTENTS

1 Population 4

2 Migration 18

3 Settlement and urban growth 30

4 Urban change 50

5 Urbanisation in developing countries 64

6 Employment structures 76

7 Farming 80

8 Energy resources 98

9 Industry 112

10 Tourism 132

11 World development and interdependence 148

12 Britain's weather and climate 160

13 World climate 170

14 Ecosystems 186

15 Rocks and soils 200

16 Plate tectonics 212

17 Drainage basins and rivers 228

18 Glaciation and coasts 246

Glossary 266

Index 271

1 POPULATION

Distribution and density

During 1998 the population of the world passed the 6,000 million mark. But where do all of these people live?

Map **A** below is a **population distribution** map. It shows how these 6,000 million people are spread out across the Earth's surface. Notice that the distribution is uneven. Some places are very crowded whilst others have hardly any people living in them. Look at Europe, for example. It is covered by many dots and is crowded. Australia, on the other hand, has only a few dots and in places is almost empty.

Population density is a measure of how crowded a place is. It is worked out by dividing the total population of a place by its area. Population density is usually given as the number of people per square kilometre (km^2). Europe has 51 people per km^2, Australia 2 per km^2 and London 4,482 per km^2.

> Places with few people and a low population density are said to be **sparsely populated.**

> Places that are crowded and have a high population density are said to be **densely populated.**

 World population distribution

Northern Canada
- Too cold for people.
- Frozen ground makes settlement and communications difficult.
- Poor, thin soil unsuitable for crops.
Sparsely populated

Europe
- Low-lying and gently sloping.
- Pleasant climate.
- Good water supply and soil for farming.
- Easy communications and many resources for industry.
Densely populated

Himalayan mountains
- Too cold for people.
- Steep slopes are bad for settlement and communications.
- Poor, thin soil unsuitable for crops.
Sparsely populated

1 dot represents 100,000 people

Amazon rainforest
- Too hot and wet for people.
- Dense forest makes settlement and communications difficult.
Sparsely populated

Bangladesh
- Low-lying and flat.
- Hot and wet with rich, fertile soil makes ideal farming conditions.
Densely populated

Central Australia
- Too hot and dry for people.
- Too dry and too little soil for crops to grow.
Sparsely populated

There are many reasons for the population distribution shown on map **A**. Some of these reasons encourage people to live in an area and are called **positive factors**. They create high population densities such as in Europe. Other reasons discourage people and are called **negative factors**. They result in low population densities such as in Australia.

Both the positive and negative factors can be described as either **physical factors** or **human factors**.

Physical factors are natural and part of the environment.
They include relief, climate, vegetation, soils, natural resources and water supply.

Human factors are made by people.
They include roads, factories, government investment, improved housing, education and healthcare.

Densely populated (positive factors)

- Pleasant climate
- Flat or gently sloping land
- Good soil for growing crops
- Open grassland for animals
- Good food supply
- Good water supply
- Money available for investment
- Good roads, railways, ports, etc.
- Natural resources for industry
- Industry and jobs

Sparsely populated (negative factors)

- Too hot or too cold
- Too wet or too dry
- Steep slopes
- Poor soils for farming
- Dense forest
- Poor water supply
- Few natural resources
- Poor transport links
- Little industry and few jobs
- Lack of investment

Population growth

Graph **A** shows that the growth in world population was slow but steady until the early 19th century. Since then it has grown at a much faster rate. Estimates suggest that, at present, it is growing by just over 90 million people each year.

Population growth has not been even throughout the world. It is more rapid in some countries than in others. As graph **A** also shows, the fastest growth has been in the world's poorer countries. Growth in the richer countries is now very slow. Some nations in north-west Europe even have a zero population growth. That means neither an increase nor a decrease.

A World population growth

[Graph showing world population growth from 1750 to 2150, with y-axis "Population in millions" from 0 to 12,000, and x-axis "Year". Labels include: Estimate, POORER COUNTRIES, TOTAL WORLD POPULATION, 6,000 million, 1998, Estimate, RICHER COUNTRIES, Slow increase, More rapid increase, Population explosion, Slow-down of growth.]

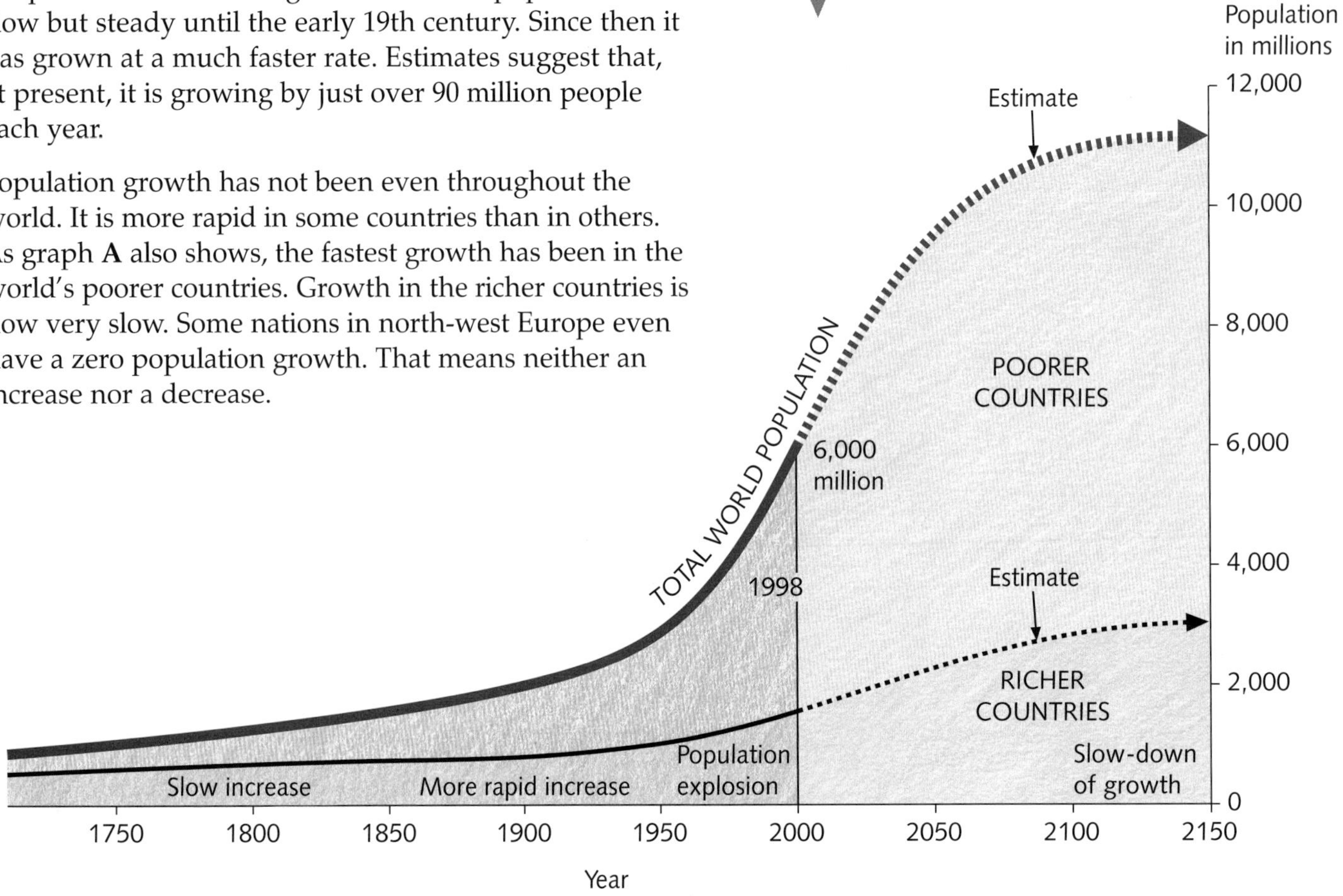

Population change

This depends mainly on the **natural increase** (or decrease), which is the difference between the birth rate and the death rate. The **birth rate** is the average number of births per 1,000 people. The **death rate** is the average number of deaths per 1,000 people.

Diagrams **B**, **C** and **D** below show how the balance between births and deaths affects population growth.

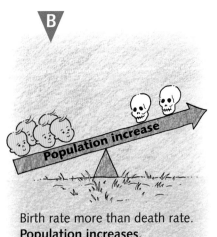

Birth rate more than death rate.
Population increases.

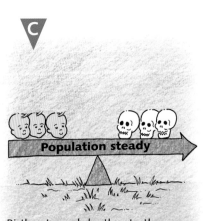

Birth rate and death rate the same.
Population stays the same.

Death rate more than birth rate.
Population decreases.

Stage	1 High stationary	2 Early expanding	3 Late expanding	4 Low stationary

Birth and death rates (per 1,000 people per year)
40 – 30 – 20 – 10 – 0 –

Birth rate
Death rate
Natural increase
Total population

Examples	A few remote groups	Egypt, Kenya, India	Brazil	USA, Japan, France, UK
Birth rate	High	High	Falling	Low
Death rate	High	Falls rapidly	Falls more slowly	Low
Natural increase	Stable or slow increase	Very rapid increase	Increase slows down	Steady or slow increase
Reasons for changes in birth rate	Many children needed for farming. Many children die at an early age. Religious/social encouragement. No family planning.		Improved medical care and diet. Fewer children needed.	Family planning. Good health. Later marriages
Reasons for changes in death rate	Disease, famine. Poor medical knowledge, so many children die.	Improvements in medical care, water supply and sanitation. Fewer children die.		Good healthcare Reliable food supply

 The demographic transition model

Population change in developing and developed countries

Diagram **E** above is called the **demographic transition model**. It shows how changes in birth and death rates can affect population growth. It also identifies four distinct stages of growth. These stages, it suggests, are linked to economic growth.

Graph **F** shows Stage 2 of the model. Many of the world's poorer countries are at this stage, with high birth rates and falling death rates. This results in rapid population growth.

Graph **G** shows Stage 4 of the model. This is more typical of the world's richer countries. Here there are low birth rates and low death rates. In this case population growth is very slow.

Some people even suggest a fifth stage to the model, with death rates greater than birth rates. This would produce a decrease in population, as shown in diagram **D**.

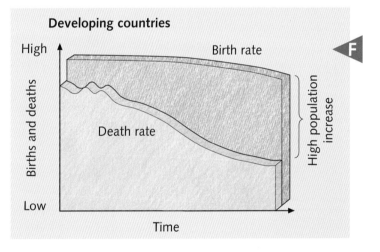

Developing countries F

High / Low
Births and deaths
Birth rate
Death rate
High population increase
Time

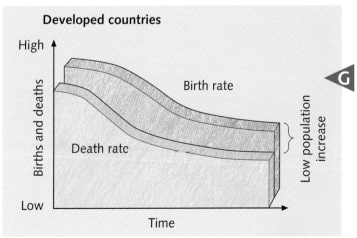

Developed countries G

High / Low
Births and deaths
Birth rate
Death rate
Low population increase
Time

Population structures

The rate of natural increase, birth rate, death rate and life expectancy all affect the **population structure** of a country. This population structure can be shown as a **population pyramid** or, as it is sometimes known, an **age–sex pyramid**. Where possible, information for a population pyramid is collected in a census. In the United Kingdom, this happens every ten years.

Look at the population pyramids for the United Kingdom and Kenya. Notice how different they are. The United Kingdom has a narrow shape whilst Kenya is more squat with a narrow top and broad base. Look carefully at the reasons for these differences.

Population pyramids show:
- the population of a country or region divided into five-year age groups.
- the percentage of people in each of these age groups
- the percentage of males and females in each age group
- changes in birth rate, death rate, life expectancy and infant mortality
- the proportion of elderly and young people who are dependent upon those of a working age – the economically active
- the effects of people migrating into or out of the country or region.

Life expectancy is the average number of years a person can expect to live.

Infant mortality is the average number of children per 1,000 born alive, who die before the age of one year.

Dependents are those people who rely upon others of working age.

Economically active are those people who work and receive a wage.

A   Population pyramid: United Kingdom 2003

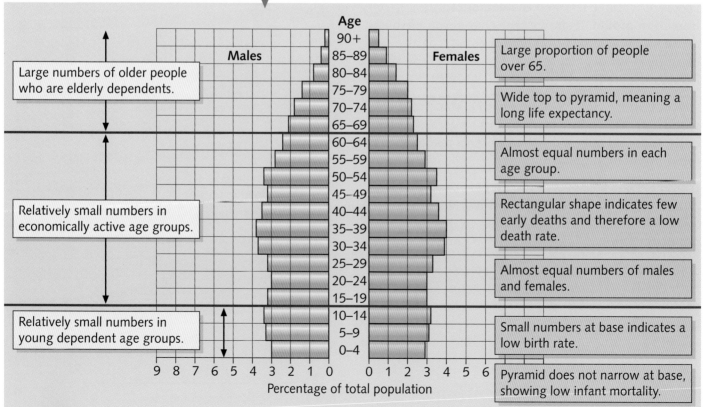

Large numbers of older people who are elderly dependents.

Relatively small numbers in economically active age groups.

Relatively small numbers in young dependent age groups.

Large proportion of people over 65.

Wide top to pyramid, meaning a long life expectancy.

Almost equal numbers in each age group.

Rectangular shape indicates few early deaths and therefore a low death rate.

Almost equal numbers of males and females.

Small numbers at base indicates a low birth rate.

Pyramid does not narrow at base, showing low infant mortality.

Percentage of total population

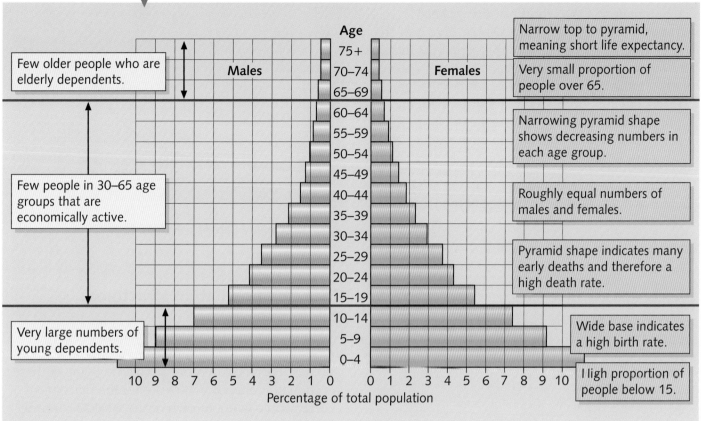

Age

Few older people who are elderly dependents.

Males | 75+ | Females
70–74
65–69

Narrow top to pyramid, meaning short life expectancy.

Very small proportion of people over 65.

60–64
55–59
50–54
45–49

Narrowing pyramid shape shows decreasing numbers in each age group.

Few people in 30–65 age groups that are economically active.

40–44
35–39
30–34

Roughly equal numbers of males and females.

25–29
20–24
15–19

Pyramid shape indicates many early deaths and therefore a high death rate.

Very large numbers of young dependents.

10–14
5–9
0–4

Wide base indicates a high birth rate.

High proportion of people below 15.

10 9 8 7 6 5 4 3 2 1 0   0 1 2 3 4 5 6 7 8 9 10
Percentage of total population

Population pyramids are useful because they enable comparisons to be made between countries, and help to forecast future trends. This can help a country identify problems and plan for the future. For example, a growth in the elderly population may mean more residential homes are needed. On the other hand, an increase in younger people may mean more schools will be required.

There are four main types of population pyramid. As with the demographic transition model (page 7), each type represents a different stage of economic development. These stages are shown in the graphs below, and can easily be identified by their shape.

C Changing population structures

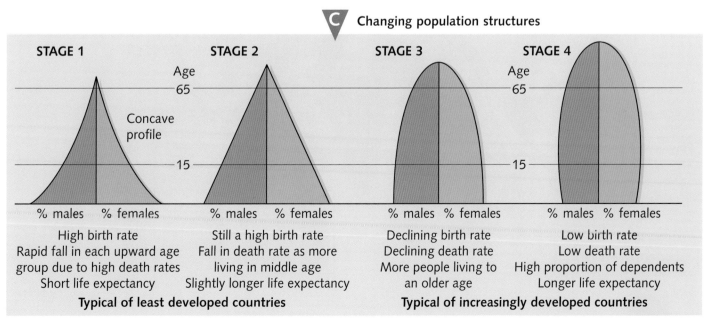

| STAGE 1 | STAGE 2 | STAGE 3 | STAGE 4 |

Age 65

Concave profile

15

% males   % females | % males   % females | % males   % females | % males   % females

High birth rate
Rapid fall in each upward age group due to high death rates
Short life expectancy

Still a high birth rate
Fall in death rate as more living in middle age
Slightly longer life expectancy

Declining birth rate
Declining death rate
More people living to an older age

Low birth rate
Low death rate
High proportion of dependents
Longer life expectancy

Typical of least developed countries | | **Typical of increasingly developed countries**

Population trends

The population of the world has always been increasing, and there are more people alive now than ever before. The problem with this is that the increase is now very rapid. Up to the year 1900, it had taken nearly a million years for the world's population to reach 2 billion. In the 100 years since then, the population has increased by a further 4 billion, and in September 1999 was estimated to have reached the 6 billion mark.

This rapid growth in population is a concern to many people, as it will lead to a shortage of food and other basic needs.

Estimating future trends, however, is very difficult. Until recently, forecasters predicted that the population growth rate would continue to increase and that by the year 2050 population would have doubled again to nearly 12 billion. Evidence now suggests that population growth has already begun to slow down and will eventually decline after peaking in 2080 at about 10.6 billion.

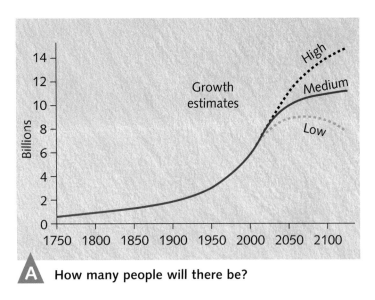

A How many people will there be?

Changing population structures
Children under 15

Not only does total population change but the number of people in different age groups also changes. This too can cause problems. Some of these are shown on map **B**, which shows the percentage of young people living in each of the world's countries.

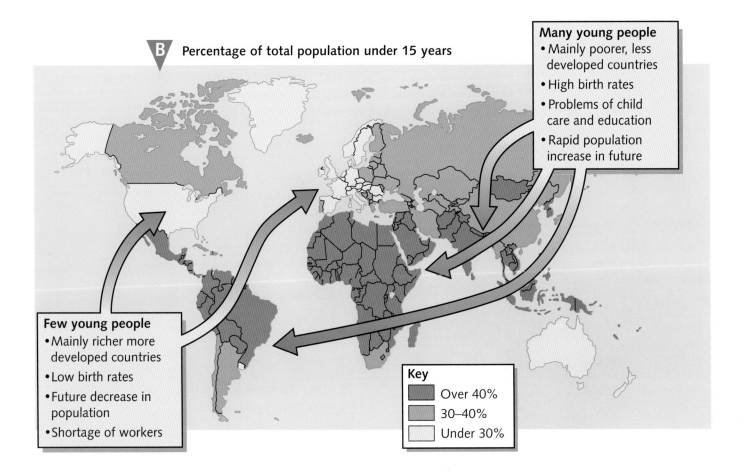

B Percentage of total population under 15 years

Many young people
- Mainly poorer, less developed countries
- High birth rates
- Problems of child care and education
- Rapid population increase in future

Few young people
- Mainly richer more developed countries
- Low birth rates
- Future decrease in population
- Shortage of workers

Key
- Over 40%
- 30–40%
- Under 30%

People aged over 65

Higher living standards and better health care mean that people are living longer. Today the average life expectancy of people living in North America and Europe exceeds 73 years, compared with just 67 in the early 1950s.

Indeed in most of the richer, more developed countries of the world, life expectancy continues to rise quickly. For these countries, nearly one in four of the population will be aged 65 and over by the year 2020. For the world as a whole this figure will be one in five, which means that a high and worrying proportion of the world's population will be dependent on younger people.

This process and the problems it causes are shown in diagram **D** below.

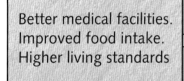

| Better medical facilities. Improved food intake. Higher living standards | → | Increased life expectancy | → | More people 65 and over | → | More money needed for pensions, health-care, residential homes and social services |

D

Overpopulation

We know that some places in the world are already very crowded. If the population of these places is also growing very quickly, it can be difficult to provide for everyone's needs. Places like this are said to be **overpopulated.**

Overpopulation is when the resources of an area cannot support the people living there. In this case **resources** are things that people need, like food, water, good soil and building materials.

Overpopulation happens mainly in the poorer countries of the world. This makes it difficult for these places to develop and improve their standard of living and quality of life.

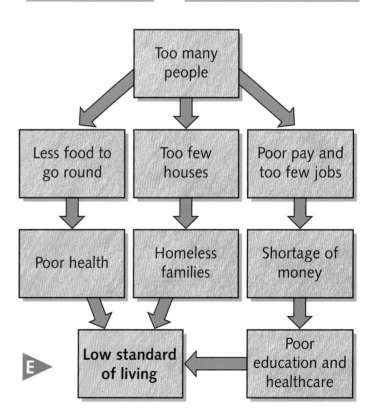

E

Too many people
→ Less food to go round → Poor health → Low standard of living
→ Too few houses → Homeless families → Low standard of living
→ Poor pay and too few jobs → Shortage of money → Poor education and healthcare → Low standard of living

11

China's one child policy

During the mid-20th century the Chinese were encouraged to have large families. The belief was that 'a large population gives a strong nation'. The result was a population growth of 55 million every three years. This is about the same as the UK's total population.

During the 1970s, China became increasingly concerned about this rapid growth rate. There were signs that the country was becoming **overpopulated** as it became more and more difficult to provide for everyone's needs.

In 1979 it was decided to try to control and reduce population growth. To do this the Chinese government introduced the **one child per family policy** and set a minimum age for marriage.

- Couples had to seek permission from the state to be married and again before having a child.
- Those who conformed were given free education, priority housing and family benefits.
- Those who did not were deprived of benefits and fined heavily.
- Women who became pregnant a second time were forced to have an abortion and persistent offenders were 'offered' sterilisation.

By 1999 the state claimed that China's population was an estimated 230 million less than it would have been had the one child policy not been introduced. Feeling confident that population growth was under control, the authorities made changes to the policy. These changes included:

- allowing all families in rural areas to have two children
- offering women a wider choice in methods of contraception
- allowing the option of voluntary family planning in 300 trial districts.

A   A one child family in Kunming, China

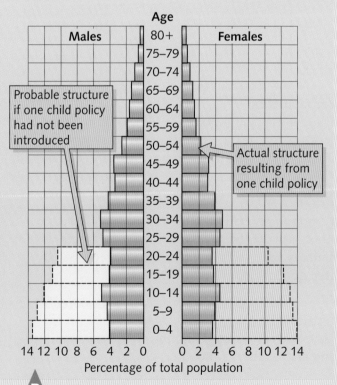

B   Population structure for China, 2000

China's ageing population

At present, China is more concerned with its **ageing population** than it is with population growth or the number of children.

China's ageing population results from an increase in **life expectancy**. Life expectancy increased from 40 years in 1950 to 70 years in 2000. In other words, a person born in 2000 could expect to live 30 years longer than someone born 50 years earlier.

Predictions suggest that the proportion of Chinese aged 65 and over will increase from 10% in 2000 to 22% by 2030. This will result in China having a very large number of **elderly dependents**. As explained on page 8, elderly dependents are those people who rely on support from others of a working age.

In 1998, the United Nations began to describe the group of people aged 80 years and over as the **oldest old**. At that time, the Chinese had 10.5 million people in that age group. As drawing **D** shows, by 2050 it can expect to have 100 million people aged 80 or more. That is almost twice the present-day population of the UK.

These changes will have a huge impact on Chinese society. It means, for example, that there must be an urgent reform in the provision of:
- pensions – there are none at present for the majority of the population
- healthcare – the need for more doctors, nurses and medical provisions
- other needs – including residential homes for the elderly, and social services.

> Ageing population is the increase in the proportion of elderly people in a country or area.

> The **oldest old** refers to the increasing number of people aged 80 years and over.

Places

C   Ageing Chinese

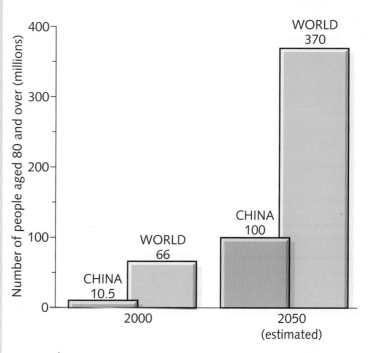

D   Population change for the 'oldest old' age group

Population: Brazil

Distribution and density

In 2003 Brazil had a population of 182 million, which is more than three times that of the United Kingdom. Map **B** below shows how these people are spread out across the country.

Notice that the distribution is uneven. Some places are crowded whilst others are almost empty. Look carefully, however, and you should be able to identify a clear pattern. Most Brazilians – over 90% of them – live near to the coast, mainly in the south-east of the country. Going inland and towards the north and west, the population decreases rapidly. Some of the most remote areas have virtually no people at all.

① South-east

This area is the most densely populated. It has a pleasant climate, reliable rainfall, good soils and plenty of raw materials. The region has the best transport system in Brazil and the greatest number of services, and receives most government help. Farming is very successful and industrial growth, particularly around the major towns, has provided many jobs.

② North-east

Away from the coast, this region is sparsely populated. Here the weather is drier than in the south-east, and poor, thin soils make farming difficult. There are few industries because there is a shortage of natural resources and poor transport links. With these largely negative factors, the region cannot support many people.

A São Paulo is the world's second largest city. It is located in Brazil's densely populated south-east region.

B Population distribution map of Brazil

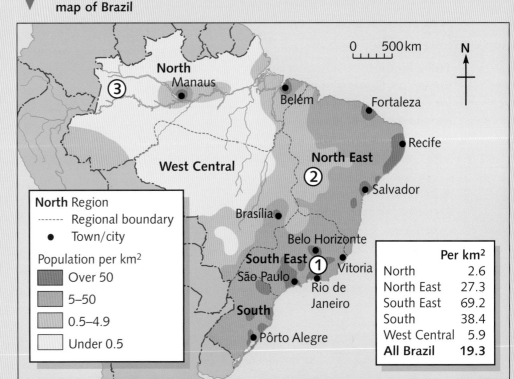

0   500 km   N

North Region
------- Regional boundary
• Town/city

Population per km²
- Over 50
- 5–50
- 0.5–4.9
- Under 0.5

	Per km²
North	2.6
North East	27.3
South East	69.2
South	38.4
West Central	5.9
All Brazil	**19.3**

③ North-west

This is Amazonia, the most sparsely populated region in Brazil. The area is covered in tropical rainforest, and is hot, wet and unhealthy. Soils are poor and most areas lack resources. Transport through the forest is difficult and much of the region lacks basic services such as health care, education and electricity. Life here is difficult, and apart from Manaus – the only major city – few people can live in the region.

C The Amazon rainforest is the largest in the world. It is Brazil's most sparsely populated region.

Structure

Figures suggest that Brazil has reached Stage 3 of the demographic transition model described on page 7. However, parts of the less well-developed interior are likely to be at an earlier stage than that. The Amazon Indians, for example, are still at Stage 1 with high birth rates, high death rates and a stable or slow natural increase.

Trends

Brazil's population structure is undergoing change as the country moves into Stage 3. Already population growth has slowed as birth rates have fallen due to improved medical care and the introduction of family planning. Improved conditions are also beginning to lengthen life expectancy and increase the number of elderly dependents in the country.

In some places, though, there has been little change and large families are still common. In the north, for example, the average family has 7 children and a quarter of them have 10 or more. It is not unusual for some mothers to be pregnant up to 16 times.

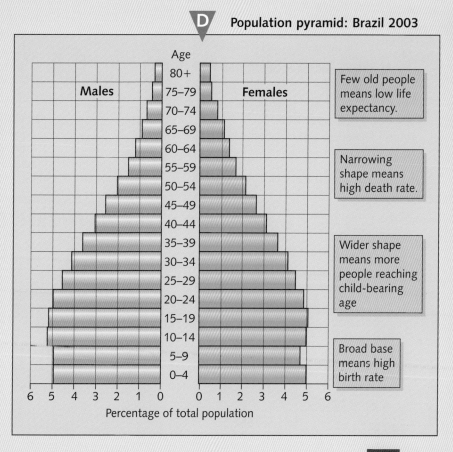

D Population pyramid: Brazil 2003

Few old people means low life expectancy.

Narrowing shape means high death rate.

Wider shape means more people reaching child-bearing age

Broad base means high birth rate

(Pages 4 and 5)

As a geographer you should be building up your geographical vocabulary. Write down the meaning of the following terms:
a) population distribution
b) population density
c) sparsely populated
d) densely populated
e) positive factors
f) negative factors
g) physical factors
h) human factors.

(Pages 4 and 5)

a) Write down three examples of physical conditions that make a place sparsely populated.
b) Write down three examples of human factors that make a place densely populated.

(Pages 6 and 7)

Write down the meaning of the following terms:
a) birth rate
b) death rate
c) natural increase.

(Pages 6 and 7)

a) What does the demographic transition model show?
b) Describe the population growth in the poorer countries. Suggest a reason for this.
c) Describe the population growth in the richer countries. Suggest a reason for this.

 (Pages 6 and 7)

a) Make a larger copy of the graph below.
b) Describe the population growth at A, B, C and D.
c) Why is 'explosion' a good description of world population changes since 1950?

 (Pages 8 and 9)

Give the meaning of the following terms:
a) life expectancy
b) infant mortality
c) dependents
d) economically active.

 (Pages 8 and 9)

Draw a diagram like the one below to show six things that population pyramids show.

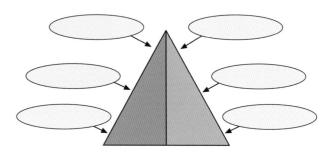

 (Pages 8 and 9)

a) Draw a simple sketch of a population pyramid for a developed country like the United Kingdom.
b) Add three labels to show the main features of the base, middle and top of the pyramid.

 (Pages 10 and 11)

a) Give two reasons why many people now live longer than they did in the past.
b) Write out the following in the correct order to show the causes and effects of longer life expectancy:

More money needed for care

Better living conditions

People live longer

More elderly people

 (Pages 14 and 15)

a) Name a part of Brazil that is densely populated. Suggest reasons for this dense population.
b) Name a part of Brazil that is sparsely populated. Suggest reasons for this sparse population.

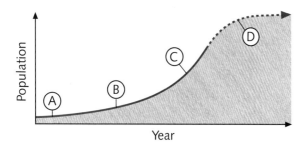

EXAMINATION QUESTIONS

1 (Pages 4, 5, 14 and 15)

a) From map **A**, give the location of two areas with a population density of over 100 inhabitants per km². **(2)**

b) Suggest two reasons why some areas of the world have a high population density. **(2)**

c) From map **A**, give the location of two areas with a low population density. **(2)**

d) Suggest two reasons why some areas of the world have a low population density. **(2)**

e) Describe the distribution of population in a named country that you have studied. **(4)**

f) Explain how the population is changing in a named country that you have studied. **(4)**

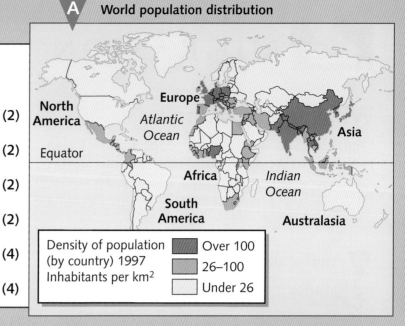

A World population distribution

Density of population (by country) 1997 Inhabitants per km²
- Over 100
- 26–100
- Under 26

2 (Pages 6 and 7)

Diagram **B** shows the demographic transition model. There are four stages, marked 1, 2, 3 and 4.

a) Which stage has high birth rates and death rates? **(1)**

b) Which stage has low birth rates and death rates? **(1)**

c) In which two stages will population increase? Give a reason for this. **(3)**

d) Which stage is typical of the world's richer countries? Give a reason for your answer. **(3)**

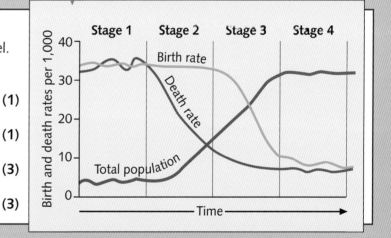

B The demographic transition model

3 (Pages 8 and 9)

Based on the evidence of the population pyramid, which of the following are correct statements for the USA?

■ 4% of males are aged 0–4
■ The largest age group is 25–29.
■ The smallest age group is 5–9.
■ Females tend to live longer than males.
■ Many people die at an early age.
■ There is a high life expectancy.
■ There is low infant mortality.
■ Birth rates are high.
■ There is a low death rate.
■ There are large numbers of elderly dependents.
(10)

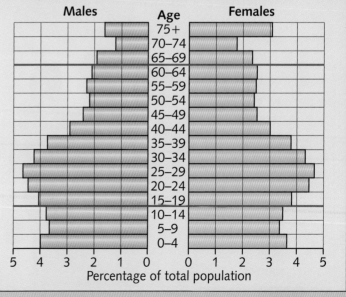

C Population pyramid for the USA

2 MIGRATION

What is migration?

Migration is the movement of people from one place to another to live or to work. Sometimes this movement may only be a short distance to a better house in the next street or nearby town. Other migrations may involve longer distances, when a family moves to a different region or even another country.

Migrations also vary in length of time. Some people may move for just a few months or years, whilst others can move permanently. Some examples of different types of migration are shown below.

 A Types of migration

Type	Description	Example
Internal	Within a small area	Family move to a bigger house on the same side of Birmingham, as their children grow up.
Rural-to-urban	From the countryside to the towns or cities	Young farmer in Cumbria leaves home and moves into Manchester to work in a factory.
Urban-to-rural	From the towns into the countryside	Wealthy family move out of the city into a larger house in a nearby village.
Regional	From one part of the country to another	Young female office worker moves from Leeds to London where she is promoted to manager.
International	From one country to another	British scientist moves to California to work on a state-funded research project.
Short-term	For several weeks or months	College student takes up holiday work in Mediterranean resort.
Long-term	For several years	Unemployed young man from Turkey migrates to Germany in search of work.

Voluntary migration is when people choose to move. This is usually because of the 'pull' or attraction of a better quality of life elsewhere.

Reasons include:
- to find a job or earn a higher salary
- to live in a better climate, especially in retirement
- to have improved amenities such as hospitals, schools and entertainment
- to be with friends and relatives

B **Forced migration** is when people have no choice and are made to move. In this case they are 'pushed' out of their homes.

Reasons include:
- religious or political persecution
- natural disasters such as floods or volcanic eruptions
- lack of food due to crop failure
- wars creating large numbers of refugees
- racial discrimination

Refugees

Refugees are people who have been forced to leave their homes because of persecution, wars, or other hazards such as famine or floods. In the mid-1990s the UN estimated that there were 15 million refugees in the world, half of whom had been forced to leave their country.

These large numbers of people, who have usually left all of their personal possessions behind, live in extreme poverty and have virtually no prospects. They are unlikely ever to return to their homeland and often live in large refugee camps where they need food, water and shelter. This has to be provided by the host country or by charities such as the Red Cross.

Over half of the world's refugee population are children, and most of the adults are women. Over 80% are from developing countries, where the shortage of money makes the problem even greater.

C

Some recent refugee movements

- 6 million Afghans forced by war to leave for neighbouring Pakistan and Iran.

- 1.5 million Ethiopians, Sudanese and Somalis driven from their homes in East Africa by drought, famine and civil war.

- The 1994 Rwandan civil war caused 1.5 million people to become refugees. One million crossed into Congo to live in refugee camps. An estimated 300,000 died of cholera and starvation.

- Half a million Chechens forced out of their capital Grozny, by an army of 100,000 Russian troops, in 1999–2000.

D Growth of the world refugee problem

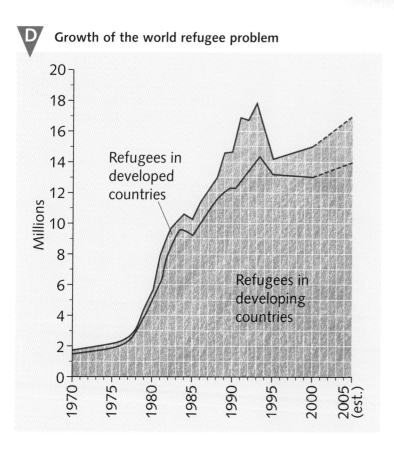

Refugees in developed countries

Refugees in developing countries

E A Rwandan refugee camp

Migration into the UK

Migrants have been arriving in Britain from other countries for more than 2,000 years. Some have come as invaders, some to escape problems in their own countries, and some simply to find jobs and enjoy a better way of life.

In fact, the UK population is made up of immigrants, and has always been a country of mixed races and cultures. The majority of UK residents are descended from Romans, Vikings, Angles, Saxons and Normans. The Irish have also settled in Britain for several centuries, while many other Europeans migrated here both during and after the Second World War.

Some of the largest groups of immigrants are from countries that were once part of the British Empire, like India, Pakistan and the West Indies. After the war there were serious labour shortages in Britain. The government of the time invited people from these countries to come and fill job vacancies. Almost 1 million responded to the call.

Most immigrants settled permanently in Britain. They had families, and along with their descendants became UK citizens. Unfortunately, many were underskilled and were forced to take poorly paid jobs.

In recent years the government has tried to restrict and control the number of non-white immigrants entering Britain. Only those with specific jobs to go to, with descendants already in the country, or genuine refugees, are now allowed access.

A Uneven concentrations of ethnic groups

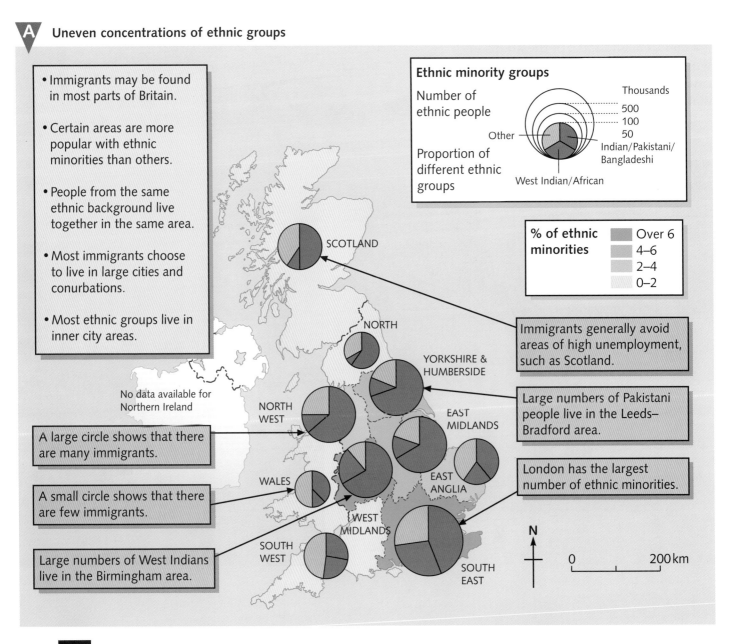

- Immigrants may be found in most parts of Britain.
- Certain areas are more popular with ethnic minorities than others.
- People from the same ethnic background live together in the same area.
- Most immigrants choose to live in large cities and conurbations.
- Most ethnic groups live in inner city areas.

Ethnic minority groups

Number of ethnic people

Proportion of different ethnic groups

Thousands
500
100
50

Other

Indian/Pakistani/Bangladeshi

West Indian/African

% of ethnic minorities
- Over 6
- 4–6
- 2–4
- 0–2

No data available for Northern Ireland

A large circle shows that there are many immigrants.

A small circle shows that there are few immigrants.

Large numbers of West Indians live in the Birmingham area.

SCOTLAND

NORTH

NORTH WEST

YORKSHIRE & HUMBERSIDE

EAST MIDLANDS

WALES

WEST MIDLANDS

SOUTH WEST

EAST ANGLIA

SOUTH EAST

Immigrants generally avoid areas of high unemployment, such as Scotland.

Large numbers of Pakistani people live in the Leeds–Bradford area.

London has the largest number of ethnic minorities.

N

0   200 km

Problems facing immigrants to Britain

The effect of migration into Britain has been considerable. It has caused an increase in numbers and altered the mix of people in the country. It has also produced a **multicultural society** where people with different beliefs and traditions live and work together.

Most people agree that this has added variety and interest to the UK. Unfortunately it has also caused problems, particularly for the immigrants themselves. Some of these are shown below.

DEFINITIONS

Multicultural – a society where people with different beliefs and traditions live and work together.

Ethnic minority – a small group of people of similar race, beliefs and traditions.

Discrimination – unfair treatment of a person or group.

Racial prejudice – the dislike and mistreatment of people from a different race.

Harassment – to trouble, torment and persistently annoy people.

Immigrant – a person who arrives in a country with the intention of living there.

B Problems facing immigrants to Britain

Difficulties with the English language, cultural difficulties and racial prejudices are major problems.

Many ethnic minorities live in overcrowded, poor-quality buildings which are cheap to buy or rent because they are in undesirable areas.

Places where ethnic minorities live have high crime rates. Violence, drug problems and muggings are a common feature.

Unemployment is often greater than 70%, and low expectations mean that immigrants develop few skills.

Many immigrants complain of police harassment. The resultant lack of trust leads to further tension.

Discrimination is common, and is considered by many to be the main reason for ethnic unhappiness.

Table **C** compares some features of white communities with those of black and Asian groups. Notice how different they are. These differences are called **inequalities**, and show that in terms of job qualifications and employment, black and Asian people in Britain are less fortunate than white people.

C

Group	% of England's population	% under 16	% over 65	% living in conur- bations	Average family size		% professional/ managerial		% semi and unskilled	Unemployed 16–29 years old	Without basic WC/hot water/bath
White 94.2	19.5	19.3	32	3.1	40	18	15	6			
Black and Asian	5.8	32.8	4.2	78	3.5 (Black) 5.9 (Asian)		14		37	25	28

Migration within the UK

Rural-to-urban migration

During the Industrial Revolution of the 19th century, many people moved from the countryside to towns and cities. This movement is called **rural-to-urban migration**. There were two main reasons for rural-to-urban migration:

1 **Push factors** forced people to leave the countryside, which caused **rural depopulation**.
2 **Pull factors** attracted people to the growing towns, which caused **urbanisation**.

The movement was greatest in the rapidly growing areas, which included:
- textile towns of Yorkshire and Lancashire
- coalfield towns of South Wales, north-east England and central Scotland (these places also produced iron and, later, steel)
- ports of London, Liverpool and Glasgow.

Regional migration

Between about 1930 and 1980 there was a steady drift of people from the north and west of Britain to the south-east of England. Map **A** below shows the change in population that this movement caused, and some of the reasons for it.

 Population change in the UK, 1961–81

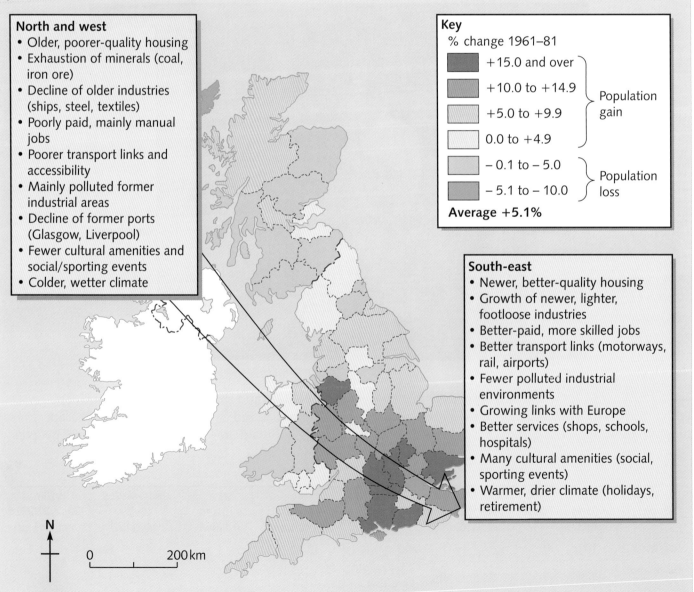

North and west
- Older, poorer-quality housing
- Exhaustion of minerals (coal, iron ore)
- Decline of older industries (ships, steel, textiles)
- Poorly paid, mainly manual jobs
- Poorer transport links and accessibility
- Mainly polluted former industrial areas
- Decline of former ports (Glasgow, Liverpool)
- Fewer cultural amenities and social/sporting events
- Colder, wetter climate

Key
% change 1961–81

+15.0 and over	⎫
+10.0 to +14.9	Population gain
+5.0 to +9.9	
0.0 to +4.9	⎭
– 0.1 to – 5.0	⎫ Population loss
– 5.1 to – 10.0	⎭

Average +5.1%

South-east
- Newer, better-quality housing
- Growth of newer, lighter, footloose industries
- Better-paid, more skilled jobs
- Better transport links (motorways, rail, airports)
- Fewer polluted industrial environments
- Growing links with Europe
- Better services (shops, schools, hospitals)
- Many cultural amenities (social, sporting events)
- Warmer, drier climate (holidays, retirement)

N

0   200 km

Counter-urbanisation

Since the 1980s there has been a movement out of the city and into the nearby countryside. This movement from urban areas into new towns and suburbanised villages in the rural areas is called **counter-urbanisation**. Who moves out, and the reasons for their movement, are shown below.

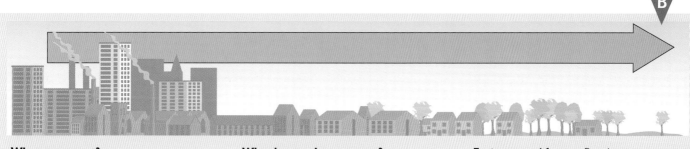

Who moves out?

- Those with higher incomes now capable of buying their own homes in suburbia.

- Those with higher skills and qualifications – especially moving to new towns.

- Parents with a young family wishing for gardens, open space and larger houses.

- Those able to commute to work in the city using public or private transport.

Why do people move out?

Employment. As industry has declined in inner city areas, it has relocated on edge-of-city sites or in smaller rural towns. People move for promotion, for better-paid jobs or simply to find work.

Housing. When people become wealthy they are likely to move from small terraced houses and high-rise flats in the inner city to larger, modern houses with better indoor amenities, garages and gardens.

Changing family status. People move as a result of an increase in family wealth or family size.

Environmental factors. People move away from the polluted and noisy city to live in rural areas where it is quieter and cleaner, and there is more open space.

Social factors. People may move out of cities due to problems with neighbours and ethnic groups. Other concerns include an above-average crime rate, vandalism and poorer educational facilities.

Cycle of change in London

Map **C** shows the outward movement of people from London. Notice that the greatest losses are from the inner city areas, often alongside the River Thames. Until the 1970s people moved from these areas to the suburbs. Since then, however, even the outer suburbs have lost population.

Very recently there has been a reversal in movement, with wealthy people returning to central London. Older, derelict property has been bought cheaply and transformed into expensive houses and flats, as in Islington, along the banks of the Thames and in the former Docklands.

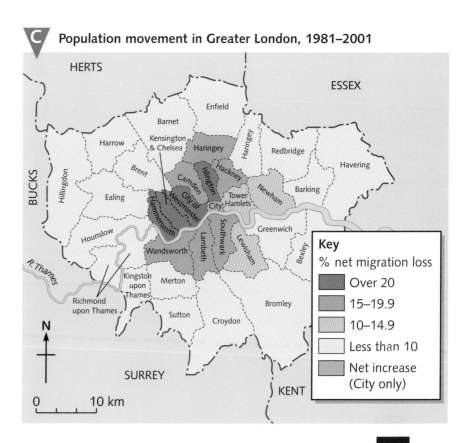

C Population movement in Greater London, 1981–2001

Key
% net migration loss
- Over 20
- 15–19.9
- 10–14.9
- Less than 10
- Net increase (City only)

Migrant workers

Turkish migrants into West Germany

In countries where there is a low standard of living and a shortage of jobs, groups of people often migrate to nearby, wealthier countries hoping to find work. One example is the movement of people from southern Europe and Turkey into what was then West Germany.

Like other West European countries, West Germany needed rebuilding when the Second World War ended in 1945. There were many more job vacancies than workers, so extra labour was needed. Later, as West Germany became increasingly wealthy, it attracted workers from the poorest parts of southern Europe and the Middle East.

Many of these migrants went into farming but soon turned to the better-paid jobs in factories and the construction industry. These jobs were not wanted by the Germans because they were dirty, unskilled, poorly paid and often demanded long and unsociable hours. By 1989 Germany had 4.5 million 'guest workers', accounting for some 7.4% of the total workforce.

Although the Turks were in full employment in the 1950s and 1960s, many found themselves out of work by the late 1980s. This was mainly due to a decline in Germany's manufacturing industry.

A **Origin and number of migrant workers to Germany**

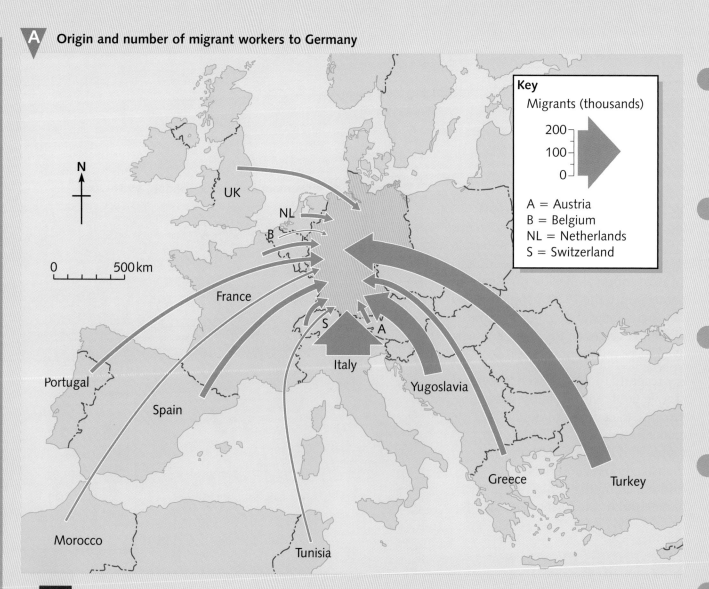

Key

Migrants (thousands)

200
100
0

A = Austria
B = Belgium
NL = Netherlands
S = Switzerland

The movement of migrant workers from one country to another can bring many benefits but can also cause problems. These can affect both of the countries involved: the country that has lost workers and the country that has received them. Some of the advantages and disadvantages for Turkey and Germany are shown in figure **B**.

B

Turkey – the country losing migrants

Advantages
- Reduces pressure on jobs and resources.
- Loses people of child-bearing age, so reduces birth rate.
- Migrants develop new skills which they may take back to Turkey.
- Some of the money earned in Germany is sent back to Turkey.

Disadvantages
- Turkey loses people in the working age groups.
- The people who leave are the ones most likely to have education and job skills.
- Most migrants are men, which causes a split in families and leaves the wife to bring up the children.
- Left with elderly population and so a high death rate.

Germany – receiver of migrants

Advantages
- Overcomes labour shortage.
- Dirty, unskilled jobs are done by immigrants.
- Immigrants are prepared to work long hours for a low salary.
- Cultural mix adds variety and interest to society.
- Many migrants are highly skilled and benefit the workforce.

Disadvantages
- Ethnic groups tend not to integrate which causes racial tension.
- May lead to the development of over-crowded, low-quality, slum accommodation.
- Can put pressure on jobs and lead to unemployment for local people.
- Development of religious and cultural traditions can cause resentment among Germans.

Places

Germany has tried to reduce the problems caused by migrant workers by banning the recruitment of foreign workers and restricting the immigration of people without a German passport.

It has also encouraged Turks to return home by offering them special payments. So far, few have taken up the offer. Most prefer to stay in a country that offers them more opportunities than they may have at home.

These policies have had some success. Unfortunately, the country still suffers social unrest, and racist attacks on immigrant groups are on the increase.

C **Turkish workers in Germany**

Immigrants into California

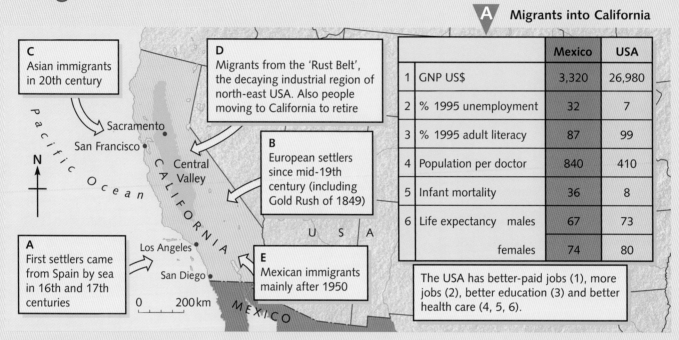

A Migrants into California

C
Asian immigrants in 20th century

D
Migrants from the 'Rust Belt', the decaying industrial region of north-east USA. Also people moving to California to retire

B
European settlers since mid-19th century (including Gold Rush of 1849)

A
First settlers came from Spain by sea in 16th and 17th centuries

E
Mexican immigrants mainly after 1950

		Mexico	USA
1	GNP US$	3,320	26,980
2	% 1995 unemployment	32	7
3	% 1995 adult literacy	87	99
4	Population per doctor	840	410
5	Infant mortality	36	8
6	Life expectancy males	67	73
	females	74	80

The USA has better-paid jobs (1), more jobs (2), better education (3) and better health care (4, 5, 6).

California has always attracted migrants. As map **A** shows, until the early 1950s most came from Europe, Asia and other parts of the USA. Since then, however, it is the Mexicans who have migrated in large numbers, to form the fastest-growing ethnic minority in the USA.

The USA has much to offer migrants. It is a place with many opportunities, high standards of living and an attractive way of life. For many people, California is the best of the USA. It is one of the wealthiest places in the world, jobs are readily available, education is good and healthcare is excellent.

Mexicans migrate to the USA for these very reasons. Most go in search of work and the chance to earn money. They hope to rid themselves of the poverty and unemployment of Mexico and replace that with what they hope will be the wealth and opportunity of the USA.

B A Mexican village

Workers leave Mexico because of a lack of jobs and low living standards.

Many migrants are Mexican farm workers on very low pay with few skills.

At one time most migrants were men who returned home when they had earned enough money.

Mexican workers

Most migrants now prefer to live permanently in California.

Some Mexican villages have lost half of their population.

Many migrants now take their families with them, although some desert their wife and children.

C Mexican migrant workers packing vegetables in California

Migrants – illegal and legal

Between 1 and 2 million Mexicans try each year to enter the USA to live and work. Estimates suggest that at least 1 million of these attempt to cross the border illegally. This is despite the USA setting up elaborate border security controls using horses, helicopters and advanced detective equipment.

Jobs taken by migrant workers

Mexican workers can be a great help to the American economy. They often provide cheap labour and work at jobs that local people are reluctant to do. Many of these jobs are hard, dirty, monotonous and even dangerous. Even in these occupations, however, they can earn more in a month than they could in a full year in Mexico.

Migrant workers do all kinds of jobs. Large numbers find seasonal work on large agricultural estates at harvest times, or work in food-processing factories. Others work in cities like Los Angeles where they find employment on construction projects and in hotels and restaurants.

D Poor-quality housing in Los Angeles

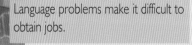

Mexicans in Los Angeles

Mainly young with little money and few qualifications.

Language problems make it difficult to obtain jobs.

Many cannot work legally, and take very low-paid jobs.

Low incomes make it difficult to obtain decent accommodation.

Illegal workers are harassed by the police.

Many are forced to live in ghettos in the poorest districts.

REVISION QUESTIONS

1 (Pages 18 and 19)
Give the meaning of the following terms:
a) Migration
b) International migration. Give an example.
c) Rural-to-urban migration. Give an example.
d) Urban-to-rural migration. Give an example.

2 (Pages 18 and 19)
a) What is the difference between voluntary and forced migration?
b) Give two reasons for forced migration.
c) Give two reasons for voluntary migration.

3 (Pages 20 and 21)
a) Give three reasons why immigrants have come to the UK.
b) Name five of the early immigrant groups.
c) Where do the most recent immigrants come from?
d) Why did the recent immigrants come to the UK?
e) Why are there fewer immigrants now?

4 Look at map **A** on page 20.
a) Which region has most migrants?
b) Which regions have fewest migrants?
c) How many migrants does Scotland have?
d) Which region has the highest proportion of West Indians and Africans?

5 (Pages 20 and 21)
a) What is a multicultural society?
b) What are the advantages of a multicultural society?

6 (Pages 20 and 21)
Draw a star diagram to show six problems facing immigrants to Britain. Write no more than 10 words for each problem.

7 (Pages 22 and 23)
a) Describe regional migration in Britain between 1930 and 1980.
b) Copy and complete the diagram below to show reasons for this migration.

Push factors (give four)
· · · ·

Pull factors (give four)
· · · ·

8 (Pages 22 and 23)
a) What is counter-urbanisation?
b) Give three reasons why it has become common in the richer countries of the world.

9 Look at map **A** on page 24.
a) From which five countries did most migrants come? List them in order, highest first.
b) How many Turkish migrants were there?
c) How many UK migrants were there?

10 (Pages 24 and 25)
a) Why did Germany want migrant workers?
b) What types of jobs did most migrants do?
c) Why did many migrants become unemployed?
d) Why did Germany try to stop the inflow of migrant workers in the 1980s?

11 (Pages 26 and 27)
a) Give two push factors and two pull factors to explain why Mexicans migrate to California.
b) Many migrants are employed in seasonal work. What is seasonal work? Give an example.
c) Give four other types of job done by migrants.

12 (Pages 26 and 27)
Suggest reasons for the following newspaper headlines:

Local businesses welcome migrants to California

'USA a great place to work' say Mexican migrants

Mexicans unhappy with life in Los Angeles

EXAMINATION QUESTIONS

1 (Pages 18 to 21)

Study graph **A**, which shows migration between the UK and some other European countries between 1985 and 1995.

a) What is a migrant? **(1)**

b) Which country has the most migrants **from** the UK? **(1)**

c) Which country has the most migrants **to** the UK? **(1)**

d) List three reasons why people migrate. **(1)**

e) Describe four problems facing immigrants to Britain. **(4)**

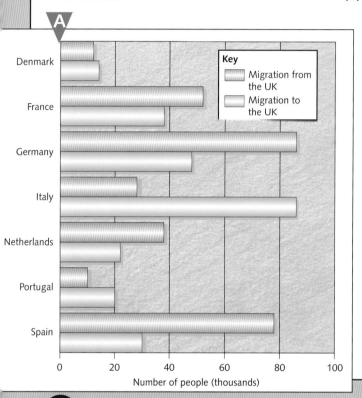

A

Key
- Migration from the UK
- Migration to the UK

Number of people (thousands)

(Denmark, France, Germany, Italy, Netherlands, Portugal, Spain; axis 0 20 40 60 80 100)

3 (Pages 24 and 25)

Look at the information below about German immigrants.

a) Which country has the lowest average income per person? **(1)**

b) Which country has the highest percentage of people working in farming? **(1)**

c) Which country has the highest percentage of people working in factories? **(1)**

d) Why do you think people have migrated from these countries to Germany? **(4)**

e) Suggest two ways that Germany might benefit from migrant workers. **(2)**

C Where immigrants to Germany have come from

Country	Employment structure (%)			Average income per person (US$)
	Primary	Secondary	Tertiary	
Germany	3	39	58	23,560
Turkey	47	20	33	2,120
Italy	9	32	59	19,620
Greece	23	27	50	7,390
Poland	27	37	36	2,270
Former Yugoslavia	No data available			No data available

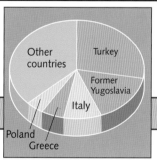

(Pie chart: Other countries, Turkey, Former Yugoslavia, Italy, Greece, Poland)

2 (Pages 22 and 23)

a) With the help of diagram **B**, list four factors about life in the urban area that might persuade people to move away (push factors). **(4)**

b) Describe three attractions that the rural/urban fringe might have for people living in large cities (pull factors). **(3)**

c) Why might people who are already living in the rural/urban fringe object to others migrating to the area in large numbers? **(3)**

B In the United Kingdom, migration from urban to more rural areas is increasing

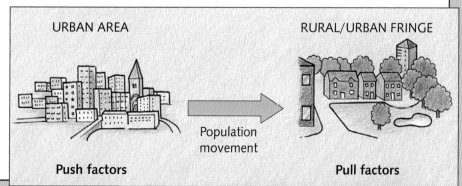

URBAN AREA

RURAL/URBAN FRINGE

Population movement

Push factors

Pull factors

A settlement is a place where people live. They have many different purposes. They are places to work in, places to shop in, places to visit and places where most people have their homes and spend most of their time. Settlements may be large, sprawling cities, small, neat villages or simply groups of scattered buildings. Although each settlement is unique, it is likely to share similar characteristics with other settlements. This chapter looks at how settlements vary in their location, shape and importance.

Site describes the point at which a settlement is located. Factors such as relief, soil, water supply and resources were important in choosing the original site of a settlement.

Situation is the location of a settlement in relation to surrounding features such as other settlements, mountains, rivers, the sea and communications.

Site and situation

The location of a settlement is related to its site and situation.

Most early settlements were established by groups of farmers who wished to be self-sufficient. The site, therefore, had to provide all the basic needs of the community. Some of these needs are shown below – they are called **location factors**. An ideal site was likely to have the benefit of several of these factors.

A Location factors

Wet point. A settlement needed to be close to a reliable source of fresh water. In early days, rivers were clean enough to give a safe, permanent supply.

A **fuel supply** was needed for heating and cooking. In earlier times in Britain, and still today in many developing countries, this would mainly be wood.

Dry point. A site had to be safe from flooding and away from marshy areas.

Food supplies were needed from land nearby. Some land would be suitable for rearing animals and some for growing crops.

Building materials. These included stone, wood and clay which had to be available locally as they were heavy and bulky to move.

Bridging point. A place where the river was shallow, and narrow enough for a bridge to be built. A route centre where valleys met was also an advantage.

Defence. Surrounding tribes were often hostile. A good defensive site would be within a river bend or on a hill with steep sides and commanding views.

Shelter and aspect. A place needed shelter from the prevailing south-westerly and cold northerly winds. A south-facing aspect gives most sunshine, heat and light.

Warkworth, Northumberland is located on a bend of the River Coquet. The site was easy to defend, had a good water supply, and the river could be bridged at this point. The site was dry, and rock outcrops and nearby forest provided building materials.

Paris had the site advantage of being located on an island in the River Seine which could be defended and which made bridging easier. Further growth resulted from its situation in the centre of a major farming area where several routes met.

Diagram **D** below shows an area of land available for early settlement. Imagine that you have been given the task of choosing a site for a settlement in the area. Look carefully at the places labelled A to E and work out the advantages and disadvantages of each site. Which do you think is the best site? Why?

Finally, remember that location factors change with time. Many of these early site factors may no longer be important. Nowadays, for example, most settlements have a piped water supply, have one or more shops to provide food, and do not need to be defended.

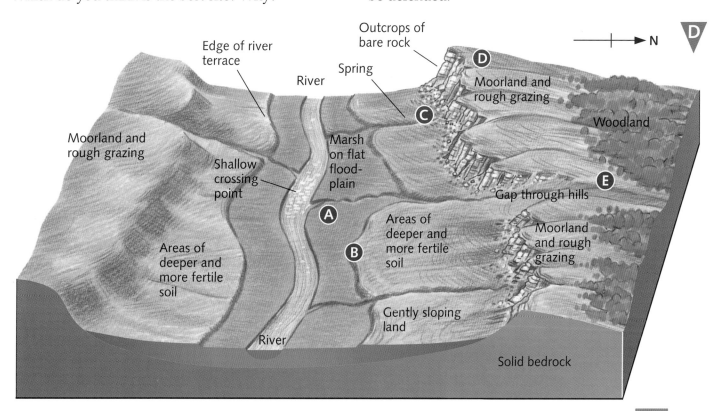

Settlement types

We usually divide settlements into two basic types. These are **rural** and **urban**. Rural settlements are found in the countryside, and include isolated farms, hamlets, villages and small market towns. Most of these settlements were originally involved in agriculture. Urban settlements are usually much larger and include towns, cities and **conurbations**. Conurbations are very large built-up areas that are a result of towns and cities spreading outwards and joining together.

Patterns

Geographers are interested in the patterns or shapes of settlements. The shape of early villages and towns was usually influenced by the physical features of the surrounding area. More recently, transport links and the availability of land for development have become important factors. Although every place is different, most settlements have a pattern which may be described as either **dispersed** or **nucleated**. Examples of these are shown in photos **A**, **B** and **C**.

A Northumberland

Dispersed settlements

These are places where the individual buildings are well spread out. They are usually isolated farms or small groups of buildings that are separated from the next group by several kilometres. Dispersed settlement patterns are typical of regions where the agricultural land is poor and large areas are needed to support each community. In Britain, these places occur mainly in the mountainous parts of Scotland, Wales and northern England, and in previously marshy areas such as the Fens.

Nucleated settlements

These are places where buildings are clustered around a central point. They developed either where defence was important, around a reliable water supply, or in places where groups of farmers worked together as a self-sufficient co-operative. Nucleated settlements may be found in most of lowland Britain, particularly in the English Midlands and East Anglia.

B Hooton Pagnell, Yorkshire

Linear settlements

These are often called **ribbon developments** because they have a long narrow shape. They occur when buildings are strung out along a line of communication such as a road, river or canal. Linear settlements are also described as nucleated because the buildings are close together.

C   Parsons Drove, Cambridgeshire

Functions

Settlements are places that are useful to people. They provide jobs, shops, offices, entertainments and other services. These are called the **functions** of the settlement. The function describes what the settlement does.

Normally the larger the settlement the more functions there are. Sometimes one function is more important than the others. The settlement then becomes known as that particular type of town. For example,

Edinburgh is a capital city, Oxford is a university town and Southampton is a port.

Settlement functions can change over time. In some cases the original function may no longer exist. For example, British towns no longer have a defensive function. In other cases the decline of an industry can cause change. A fishing village might abandon fishing and become a tourist resort, or a mining town that is short of raw materials may develop high-tech industries.

 D

Main function	Description	UK example	World example
Capital	Important for administration and government	London	Moscow, Russia
Market town	A collecting and distribution centre	York	Winnipeg, Canada
University	Place with a reputation for educational services	Cambridge	Paris, France
Industrial	Place where manufacturing is the main employer	Birmingham	Pittsburgh, USA
Port	Coastal town important for trade	Southampton	Rotterdam, Netherlands
Resort	Holiday centre popular with tourists	Blackpool	Orlando, USA
Religious	A place where religion is important	Canterbury	Mecca, Saudi Arabia
Residential	Where the majority of residents live, but work elsewhere	Telford	Marne-la-Vallée, France

Hierarchies

A **hierarchy** is a way of organising things into a certain order. A school has a hierarchy. As diagram **A** shows, the head teacher is at the top and the subject staff and tutors at the bottom. Notice that the structure looks like a pyramid. As you progress up the pyramid, each level becomes more important but has fewer members of staff.

A settlement hierarchy is similar to a school hierarchy, but in this case cities, towns and villages are organised in order of importance. There are several ways of doing this. The three most common are:

1. by population size
2. by the number and range of services provided
3. by the sphere of influence.

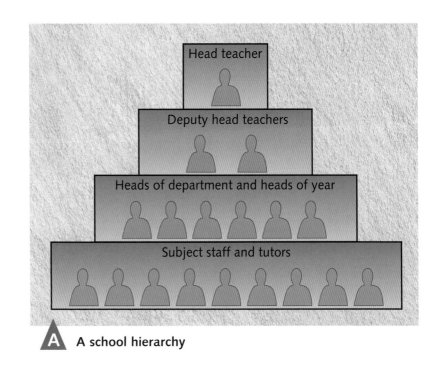

A A school hierarchy

B A settlement hierarchy

Distance apart		Population
Usually over 200 km	Two or three **conurbations**	Over a million people
100–200 km	Several **cities**	Up to a million people
50–100 km	Many **large towns**	Up to 100,000 people
20–50 km	Hundreds of **small towns**	Up to 10,000 or 20,000 people
5–10 km	Thousands of **villages**	Up to several hundred people
2–3 km	Several thousand **hamlets**	5 or 6 buildings and families

1 Population size

Diagram **B** shows a settlement hierarchy based on population size. Like the school hierarchy, it is drawn as a pyramid. As well as population size, the drawing also shows the approximate number of settlements in each group and the distance apart that they might be. The figures are approximate.

A conurbation is at the top of the hierarchy because it has the highest population. Notice also that there are very few conurbations and they are located well apart. A hamlet is at the bottom of the hierarchy because it is the settlement with the fewest people. There are large numbers of hamlets and they are generally quite close together.

Two points to remember from the drawing are:

1. As settlement size increases, the number of settlements decreases – so there are many hamlets and villages but few conurbations.
2. As settlement size increases, so the distance between them increases.

2 Range and number of services

The size of a settlement can affect the type and number of shops and services it provides. The smallest settlements are hamlets with no more than 100 people and perhaps just one or two services, if any. Villages are larger and will usually have a number of basic services and several shops. Settlements that have grown into towns and cities provide a larger number of shops and services, and offer a wider range and greater choice.

Table **C** shows some of the shops and services that may be found in different types of settlement. They form a settlement hierarchy based on services. In general, the larger the settlement, the more goods and services it provides.

Settlement	Typical shops and services
• Hamlet	Possibly a church, pub or telephone but often none at all
• Village	Church, post office, pub, shop for daily needs, primary school, village hall
• Small town	All of the above plus supermarket, many shops, banks, health centre, leisure centre, secondary school, cafés and restaurants, railway station
• Large town	All of the above plus several shopping arcades, hypermarket, cinemas, main railway station, hotels, small hospital, small football team
• City	All the above plus cathedral, university, theatre, county hall, airport
• Capital	All the above plus government buildings, banking headquarters, museums and art galleries, several universities

C

3 Sphere of influence

The shops and services of a hamlet or small village are used mostly by local people. The **sphere of influence** of those places is therefore very small. However, a large town serves the needs of its local inhabitants but also has sufficient shops and services to attract people from far away. It therefore has a large sphere of influence.

Map **D** shows the sphere of influence for some shops and services based in Exeter. Notice that people are willing to travel much further for some shops and services than for others. The shops and services with the greatest **range** are usually located in the largest settle-ments, which further increases their market area.

The sphere of influence is a useful way of organising cities, towns and villages into a settlement hierarchy. In general, the larger the settlement the larger the sphere of influence.

Sphere of influence is sometimes called the **market area** and is the area affected or served by a settlement.

Range is the maximum distance people are prepared to travel to buy goods or use a service.

Threshold is the minimum number of people needed to support a shop or service.

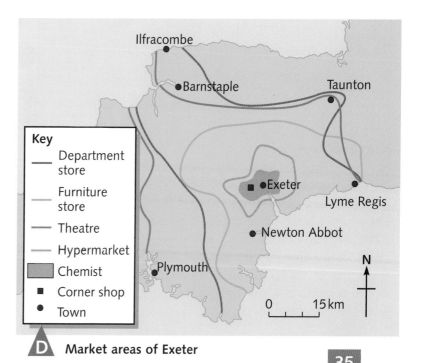

D Market areas of Exeter

Settlements and the OS map

The maps on these two pages show settlements around Hull in East Yorkshire. The area is very flat and low-lying with a scattering of small towns and villages. Farming is the main occupation of the rural areas, whilst Hull, with a population of 254,000, is the main city and Bridlington an important coastal tourist resort.

Site

Although the Ordnance Survey (OS) map on the opposite page shows the area in the 2000s, some of the early site factors for the various settlements are still visible. Map **A** shows some of these factors for Hedon, a village just east of Hull. Hedon's present development probably depends more on its closeness to Hull and its **function** as a **residential** settlement for that city.

Patterns

Settlements in this part of East Yorkshire show both dispersed and nucleated patterns. Most locations in the area have a reliable water supply, flat land, good farming and easy communications. This gave early settlers a wide choice of location, and a variety of settlement patterns were able to develop. The following are some examples from the OS map:

Dispersed Preston Field (1732), Manor Farm (1932)

Nucleated Hedon (1928), Thorngumbald (2026)

Linear Humbleton (2234), Elstronwick (2232).

Hierarchies

Hull is by far the largest settlement in the area. It has the greatest range and number of services, and the largest sphere of influence. Map **B** shows the settlement hierarchy of the area, by size. Notice that there are many more small settlements than large ones. Notice also that the smaller settlement are closer together and the large ones far apart. This would seem to confirm the points made about settlement hierarchies on page 34.

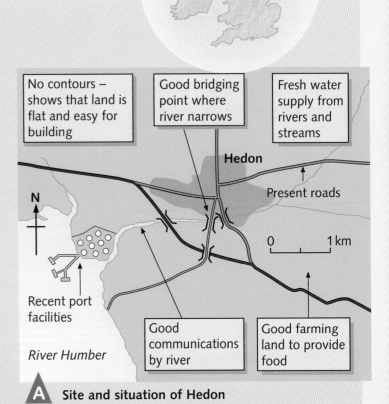

No contours – shows that land is flat and easy for building

Good bridging point where river narrows

Fresh water supply from rivers and streams

Present roads

Recent port facilities

River Humber

Good communications by river

Good farming land to provide food

A Site and situation of Hedon

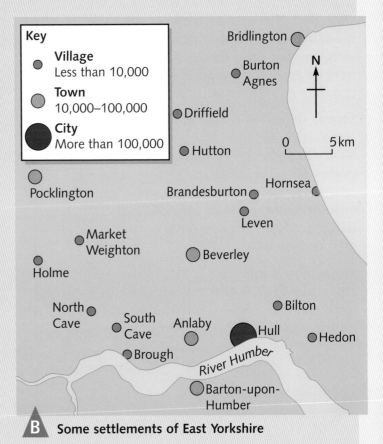

Key

● Village
Less than 10,000

● Town
10,000–100,000

● City
More than 100,000

Bridlington

Burton Agnes

Driffield

Hutton

Pocklington

Brandesburton

Hornsea

Leven

Market Weighton

Beverley

Holme

North Cave

South Cave

Anlaby

Bilton

Hull

Hedon

Brough

River Humber

Barton-upon-Humber

B Some settlements of East Yorkshire

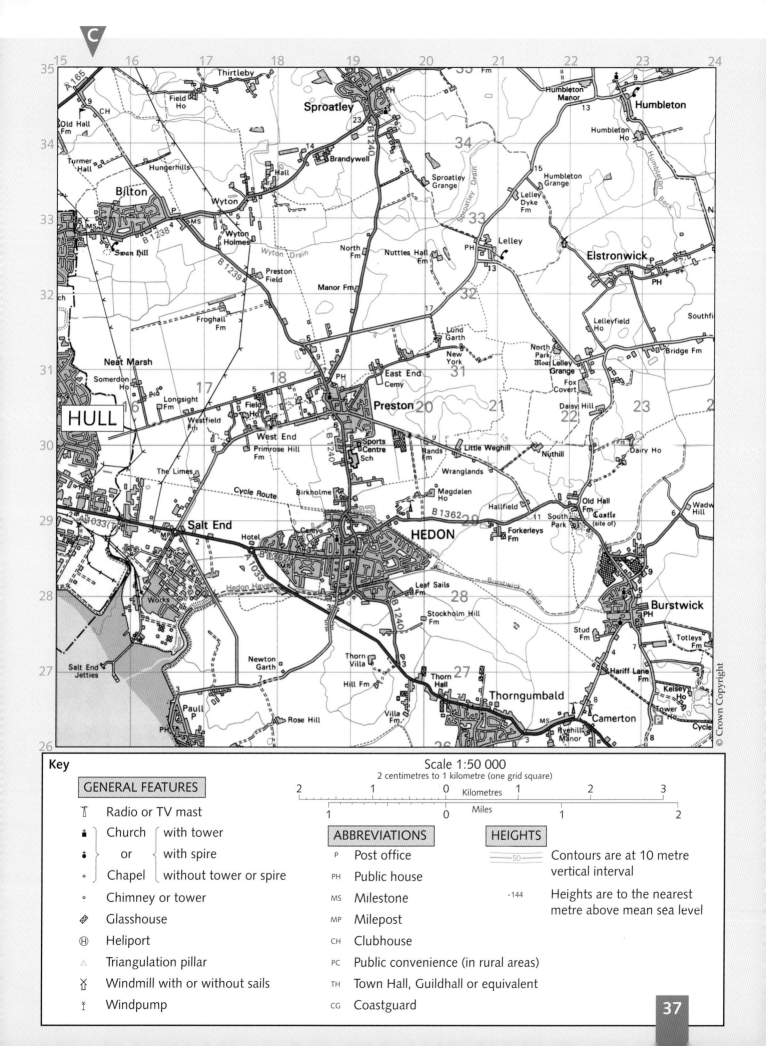

Key

GENERAL FEATURES

- ⌐ Radio or TV mast
- ⌐ Church { with tower
- ⌐ or { with spire
- + } Chapel { without tower or spire
- ○ Chimney or tower
- ⌖ Glasshouse
- Ⓗ Heliport
- △ Triangulation pillar
- ⌐ Windmill with or without sails
- ⌐ Windpump

Scale 1:50 000
2 centimetres to 1 kilometre (one grid square)

Kilometres: 2 1 0 1 2 3

Miles: 1 0 1 2

ABBREVIATIONS

- P Post office
- PH Public house
- MS Milestone
- MP Milepost
- CH Clubhouse
- PC Public convenience (in rural areas)
- TH Town Hall, Guildhall or equivalent
- CG Coastguard

HEIGHTS

—50— Contours are at 10 metre vertical interval

·144 Heights are to the nearest metre above mean sea level

© Crown Copyright

Urban growth

Towns and cities are popular places in which to live. They can provide housing, jobs, education, medical care and a better chance of getting on and enjoying life. More than half the world's population now live in cities, and the number is increasing all the time.

Although towns existed even in early civilisations, in the past farming and the production of food was most important, so most people lived in rural areas. It was not until the rapid growth of industry in the 19th century that the movement of people to towns began on a large scale.

Urbanisation is the increase in the proportion of people living in towns and cities.

Urban growth is when towns and cities get larger.

Urban population is the proportion of a country's population living in towns or cities. The UK's urban population is 90%.

Urban land use models

A city is usually divided into recognisable areas or zones. Each area serves a function or purpose. The main types of function are shops and offices, industry, housing, and open space. Although different in some ways, towns and cities all tend to be set out in a similar way. For example, the main shopping areas are found in the centre, and the newest housing is on the outskirts. Any industries are usually grouped together.

When a very simple map is drawn to show these similarities in land use, it is called an **urban land use model**. A model is when a real situation is made simple so that it is easier to understand. The two simplest land use models that apply to the richer, more developed cities of the world are shown in diagram **A**.

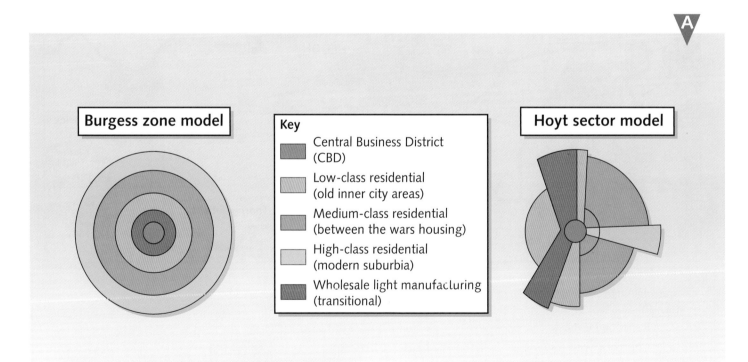

Burgess zone model

Key
- Central Business District (CBD)
- Low-class residential (old inner city areas)
- Medium-class residential (between the wars housing)
- High-class residential (modern suburbia)
- Wholesale light manufacturing (transitional)

Hoyt sector model

At the centre of the Burgess model is the Central Business District (CBD) of shops and offices. As towns developed, they grew in a series of concentric circles or rings outwards from the CBD. The oldest part of the city is therefore at the centre and the newest part on the outer edge.

Hoyt considered transport and physical features to be important. In his model, factories grew up along roads, rivers and canals in wedge-shaped sectors leading out of the city. Housing then developed alongside these industrial sectors.

Urban land use and functional zones

The main purpose of towns and cities is to provide shops and offices, industry, housing and open space. The location of these functions is related to three main factors:

- **Land values and space** – how expensive the land is and who can afford to locate there.

- **Accessibility** – how easy it is to get to a place and how important that is to a land user.

- **Age** – whether land users want to be in old areas of the city, or in newer more pleasant locations on the outskirts.

Eventually each town develops its own pattern of land use, which will be similar to that suggested by Burgess and Hoyt but much more complex. A more realistic picture of land use is shown in drawing **B** below. Part of the town has been left blank to help you see the model shape.

A simplified land use model of a city B

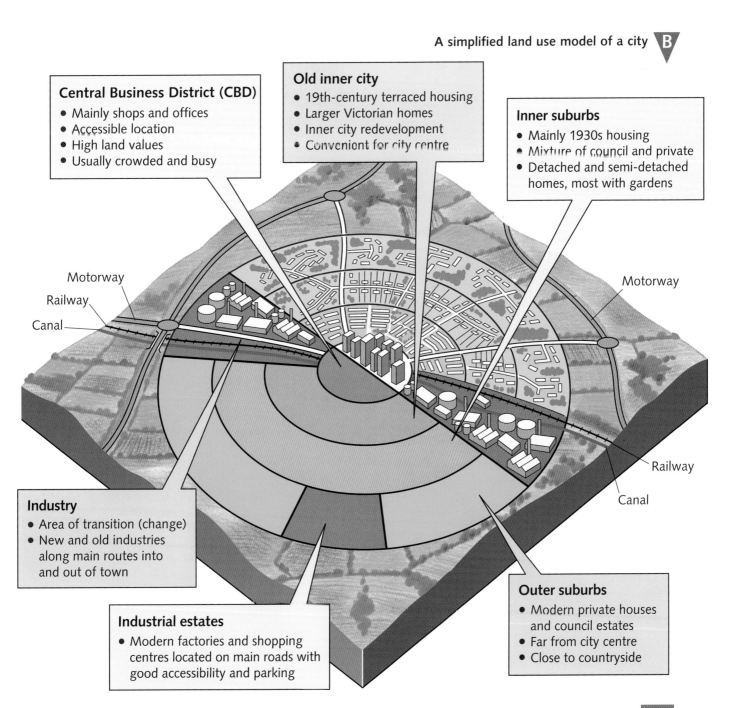

Central Business District (CBD)
- Mainly shops and offices
- Accessible location
- High land values
- Usually crowded and busy

Old inner city
- 19th-century terraced housing
- Larger Victorian homes
- Inner city redevelopment
- Convenient for city centre

Inner suburbs
- Mainly 1930s housing
- Mixture of council and private
- Detached and semi-detached homes, most with gardens

Motorway
Railway
Canal

Motorway

Railway

Canal

Industry
- Area of transition (change)
- New and old industries along main routes into and out of town

Industrial estates
- Modern factories and shopping centres located on main roads with good accessibility and parking

Outer suburbs
- Modern private houses and council estates
- Far from city centre
- Close to countryside

The CBD and old inner city

The CBD

The central business district (CBD) became the most accessible part of a town or city. Because most road and rail routes met there, this meant that it could easily be reached by people living throughout the urban area and beyond.

The major land users in the CBD became shops, banks and offices. They located here mainly because they needed to be accessible to large numbers of people and could afford the high cost of land.

In time, CBDs became increasingly congested with pedestrians and traffic. This reduced their accessibility as well as their attractiveness as a place to either shop or work.

Old inner city areas

These areas are located close to the city centre. As with CBDs, they have experienced much change over the years. Some of the features and changes in these areas are described in diagram **B** below.

 **A traditional city centre**

Origin

Most British towns began to grow rapidly in the 19th century. The growth was linked to the development of industry and the huge demand for workers. This demand was met by large numbers of people leaving the rural areas to live and work in the cities. They needed low-cost houses in which to live.

The first developments took place in the areas next to the city centre – places now called the inner city. Large factories and houses were built close together so that workers who in those days had no other form of transport, could walk to work easily.

Development then was rapid. As there were no planning controls, little thought was given to building a quality environment. Only the most basic needs at the lowest possible cost were provided.

Features

The inner city areas were crowded places with little open space. Houses were built in terraces and packed close together. Bathrooms were almost unknown and toilets were usually outside in the back yard. Most factories were built beside railways and canals and right next to the houses. A typical street would have a factory at one end, a pub or shop at the other, and 100–200 small terraced houses in the middle.

The canals and any river were usually badly polluted by industrial waste, whilst the burning of coal in factories and homes added to the air pollution.

Despite these difficult living conditions, the local people often created a strong community spirit and were friendly and supportive to each other.

C Inner city in the early 20th century

Crowded, high-density housing

Narrow, unplanned streets

Rows of terraced houses

Smoky chimneys

Railway sidings

Little open space

Large factories

Polluted canal

Decline

Industry in the inner city declined as old factories closed down. There were several reasons for these closures:

- Most factories were simply too old and used outdated methods of production.
- There was strong competition from new factories and new products elsewhere.
- The sites were crowded and poorly organised with no room for expansion.
- Transport facilities were poor, with canals and railways closed and roads narrow and congested.
- The environment was unattractive and unpleasant to work in.

As industry declined, many factories closed down and became derelict. These were either vandalised or pulled down and the land left unused. This further added to the area's visual decay.

Effects

Housing in many cities had become slum-like by the 1960s. Many houses were already a hundred years old and had been built before such amenities as electricity, running water and indoor toilets were considered essential.

The environment was polluted and houses blackened by smoke from domestic and factory chimneys. Empty buildings were vandalised whilst sites of demolished buildings became rubbish tips.

Some terraced housing was eventually replaced by high-rise flats. Whilst more modern in design and amenity provision, they were unpopular and created social problems.

The inner city is now an area of cheap housing. This has attracted people with low incomes such as pensioners, single-parent families and first-time home buyers. It is also a place where ethnic groups tend to concentrate.

Suburbia and the rural–urban fringe

Suburbia

Suburbia was the name given to areas that developed during the 1920s and 1930s. Urban areas grew rapidly at this time due mainly to the introduction of public transport and the private car. These improvements in transport allowed people to live further away from the city centre where most work and amenities were located.

This outward growth, known as **urban sprawl**, led to the building of numerous private housing estates. Many of the houses were semi-detached and had bay windows, garages and front and back gardens.

As each new housing estate was built, its distance from the CBD and shops increased. This led to the growth of shopping parades within the estates. These parades were visited by local residents several times a week. They saved people time in travelling and reduced transport costs.

Suburbia is the outer area of a town or city. It is usually residential and developed mainly during the 1920s and 1930s.

The rural–urban fringe is where the city and countryside meet.

Urban sprawl is when a city grows unchecked and gradually takes up more of the surrounding countryside.

The estates of the 1920s and 1930s rarely had industry nearby so residents had to travel long distances to their place of work. This process became known as **commuting**.

A Typical housing in suburbia

B Suburban shopping parade

The rural–urban fringe

After the 1960s, urban sprawl continued, with land on the rural–urban fringe being used mainly for:

- private estates with low-density, high-quality housing

- outer city council housing estates built to re-house people from slum areas of the old inner city

- new industrial estates with modern buildings and easy access to motorways.

Recent developments

An increasing number of land users see the rural–urban fringe as the ideal location for future developments. This location is less congested, has easier access, provides cheaper land and is more attractive than places near to the city centre

However, many people are not happy with these developments. They don't want to see urban areas spreading out any further. They wish to protect the rural environment and

C A modern estate on the rural–urban fringe

retain the pleasant and attractive countryside that surrounds most towns. Drawing **D** shows some of the problems of the rural–urban fringe.

D Competition for land on the rural–urban fringe

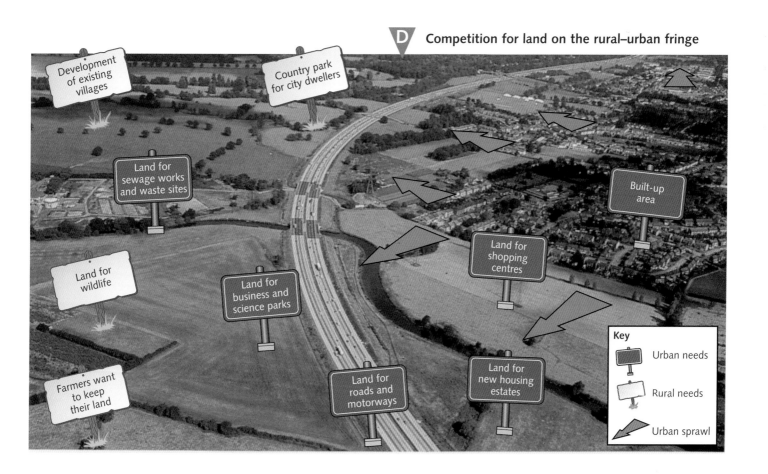

Development of existing villages

Country park for city dwellers

Land for sewage works and waste sites

Built-up area

Land for wildlife

Land for shopping centres

Land for business and science parks

Land for roads and motorways

Land for new housing estates

Farmers want to keep their land

Key

Urban needs

Rural needs

Urban sprawl

Residential environments in British cities

A Old inner city area

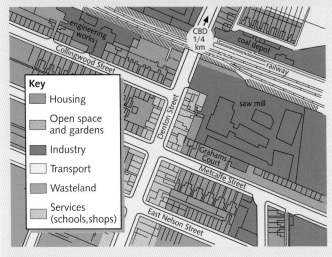

Key
- Housing
- Open space and gardens
- Industry
- Transport
- Wasteland
- Services (schools, shops)

- Built some 100 years ago for factory workers.
- Located close to city centre near factories.
- Mainly long straight rows of terraced housing.
- Cheap, high-density, and overcrowded.
- Few amenities, no gardens, little open space.
- Now being improved and modernised.

Tenure (house ownership)
- Council 8%
- Owner-occupied 30%
- Rented 62%

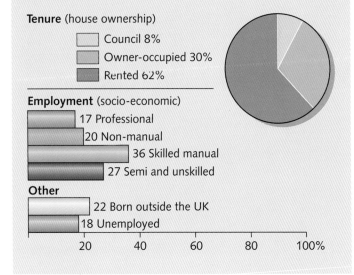

Employment (socio-economic)
- 17 Professional
- 20 Non-manual
- 36 Skilled manual
- 27 Semi and unskilled

Other
- 22 Born outside the UK
- 18 Unemployed

20 40 60 80 100%

B Inner city redevelopment

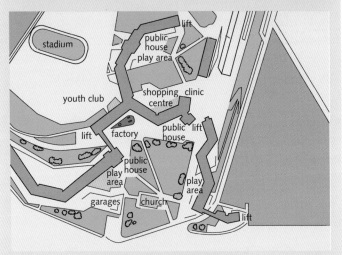

stadium, lift, public house, play area, youth club, shopping centre, clinic, lift, factory, public house, lift, public house, play area, play area, garages, church, lift

- Built in the 1950s and 1960s.
- Located close to city centre.
- Mainly high-rise buildings of apartments and flats.
- Replaced old terraced housing that was cleared.
- Many lifts, stairs and dark, narrow corridors.
- Modern amenities but crowded and unpopular.

Tenure (house ownership)
- Council 86%
- Owner-occupied 3%
- Rented 11%

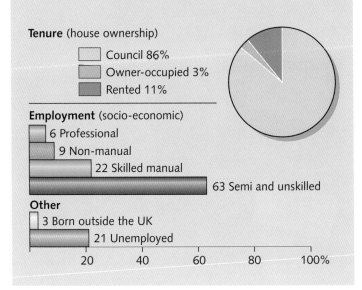

Employment (socio-economic)
- 6 Professional
- 9 Non-manual
- 22 Skilled manual
- 63 Semi and unskilled

Other
- 3 Born outside the UK
- 21 Unemployed

20 40 60 80 100%

C Suburbia

- Built from the 1930s to the present day.
- Located on edge of city near to countryside.
- Linked to introduction of public transport and cars.
- Mainly detached and semi-detached houses.
- Most with gardens and near to open space.
- Generally well planned, spacious and popular.

Tenure (house ownership)

- Council 5%
- Owner-occupied 70%
- Rented 25%

Employment (socio-economic)

- 29 Professional
- 30 Non-manual
- 29 Skilled manual
- 12 Semi and unskilled

Other

- 6 Born outside the UK
- 4 Unemployed

20   40   60   80   100%

D Outer city council estate

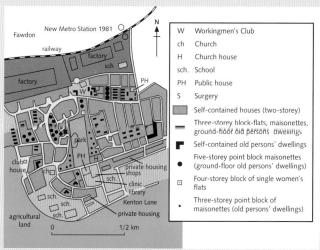

W	Workingmen's Club
ch	Church
H	Church house
sch.	School
PH	Public house
S	Surgery

- Self-contained houses (two-storey)
- Three-storey block-flats, maisonettes, ground-floor old persons' dwellings
- Self-contained old persons' dwellings
- Five-storey point block maisonettes (ground-floor old persons' dwellings)
- Four-storey block of single women's flats
- Three-storey point block of maisonettes (old persons' dwellings)

- Built by local councils in the 1950s and 1960s.
- Rehoused people from slum areas of inner city.
- Located on greenfield sites on edge of city.
- Mixture of high-rise, low-rise and terraces.
- Modern amenities but unpopular high-rise.
- Far from city centre but close to countryside.

Tenure (house ownership)

- Council 100%
- Owner-occupied 0%
- Rented 0%

Employment (socio-economic)

- 4 Professional
- 18 Non-manual
- 43 Skilled manual
- 35 Semi and unskilled

Other

- 2 Born outside the UK
- 15 Unemployed

20   40   60   80   100%

New York

Manhattan Island

Manhattan Island was the original site of New York. To most visitors Manhattan *is* New York, although in reality it is just one of five boroughs that make up the city.

Photo **A** is a view of Manhattan looking north-east. Notice the many bridges, port facilities and groups of skyscrapers. Also notice the grid pattern of the roads. There are 12 'avenues' that run north to south and 219 'streets' that run across the island from east to west. Finding your way around is very easy. The Empire State Building is 'on Fifth Avenue at 34th Street'.

New York is the world's third largest city. Like most other large cities in developed countries, it has many problems. This case study is mainly about these problems and therefore gives a rather negative view of the city. In reality, modern New York is much changed and much improved. Many of the problems of the past have been sorted out and the city has become an interesting, exciting and relatively safe city to live in or visit.

Problems resulting from the growth of New York

High cost of land. The lack of space and huge cost of land has led to skyscraper development especially in Middle and Downtown Manhattan. Only highly successful firms like banks and giant oil corporations can locate here. Many small companies have closed down or had to move to less expensive sites.

A Aerial view of Manhattan

Key
Buildings:
1 Empire State
2 Chrysler
3 United Nations
4 Wall Street

Urban decay. Many areas of inner city housing such as Harlem are now very old and have suffered years of neglect. Some have become 'ghettos' with living conditions below acceptable levels. They became home for the very poorest families – ethnic minorities, the unskilled and unemployed (diagram **C**).

Immigrants. America has always welcomed large numbers of immigrants but has not always been able to offer them equal opportunities. Over a period of time many immigrants find jobs and are able to enjoy successful lives. Others are unable to find work and find themselves trapped in a life of poverty. Estimates suggest that New York has over 50,000 homeless people.

Traffic congestion. Each morning up to 2 million commuters travel into the Manhattan area. About 75% use public transport, mainly the underground, or subway as it is called. Roads become blocked with cars, buses and yellow taxis. Congestion is worst around access points to the many bridges, tunnels and ferry terminals.

Unemployment. During the 1980s up to 1.5 million New Yorkers were unemployed. Unemployment was mainly due to decline in the port, in associated industries and in the clothing industry. New industries tend to be high-tech and in finance – jobs that require skills not possessed by many of the unemployed.

Crime. By the late 1980s crime had become, arguably, the greatest single problem. Street violence, subway muggings, drug related crimes and murder (on average, one every five hours) had turned certain parts of Manhattan into 'no-go' areas.

Pollution. New York has a severe refuse collection and disposal problem. Vehicles cause air and noise pollution, while run-down houses and graffiti cause visual pollution.

However, New York is now a much changed city. This is due largely to a programme of improvements introduced by Mayor Giuliano. These have reduced crime, created jobs by improving houses and tidying up streets, and reduced the number of homeless people.

B

The Empire State Building

C ◢ **The 'vicious circle' of the ghetto**

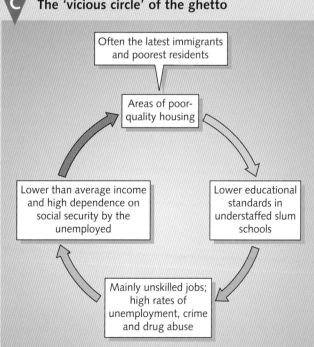

Often the latest immigrants and poorest residents

Areas of poor-quality housing

Lower educational standards in understaffed slum schools

Mainly unskilled jobs; high rates of unemployment, crime and drug abuse

Lower than average income and high dependence on social security by the unemployed

D ◢ Graffiti on the subway in 1996 (the subway is now clean, safe and efficient)

1 (Pages 30 and 31)
What is the difference between **settlement site** and **settlement situation**?

2 (Pages 30 and 31)
Draw a star diagram to show eight location factors that may have been considered by early settlers choosing a site for a settlement.

3 (Pages 32 and 33)
Look at the OS map on page 37. Find examples of dispersed, nucleated and linear settlement patterns. For each type, draw a simple map, add a title and describe its main features.

4 (Pages 32 and 33)
a) What factors led to the development of dispersed settlement patterns?
b) What factors led to the development of nucleated settlement patterns?

5 (Pages 32 and 33)
a) What is meant by the **function** of a settlement?
b) Give four different settlement functions. Name a town that is known for each one.
c) Give an example of how a settlement function might change over time.

6 (Pages 34 and 35)
a) What is a **hierarchy**?
b) Make a larger copy of the settlement hierarchy diagram below. On your diagram:
   ▪ name and describe the type of settlement at the top of the hierarchy
   ▪ name and describe the type of settlement at the bottom of the hierarchy.

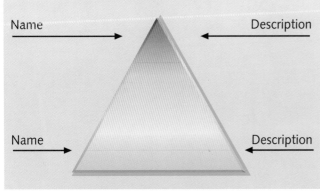

Name →   Description ←

Name →   Description ←

A settlement hierarchy

7 (Pages 34 and 35)
Copy and complete the table below by putting the following in the correct places. Most will be used more than once.

- government buildings ● cinema ● church
- primary school ● museums ● university
- hypermarket ● pub ● cathedral
- village hall ● main railway station

Settlement	Typical features
Village	
Large town	
Capital city	

A settlement hierarchy

8 (Pages 38 and 39)
Write down the meaning of the following terms:
a) urban growth
b) urbanisation
c) urban land use model
d) accessibility.

9 (Pages 38 and 39)
Make a larger drawing of this land use model. Name each of the zones marked at places A, B, C, D and E. Choose from this list:
▪ Inner suburbs ▪ CBD
▪ Outer suburbs ▪ Industry
▪ Old inner city.

10 (Pages 38 to 45)
Describe the main features of these residential areas:
a) Old inner city
b) Inner city redevelopment
c) Suburbia.

11 (Pages 40 and 41)
a) Why did most British towns grow rapidly in the 19th century?
b) Give four features of inner city areas.
c) Give four reasons for the decline of inner city areas.

EXAMINATION QUESTIONS

1 (Pages 30 and 31)

Study map **A**, which shows the site of Paris.
a) Suggest two ways that the river may have been used by the original settlers. **(2)**
b) Suggest two ways that the river may have caused problems for the original settlers. **(2)**
c) The original settlement was sited at a bridging point across the River Seine. Suggest why this was a good place to build a bridge. **(1)**
d) For a town or village that you have studied, draw a simple map and label the features that made it a good place to build a settlement. **(3)**

Original site of Paris, France

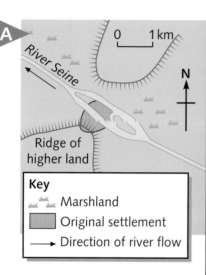

Ridge of higher land

Key
- Marshland
- Original settlement
- → Direction of river flow

River Seine

2 (Pages 34 and 35)

Study map **B**, which shows the hierarchy of settlements in part of East Anglia.
a) What is the most common type of settlement? **(1)**
b) What type of settlement is at the top of the settlement hierarchy shown here? **(1)**
c) Describe the size and spacing of the settlements. **(3)**
d) Why are there more shops and services in cities than in smaller settlements? **(3)**

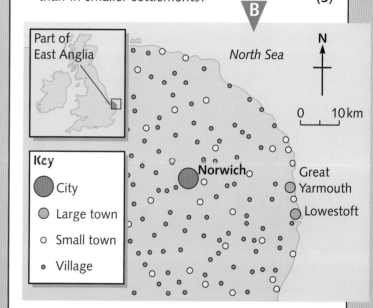

Part of East Anglia

North Sea

Norwich

Great Yarmouth

Lowestoft

Key
- ● City
- ● Large town
- ○ Small town
- • Village

3 (Pages 38 and 39)

Look at diagram **C**.
a) What do the letters CBD stand for? **(1)**
b) Give two main functions of the CBD. **(2)**
c) Which zone is mainly industrial? **(1)**
d) Which zone is the old inner city? **(1)**
e) In which zone is the most expensive land? **(1)**
f) Which is the oldest and most crowded zone? **(1)**

C A section through a British city

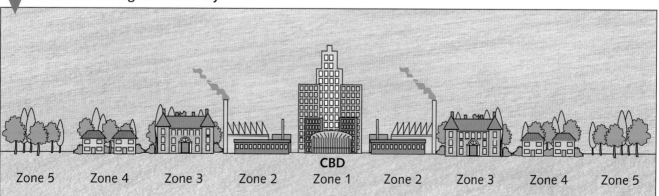

CBD

| Zone 5 | Zone 4 | Zone 3 | Zone 2 | Zone 1 | Zone 2 | Zone 3 | Zone 4 | Zone 5 |

4 URBAN CHANGE

Changes in the CBD

City centres are always changing. Before the rapid growth of the 19th century they were mainly open-air markets selling animals, farm produce and household goods. By the 20th century the most important types of land use had become shops, offices and commercial buildings.

Nowadays, city centres have also become places for entertainment and leisure, with cinemas, theatres, restaurants and bars. They have also become busier and more congested.

These changes have caused problems in the CBD. Diagram **A** shows some of the problems that have affected cities in more recent times.

During the 1990s, major changes began to occur in most city centres as authorities looked at ways of improving their CBDs. The main aims of these changes were:
- to reduce traffic congestion and pollution
- to separate shoppers and traffic
- to create a safer and more pleasant environment
- to provide more leisure amenities
- to revitalise CBDs, many of which had lost businesses to the rural–urban fringe.

Some of the schemes that have been introduced are shown in diagram **B**.

Problems

A

- Many older properties were in need of improvement and modernisation.
- The narrow streets, built before the invention of the car, bus and delivery lorry, were often congested.
- The large volume of traffic caused air pollution and was a danger to health and safety.
- There was insufficient space for car parks, and buses found it difficult to keep to time.
- Larger shops moved out and relocated on less congested sites.
- Smaller shops were forced to close as costs increased.
- The unplanned growth of the CBD made it unsuitable and unattractive to modern needs.

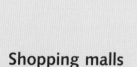

B

Pedestrianised zones

These are areas that are either traffic-free or allow only limited access to delivery vehicles and public transport. They improve safety for pedestrians and reduce traffic pollution (air, noise and visual). Overall, they make the area a more pleasant and enjoyable place in which to shop or work.

Shopping malls

These malls are built under cover and have air conditioning. They protect people from the weather and provide a warm, dry and comfortable shopping environment. They are pedestrianised and the shops are close together so reducing the distance to travel. This makes shopping both safer and easier.

Improved environment

This has been done by providing sitting areas, erecting hanging baskets, planting flower beds and shrubs and adding small areas of grass. Leisure amenities have been increased by opening cafés with outside tables, small restaurants and theme bars. More staff are employed to ensure that the place is clean and undamaged.

Changes in old inner city areas

Urban Development Corporations (UDCs)

Inner city areas have many problems. Houses are old and are often in need of repair. Factories have closed, and there is high unemployment. The environment is polluted and there is little open space for leisure. Over the years most cities have tried to improve conditions in these areas but with varying success.

Urban Development Corporations (UDCs) were set up by the government in 1981 in an attempt to regenerate inner cities and so improve conditions for people living there. One of the biggest UDC schemes was in London Docklands, an area that had long been suffering inner city decline and decay.

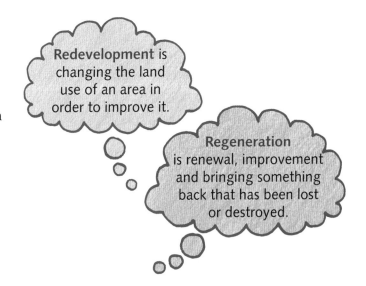

Redevelopment is changing the land use of an area in order to improve it.

Regeneration is renewal, improvement and bringing something back that has been lost or destroyed.

London Docklands – the problem

Up to the early 1950s, London was the busiest port in the world and the Docklands a thriving industrial zone. For a number of reasons, shipping on the Thames went into decline, and by 1981 the docks were virtually abandoned and derelict. By that time there were very few jobs, many of the old terraced houses needed urgent repair, transport was poor and there was a lack of basic services. The Docklands UDC was set up to try to solve these problems.

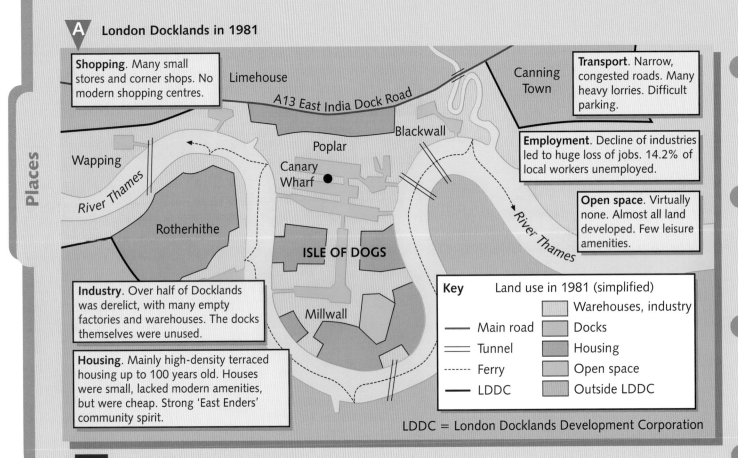

A London Docklands in 1981

Shopping. Many small stores and corner shops. No modern shopping centres.

Transport. Narrow, congested roads. Many heavy lorries. Difficult parking.

Employment. Decline of industries led to huge loss of jobs. 14.2% of local workers unemployed.

Open space. Virtually none. Almost all land developed. Few leisure amenities.

Industry. Over half of Docklands was derelict, with many empty factories and warehouses. The docks themselves were unused.

Housing. Mainly high-density terraced housing up to 100 years old. Houses were small, lacked modern amenities, but were cheap. Strong 'East Enders' community spirit.

Limehouse · A13 East India Dock Road · Canning Town · Blackwall · Poplar · Canary Wharf · Wapping · River Thames · Rotherhithe · ISLE OF DOGS · Millwall

Key Land use in 1981 (simplified)

— Main road
= Tunnel
------ Ferry
— LDDC

Warehouses, industry
Docks
Housing
Open space
Outside LDDC

LDDC = London Docklands Development Corporation

Places

London Docklands – the solution

B London Docklands in 2005

Transport links have been improved by the building of new roads, the Docklands Light Railway, and a City Airport.

The area is now more attractive as derelict land has been reclaimed, trees planted and parklands created.

Over 20,000 new houses and flats have been built. Many of the old terraces have been cleared or renovated.

Huge new office blocks like Canary Wharf Tower have been built.

By 2004 the scheme had helped provide over 21,000 new jobs.

Financial and high-tech industries have been attracted to the area with the promise of low rates.

New leisure facilities include an indoor sports centre and water sports complex.

New shopping facilities have been built at Canary Wharf, Surrey Quays and Tobacco Wharf.

Many people have benefited from the Docklands redevelopment and are in favour of the scheme. Others, however, are less happy and are against it. Local people in particular feel disadvantaged. They say that the housing is too expensive for them, that money has been spent on facilities for the rich rather than services for the poor, and that most new jobs are inappropriate to their needs. They also think that the 'yuppie' newcomers rarely mix with local people and that the 'East Enders' community has been broken up.

C Canary Wharf, Isle of Dogs, London

Changes at the rural–urban fringe

For some time now, cities have been spreading out at an alarming rate. This process, called **urban sprawl**, has resulted in a gradual loss of countryside and a spoiling of the environment.

Planners have tried many different ways of stopping cities from spreading outwards. One of the most successful has been by the use of **green belts**. A green belt is a broad ring of land around a city which is protected from development and on which almost all new building is banned.

The main aims of green belts are to restrict urban sprawl, protect the countryside and prevent neighbouring towns from merging into one another. They were created by the Town and Country Planning Act of 1947 and now surround most of the UK's large cities.

Green wedges may also help control sprawl. These wedges would allow growth to take place in certain directions whilst at the same time maintaining green areas close to the urban centre itself.

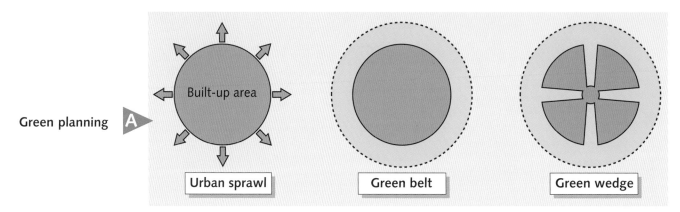

Green planning **A**

Urban sprawl   Green belt   Green wedge

Recently there has been increasing competition for the use of land at the rural–urban fringe. The main reasons are that at the fringe there is:
- cheaper land
- less traffic congestion and pollution
- easier access to surrounding settlements
- a pleasanter environment with more open space.

Because of this increased competition, planners have come under considerable pressure to release green belt land for more housing, jobs and roads. Some of the developments keen to locate in the open countryside of the rural–urban fringe are shown in drawing **B** below.

B Developments at the rural–urban fringe

Housing developments around nearby villages

Science and business parks with high-tech firms

Retail parks and shopping centres such as the MetroCentre

Office developments that no longer need to be in the CBD

Hotels and conference centres with landscaped gardens

Road developments such as motorways and by-passes

Sewage works and landfill sites for urban waste

Recreational areas such as country parks and sports stadiums

Out-of-town shopping centres

MetroCentre in Gateshead

The MetroCentre opened in 1983 and was the first out-of-town shopping centre in Britain. At the time it was the largest new shopping complex in Europe, and was immediately successful. Sir John Hall, who was responsible for the centre's development has said, 'The main aim of the MetroCentre is to create a day out for the family, with the emphasis on family shopping and leisure activities'.

C   Advantages of the site

Next to a bypass that links with the North East's modern road network.

1.3 million people live within 30 minutes' drive.

In an Enterprise Zone which provided a relaxation in planning controls and exemption from rates.

The area was previously marshland and cheap to buy.

A large flat site was available with plenty of room for expansion.

Next to a main railway line.

D

MetroCentre

Main features

- Pedestrianised with wide, tree-lined malls.
- Contains a funfair, 10-screen cinema and hotel.
- Started with 300 shops and now has over 500.
- Major stores such as Marks & Spencer and House of Fraser.
- New developments include Asda and Ikea.
- Several cafés, restaurants and bars.
- Pleasant, bright and cheerful interior.
- Children's play area and crèche.
- All indoors with climate control.
- Extensive free parking.
- Own railway station.
- Own bus station.

Suburbanised villages

Many people now find life in towns and cities unattractive, and move out to live in nearby villages. This movement has led to a change in the character of these small settlements and they have become **suburbanised**. They take this name because they gradually become urban areas in countryside surroundings. Suburbanised villages are also called **commuter settlements** or **dormitory towns**, because many residents who live and sleep there travel to nearby towns and cities for work.

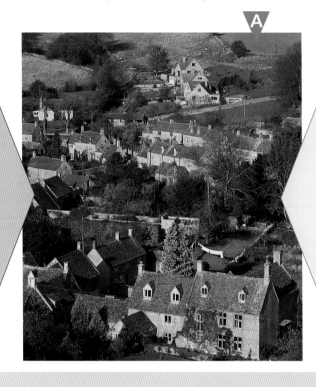

A

Who moves into the villages?
- The more wealthy urban residents who can afford the larger and often more expensive housing and the cost of travel to work, shops and amenities in the city.
- Those wishing to move to more attractive surroundings with less pollution and more open space.
- Elderly people who have retired and wish to live in a quieter environment.

How do the villages change?
- Newcomers begin to out-number the original residents, so creating social problems.
- House prices increase and local people can no longer afford to buy them.
- An increase in primary school population and a need for more shops.
- More cars, causing congestion on narrow lanes and the need for wider roads.

Braithwaite

Braithwaite is a small village in the English Lake District. In 1925 it consisted of a few farms, outbuildings and terraced cottages along narrow lanes. The village was self-contained and had a church, chapel, village hall, school and inn. Employment was in farming, in the the woollen, pencil and flour mills, or in the nearby mines.

Today the village is surbanised mainly because it is close to the tourist centre of Keswick. It is also located on a good road system, which makes access to other places very easy. The old village still remains but is now surrounded by modern houses and accommodation for tourists. Most of the residents are newcomers, and few are employed in the village.

B

Places

Key

— New or improved roads

Buildings and built-up areas in 1925

Buildings and built-up areas since 1925

N   0   100 m

A66

Motel
Church
Local authority housing
School
Inn
Café
Chapel
Semi-detached houses
Caravan site
Hotel
Campsite
Post office
Bungalows
Hotel
Coledale Beck
Large detached houses
Large houses

Brownfield and greenfield sites

Britain is short of houses. Estimates suggest that 4.9 million new homes could be needed by 2020. Assuming that this prediction is correct, the question then is: 'Where will all these houses be built?'

In 2004 the government put forward proposals for a number of development corridors, several new towns and dozens of housing estates. It was hoped that 60% of the building would be on brownfield sites and 40% on greenfield sites.

The proposals were strongly criticised by people wanting to 'save the countryside'. It was also pointed out that in south-east England where most houses are needed, there are limited brownfield sites available.

Diagram **C** gives some of the arguments as to why some groups of people would prefer most of the new developments to be brownfield sites and why other groups favour greenfield sites.

> A **brownfield site** is an area of disused and derelict land in an urban area that is available for redevelopment.

> A **greenfield site** is an area of countryside or open space that has not yet been built upon.

C

Why build on brownfield sites?

Supporters of the countryside say that:
- there are already over a million unoccupied houses in cities that could be upgraded
- a further 1.3 million could be created by using empty space above shops and offices
- 1.6 million homes could be built on derelict land and by re-using old industrial premises
- urban living reduces the need to use a car and supports shops and other services in city centres
- 80% of the demand for new houses will come from single-parent families who prefer, or need, to live in cities.

Why build on greenfield sites?

Developers claim that:
- most people want their own home, complete with garden, set in a rural location
- people are healthier and generally have a better quality of life in rural areas
- at present, for every three people moving into cities, five move out – this gives a total loss to urban areas of 90,000 a year (most people simply prefer countryside living)
- greenfield sites are cheaper to build on than brownfield sites because they are likely to have lower land values and less likely to need expensive clearing-up operations.

Transport in urban areas

The urban traffic problem

Traffic congestion is a major problem in most large cities. Since the 1960s car ownership has increased rapidly and today, three out of every five families in the UK own a car. The car gives people freedom to travel as they please. Unfortunately, the resulting traffic congestion wastes time, costs money and causes pollution.

Commuting

Urban traffic problems are often at their worst during the early morning and late afternoon. This is when commuters are travelling to and from work. Commuters are people who live in one place and travel to their place of work somewhere else. Typical commuters are those people who live on the edge of the city and travel each day to work in the centre.

Traffic congestion in London **A**

B The urban traffic problem

Causes

- Greater wealth has increased car ownership. Many families even have two cars.
- People commuting to work or travelling to city centres for shopping or entertainment.
- Reduction of public transport at the expense of private cars.
- More vans and lorries delivering goods to city locations.

Effects

Environment
- Air pollution from vehicle exhausts.
- Noise pollution from cars, lorries and buses.
- Visual pollution of motorways and car parks.

Economy
- Time wasted sitting in traffic jams.
- Cost of building and maintaining new roads.
- Use of non-renewable resources.

People and buildings
- Danger of accidents and stress to drivers.
- Destruction of property to make way for new roads and car parks.
- Damage to foundations caused by traffic vibration.

Solutions

Cities have responded to the urban traffic problem in a number of ways. They have built bypasses to divert traffic from the centre, and expressways to improve access to the centre. They encourage motorists to leave their cars in the suburbs with park-and-ride schemes. They discourage the use of cars by restricting parking and increasing charges. Some cities have invested in new public transport systems, such as the Tyne and Wear Metro, Sheffield Supertram and Manchester Metrolink.

BART – the San Francisco Bay Area Rapid Transit System

Like most large towns, San Francisco receives thousands of commuters every weekday. Unfortunately the situation of the city on a huge bay with just five major road bridges, makes travel in the area even more difficult.

During the 1960s an increasingly large percentage of people travelled by car causing congestion, accidents and pollution. At peak times it could take an hour to cross the 5 km long Oakland Bridge.

San Francisco's answer to the problem was to build the Bay Area Rapid Transit system (BART), which opened in 1974 and has since been extended. The system consists of 120 km of electric railway. Trains travel both above and below the ground, as well as in a tunnel under San Francisco Bay. The railway is earthquake-proof, and experienced no problems during the 'quake of 1989, when several car drivers were killed as part of the Bay Bridge and two-level freeway collapsed.

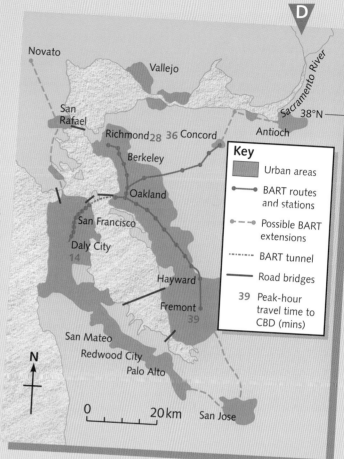

D

Key

- Urban areas
- BART routes and stations
- Possible BART extensions
- BART tunnel
- Road bridges
- 39 Peak-hour travel time to CBD (mins)

BART has certainly reduced traffic congestion in the Bay area and has been particularly successful in linking the more distant commuter locations with San Francisco's commercial centre. There are still concerns about the lack of adequate parking at some stations, and the cost of running the system.

C

Advantages

- Electric, so pollution free.
- Is able to carry over 35,000 commuters a day.
- Very fast, with speeds up to 120 km/hr.
- Efficient service with trains every 2 minutes at peak times.
- Comfortable, air-conditioned, noiseless carriages.
- Fully automatic and computerised system.
- Long platforms for easy alighting and boarding.
- Lower fares than buses to attract users off road.
- Car parking at suburban stations.
- Covers main out-of-town commuter areas.

E BART train

Osaka–Kobe
Some problems

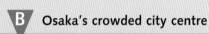

The twin cities of Osaka–Kobe are located in the Kansai region of the Japanese island of Honshu. They lie on a small area of flat land between the mountains and Osaka Bay.

The area has a population of over 9 million, and is a world leader in education, science, business technology and industry – but this success has not been achieved without creating problems.

Housing. Osaka and Kobe have grown rapidly in the last 50 years. Most of the available flat land has now been used up. This has led to a very high housing density and very small homes. The average house size is eight times smaller than a UK house.

Transport. The unplanned growth and rapid increase in road traffic has caused major transport problems. Roads are congested and vehicle exhausts cause severe air pollution.

Port. Osaka port is very busy, with 1,400 ships a day entering the docks. The ships bring in oil and other raw materials. The main exports are manufactured goods.

Industry. Most industry is concentrated along Osaka Bay where there are oil refineries, steelworks and other industries

processing raw materials. The main problem is a lack of space for factories and storage.

Pollution. The large volume of road traffic and smoke from heavy industries cause serious air pollution. Rubbish dumped at sea and oil spilled from ships pollutes Osaka Bay.

Physical environment. Japan is on a destructive plate boundary and suffers regular earthquakes and volcanic eruptions. The 1995 Kobe earthquake killed 5,500 people and destroyed large areas of the city. Japan is also affected by tropical storms which bring heavy rain and hurricane-force winds.

A

HOKKAIDO

N

HONSHU

● Tokyo

■ Osaka–Kobe

SHIKOKU

KYUSHU

B Osaka's crowded city centre

Osaka–Kobe
Some solutions

Housing. Two huge islands have been made in Osaka Bay by reclaiming land from the sea. Much of Rokko Island is a new town, with housing in the form of flats. These are close to schools, shopping centres, hospitals, parks and places of entertainment. Traffic is segregated from housing, whilst a railway takes commuters to Kobe.

Transport

- **Rail** – the Shinkansen or 'bullet train' provides one of the fastest and most reliable rail journeys in the world. It travels at speeds up to 300 km/hr and carries 275 million people a year.
- **Road** – a new road links Osaka–Kobe with the islands of Awaji and Shikoku. A further extension to Kyushu is planned.
- **Air** – Kansai International Airport has been built on land reclaimed from the sea. The terminal handles 30 million passengers a year.

Port development. Land has also been reclaimed from the sea for port extensions. Kobe's new container facility is on Port Island, which stretches some 7 km out to sea.

Industry. Industrial development has taken place at four locations:

1 On land next to Osaka Bay previously used by the Nippon steelworks.
2 On land reclaimed from Osaka Bay by levelling inland areas and depositing the waste material on the sea bed.
3 In 'science cities' created on the newly levelled sites.
4 Alongside major motorways.

Pollution. Japan – a rich country – has made serious attempts to clean up some of its pollution. The Inland Sea, once a 'dead' sea, now has fish and oyster farms. The new industries are cleaner than the old, and nuclear energy, despite the risks, causes less air pollution than fossil fuels.

Physical environment. Earthquakes and tropical storms cannot be controlled, but attempts can be made to reduce their effects. New buildings and bridges are now designed to withstand both earthquakes and hurricane-force winds.

D | Kansai International Airport on reclaimed land in Osaka Bay

REVISION QUESTIONS

1 (Pages 50 and 51)
a) List the problems of the CBD under the following headings:

Traffic   Shopping   Environment

b) Use the same headings to describe what has been done to reduce these problems.

2 (Pages 52 and 53)
a) What was the main reason for the decline of London Docklands?
b) What was Docklands housing like in 1981?
c) Describe four other problems in Docklands.
d) Describe four good points about the Docklands development scheme.
e) Why are some people against the Docklands development?

3 (Page 54)
a) What is a green belt?
b) Give three aims of green belts.
c) What are the advantages of green wedges?

4 (Page 54)
a) Make a copy of the diagram below and add four reasons to explain why the rural–urban fringe is attractive to developers.

1............   3............
2............   4............
Advantages for development

b) List the developments keen to locate on the rural–urban fringe that:
 - may provide employment for people
 - could improve people's quality of life.

5 (Page 55)
Give six advantages of building the MetroCentre on the outskirts of Gateshead.

6 (Page 56)
a) What are suburbanised villages?
b) Describe Braithwaite using these headings:
 - Braithwaite in 1925
 - Braithwaite today
 - Changes due to suburbanisation.

7 (Page 57)
a) What is the difference between a brownfield site and a greenfield site?
b) Do you think development should be mainly on brownfield sites or on greenfield sites?

8 (Page 59)
Use the following headings to describe urban traffic problems in San Francisco:

Causes   Effects   Solutions

9 (Pages 60 and 61)
a) Briefly describe the main features of Osaka–Kobe.
b) Copy and complete the table to show the city's problems and attempts to solve these problems.

Osaka–Kobe		
Feature	**Problem**	**Solution**
Housing		
Transport		
Port		
Industry		
Pollution		
Environment		

EXAMINATION QUESTIONS

1

(Pages 52 and 53)

a) Look at the information about Dunbar Wharf.
- In which part of London is Dunbar Wharf? (1)
- On which street is Dunbar Wharf located? (1)
- Give four advantages of living in Dunbar Wharf. (4)

b) Describe four problems of living in the Docklands area before it was redeveloped. (4)

c) Describe four ways in which the Docklands area has been improved. (4)

d) Suggest why some local people have been against the redevelopment. (2)

DUNBAR WHARF

Located in London's Docklands, Dunbar Wharf is a collection of large, luxury apartments. Each apartment has a balcony or terrace with spectacular views of the River Thames. Facilities include a gymnasium, secure parking and a riverside restaurant. Apartments are available now and priced from £460,000.

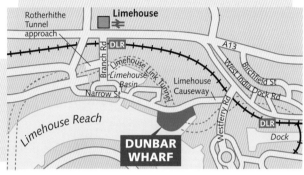

2

(Pages 54, 55 and 57)

a) Look at the locations marked J to N on map **B**. Which locations are likely to be:
- in the green belt
- possible brownfield sites
- possible greenfield sites? (3)

b) Why are greenfield sites on the rural–urban fringe attractive to developers? (4)

c) Five possible sites for an out-of-town shopping centre are numbered 1 to 5 on map **B**. Which site do you think is the best location? Give four reasons for your answer. (4)

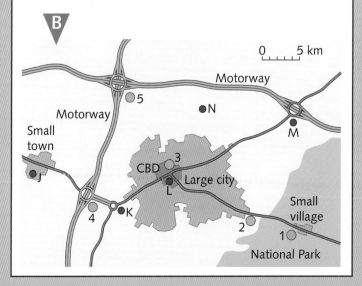

B

3

(Pages 58 and 59)

a) What was the traffic index in 1990? (1)

b) In which year had the traffic index doubled to 200? (1)

c) Give two reasons for the increase in traffic flow in cities such as Cambridge. (2)

d) Suggest four problems that would be caused by the increase in traffic in a city like Cambridge. (4)

e) Describe a scheme to reduce traffic congestion in a named town or city that you have studied. (4)

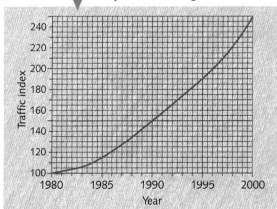

C   Traffic movement in the city of Cambridge, 1980–2000

The traffic index is a measure of the amount of traffic. It begins in 1980 with 100 vehiclies

5

URBANISATION IN DEVELOPING COUNTRIES

Growth of cities

More and more people are choosing to live in cities. This **urbanisation** process, as it is called, was most rapid in the richer, more developed countries during the Industrial Revolution of the 19th century. At that time, people moved from the countryside to work in factories, mines and shipyards that were located in the towns and cities. The UK's urban population has now reached 90%, but as graph **A** shows, urbanisation in developed countries has slowed down.

Nowadays, urbanisation is most rapid in the poorer, less developed countries. Here, urban growth is more to do with difficult conditions in the countryside forcing people to move into cities in the hope of improving their chances in life. Unfortunately this hope is rarely fulfilled as there are just too many newcomers for the city authorities to cope with, and not enough work for them to earn a living. Despite these problems, people continue to flood into cities throughout the developing world.

> Urbanisation is the increase in the proportion of people living in towns and cities.

> A developing country is often quite poor, has few services and a low standard of living.

A Percentage of population living in urban areas

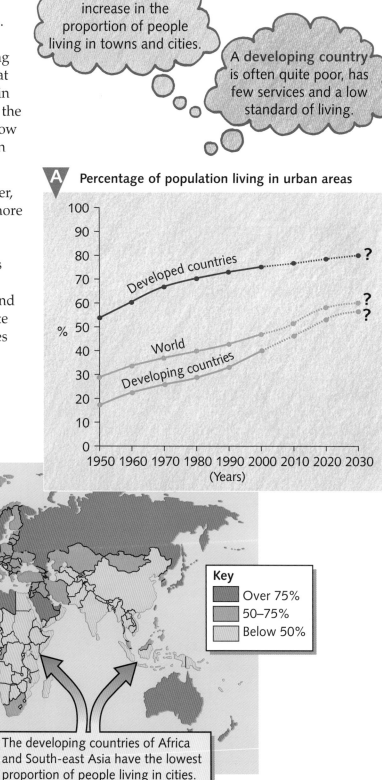

B People living in urban areas

The developed countries of North America and Western Europe have the highest proportion of people living in cities.

Countries in South America are generally poor but many are developing rapidly and already have over 75% of their people living in cities.

The developing countries of Africa and South-east Asia have the lowest proportion of people living in cities.

Key
- Over 75%
- 50–75%
- Below 50%

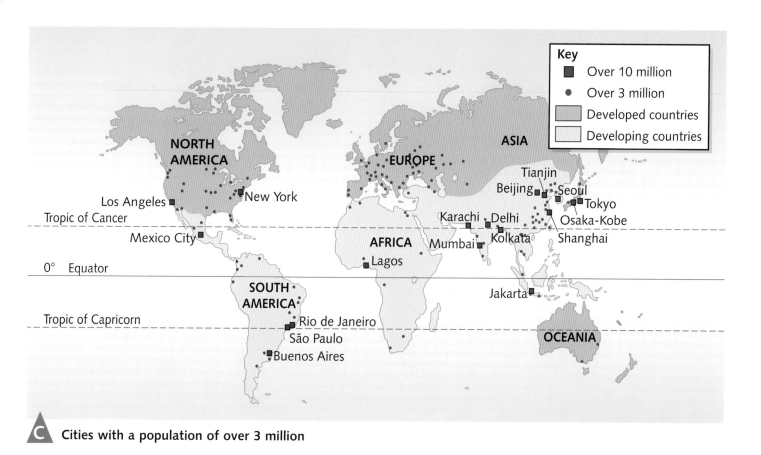

C Cities with a population of over 3 million

Key
■ Over 10 million
• Over 3 million
▨ Developed countries
☐ Developing countries

Million cities and megacities

Not only have cities become popular places in which to live, but in the last 30 years there has also been a large increase of **million cities** – that is, places with a population of more than 1 million. The most rapidly growing cities of all, though, are the **megacities** or **super cities** whose populations exceed 10 million. At the moment, the largest of these are Tokyo, Mexico City and New York.

Before 1950 most very large cities were in the richer and more developed countries of the North. Beyond the year 2010, however, there will probably be more than 30 super cities, most of them in the less developed countries of the South.

Fastest growing cities

Many people are concerned about how quickly some cities are growing. The populations of most of the cities shown on map **D** are expected to double in the next 10 years. This will produce some very large cities and cause many problems, particularly in the poorer countries of the world.

Take Dhaka, for example, the capital city of Bangladesh. At the moment just over 6 million people live there, but the population is increasing by almost a million every year. That is the same as all the inhabitants of Liverpool or Glasgow suddenly arriving in Dhaka in a single year. Think of the problems that must cause for newcomers, the existing inhabitants and the city authorities.

D Ten of the world's fastest growing cities

1 Mexico City	6 Kinshasa
2 Bogota	7 Addis Ababa
3 Lima	8 Madras
4 Belo Horizonte	9 Dhaka
5 São Paulo	10 Seoul

Key
▨ Richer, more developed countries
☐ Poorer, less developed countries

Urban growth

The movement of people from countryside areas to cities is called **rural-to-urban migration**. In the developing world, this started about a hundred years ago, at the beginning of the 20th century. Since then the movement has increased so rapidly that during the past 10 years some places have almost doubled their population.

People move or migrate from one place to another for two reasons. Firstly they may wish to get away from things they do not like. These are called **push factors**. Secondly, people are attracted to things that they do like. These are called **pull factors**. Some of these factors are shown in figures **A** and **B**.

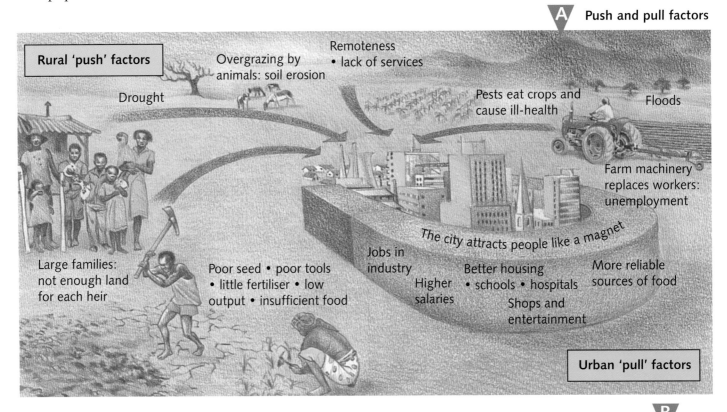

A **Push and pull factors**

Rural 'push' factors

Drought

Overgrazing by animals: soil erosion

Remoteness
• lack of services

Pests eat crops and cause ill-health

Floods

Farm machinery replaces workers: unemployment

Large families: not enough land for each heir

Poor seed • poor tools • little fertiliser • low output • insufficient food

Jobs in industry

The city attracts people like a magnet

Higher salaries

Better housing • schools • hospitals

Shops and entertainment

More reliable sources of food

Urban 'pull' factors

B

PUSH factors

PULL factors

- Poor wages and shortage of jobs.

- Chance of natural disasters and crop failures.

- Difficult conditions, with poor housing and low standards of living.

- Lack of services such as schools, hospitals, clean water and electricity.

- Limited food production and possible starvation due to overgrazing and land misuse.

- Country life is hard work, with little chance to enjoy oneself.

- Unhappy life with few opportunities for personal progress.

- More job opportunities in industry and services, with higher wages.

- Fewer natural disasters in cities.

- Better housing and a better quality of life.

- Better chance of services such as schools, medical care, water and electricity supply.

- More reliable sources of food.

- Attraction of 'bright lights' and entertainment.

- More opportunities and a better chance of enjoying life.

C The dream – glittering skyscrapers in Hong Kong

People migrate in the hope of improving their living conditions and having a better chance in life. They expect, or are led to believe, that the city will provide everything they need. They dream of the good life and a bright future for themselves and their family.

The reality is often very different. New arrivals to the city are unlikely to have any money and are usually poorly educated and without work skills. They are unable to buy a house and have to make a temporary shelter from cheap or waste material. Few people find jobs, and almost all remain very poor.

D The reality – slum houses in Ho Chi Minh City, Vietnam

Problems in residential areas

Although different in some ways, towns and cities all tend to be set out in a similar way. For example, the main shopping areas are found in the centre and housing around the outskirts. Any industries are usually grouped together near the city centre or along routeways leading out of town. When a simple map is drawn to show these patterns, it is called an **urban land use model**.

Diagram **A** shows the pattern of land use for a city in the developing world. Look carefully at the residential areas: you should see marked differences in their quality and location. However, these differences are not the same as those found in cities of the developed world shown on pages 38 and 39. There are three main differences:

1 The gap between the wealth of the rich and the poor is much greater than in the developed world. This means that the contrast between rich and poor housing, in terms of quality and amenity provision, is also greater.
2 Most better-off areas are near to the city centre whilst poorer areas are near to the edge of the city.
3 Many people live in slum areas called shanty towns.

Self-help schemes

Large numbers of people in developing cities live in slum areas called **shanty towns** or **squatter settlements**. A shanty town is a collection of shacks and poor-quality housing which often lack electricity, a water supply or sewage disposal.

Most local authorities would prefer not to have shanty towns, but they cannot afford to provide new, high-quality housing to replace them. To overcome this problem, they encourage people to improve their own property through **self-help schemes**. In these schemes, the authority provides land, a small loan, cheap building materials and basic services. The squatters then help each other to build their own homes and improve their living conditions.

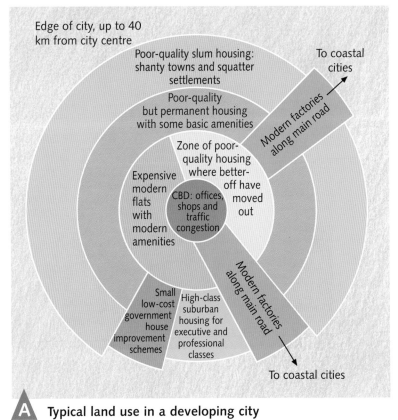

A Typical land use in a developing city

B A self-help housing scheme in São Paulo – a 'slum of hope'

São Paulo

São Paulo is the largest and richest city in Brazil. Its recent growth has been due mainly to the arrival of migrants from the rural areas. With a population increasing from 7 million to 23 million in the last 30 years, the city authorities have an almost impossible task of providing sufficient housing and services.

Housing for the well-off

These people live in elegant, expensive houses with large gardens and swimming pools. The properties are protected by security guards and located near to the CBD.

Housing for the poor (favelas)

Location. Favelas are located on land that no one else will use. Typically these are in marshy areas, on steep hillsides and even on rubbish tips. Most are on the edge of the city.

Features. The housing is a collection of primitive shacks made from wood, corru-gated iron, cardboard, sacking or anything else available. Some may have only one room in which everyone has to live, eat and sleep. Disease is common, with open sewers and no rubbish collection.

The people. Most are newcomers to the city with large families and no money or jobs. They are squatters with no legal right to the land they occupy, and can be forced off at any time.

South America

Equator

BRAZIL

N

São Paulo • • Rio de Janeiro

Atlantic Ocean C

0   800 km

D A favela in São Paulo – a 'slum of despair'

E Self-help schemes

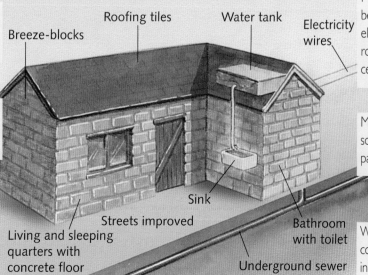

Groups of people work together to build or improve their own homes.

Local authority provides building materials and the group provides labour.

Roofing tiles

Breeze-blocks

Water tank

Electricity wires

Money saved by authority can be spent on providing electricity, clean water, tarred roads and a community centre.

Most inhabitants will have some employment and pay a low rent.

Advantages:
- can be done in stages
- creates community spirit
- is relatively cheap, so more houses can be provided.

Sink

Streets improved

Living and sleeping quarters with concrete floor

Bathroom with toilet

Underground sewer

Improved road

Water tank collects rainwater and is connected to outside wash basin and indoor bathroom.

Problems in developing cities

Kolkata (Calcutta)

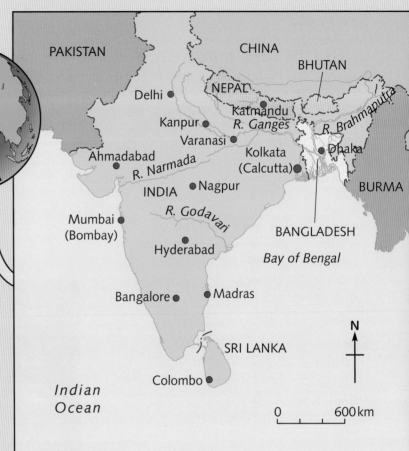

A Location of Kolkata

Kolkata (Calcutta) is a good example of how problems are created when cities grow too quickly. The city is built on flat, swampy land alongside the River Hooghly, which is part of the Ganges Delta. It is India's largest city with a population of over 16 million. This population has increased by more than 9 million in the last 30 years. The city authorities have no hope of providing enough new homes, jobs or services for the increasing population.

Housing. Over a quarter of a million people sleep in the open, covered only by bamboo, sacking, polythene sheets or cardboard. A further 3 million live in **shanty towns** called **bustees**. Here, the shacks are built of mud, straw and scrap materials. The houses are packed tightly together and are separated by narrow alleys. Inside each house there is probably only one room in which the whole family, perhaps 10 in number, have to live, eat and sleep. Despite the overcrowding, most houses are clean and tidy.

B Street dwellers in Kolkata

Services. Houses lack electricity, running water and sewage disposal. There are very few schools and a lack of doctors and hospitals. Public transport is often absent or totally overcrowded.

Sanitation and health. One water tap and one toilet in each alley may serve up to 100 people. Sewage often flows down the alley and may pollute drinking water, causing cholera, typhoid and dysentery. Rubbish dumped in the street, provides an ideal breeding ground for disease.

Transport. Most people have to walk or use the overcrowded public transport system. Both buses and trains are old and dangerous. They are always overcrowded, and passengers sit on the roof and hang onto the outside. Traffic noise and congestion continue, despite a new bridge over the Hooghly and an underground rail system.

Employment. Those with jobs often use their homes as a place of work. The front of the house can be opened up to allow the occupants to sell food, wood, clothes and household utensils. Almost everyone in the bustees does some work, but most jobs only occupy a few hours a week and earn very little money.

Improvements. Several organisations have been set up in recent years to try to make the bustees more habitable, by paving alleys, digging drains and providing more taps and toilets.

Prefabricated houses have been built and a better community atmosphere created. Even so, the lack of money has meant that only relatively small areas have been improved.

Key

- Upper class
- Middle class
- Artisan class
- Farmers and scheduled castes
- Central industrial area
- Migrants in shanty towns

Howrah

Hooghly Bridge

City centre

R. Hooghly

Maidan

City boundary

N

0   3 km

C Kolkata's residential areas

D Problems with clean water

E Traffic problems

Places

71

Rio de Janeiro

Some problems

Rio de Janeiro is situated around the huge natural harbour of Guanabara Bay in south-east Brazil. It is one of the world's **megacities**, with a population of around 10 million people which is increasing rapidly every day.

Housing. Over a half a million people in Rio have no homes at all and sleep in the street. A further 2 million live in **shanty towns** called **favelas**.

Many of the favelas are huge, with up to 100,000 people living in them. The houses are crowded together, and have no piped water or sewerage. They are constructed from wood, corrugated iron, broken bricks and any other materials available.

Most favelas in Rio are built on hillsides which are con-sidered too steep for normal houses. When it rains, flash floods can cause mudslides and carry away the flimsy homes. Over 200 people died in a mudslide in 1988.

Crime. Rio has a bad reputation for crime, and drug trafficking is a particular problem. The favelas are the worst areas for organised crime and violence. Tourists visiting the city centre and famous beaches of Copacabana and Ipanema are warned not to take valuables with them or wear jewellery or watches.

Traffic. Although the mountains add to Rio's attractiveness, they channel traffic along a limited number of routes, which causes severe congestion.

Pollution. An industrial haze intensified by traffic fumes is a permanent feature of the city. In addition, much of Guanabara Bay is polluted by open sewers pouring waste products directly into the sea.

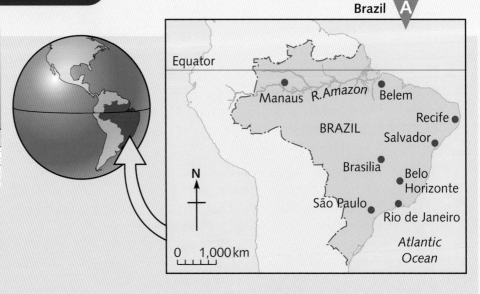

Brazil **A**

B A favela on a steep hillside

Rio de Janeiro

Some solutions

Self-help housing schemes.
Improvements have been made
to some slum housing through
self-help schemes. With help
from the local authorities the
people of Rocinha have
transformed their favela into a
small city:

- The old wooden buildings
  have been upgraded to brick
  and tile.
- Shops and places of entertainment have been opened.
- Small informal industries
  have been set up to create
  jobs.
- Electricity, paved roads and
  piped water have been
  provided.

The Favela Bairro project. The
city authorities have recently set
aside £200 million to improve
living conditions in 60 of the
600 favelas. The plan includes:

- replacing wooden shacks
  with larger brick and tile
  buildings
- widening streets so that
  emergency services and
  waste collection vehicles can
  have access
- laying pipes for clean water
  provision and cables for
  electricity
- improving sanitation and
  adding health facilities.

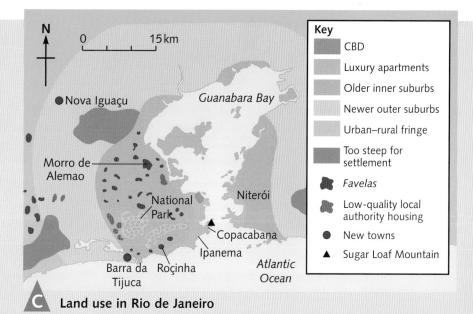

C   **Land use in Rio de Janeiro**

By using local labour to complete
the scheme, residents have
developed new skills, and now
have a feeling of ownership.

**The new town of Barra da
Tijuca.** Barra da Tijuca is a self-
contained city built along the
coastal motorway some 20 km
west of Rio. Its main features
include:

- 5 km of shops, schools,
  hospitals, offices and places
  of entertainment

- high-rise apartments with
  spacious, luxury
  accommodation and security
  guard protection
- large areas of single and two-
  storey houses with every
  possible amenity
- an efficient bus service linking
  the apartments, shops and
  leisure amenities.

Sadly, Barra already has its
new favelas. These house the
cleaners, housekeepers, cooks
and gardeners who work for
the rich people.

D   **View of Barra da Tijuca new town**

1 (Pages 64 and 65)
Write down the meaning of the following terms:
a) urbanisation   b) millionaire city
c) megacity.

2 (Pages 64 and 65)
a) When was urbanisation most rapid in the richer, more developed countries? Give a reason for this.
b) When was urbanisation most rapid in the poorer, less developed countries? Give a reason for this.

3 (Pages 64 and 65)
a) Name the largest cities in the developing world.
b) How has the distribution of the world's largest cities changed over time?

4 (Pages 66 and 67)
Give the meaning of the following terms:
a) rural-to-urban migration
b) push factors
c) pull factors.

5 (Pages 66 and 67)
Sort the following statements into **push factors**, **pull factors**, or both **push and pull factors**:

a) I was forced off my land. I had to leave.

b) A friend offered me a job and a place to live.

c) My sons were ill. There was no healthcare.

d) I moved to the city for a more interesting life.

e) Our village was washed away by floods.

f) I had no work and my family were in the city.

6 (Pages 68 and 69)
This diagram is a land use model for a city in the developing world. Match the following with letters A, B, C, D, E and F on the model:
■ Squatters who have built shanty towns
■ A large shopping centre and office blocks
■ Factories along main roads
■ Improved housing with some basic amenities
■ Modern, luxury high-rise flats
■ Low-cost government housing scheme

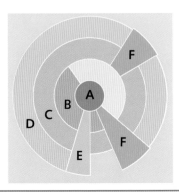

7 (Pages 38, 39, 68 and 69)
Give two ways that the pattern of land use in a developed city is different from that of a developing city.

8 (Pages 68 and 69)
Describe the shanty towns of São Paulo, using these headings:
■ Shanty town definition
■ Reason for shanties
■ Location
■ Features
■ People.

9 (Pages 68 and 69)
Use the following headings to describe how self-help schemes can help improve living conditions in shanty towns:

| Definition | Features | Advantages |

10 (Pages 70 and 71)
a) Describe Kolkata's location.
b) Why have the authorities little chance of improving conditions in Kolkata?
c) Describe the problems caused by rapid urbanisation in Kolkata.

11 (Pages 72 and 73)
a) Describe Rio de Janeiro's location.
b) Draw a star diagram to show some of Rio's problems.
c) Describe three schemes that have helped improve housing in Rio de Janeiro.

EXAMINATION QUESTIONS

1

(Pages 64 and 65)

a) Use map **A** to answer these questions. Write out each sentence using the correct word from the brackets.
- The city with the largest population in 1990 was (Mexico City **or** New York **or** Tokyo). (1)
- The city with the largest population in 2015 will be (Mexico City **or** Bombay **or** Tokyo). (1)
- The city with the largest population growth between 1990 and 2015 is (Cairo **or** Mumbai). (1)
- The city with the smallest population growth between 1990 and 2015 is (Mumbai **or** London). (1)
- Most of the fastest growing cities are in the (richer **or** poorer) countries of the world. (1)

b) What is meant by **urbanisation**? (1)

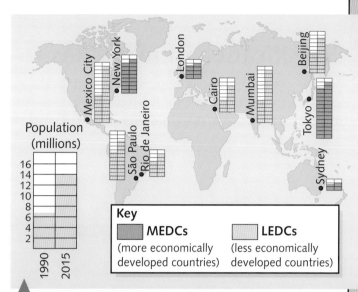

Key

| MEDCs (more economically developed countries) | LEDCs (less economically developed countries) |

Population (millions)
16
14
12
10
8
6
4
2

1990 2015

A Population in 10 cities: 1990 and 2015 (projected)

2

(Pages 66 and 67)

One reason why cities in the world's poorer countries are growing quickly is migration from the countryside. Diagram **B** shows some reasons for this migration.

a) What is migration? (1)
b) What are push factors? (1)
c) Give two more push factors. (2)
d) What are pull factors? (1)
e) Give two more pull factors. (2)
f) Give three problems caused by this migration. (3)

PUSH PULL

- Lack of opportunities
- Unhappy life

Hope for:
- *better way of life*
- *better living conditions*

B

3

(Pages 68–73)

The very fast growth of cities in poorer countries can lead to the growth of shanty towns.

a) Describe three features of the shanty town home shown in photo **C**. (3)
b) Describe three difficulties for people who live in the shanty towns. (3)
c) Use a named example that you have studied to explain how a shanty town can be improved. (3)

A home in a shanty town **C**

EMPLOYMENT STRUCTURES

Classification of industries

Most people have to **work** to provide the things they need in life. Another name for the work they do is **industry**. There are so many different types of work and industry that it is helpful to put them into groups. Traditionally, there were three main groups: **primary**, **secondary** and **tertiary** industries. Since the 1980s a fourth group has been added: this is called **quaternary** industries.

A

Primary industries employ people to collect or produce natural resources from the land or sea. Farming, fishing, forestry and mining are examples of primary industries.

B

Secondary industries employ people to make things. These are usually made from raw materials or involve assembling several parts into a finished product. Examples are steelmaking, house construction and car assembly plants. **Manufacturing** is another name for this industry.

C

Tertiary industries provide a service for people. They give help to others. No goods are made in this industry. Teachers, nurses, shop assistants and entertainers are examples of people in tertiary industry occupations. This is sometimes called a **service** industry.

D

Quaternary industries are a type of service industry. People working in quaternary industries carry out research, provide information and give advice. They include financial advisers, research scientists, market researchers and football agents.

Employment structures

The proportion of people working in primary, secondary and tertiary jobs in any place is called the **employment structure**.

Employment structures change over a period of time and vary from one place to another. They also give an indication of how rich or how poor a country is. Poorer, developing countries tend to have most people working in primary industries such as farming. Richer, more developed countries, have their highest percentage of workers in the tertiary sector.

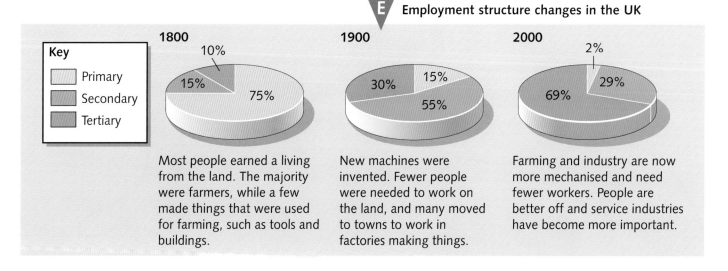

E Employment structure changes in the UK

Key
- Primary
- Secondary
- Tertiary

1800
10%
15%
75%

Most people earned a living from the land. The majority were farmers, while a few made things that were used for farming, such as tools and buildings.

1900
15%
30%
55%

New machines were invented. Fewer people were needed to work on the land, and many moved to towns to work in factories making things.

2000
2%
29%
69%

Farming and industry are now more mechanised and need fewer workers. People are better off and service industries have become more important.

Change over time

Employment structures change as a country develops. Graph **E** shows these changes for the UK.

Changes between places

Employment structures vary between countries, between regions and even within regions. Map **F** compares regional employment structures in the UK.

Notice that every region has fewest workers in the primary sector and most in the tertiary sector. This is typical of a richer, more developed country.

Notice also, though, that the proportion in each region varies considerably. For example, compare south-east England with the West Midlands.

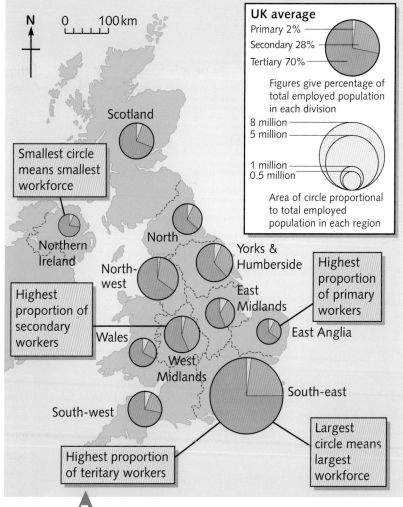

N   0   100 km

UK average
Primary 2%
Secondary 28%
Tertiary 70%

Figures give percentage of total employed population in each division

8 million
5 million

1 million
0.5 million

Area of circle proportional to total employed population in each region

Scotland

Smallest circle means smallest workforce

Northern Ireland

North

Yorks & Humberside

North-west

Highest proportion of secondary workers

Wales

East Midlands

Highest proportion of primary workers

East Anglia

West Midlands

South-east

South-west

Highest proportion of teritary workers

Largest circle means largest workforce

F Employment structures for the UK, 2003

Employment structures and development

World employment structures

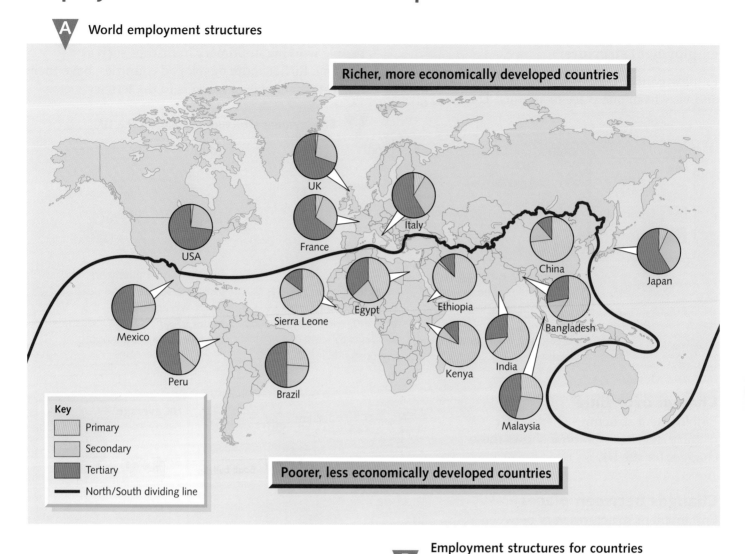

Richer, more economically developed countries

Key
- Primary
- Secondary
- Tertiary
- North/South dividing line

Poorer, less economically developed countries

Usually there is a link between the employment structure of a country and its level of development.

The **richer, developed countries** have:
- a very high percentage in the tertiary sector
- a high percentage in the secondary sector and
- a very low percentage in the primary sector.

The **poorer, developing countries** have:
- a very high percentage in the primary sector
- a low percentage in the secondary sector and
- a low percentage in the tertiary sector.

Look at map **A**. It compares employment structures for several countries. Notice how the UK and USA closely fit the description of developed countries. Kenya and Sierra Leone are good examples of developing countries.

Graph **B** ranks the countries according to the proportion of people employed in the primary sector.

B Employment structures for countries at different levels of development

% employed

	0	10	20	30	40	50	60	70	80	90	100
Ethiopia											
Kenya											
China											
Sierra Leone											
Bangladesh											
India											
Egypt											
Peru											
Malaysia											
Mexico											
Brazil											
Italy											
Japan											
France											
USA											
UK											

78

REVISION QUESTIONS

1 (Pages 76 and 77)
Write a definition of the four main types of industry, and give an example of each:
a) primary
b) secondary
c) tertiary
d) quaternary.

2 (Pages 76 and 77)
a) What is meant by **employment structure**?
b) What was the UK's main employment type:
- in 1800
- in 2000?
c) Why is the UK's employment structure different in 2000 from the structure in 1800?

3 (Page 78)
Make a larger copy of the drawing below.
a) Name country A and country B. (Choose from the countries on map **A** on page 78.)
b) Give three facts about the employment structure for each country.

A Developed country   B Developing country

EXAMINATION QUESTIONS

1 (Page 76)
Make a larger copy of the table below.
a) Give a short definition for each type of job. (4)
b) Write the jobs from drawing **A** into the correct columns. (5)

Primary	Secondary	Tertiary	Quaternary

Boat builder
Football star
Bank manager
Oil rig worker
Film star agent
Shepherd
Bricklayer
Medical research worker
Copper miner
Truck driver

JOB CENTRE
VACANCIES

2 (Pages 76 to 78)
Look at graph **B**.
a) What percentage of primary jobs are there in the LEDC countries? (1)
b) What percentage of tertiary jobs are there in the MEDC countries? (1)
c) Complete the following sentences using the correct words from the brackets:
- In an LEDC, most people have a (primary **or** tertiary) job. This is because there are (few **or** many) machines to do the work on farms.
- In an MEDC, most people have a (primary **or** tertiary) job. There are many machines to do the work in factories. This means that secondary employment is likely to be (increasing **or** decreasing). (4)

B   A less economically developed country (LEDC)

0 10 20 30 40 50 60 70 80 90 100%

A more economically developed country (MEDC)

0 10 20 30 40 50 60 70 80 90 100%

Key
Primary   Secondary   Tertiary

Farming systems

Farming, or **agriculture**, is the way that people produce food by growing crops and raising animals. A farm is really just a factory. The things it needs to make it work are called **inputs**. What happens on the farm are its **processes**. What it produces are called **outputs**. When put together, these three things are called a **farming system**.

Diagrams **A** and **B** below show farming systems for two different types of farm. Notice that some features are the same but others are different.

The farmer as a decision maker

The main aims of the farming industry are to produce food and make a profit. To do this, a farmer must choose carefully what crops to grow, what animals to rear and what methods to use. These decisions depend on several different factors.

Of these, physical factors are probably the most important. They include temperature, rainfall, sunshine, soil type and whether the land is flat or hilly. Economic conditions such as market demand, input costs and transport expenses must also be considered.

A Simple farming system for an arable farm

Inputs	Processes	Outputs
• Sunshine		• Wheat, barley
• Rainfall		• Potatoes
• Flat land		• Vegetables
• Good, deep soils		• Flowers
• Seeds		• Profit
• Fertiliser		
• Machinery		
• Labour		
• Money		

Processes:
• Ploughing • Planting
• Crop spraying • Harvesting

B Simple farming system for a pastoral farm

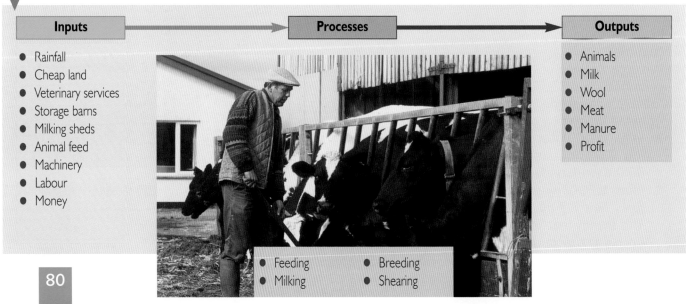

Inputs	Processes	Outputs
• Rainfall		• Animals
• Cheap land		• Milk
• Veterinary services		• Wool
• Storage barns		• Meat
• Milking sheds		• Manure
• Animal feed		• Profit
• Machinery		
• Labour		
• Money		

Processes:
• Feeding • Breeding
• Milking • Shearing

Types of farming

In Britain there are three main types of farming:

- **Arable** is the ploughing of the land and growing of crops.
- **Pastoral** is leaving the land under grass and the rearing of animals.
- **Mixed** is when crops are grown and animals are reared in the same area.

Distribution

Map **C** below shows the distribution of the main types of farming in the UK. Their location is due mainly to physical factors. The cool summers, heavy rainfall and hilly conditions of the north and west are most suited to pastoral farming. The south and east with its warm summers, dry climate and low-lying flat land is more suited to arable and mixed farming.

Classification of types of farming

On a world scale there are many other different types of farming. Some of these are shown below, and explained through examples in the following pages.

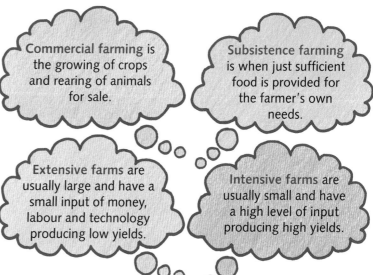

Commercial farming is the growing of crops and rearing of animals for sale.

Subsistence farming is when just sufficient food is provided for the farmer's own needs.

Extensive farms are usually large and have a small input of money, labour and technology producing low yields.

Intensive farms are usually small and have a high level of input producing high yields.

C Farming in the UK

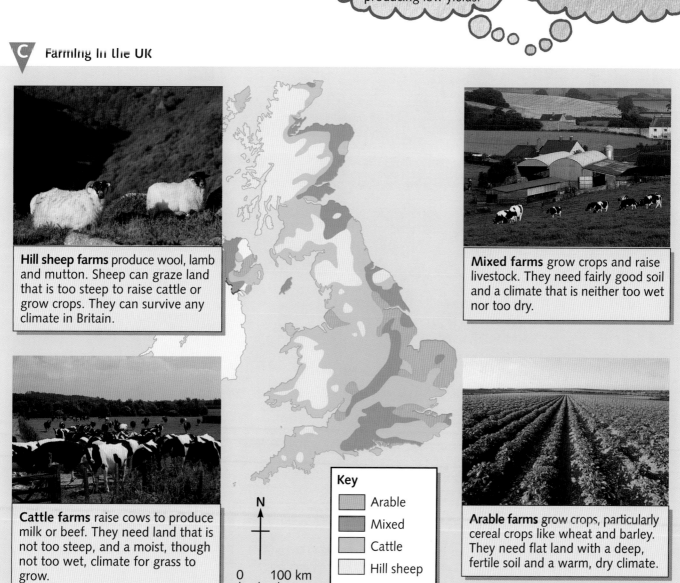

Hill sheep farms produce wool, lamb and mutton. Sheep can graze land that is too steep to raise cattle or grow crops. They can survive any climate in Britain.

Mixed farms grow crops and raise livestock. They need fairly good soil and a climate that is neither too wet nor too dry.

Cattle farms raise cows to produce milk or beef. They need land that is not too steep, and a moist, though not too wet, climate for grass to grow.

Arable farms grow crops, particularly cereal crops like wheat and barley. They need flat land with a deep, fertile soil and a warm, dry climate.

Key

	Arable
	Mixed
	Cattle
	Hill sheep

N

0   100 km

Factors affecting farming

To be successful, a farmer must choose carefully what crops to grow, what animals to rear and what farming methods to use. The type of farming most suited to an area depends on both the physical and human conditions at that location. This means that certain areas will be more suited to one type of farming than another. Groups of farmers in this area therefore tend to specialise in that one type.

Map **A** shows the distribution of major farming types in the EU. It is a very simplified map but allows broad patterns to be identified.

A Farming in the EU

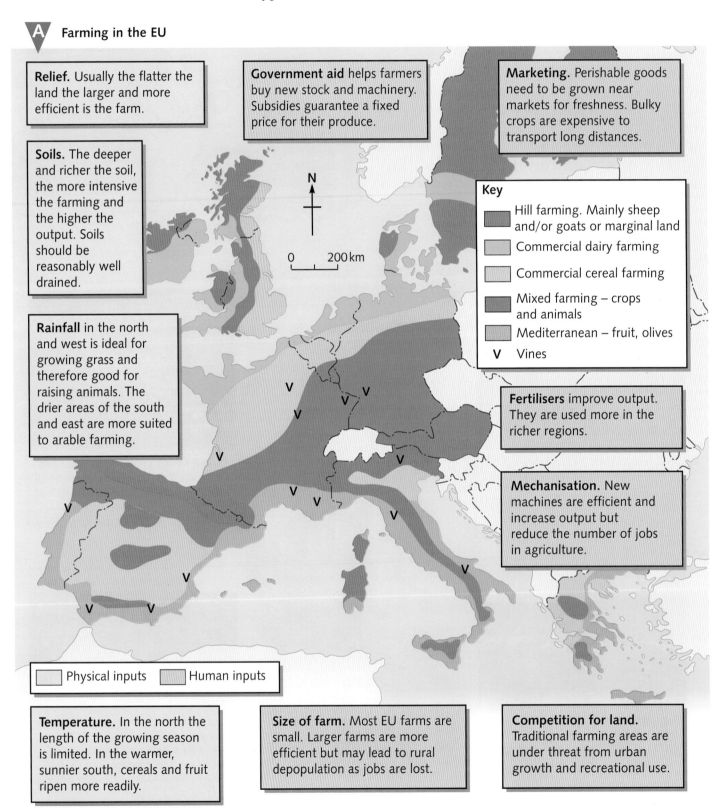

Relief. Usually the flatter the land the larger and more efficient is the farm.

Soils. The deeper and richer the soil, the more intensive the farming and the higher the output. Soils should be reasonably well drained.

Rainfall in the north and west is ideal for growing grass and therefore good for raising animals. The drier areas of the south and east are more suited to arable farming.

Government aid helps farmers buy new stock and machinery. Subsidies guarantee a fixed price for their produce.

Marketing. Perishable goods need to be grown near markets for freshness. Bulky crops are expensive to transport long distances.

Key

- Hill farming. Mainly sheep and/or goats or marginal land
- Commercial dairy farming
- Commercial cereal farming
- Mixed farming – crops and animals
- Mediterranean – fruit, olives
- **V** Vines

Fertilisers improve output. They are used more in the richer regions.

Mechanisation. New machines are efficient and increase output but reduce the number of jobs in agriculture.

Physical inputs   Human inputs

Temperature. In the north the length of the growing season is limited. In the warmer, sunnier south, cereals and fruit ripen more readily.

Size of farm. Most EU farms are small. Larger farms are more efficient but may lead to rural depopulation as jobs are lost.

Competition for land. Traditional farming areas are under threat from urban growth and recreational use.

Common Agricultural Policy (CAP)

The UK is a member of the European Union (EU), a group of countries that work together in order to improve their trade and living standards. One of the aims of the EU is 'to develop and improve farming across the whole of the EU'. To do this, a **Common** **Agricultural Policy** has been introduced which tries to help farmers provide an efficient and reliable way of producing food production within the EU. The CAP has been successful in many ways, but has also created problems and disagreements between member states.

1970s and 1980s – increasing concerns over the CAP

- 70% of the budget was spent on farming but farming only provided 5% of the income.
- Improved farming methods produced too much food, which was wasteful and brought prices down.
- Imports were subject to duties to make them less competitive. This caused problems for less developed countries.
- Farms became larger and more efficient but only the richer farmers benefited.

1992 – agricultural reform

Five aims were introduced to improve the CAP:

- To improve competitiveness by concentrating on quality rather than quantity, and training young farmers.
- To control overproduction by reducing financial support given to products that had a surplus.
- To ensure a fair standard of living for farmers by providing income support and early retirement.
- To maintain jobs in rural areas by introducing alternative forms of land use.
- To protect and enhance the environment by paying farmers to 'set aside' land to its natural state.

Successes

- Achieved increased self-sufficiency with less reliance on imports.
- Created higher yields due to new machinery and fertilisers.
- Produced more of the food that we need and less of that we don't need.
- Provided the opportunity for farmers to increase their income.
- Reduced the risk of farmer unemployment in some rural areas.

Problems

- Increased food prices, particularly in the UK and Germany.
- Large sums of money spent on subsidies to support farmers.
- Destruction of hedges destroyed wildlife and increased soil erosion.
- Uneven share of benefits, with some farmers and areas receiving little help.
- Reduced imports from developing countries has restricted their progress.

Pastoral farming in the Lake District

Harsh conditions and poor-quality land make farming difficult in the Lake District. Hill sheep like the **Herdwick** and **Swaledale** graze land that is too steep and infertile to raise cattle or grow crops. The low-lying, flatter valley floors have good-quality grass and are suitable for cattle rearing. A few crops like oats, barley and turnips are also grown here.

The farmer earns most of his money in autumn when lambs and four-year-old sheep are taken to market. Wool is sold in summer but is no longer a main source of money. Dairy cattle are milked daily and provide a small but regular income. The crops are grown in summer and given to the sheep and cattle as winter feed.

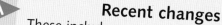

A

Recent changes

These include:

- a fall in the prices of lamb, sheep and wool has reduced profits to a minimum
- some marginal land has been taken out of production to save costs
- more farms have turned to other forms of income such as tourism, caravan sites and craft shops.

Physical inputs

- Heavy rainfall throughout the year
- Cool and cloudy summers
- Cold and often windy winters
- Steep valley sides with exposed rock
- Small areas of flat land on valley floors
- Thin, poor soils on hills support only rough grasses and heather
- Fertile but boggy soil on valley floors supports good-quality grass

B

Pastoral farming in the Lake District

Human inputs

- Poor communications with many narrow roads
- Long distances to markets
- Land unsuited to large-scale modern machinery
- Limited capital in area to fund improvements
- Farmers receive subsidies from the government and European Union

C A hill sheep farm in the Lake District

Arable farming in East Anglia

The climate, relief and soils of East Anglia are ideal for growing crops. These include cereals (mainly wheat and barley), root crops (potatoes and sugar beet) and vegetables (peas and beans).

Farms in the area are efficient and use modern methods. Many are owned by a company and run by a professional manager. Much use is made of machines such as combine harvesters and sprayers. Chemical fertilisers and pesticides are used to improve output.

The farmer makes his money, of course, from selling crops. Some crops, such as peas, go direct to large processing companies such as Bird's Eye. Others are kept in huge refrigerated stores and sold to wholesalers and supermarkets such as Tesco and Asda when prices are favourable.

 D

Recent changes

These include:

- larger farms encouraged by the EU
- larger fields for larger machinery
- increased use of fertiliser
- reduced subsidies to reduce overproduction in the EU
- increase in set-aside land (page 91).

Places

Physical inputs

- Rainfall is the lowest in the UK
- Most rain falls in the summer growing season
- Summers are warm and sunny
- Winters are cold with hard frosts that help break up the soil
- The land is flat or gently sloping
- Soils are deep, fertile and well drained

 E

Arable farming in East Anglia

Human inputs

- Good road and rail links save time and costs
- Large nearby markets in south-east England
- The land is ideal for the use of large-scale machinery
- Farms are large, efficient and use modern methods
- The region has considerable capital to fund improvements

Harvesting wheat on a large farm in East Anglia **F**

Farming in southern Italy

The Mezzogiorno before 1960

Map **A** shows the part of Italy that is known as the Mezzogiorno – 'the land of the midday sun'. It lies south of Rome and includes the two islands of Sicily and Sardinia. The Mezzogiorno is one of the poorest parts of the EU, with Basilicata described as 'the most disadvantaged of all the 160 EU regions'.

Farming is very difficult in the area. The landscape is mountainous and there is a shortage of good, flat land. Summers are very hot and dry, with drought conditions a common problem. The clay hillsides suffer erosion by the heavy winter rains, and the river valleys and coasts were, until recently, disease-ridden swamps. Land ownership was also a problem, with foreign landlords charging high rents to peasant farmers.

The South was also remote and cut off from the rest of Europe and had few decent roads or railways. There was little profitable industry and insufficient money to improve conditions.

Life was very tough for the local people. They worked long hours, produced little food and often suffered from ill-health. They had few opportunities in life. Many moved out of the rural areas to the big cities, or to the north of Italy. Rural depopulation left many villages with an elderly population and few people of working age.

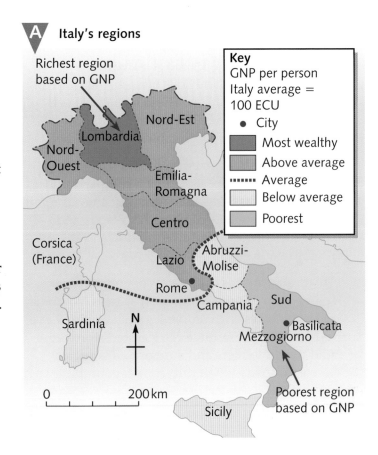

A Italy's regions

Richest region based on GNP

Key
GNP per person
Italy average = 100 ECU
- City
  Most wealthy
  Above average
  Average
  Below average
  Poorest

Nord-Est
Lombardia
Nord-Ouest
Emilia-Romagna
Centro
Corsica (France)
Lazio
Abruzzi-Molise
Rome
Campania
Sud
Sardinia
Basilicata
Mezzogiorno
N
0   200 km
Poorest region based on GNP
Sicily

B Peasant farming in southern Italy

The Mezzogiorno before 1960
- Water shortages in summer
- Wet and windy winters
- Few streams or rivers
- Poor-quality vegetation
- 85% of land hilly or mountainous
- Winter landslides and soil erosion
- Rough tracks and poor roads
- Landlords unhelpful to farmers
- Lack of skilled labour and industry
- Poverty and high unemployment
- Shortage of raw materials

Farming in the Mezzogiorno today

From 1950 until 1985, several organisations were set up by the Italian government to improve conditions in the Mezzogiorno. The European Union (EU), through the Common Agricultural Policy (CAP), also put in huge sums of money.

Most schemes tried to improve the services and industries of the Mezzogiorno as well as the agriculture. Fast new roads have been built and water and electricity supplies improved. Tourism has been encouraged by the opening of new hotels along the coast and in the mountains. New factories close to many of the towns have provided jobs and brought wealth to the area.

Agriculture has been improved by land reform which took away land from the rich and gave small plots to poor farm labourers. More intensive and efficient farming methods have been encouraged, with sprinkler systems and irrigation schemes enabling peaches, pears, oranges and lemons to be grown on a commercial scale.

Although some areas benefited from these developments, many mountainous areas saw little improvement. Whilst the region as a whole is certainly wealthier than in the 1950s, most of the Mezzogiorno remains poor by EU standards.

C

Some remaining problems
- Farming tends to be done by the older generation. It attracts few young people.
- Subsistence farming, which requires hard work and produces low yields, still exists.
- Increased mechanisation has led to further unemployment and abandoned farms.
- Many poor immigrants from Africa and the Middle East have arrived.
- The ground is unstable with soil erosion, landslides and earthquakes still a problem.
- The region is a long way from most EU markets. It has received little real help from the CAP.
- Many areas have been largely untouched by developments, and they remain backward.

D Vine growing in southern Italy

The Mezzogiorno today
- Improved roads to villages
- New schools and medical centres
- Piped water and improved sanitation
- Marsh areas drained
- Afforestation to reduce soil erosion
- Reservoirs provide HEP and irrigation
- New motorway link to rich North
- Large estates made into small farms
- Farmers' salaries increased by 25%
- Intensive farming introduced
- Increase in food production

Subsistence rice farming in the Lower Ganges Valley

The Ganges is one of the world's longest rivers. It drains an area more than four times the size of Britain. The river flows south-eastwards from the Himalayas across India and Bangladesh to its mouth in the Bay of Bengal. The **alluvium** or **silt** which it carries has been deposited over many centuries to form a flat river plain and large **delta**.

The plain and delta is one of the most densely populated parts of the world. Many of the people who live here are **subsistence** farmers who work exceptionally hard but produce only enough food for their own family. They grow mainly rice on an **intensive** scale. Rice has a high nutritional value and can form over three-quarters of the total diet needs. It is a **sustainable** form of farming.

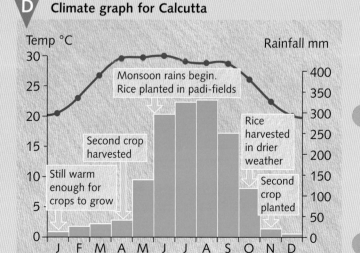

A Lower Ganges Valley

Intensive farms have a high level of input and produce high yields.

Sustainable farming provides food without wasting resources or harming the environment.

Physical inputs

- Silt deposited by the Ganges during monsoon floods provides deep, rich soil.
- High temperatures and monsoon rainfall provide ideal rice growing conditions.
- Continuous growing season allows two crops to be grown each year.
- During the dry season some vegetables and cereal crops are grown.

B

Subsistence rice farming

Human inputs

- Much manual effort is needed to construct embankments, build canals and level padi fields.
- Rice farming is labour-intensive, with field preparation, planting, weeding and harvesting all done by hand.
- Farms are very small – usually less than a football pitch in size – and divided into further tiny plots.
- Small farms and poverty mean that hand-labour rather than machines is used.

C Rice cultivation on the floodplain of the River Ganges

D Climate graph for Calcutta

Temp °C

Rainfall mm

Monsoon rains begin. Rice planted in padi-fields

Second crop harvested

Rice harvested in drier weather

Still warm enough for crops to grow

Second crop planted

J F M A M J J A S O N D

The Green Revolution

The Green Revolution is the name given to the introduction of modern farming methods to the poorer countries of the world, in order to increase food production.

Green Revolution research first started in 1940, when a group of American scientists developed new varieties of wheat and maize for Mexico. Encouraged by their success, a research centre was set up in the Philippines in the 1960s to produce improved strains of rice. The immediate effect was to increase rice yields sixfold at its first harvest.

There are four main parts to the Green Revolution:

1 the use of scientifically bred, high-yielding varieties of plants (HYVs)
2 the introduction of efficient irrigation schemes
3 the use of large quantities of chemical fertiliser
4 the use of chemicals to control pests and disease.

E

Benefits

- HYVs have increased food production. For example, India used to experience food shortages until the 1960s but is now self-sufficient in cereals.
- The increase in yields led to a fall in prices, which makes it easier for the poor to buy food.
- Faster-growing varieties allow an extra crop to be grown each year.
- Yields are more reliable as many new varieties are more disease-resistant.
- Higher yields allow other crops such as vegetables to be grown. This varies the local diet.
- HYVs allow the production of some commercial crops, which brings money to the area.
- HYVs are not so tall as traditional varieties. This enables them to withstand wind and rain.
- Many of the more well-off farmers who could afford seed, fertiliser and tractors have become richer.

Problems

- HYVs need large amounts of fertiliser and pesticides, which increase costs, encourage weeds and can harm water supplies.
- HYVs need a more reliable and controlled supply of water. They are badly affected by drought and waterlogging. Irrigation, where it is used, increases costs and can cause salinisation.
- HYVs are more easily attacked by pests and diseases.
- Many of the less well-off farmers cannot afford seeds, fertiliser and tractors, and have become much poorer.
- Mechanisation has increased rural unemployment and caused people to migrate to cities for work.
- Farming has become less sustainable.

Changes in farming in the UK

Farming, like any industry, has to change with the times. It has to keep up with modern methods, provide the produce that people want, look after the countryside, and ensure a living for its workers.

The changes have brought both advantages and disadvantages. They have certainly increased outputs, improved quality and reduced food costs in the UK. People are worried, however, that many farmers now struggle to make a living and some have been forced out of business. There is also concern that they have caused serious environmental problems, as shown on page 92.

A

- Many of the changes in farming have been a result of directives issued by the European Union (EU) – see page 83.
- These have encouraged the use of new farming methods and, to a large extent, determined what farmers produce.

B

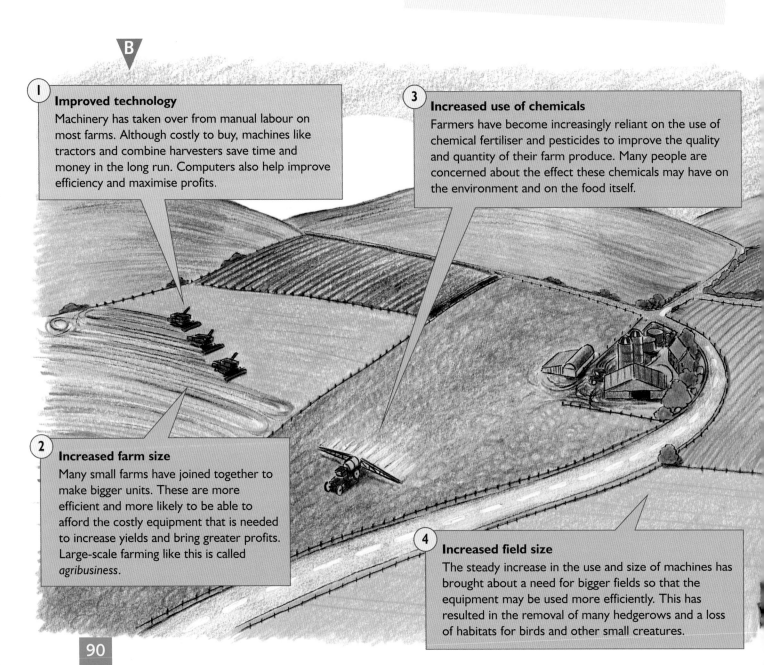

1 Improved technology
Machinery has taken over from manual labour on most farms. Although costly to buy, machines like tractors and combine harvesters save time and money in the long run. Computers also help improve efficiency and maximise profits.

3 Increased use of chemicals
Farmers have become increasingly reliant on the use of chemical fertiliser and pesticides to improve the quality and quantity of their farm produce. Many people are concerned about the effect these chemicals may have on the environment and on the food itself.

2 Increased farm size
Many small farms have joined together to make bigger units. These are more efficient and more likely to be able to afford the costly equipment that is needed to increase yields and bring greater profits. Large-scale farming like this is called *agribusiness*.

4 Increased field size
The steady increase in the use and size of machines has brought about a need for bigger fields so that the equipment may be used more efficiently. This has resulted in the removal of many hedgerows and a loss of habitats for birds and other small creatures.

C Kilnsey Trout Farm, Yorkshire

D A Center Parcs holiday village

5 Organic farming

Organic farming is a form of food production that does without chemicals. Much less damage is done to the environment as fewer toxic chemicals are released into the soil or find their way into rivers. Prices are higher and yields are lower than for traditional farming.

6 Natural environments

More efficient farming has led to a surplus of food being produced. Set-aside and farm woodland schemes encourage farmers to stop growing crops by offering grants. The land may then return to its natural state or trees may be planted to enhance the landscape.

7 Changes in land use

Farmers now use their land in different ways. For example, the EU has encouraged farmers to grow crops such as oilseed rape in place of barley or oats. It has also put limits on milk production so there is now less dairy farming than in the past.

8 Diversification

In the last few years most farmers have seen a rapid decline in their income. Many have had to diversify and seek income from other sources. Some have moved into the leisure industry and provide holiday accommodation and recreational facilities for visitors.

Farming and the environment

Farmers are continually trying to make their farms more efficient and improve the quality of their produce. Unfortunately many of the methods used by farmers to increase productivity have had a damaging effect on the environment.

It has only recently been realised that changes in farming methods, such as the increased use of chemicals and the removal of hedgerows and natural vegetation, can be harmful to the environment. Nowadays, greater care is taken to try and ensure that new developments in farming are **sustainable** and will use the environment but not damage it.

The use of chemicals and farm waste

Pesticides, fertilisers and slurry are used by farmers to improve output on their farms.

- **Pesticides** are used to help control pests, diseases and weeds. Scientists estimate that if pesticides were not used, up to 45% of crops would be lost.
- **Fertilisers** contain minerals that are necessary for plant growth. Although it is expensive to use, chemical fertiliser replaces nutrients which may have been removed from the soil. This helps to give healthier crops and so increases yields.
- Farmers also spread **slurry** over their fields. Slurry is animal waste. It is a natural fertiliser so is cheaper to use than chemical fertiliser, and is just as effective.

The use of pesticides, fertilisers and farm waste can cause problems, as the chemicals they contain seep into water systems and pollute the air. For example:

- Polluted water supplies harm wildlife and may cause illnesses in people.
- Fertilisers washed into lakes and rivers encourage the growth of algae and plants. These use up oxygen, leaving too little for fish life to survive.
- Pesticide sprays kill many harmless insects, such as bees, butterflies and ladybirds which are beneficial to the countryside.
- Over 300 of Britain's plants and wildflowers are now listed as endangered. This is largely due to the effects of chemicals used in farming.

A Algae forming on a river during hot, sunny weather

B Spraying pesticide

Removal of hedgerows and vegetation

Hedges were planted to stop animals from wandering and to show boundaries of land. Many people consider hedges to be important to the environment because they are attractive and provide a **habitat** for wildlife. While farmers may share these views, it is their land that is taken up by hedges and their job to look after them. Despite opposition from conservation groups, more than half of Britain's hedges have been removed during the last 50 years.

C Advantages and disadvantages of hedges

- Well looked-after hedges are attractive.
- Hedgerows provide a home for wildlife – birds, animals, insects and plants.
- Hedgerow insects help pollinate crops.
- Hedge roots hold the soil together and reduce erosion.
- Hedges protect crops from the wind.

- Hedge-cutting machinery is very expensive.
- Hedges get in the way of big machinery in fields.
- Hedge control takes up a farmer's time.
- Hedges harbour insect and animal pests as well as weeds.
- Hedges use up land that could be farmed.

Irrigation

Irrigation is the artificial watering of the land. It enables plants to grow in areas that are too dry, and helps improve the quality of the produce. If irrigation is not well managed, however, a problem called **salinisation** can occur.

Water that is channelled onto the land contains salts. In good irrigation schemes the water is drained away and the salts are taken with it. In this case the plants flourish and a good crop results.

In bad schemes the salts are not drained away. Instead they form a crust on the surface and soak into the soil, where they collect around the plant roots. In both cases, as most plants dislike salt, they die and crops may no longer be grown. This is salinisation.

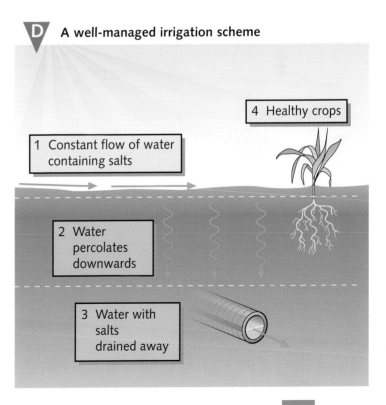

D A well-managed irrigation scheme

1 Constant flow of water containing salts

2 Water percolates downwards

3 Water with salts drained away

4 Healthy crops

Food supply and malnutrition

As the population of the world continues to grow, many people are concerned that there is not enough food for everyone, and many people in the world are starving. However, evidence suggests that due to the steady increase in food production since the 1960s, there should be enough to provide every person with 3,000 calories a day – the amount the average person in Britain eats.

Yet television pictures show clearly that many millions of people in the world are indeed starving. The cause of this is not a shortage of food, but a problem with distribution and supply. Some places actually have too much food whilst others do not have enough.

The rich, developed world, for example, has just one-quarter of the world's population but more than half the world's food. On the other hand the poorer, less developed nations have three-quarters of the population but less than half the food.

Most people now agree that food shortages and **malnutrition** are a result of poverty and an inability of people to buy or produce their own food. As diagram **A** shows, poverty leads to malnutrition which reduces people's ability to resist diseases and to work. This causes further poverty, and so the cycle goes on.

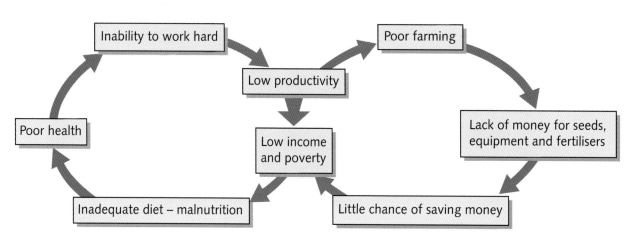

 A Cycles of poverty and malnutrition

Dietary Energy Supply (DES)

Dietary Energy Supply, or DES, is the number of calories per person available each day in a country. Graph **B** compares this daily calorie supply for a selection of countries.

Notice that the richer, more developed countries like the USA and UK have an intake of over 3,000, which is more than adequate for a healthy active life. Countries like India and Ethiopia have an intake below 2,400, at which level malnutrition begins to be a problem. It is estimated that over 20% of people living in the poorer, developing countries now suffer from serious malnutrition.

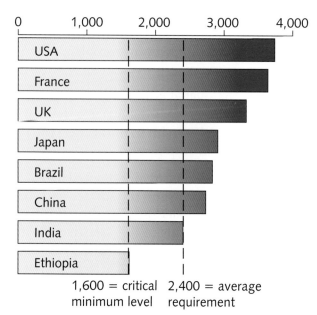

B Daily calorie supply (per capita)

1,600 = critical minimum level 2,400 = average requirement

Malnutrition in children

Malnutrition is most serious in children. It rarely results in starvation and death, but can retard mental and physical development. It may also cause illnesses which themselves may be life threatening.

Children under the age of 5 are most at risk. Estimates suggest that in 2005, 35% of youngsters in this age group in the poorer countries of the world were considered to be underweight. Children fall ill either because their diet contains too few proteins, which are particularly important during early stages of growth, or too few calories. The two main diseases caused by a shortage of proteins are marasmus and kwashiorkor.

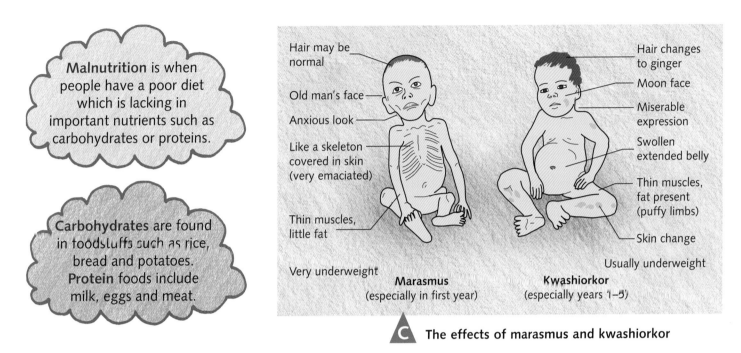

> **Malnutrition** is when people have a poor diet which is lacking in important nutrients such as carbohydrates or proteins.

> **Carbohydrates** are found in foodstuffs such as rice, bread and potatoes. **Protein** foods include milk, eggs and meat.

Hair may be normal
Old man's face
Anxious look
Like a skeleton covered in skin (very emaciated)
Thin muscles, little fat
Very underweight

Marasmus
(especially in first year)

Hair changes to ginger
Moon face
Miserable expression
Swollen extended belly
Thin muscles, fat present (puffy limbs)
Skin change
Usually underweight

Kwashiorkor
(especially years 1–5)

C The effects of marasmus and kwashiorkor

Some causes of malnutrition in sub-Saharan Africa

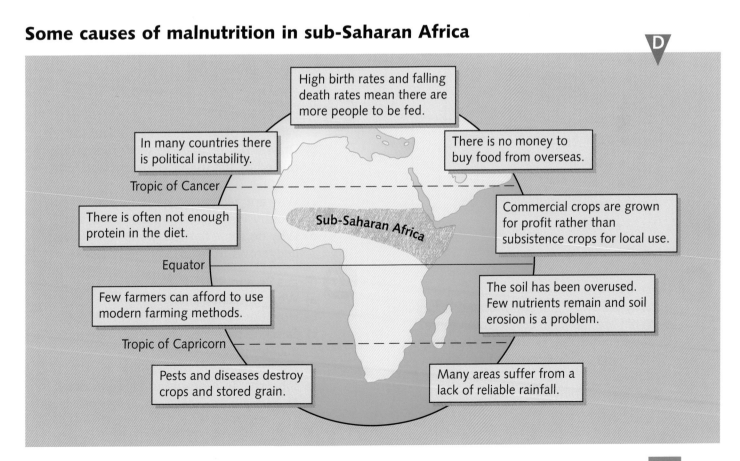

D

High birth rates and falling death rates mean there are more people to be fed.

In many countries there is political instability.

There is no money to buy food from overseas.

Tropic of Cancer

There is often not enough protein in the diet.

Sub-Saharan Africa

Commercial crops are grown for profit rather than subsistence crops for local use.

Equator

Few farmers can afford to use modern farming methods.

The soil has been overused. Few nutrients remain and soil erosion is a problem.

Tropic of Capricorn

Pests and diseases destroy crops and stored grain.

Many areas suffer from a lack of reliable rainfall.

1 (Pages 80 and 81)
a) Make a list of the inputs to a farm under the headings 'Human' and 'Physical'.
b) What are farming processes? Give two examples.
c) List three factors affecting a farm which are outside the farmer's control.

2 (Pages 80 and 81)
What is the difference between:
a) commercial farming and subsistence farming?
b) extensive farming and intensive farming?

3 (Pages 82 and 83)
a) What is the main aim of the EU's Common Agricultural Policy (CAP)?
b) Briefly describe the successes and problems of the CAP.

4 (Page 84)
a) What is pastoral farming?
b) Why is farming difficult in the Lake District?
c) Describe the main features of farming in the Lake District using the headings shown here.

- Location
- Main farming type
- Relief
- Soils
- Climate
- Main human inputs
- Use of machinery
- Sources of income
- Changes

5 (Page 85)
a) Why is East Anglia good for arable farming?
b) What are the main crops grown there?
c) Describe the main features of farming in East Anglia, using the headings shown above.

6 (Pages 86 and 87)
Briefly describe farming in Italy's Mezzogiorno, using these headings:
a) Location of the Mezzogiorno
b) Farming problems
c) Improvements
d) Remaining problems.

7 (Pages 88 and 89)
a) What is the Green Revolution?
b) Give five reasons why the Green Revolution was successful, and five why it was not.

8 (Pages 90 and 91)
Complete the five headlines below by matching each beginning with the correct ending.

Farming jobs lost as

into leisure industry

Profits increase as

new technology introduced

Farmers branch out

machines take over

causes environmental problems

Set-aside scheme

restores natural environment

Increase in chemical use

9 (Pages 92 and 93)
a) What are pesticides, fertilisers and slurry?
b) Draw a star diagram to show four problems caused by the use of chemicals and farm waste.
c) Why are hedgerows good for the countryside?
d) Why do some farmers prefer to remove hedgerows from around their fields?

10 (Pages 94 and 95)
a) What is malnutrition?
b) How does malnutrition affect children?
c) Describe two child illnesses caused by malnutrition.
d) List the causes of malnutrition in sub-Saharan Africa using these headings:
  ■ Farming problems ■ Other problems.

EXAMINATION QUESTIONS

1
(Pages 80 and 81)

a) Match the following words with the letters on diagram **A**. (3)

ploughing wheat harvesting soil labour barley

b) What is arable farming? (1)
c) Give three outputs of a hill sheep farm. (3)
d) Complete the following sentence using the correct words from the brackets. (2)

Hill sheep farming is an example of extensive farming where a (small **or** large) area of land is used with (small **or** large) amounts of labour and capital.

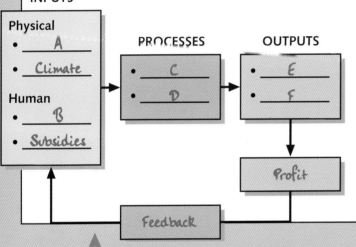

INPUTS

Physical
• _____A_____
• Climate

Human
• _____B_____
• Subsidies

PROCESSES
• _____C_____
• _____D_____

OUTPUTS
• _____E_____
• _____F_____

Profit

Feedback

A Farming system for an arable farm

3
(Pages 88 and 89)

a) Match the following words with the letters on diagram **C**. (3)

Poor diet Little money Cannot work hard

b) What is subsistence farming? (1)
c) Name an area of the world that you have studied where subsistence farming is common. (1)
d) What is the Green Revolution? (1)
e) How can the Green Revolution help subsistence farmers? (4)

C Problems of subsistence farming

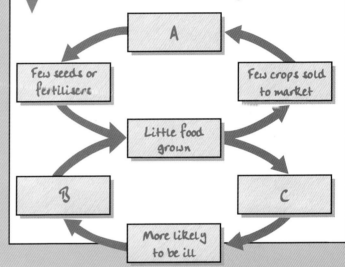

A

Few seeds or fertilisers

Few crops sold to market

Little food grown

B

C

More likely to be ill

2
(Pages 83, 86 and 87)

a) Look at the drawings below. State three changes that happened between 1955 and 2005. (3)

b) For each of the changes, explain how it has increased farm production. (3)

c) Give three examples of how the European Union agricultural policies have helped farmers. (3)

B An area of Italy's Mezzogiorno in 1955

Cut-down trees
Olive trees
Road
Large estate
River
Olive trees
Marshland

The same area in 2005

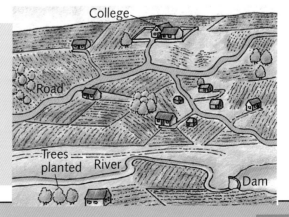

College
Road
Trees planted
River
Dam

8 ENERGY RESOURCES

What are resources?

Resources can be defined as any material or product that people find useful. Stone, for example, becomes a resource when people use it to build houses. Grass is a resource when cows eat it and produce meat and milk. Attractive countryside is a resource for people relaxing in their leisure time.

Resources may be either natural or human. **Natural resources**, which this chapter is mainly concerned with, are physical features such as climate, vegetation, soils and raw materials such as minerals and fuel. **Human resources** include the workforce, skilled labour, machinery and money.

Natural resources are usually described as **non-renewable** or **renewable**. These are shown in diagram **A** below.

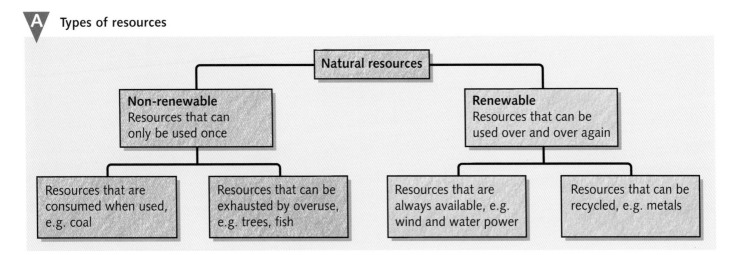

A Types of resources

Natural resources

Non-renewable
Resources that can only be used once

Renewable
Resources that can be used over and over again

Resources that are consumed when used, e.g. coal

Resources that can be exhausted by overuse, e.g. trees, fish

Resources that are always available, e.g. wind and water power

Resources that can be recycled, e.g. metals

Managing resources

The demand for and use of the world's resources continue to grow at an increasingly rapid rate. This is mainly due to:

- population growth as the world's population increases
- economic development as more countries try to develop their industry and wealth.

As the demand for resources grows, there is an increasing need to manage their use and look after them more carefully. If this is not done, two problems may result. The first is that some resources will simply run out. The second is that the environment will become damaged and polluted.

Diagram **B** shows some methods of managing resources in a **sustainable** way. Sustainable methods use resources sensibly and in a way that does not waste them or cause damage to the environment.

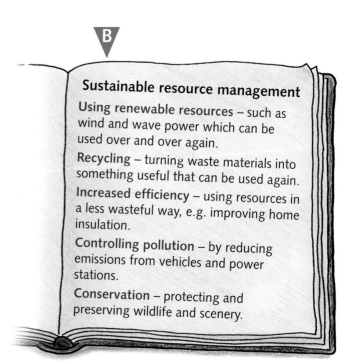

B

Sustainable resource management

Using renewable resources – such as wind and wave power which can be used over and over again.

Recycling – turning waste materials into something useful that can be used again.

Increased efficiency – using resources in a less wasteful way, e.g. improving home insulation.

Controlling pollution – by reducing emissions from vehicles and power stations.

Conservation – protecting and preserving wildlife and scenery.

Energy resources

Energy is very important to us. It provides lighting and heating in our homes and offices. It powers computers, televisions, and factory machinery. It fuels transport and has helped us develop and improve the quality of life on our planet.

Table **C** shows the world's main sources of energy. Some of these are non-renewable sources and some are renewable.

Non-renewable energy resources

So far, non-renewable resources have been easy and quite cheap to use. Coal, oil and natural gas are called **fossil fuels** because they come from the fossil remains of plants and animals.

In the late 1990s, fossil fuels provided 85% of the world's energy needs, and each year the world consumes an amount of fossil fuel that took nature 1 million years to provide. Unfortunately fossil fuels create a lot of pollution and are also causing changes in the world's climate.

Renewable (alternative) energy resources

Renewable energy resources are mainly forces of nature, like water, wind and the sun, which can be used over and over again. They tend to be difficult and expensive to use but cause little pollution and are a sustainable form of energy.

 World energy sources in 1960 and 2003

Source	% of world consumption	
	1960	2003
Coal	49	24
Oil	30	42
Natural gas	11	19
Hydro-electric power	2	3
Nuclear	1	5
Fuelwood	6	6
Other renewables	1	1

░ Non-renewable ░ Renewable

At present, only hydro-electric power from running water is a significant source of energy. The others suffer technical problems which make them difficult to use on a large scale. Eventually, as fossil fuels run out, renewable sources will become more important as a global source of energy.

D The need for sustainable management

This ...

... or this?

Non-renewable energy resources

Coal

Coal was the major fuel of the Industrial Revolution in the 19th and 20th centuries. Coalfields became the sites of vast industrial areas as Europe moved into the modern world. In 1913, over 1 million miners worked in the British coal industry. By the year 2000, fewer than 9,000 miners remained as the industry suffered rapid decline. The reasons for decline included the exhaustion of supplies, increased cost of production, and competition from cleaner, safer fuels such as oil and natural gas.

Advantages
- World reserves are likely to last over 300 years.
- Modern methods have increased outputs.
- Coal is used for electricity and heating.

Disadvantages
- Production costs have risen.
- Burning coal causes air pollution and global warming.
- Deep mining is dangerous.
- Opencast mining harms the environment.

Oil and natural gas

Many countries have come to rely upon either oil or natural gas as their main source of energy. Thanks to North Sea oil, the UK is one of very few countries that have sufficient reserves of their own.

Advantages
- Oil and gas are cheaper and cleaner than coal.
- Both are easy to transport by pipeline or tanker.
- Both are less harmful to the environment than coal.
- They are safer than nuclear energy.
- Both may be used for electricity and heating.
- Oil is the basis of the petrochemical industry.

Disadvantages
- Reserves may only last another 50–70 years.
- New fields are difficult to discover and exploit.
- Burning oil and gas causes acid rain.
- Oil spillage and gas leaks are dangerous.
- Terminals and refineries take up much space.
- Both are affected by global price rises and politics.

A Opencast mining in Nottinghamshire

B A marine oil platform in the North Sea

Nuclear energy

People have strong views about nuclear energy. Some think it is dangerous and want it banned. Others see it as a clean and modern source of energy which can provide our needs for many years to come. Many countries that are short of fossil fuels, such as France, Belgium, Japan and South Korea, are turning increasingly to nuclear power, despite fears about its safety.

Advantages

- Only limited raw materials are needed.
- Many safeguards make the accident risk minimal.
- Underground storage of nuclear waste is possible.
- It is not a main cause of acid rain or global warming
- It receives most of Britain's energy research.
- It is supported by large firms and by the government.

Disadvantages

- It is still not clear how safe nuclear power is.
- Concern over disastrous effects if there is an accident.
- Worries over health risks for those living nearby.
- Cannot be used for heating or transport.
- Waste is radioactive and dangerous for many years.
- High cost of decommissioning old power stations.

C Sizewell B nuclear power station

Fuelwood

Fuelwood is the most important source of energy for people living in the rural areas of the poorer countries of the world. Here they either collect the wood themselves or buy it to burn at home for heating and cooking. In some places, such as Kenya, more efficient cooking stoves have been introduced, which burn more efficiently and use less wood.

Advantages

- Cheap and readily available fuel source.
- Easy to use and store.
- Can be renewable if managed carefully.

Disadvantages

- Collecting fuel is very time-consuming for women and children.
- Results in loss of forested areas.
- Deforestation causes soil erosion.
- Trees are rarely replanted, so supplies run out.

D Collecting wood for fuel in Kenya

Renewable energy resources

Hydro-electric power

Hydro-electric power (HEP) is the most important of the renewable energy resources. A reliable supply of fast-flowing water is needed to produce hydro-electricity. This may be at a natural waterfall such as Niagara Falls, or where a dam has been built across a valley such as at Aswan on the River Nile.

Advantages
- Cheap to produce.
- Creates very little pollution.
- HEP dams help reduce the risk of flooding.
- Reservoirs help reduce the risk of water shortages.
- Reservoirs may be used for recreation.

Disadvantages
- Dams are expensive to build.
- Limited choice of suitable sites.
- Large areas of farmland are flooded.
- Wildlife habitats are lost.

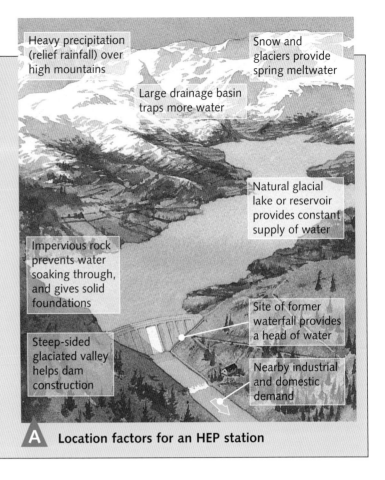

Heavy precipitation (relief rainfall) over high mountains

Snow and glaciers provide spring meltwater

Large drainage basin traps more water

Natural glacial lake or reservoir provides constant supply of water

Impervious rock prevents water soaking through, and gives solid foundations

Site of former waterfall provides a head of water

Steep-sided glaciated valley helps dam construction

Nearby industrial and domestic demand

A Location factors for an HEP station

Itaipù, Brazil

In 1982 a dam was completed across the River Parana at Itaipù, on the border of Brazil and Paraguay. The lake behind the dam is 180 km long and the 18 turbines make it the world's largest HEP scheme. Paraguay receives its needs from just one turbine. The remainder is used by Brazil and transmitted to the São Paulo area.

Advantages
- Created many jobs during construction.
- Provides a clean and reliable form of energy.
- Provides cheap electricity for Paraguay and Brazil.

Disadvantages
- Farmland and wildlife habitats flooded.
- Flooding caused 42,000 people to be relocated.
- Few jobs created despite huge cost of scheme.
- Little benefit to local residents of Itaipù.

Location of Itaipù **B**

0   10 km

N

Itaipù Reservoir

BRAZIL

Iguaçu National Park

River Iguaçu

Friendship Bridge

Foz do Iguaçu

River Parana

PARAGUAY

ARGENTINA

C The dam and lake at Itaipù

Geothermal energy

Geothermal means 'heat from the Earth'. In geothermal power stations, high-temperature geothermal steam is produced when water comes into contact with heated rocks below the ground. This steam can be used for heating or to power turbines and generate electricity. In some cases the steam is produced naturally as geysers or hot springs. In other cases cold water is pumped downwards through boreholes (diagram **D**).

Advantages
- Is renewable and causes little pollution.
- Is reliable and provides a constant energy supply.
- May be used for heating and electricity.

Disadvantages
- Limited choice of suitable sites.
- High cost of construction and maintenance.
- Possible danger from eruptions and earthquakes.
- Emission of sulphuric gases.

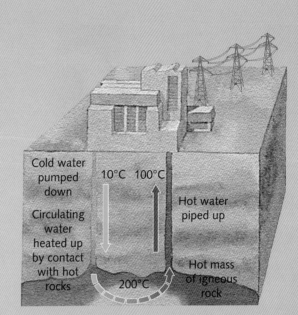

 How geothermal energy is produced

New Zealand

The Taupo area of New Zealand's North Island is an active volcanic zone. Tourists flock to the area to view the volcanoes, geysers, hot springs and mud pools, particularly around Rotorua and Taupo.

Geothermal power stations have been built at Wairakei and Ohaaki. Here, geothermal steam is used to power generators and produce electricity.

Wairakei and Ohaaki were chosen because they are in the centre of the geothermal field and next to the Waikato River, which provides water for cooling.

Throughout the area, hot steam is also piped to local towns and villages where it is used for both domestic and industrial heating.

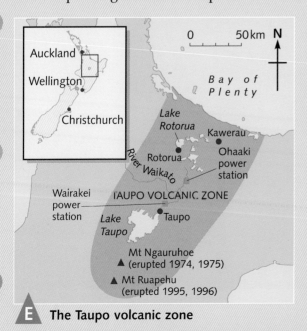

E The Taupo volcanic zone

F Wairakei geothermal power station

Places

Renewable energy resources

Wind

The wind has been used for thousands of years as a source of energy for sailing ships and windmills. Nowadays, huge wind turbines have been developed which can generate electricity from the power of the wind.

The turbines need to be in areas with strong winds that blow on a regular basis. Such places are usually found on exposed coasts or in upland parts of western Britain. As 30 metre tall wind turbines are expensive to build and maintain, it is usual to group several together to form a 'wind farm'.

Britain's first wind farm was opened in 1991 near Camelford in Cornwall. In the year 2000 there were 70 wind farms working or planned in Britain. They contributed about 0.2% of the UK's energy needs. Estimates suggest that 100,000 wind farms would be needed to produce 20% of the country's total energy supply.

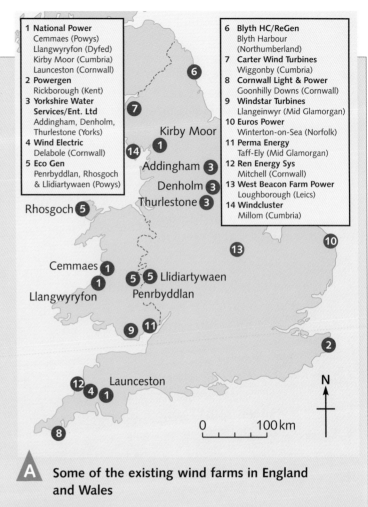

1 **National Power**
Cemmaes (Powys)
Llangwyryfon (Dyfed)
Kirby Moor (Cumbria)
Launceston (Cornwall)
2 **Powergen**
Rickborough (Kent)
3 **Yorkshire Water Services/Ent. Ltd**
Addingham, Denholm, Thurlestone (Yorks)
4 **Wind Electric**
Delabole (Cornwall)
5 **Eco Gen**
Penrbyddlan, Rhosgoch & Llidiartywaen (Powys)

6 **Blyth HC/ReGen**
Blyth Harbour (Northumberland)
7 **Carter Wind Turbines**
Wiggonby (Cumbria)
8 **Cornwall Light & Power**
Goonhilly Downs (Cornwall)
9 **Windstar Turbines**
Llangeinwyr (Mid Glamorgan)
10 **Euros Power**
Winterton-on-Sea (Norfolk)
11 **Perma Energy**
Taff-Ely (Mid Glamorgan)
12 **Ren Energy Sys**
Mitchell (Cornwall)
13 **West Beacon Farm Power**
Loughborough (Leics)
14 **Windcluster**
Millom (Cumbria)

A Some of the existing wind farms in England and Wales

B Wind farm near Camelford, Cornwall

Advantages
- Wind turbines do not cause air pollution.
- Winds are stronger in winter when demand for electricity is greatest.
- Running costs are very low.
- Wind farms can produce income for farmers.
- Wind could generate 10% of the UK's electricity.

Disadvantages
- Wind does not blow all the time.
- Wind farms spoil the look of the countryside.
- Large numbers of turbines are needed.
- Wind turbines are noisy and can interrupt TV and radio.

Solar energy

Solar energy uses silicon cells to convert the sun's energy into electricity. Small solar power units are quite common and are used to power watches, calculators, electric fences and navigation beacons, for example.

Unfortunately, using solar power on a large scale is very expensive. Further advances in technology are needed before it can be used extensively. For Britain, the solar option is further limited by a lack of sunshine and short winter days. The most likely users of solar energy are the developing countries. Many of these have a sunny climate, and their needs are often for small-scale energy sources in isolated rural areas.

Advantages
- Unlimited supply and causes no pollution.
- Ideal for small scale-energy needs.

Disadvantages
- Needs sunshine, so limited choice of suitable sites.
- Very expensive and still requires new technology.

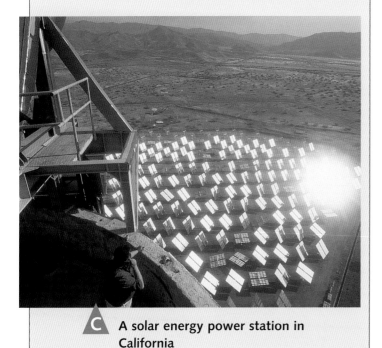

C A solar energy power station in California

Waves, tidal, biogas and biomass energy

Waves. Waves are very powerful and may be used to produce electricity. Unfortunately, building machinery that can survive the full force of waves without being damaged has proved difficult.

Tidal. Like the Rance in Brittany (map **D**), many British rivers have a large tidal range which could generate electricity. However, schemes such as the proposed Severn Barrage would be expensive to build. They would also destroy important wildlife habitats, and could disrupt local shipping.

Biogas. Rotting animal dung gives off methane gas which in developing countries can be burned and used instead of fuelwood. This is a cheap source of energy, but it means that the dung can no longer be used as a fertiliser.

Biomass. Crops like sugar cane, cassava and maize contain starch. If fermented this can produce a type of alcohol which can be used to power cars.

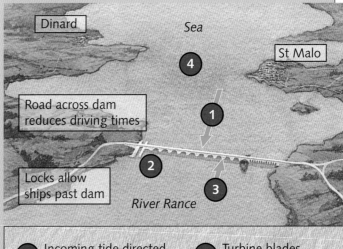

Dinard
Sea
St Malo
4
Road across dam reduces driving times
1
Locks allow ships past dam
2
3
River Rance

1 Incoming tide directed into 24 tunnels, each of which has a turbine

2 Fast-moving water turns the turbine blades to generate electricity

3 Turbine blades reversed for outgoing tide

4 Twice-daily tides generate electricity throughout the day

D The Rance tidal barrage in France

Energy and the environment – oil in Alaska

In 1968 the largest oilfield in North America was discovered at Prudhoe Bay in the far north of Alaska. The field contained one-third of the USA's oil reserves, but the problem was how to move the oil to refineries elsewhere in the USA.

Tankers were of little use because the Arctic Ocean is frozen for much of the year. The decision was made to build a pipeline, 1,242 km in length, southwards to the ice-free port of Valdez. The route faced such enormous physical difficulties and environmental opposition that it was not until 1977 that the first oil was pumped along it.

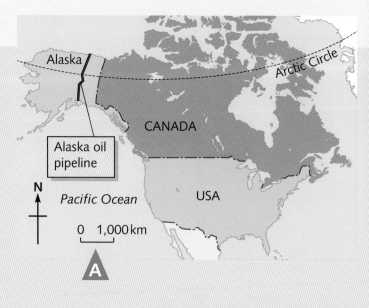

A

B Physical problems and environmental concerns

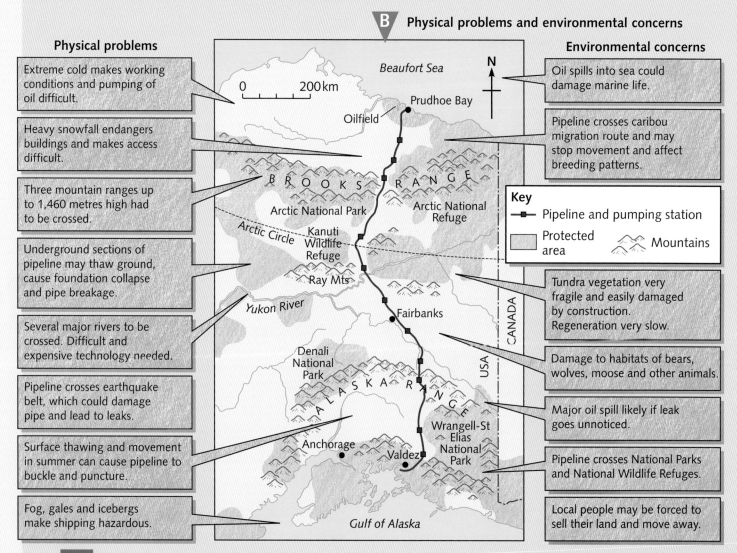

Physical problems

Extreme cold makes working conditions and pumping of oil difficult.

Heavy snowfall endangers buildings and makes access difficult.

Three mountain ranges up to 1,460 metres high had to be crossed.

Underground sections of pipeline may thaw ground, cause foundation collapse and pipe breakage.

Several major rivers to be crossed. Difficult and expensive technology needed.

Pipeline crosses earthquake belt, which could damage pipe and lead to leaks.

Surface thawing and movement in summer can cause pipeline to buckle and puncture.

Fog, gales and icebergs make shipping hazardous.

Environmental concerns

Oil spills into sea could damage marine life.

Pipeline crosses caribou migration route and may stop movement and affect breeding patterns.

Tundra vegetation very fragile and easily damaged by construction. Regeneration very slow.

Damage to habitats of bears, wolves, moose and other animals.

Major oil spill likely if leak goes unnoticed.

Pipeline crosses National Parks and National Wildlife Refuges.

Local people may be forced to sell their land and move away.

Key

- Pipeline and pumping station

Protected area   Mountains

Some attempted solutions

As map **B** shows, pipeline builders had many problems to overcome. One of the most difficult was permafrost. Permafrost is permanently frozen ground. It is difficult to build any structure on it because the warmth of the structure melts the permafrost and can cause movement and subsidence. Drawing **D** below shows how the builders overcame these problems.

Since 1996, more sections of the pipeline have been sunk underground in river gravels or encased in concrete. These improvements have helped reduce environmental damage and prevented the oil from freezing.

To a large extent the pipeline has been successful. Although there have been reports of some 300 minor leaks, these have been repaired quickly and caused no serious damage. Recent evidence also suggests that the pipeline has caused little permanent damage to the environment. A 1998 National Park survey reported that wildlife is relatively unaffected, and the natural vegetation in most places has largely recovered.

The Alaska oil pipeline near the Brooks Range **C**

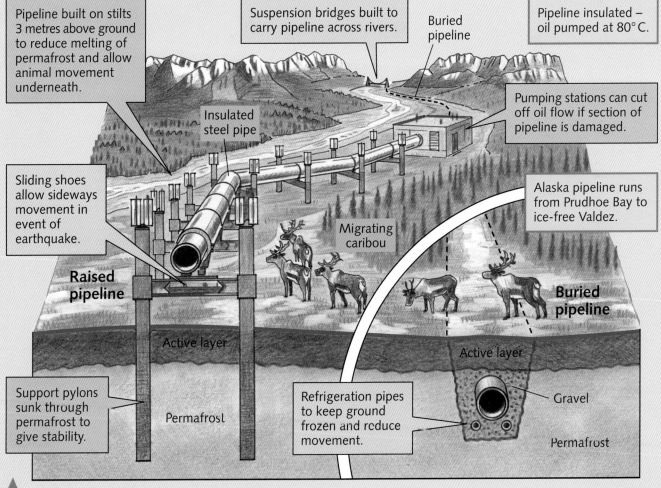

Pipeline built on stilts 3 metres above ground to reduce melting of permafrost and allow animal movement underneath.

Suspension bridges built to carry pipeline across rivers.

Buried pipeline

Pipeline insulated – oil pumped at 80°C.

Insulated steel pipe

Pumping stations can cut off oil flow if section of pipeline is damaged.

Sliding shoes allow sideways movement in event of earthquake.

Alaska pipeline runs from Prudhoe Bay to ice-free Valdez.

Raised pipeline

Migrating caribou

Buried pipeline

Active layer

Active layer

Support pylons sunk through permafrost to give stability.

Permafrost

Refrigeration pipes to keep ground frozen and reduce movement.

Gravel

Permafrost

D Alaska oil pipeline – attempted solutions

The Exxon Valdez oil spill, 1989

Valdez is the ice-free port at the end of the Alaska pipeline. To reach the open sea, oil tankers have to follow a dangerous route which takes them through Prince William Sound and into the Gulf of Alaska.

On 24 March 1989, in near perfect weather conditions, the supertanker *Exxon Valdez* strayed off-course and ran aground on Bligh Reef. The ship was badly holed and its cargo of 50 million tonnes of oil began to pour into the sea.

The disaster was not due to any of the physical dangers shown in map **B**, but to human error. At a later court case it was found that the captain was drunk and an inexperienced third mate had been left in charge of the ship.

A Oil tanker leaving Valdez

The effects of the spill were massive, deadly and longlasting. An oil slick 10 cm thick quickly spread out from the stricken tanker, eventually reaching 1,000 km to the south-west. An estimated 1,700 km of coastline was oiled, and within days more than 10 million birds were reported dead. Much of the marine life was poisoned and virtually wiped out.

B The Exxon Valdez disaster

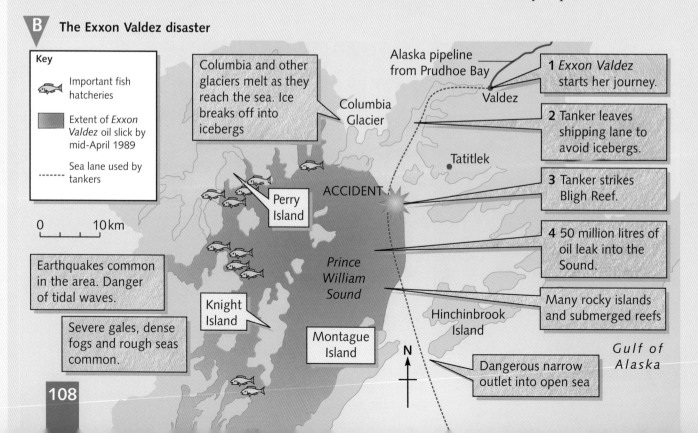

The clean-up operations were complicated, costly and not totally successful. Exxon, the company found to be at fault, spent £843 million and employed 11,000 people to clear oil from the beaches. They also agreed to spend a further £600 million over the next 10 years to restore the environment to its original state. Sadly this has not yet happened. Oil remains on the coastline and the wildlife and their habitat have still not fully recovered. Many doubt if they ever will.

C **Effects of the Exxon Valdez oil spill**

Large areas of coastline and sea covered in oil

Destruction of fragile ecosystem

10 million shore birds and water fowl dead

Commercial salmon hatcheries polluted

Land-based animals such as caribou poisoned by eating seaweed

At least 13 whales killed. Reduction in number of births since disaster

Loss of business for tourist industry

Over 5,000 sea otters killed

Serious loss of coastline vegetation and seaweeds

Local fishing industry ruined

Today and the future

The *Exxon Valdez* incident has made people think carefully about the impact of economic activity on the environment. There is no doubt that the oil industry has brought many social and economic benefits to Alaska and the USA as a whole. However, it has also caused serious and irreparable damage to a fragile environment.

People have to choose which is more important: to use these resources, or to protect and conserve the environment.

 D **Arguments for and against oil production in Alaska**

For (mainly economic and social)	Against (mainly environmental)
• Most Alaskans see oil as their main source of jobs and wealth.	• Environmental groups think it is important to protect the fragile Arctic from all forms of development.
• Oil income has been used to build schools, hospitals, public buildings, roads and water supply schemes.	• Some Native American groups claim they would prefer to live their traditional way of life rather than benefit from oil income.
• Alaska provides a third of the USA's total oil reserves.	
• Alaskans see little point in protecting 'flea-ridden caribou seen by only a few hundred humans'.	• There is some evidence of companies dumping toxic waste and damaging the environment.

1 (Pages 98 to 99)
a) What are resources?
b) What is the difference between a renewable resource and a non-renewable resource?
c) Why is the management of renewable resources so important?

2 (Pages 98 to 100)
a) Is coal a renewable or non-renewable energy resource? Give reasons for your answer.
b) Give three reasons for the decline of the UK's coal industry.
c) What are the advantages and disadvantages of coal as an energy resource?

3 (Pages 99 and 100)
a) Oil and gas are fossil fuels. What are fossil fuels and what are they formed from?
b) As well as fuel, what else is oil used for?
c) Why are oil and gas considered to be better energy resources than coal? Give four reasons.
d) Give two ways in which the use of oil and gas may damage the environment.

4 (Page 101)
a) Copy and complete the diagram below to show the advantages and disadvantages of nuclear energy.
b) Suggest three reasons why countries like France and Japan are turning to nuclear energy.

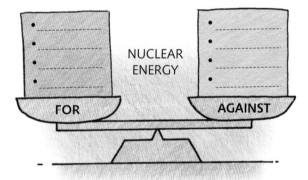

5 (Page 101)
Describe how fuelwood is used as an energy resource in some parts of the world.

6 (Page 102)
a) What is hydro-electric power?
b) Describe the ideal site for an HEP station using these headings:

Water sources   Storage   Location   Market

c) Reservoirs for HEP schemes flood large areas of land. Why does this matter?

7 (Page 102)
Describe the Itaipù hydro-electricity scheme using the following headings:
a) Location   b) Main features
c) Advantages   d) Disadvantages.

8 (Page 103)
a) What is geothermal energy?
b) How is geothermal energy produced?
c) Give three advantages and three disadvantages of geothermal energy.

9 (Page 104)
a) Where are most wind farms found?
b) Give four advantages of wind power.
c) Why might people prefer not to live near to a wind farm?

10 (Page 105)
a) What is solar energy?
b) Give three reasons why Britain uses relatively little solar energy.

11 (Pages 106 and 107)
a) List four environmental problems faced by pipeline builders in Alaska.
b) Why was permafrost a problem in Alaska? What was done to overcome this problem?

12 (Pages 108 and 109)
a) Give four dangers faced by oil tankers in Prince William Sound.
b) Draw a star diagram to show six effects of the Exxon Valdez oil spill.
c) Do you think that oil production should continue in places like Alaska? Give reasons for your answer.

EXAMINATION QUESTIONS

1

(Pages 98 to 105)

a) What is the meaning of the term 'renewable energy'? **(1)**

b) What are non-renewable energy resources? **(1)**

c) What are fossil fuels? **(1)**

d) Complete table **A** by putting each energy source in the correct column. (Some may fit into more than one column.) **(6)**

e) Sustainable resource management is a way of using resources sensibly and without waste or damage. Suggest four methods of managing resources in a sustainable way. **(4)**

A

Non-renewable	Fossil fuels	Renewable

- coal
- nuclear energy
- fuelwood
- tidal
- hydro-electric power
- oil
- natural gas
- geothermal
- wind
- solar
- waves

2

(Pages 98 and 99)

Look at the graph in **B**.

a) Which type of energy was most used in 1990? **(1)**

b) What percentage of energy came from coal in 1990? **(1)**

c) What is likely to happen to the percentage of coal used between 1990 and 2005? **(1)**

d) Which two types of energy are likely to increase in importance between 1990 and 2005? **(2)**

e) Suggest two reasons why there is likely to be a big increase in the use of energy in the future. **(2)**

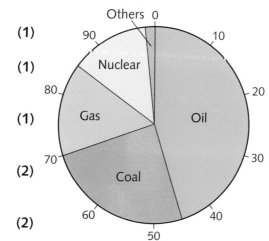

B Types of energy used in Europe in 1990

Types of energy expected to be used in Europe in 2005

Type of energy	Percentage
Oil	42
Coal	17
Gas	24
Nuclear	12
Others	5

3

(Pages 106 to 109)

a) Give four physical problems faced by oil companies in Alaska. **(4)**

b) Give two reasons why people in Alaska may be in favour of the oil industry. **(2)**

c) Give two reasons why some people are against oil production in Alaska. **(2)**

d) Do you think that oil companies should be allowed to explore new areas for oil? Give reasons for your answer. **(3)**

STOP! before it's too late

Oil benefits shared by all

Oil is our future

When's the NEXT disaster?

Oil spill hits Alaska

C

9 INDUSTRY

Industry as a system

Industry is any form of employment that involves using or producing goods and services. It includes manufacturing, farming, tourism, mining, education, and many other activities.

Industry as a whole, or a factory as an individual unit, can be regarded as a **system**. The things that a system needs to work are called **inputs**. What happens in the industry are called **processes**. What it produces are called **outputs**. The finished product is sold and the money earned is re-invested in the industry. This money buys more raw materials, pays wages and repays any loans. For an industry to be profitable and remain in business, the value of its outputs must be greater than the cost of its inputs.

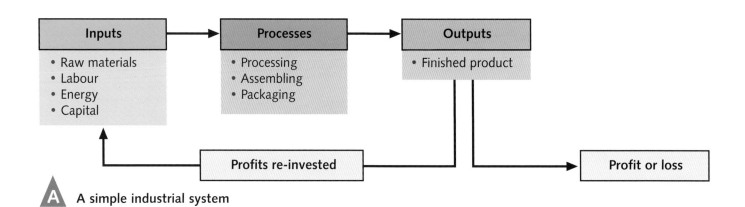

A A simple industrial system

Location of industry

Before building a factory or opening a business, the best possible site has to be found for its location. This will be where the cost of raw materials, energy, labour, land and transport is lowest and where there is a large market for the product. It is unlikely that all these factors will be available at one particular site, so the correct decision is often very hard to make. A wrong decision could mean failure for the industry, and lead to closure and a loss of jobs.

B

INDUSTRIAL LOCATION FACTORS

Physical factors
- **Raw materials.** The factory needs to be close to these if they are heavy and bulky to transport.
- **Power – energy.** This is needed to work the machines in a factory. Early industries were near to coalfields. Today, electricity allows more freedom.
- **Natural routes.** River valleys and flat areas make the movement of goods easier.
- **Site and land.** Most factories require large areas of cheap, flat land.

Human and economic factors
- **Labour.** A suitable workforce is needed. Cost and skill levels are important.
- **Capital.** Money may be available from banks and government in certain areas.
- **Markets.** An accessible place to sell the goods or services is needed.
- **Transport.** A good transport network helps reduce costs.
- **Government policies.** Development is encouraged in some areas and restricted in others.
- **Environment.** Pleasant surroundings with good leisure facilities help attract a workforce.

Location of industry in the UK

During the Industrial Revolution of the 19th century, new industries mainly needed power supplies, raw materials and port facilities to export their products. So major industrial areas tended to be located on coalfields or near the coast, particularly in the north of the country.

Recently, there have been many changes in the location and type of Britain's industries. For a variety of reasons many coalmines, textile mills, shipyards and steelworks have now closed down. These have largely been replaced by modern industries, many of which are high-tech and connected to electronics. They employ fewer people and are often located well away from traditional manufacturing areas.

These industries are called **footloose** because they are not tied down by raw materials and have a wider choice of location. Footloose industries usually seek a location in an attractive environment that has good transport links and is close to their market.

Industry provides jobs for people and enables them to earn a living. Changes in industry and the closure of factories and businesses can unfortunately lead to job losses and unemployment. Table **C** shows some of the causes of job losses.

C

Reasons for job losses	Example
• Exhaustion of resources	Pits close as coal runs out
• New machinery or new methods	Automated car manufacture needing fewer workers
• Fall in demand for product	New materials cause closure of textile mills
• Site needed for other uses	Old factories replaced with shopping complex
• Lack of money for investment	Closure of old, inefficient steelworks
• Competition from overseas	Cars from Japan
• Political decisions	Government failing to help companies in difficulties

D Traditional industrial areas before 1970

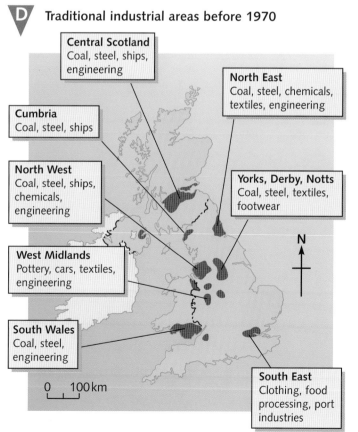

Central Scotland
Coal, steel, ships, engineering

North East
Coal, steel, chemicals, textiles, engineering

Cumbria
Coal, steel, ships

North West
Coal, steel, ships, chemicals, engineering

Yorks, Derby, Notts
Coal, steel, textiles, footwear

West Midlands
Pottery, cars, textiles, engineering

South Wales
Coal, steel, engineering

South East
Clothing, food processing, port industries

0   100 km

E Present-day industrial areas

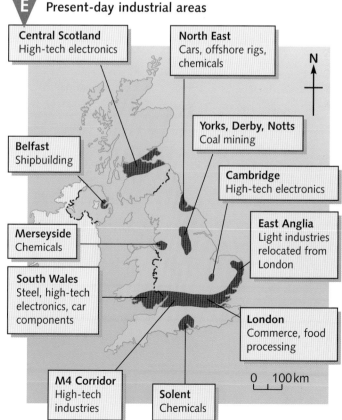

Central Scotland
High-tech electronics

North East
Cars, offshore rigs, chemicals

N

Belfast
Shipbuilding

Yorks, Derby, Notts
Coal mining

Cambridge
High-tech electronics

Merseyside
Chemicals

East Anglia
Light industries relocated from London

South Wales
Steel, high-tech electronics, car components

London
Commerce, food processing

M4 Corridor
High-tech industries

Solent
Chemicals

0   100 km

Changing locations –
the iron and steel industry

Iron and steel in South Wales

In 1860 there were 35 ironworks in the valleys of South Wales. The area was one of Europe's most important iron producers, and whole villages were totally dependent upon the local coalmines and ironworks.

South Wales had been the ideal location for making iron. Coal and iron ore were often found together on valley sides. Limestone was quarried nearby. Fast-flowing rivers provided water to turn the early water-wheels. The valleys themselves led to coastal ports where iron products and surplus coal were exported to many parts of the world.

The iron industry became centred on places like Ebbw Vale and Merthyr Tydfil. In 1856 an improvement in the method of iron smelting meant that it was possible to manufacture steel rather than brittle iron. After 1860, steelworks slowly began to replace iron foundries.

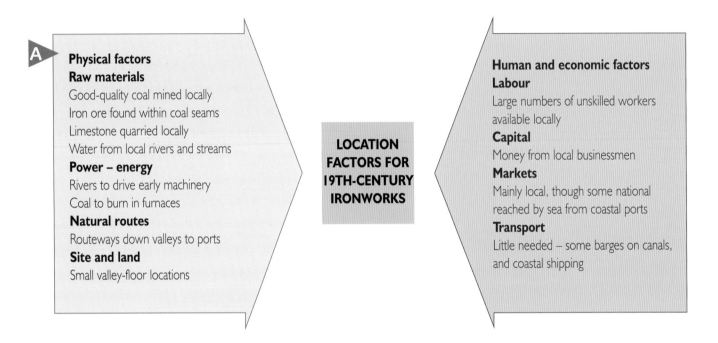

A

Physical factors
Raw materials
Good-quality coal mined locally
Iron ore found within coal seams
Limestone quarried locally
Water from local rivers and streams
Power – energy
Rivers to drive early machinery
Coal to burn in furnaces
Natural routes
Routeways down valleys to ports
Site and land
Small valley-floor locations

LOCATION FACTORS FOR 19TH-CENTURY IRONWORKS

Human and economic factors
Labour
Large numbers of unskilled workers available locally
Capital
Money from local businessmen
Markets
Mainly local, though some national reached by sea from coastal ports
Transport
Little needed – some barges on canals, and coastal shipping

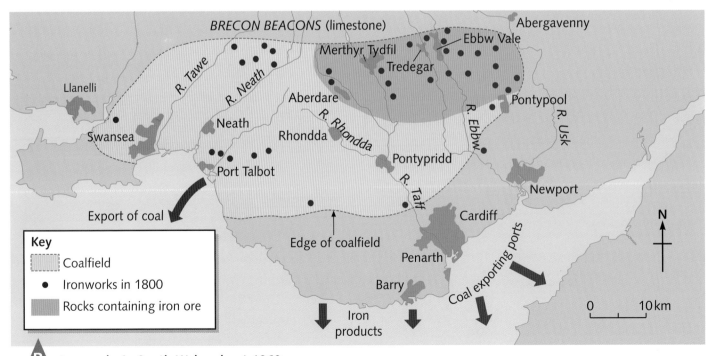

Key
- Coalfield
- • Ironworks in 1800
- Rocks containing iron ore

B Ironworks in South Wales about 1860

114

By the 1990s there were only two steelworks left in South Wales. They were not in the valleys, though, but on the coast at Port Talbot and Llanwern. This was mainly because the coal and iron ore once found in the valleys had been exhausted and without these raw materials, the old steelworks were forced to close.

The British government decided that there was a need to retain a steel industry in the area, and chose sites at Port Talbot and Llanwern for new steelworks. Port Talbot has its own harbour and docks for the import of coal and iron ore. It is an **integrated** steelworks using advanced technology. An integrated steelworks is where all the stages in steel manufacture take place on the same site. The Llanwern steelworks closed in 2001 due to overseas competition, global overproduction and a fall in steel prices.

In the 19th century, it was physical factors such as the source of raw materials and energy that determined industrial locations. This was why the original ironworks of South Wales were located in the valleys near to the coal and iron ore. Nowadays, market demand and government decisions are more important, which is why the new steelworks are on coastal sites.

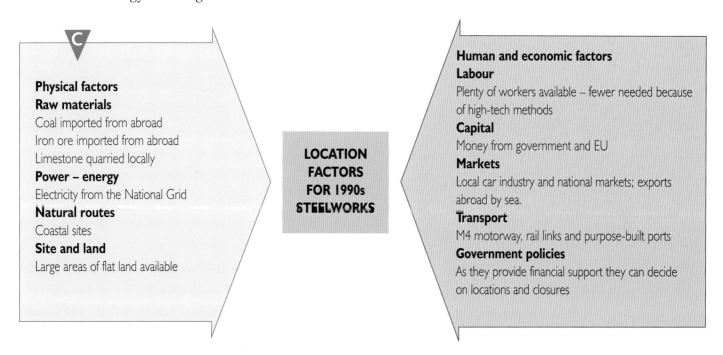

C

Physical factors
Raw materials
Coal imported from abroad
Iron ore imported from abroad
Limestone quarried locally
Power – energy
Electricity from the National Grid
Natural routes
Coastal sites
Site and land
Large areas of flat land available

LOCATION FACTORS FOR 1990s STEELWORKS

Human and economic factors
Labour
Plenty of workers available – fewer needed because of high-tech methods
Capital
Money from government and EU
Markets
Local car industry and national markets; exports abroad by sea.
Transport
M4 motorway, rail links and purpose-built ports
Government policies
As they provide financial support they can decide on locations and closures

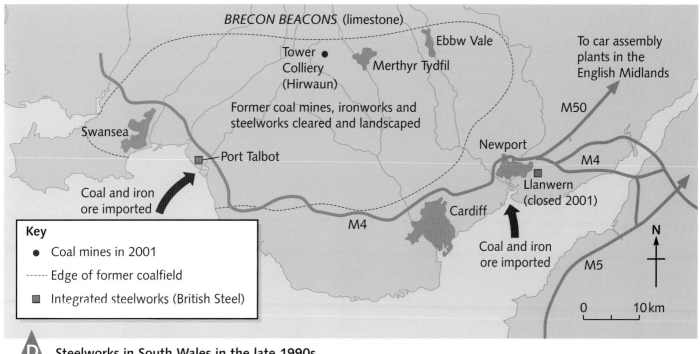

D Steelworks in South Wales in the late 1990s

Changing location – high-technology industries

High-technology or **high-tech** industries make high-value products such as electronics equipment and computers. This recent growth industry now provides more than 25% of the UK's manufacturing jobs.

High-tech companies use the most advanced manufacturing methods. They put great emphasis on the research and development of new pro-ducts, and employ a highly skilled and inventive workforce. Many high-tech factories are simply assembly plants which put together components that are made elsewhere. These components are light and easy to transport, so the industry is **footloose** and has a wide choice of location.

As high-tech industries need to attract a highly talented workforce, they are normally located in areas where the researchers and operators can enjoy a pleasant environment and a good quality of life. Such areas include Silicon Valley in California, the M4 Corridor between London and South Wales, and Silica Fen near Cambridge.

Business and science parks

Firms that make high-tech products often group together on pleasant, newly developed **science** or **business parks**. These parks are often on the edge of the city where there is plenty of space. The buildings are modern, there is plenty of parking, and the parks are landscaped, often with woodland, gardens, lakes and ponds.

All firms on science parks are high-tech and have links with a university. Business parks do not have links with universities and may include superstores, hotels and leisure centres.

Why do similar industries group together?

It is common for high-tech industries to locate close to each other. The advantage of this is that the companies are able to:

- exchange ideas and information with nearby companies
- share maintenance and support services
- build up a pool of highly skilled workers.

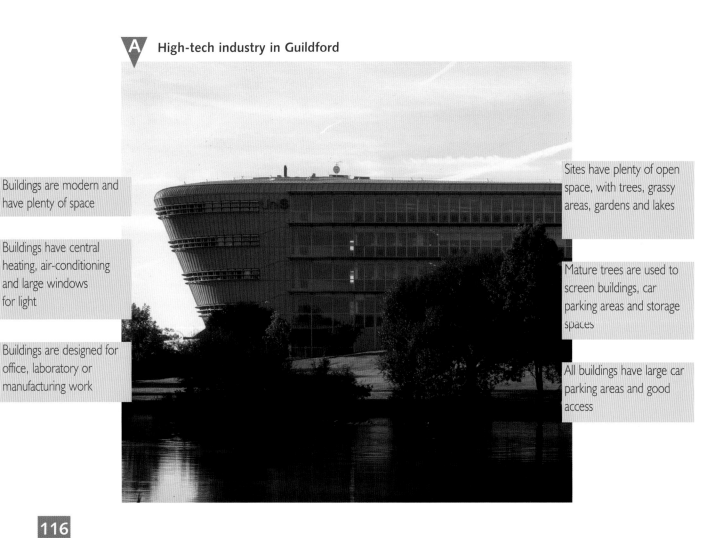

A High-tech industry in Guildford

Buildings are modern and have plenty of space

Buildings have central heating, air-conditioning and large windows for light

Buildings are designed for office, laboratory or manufacturing work

Sites have plenty of open space, with trees, grassy areas, gardens and lakes

Mature trees are used to screen buildings, car parking areas and storage spaces

All buildings have large car parking areas and good access

Cambridge Science Park

One of Britain's first science parks was established in 1970 by Trinity College, Cambridge. It is a low-density development in a park-like setting. The area is landscaped with trees, lakes and ornamental gardens. A conference centre provides sporting and social activities. Nearby are attractive countryside, pretty villages and high-quality residential areas.

Over 150 companies and organisations are located at the park. Their work ranges from the research and development of medical products such as animal vaccines and kidney dialysis machines, to computers, lasers and information technology products. Over half the employees are university graduates.

B Cambridge Science Park

Cambridge is one of Britain's largest and most successful science parks. Some factors that attract companies to the park are shown in diagram **C**.

C

Good leisure facilities in nearby Cambridge

Closely linked with excellence of Cambridge University

Attractive site impresses clients and creates good image

Pleasant housing and open space nearby

Links with university departments and research teams

Attractions of Cambridge Science Park

Near to Stansted Airport for international links

Highly qualified and skilled workforce available

Close to M11 and M25 motorways

Room on site for further expansion

Links with other companies on the site

Changing location – government policies in the UK

Some areas of the UK have higher unemployment than others. This may be due to changes in industry, the closure of factories and businesses, or an increase in the working population of an area.

The government tries to reduce unemployment by encouraging new industries to locate in areas where there are job shortages. Some of the ways that this can be done are shown in diagram **A**.

The size and location of places with high unemployment change over time. Map **B** shows the areas that were regarded as needing the most assistance in the year 2000.

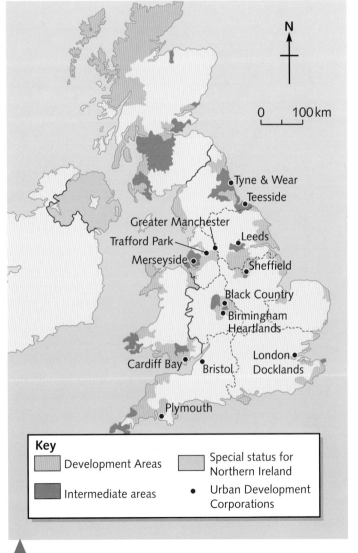

A

Government aid
- New towns to improve living and working conditions
- Ready-built premises with low rents
- Financial aid for new businesses
- Training schemes to improve workforce skills
- Subsidies to help struggling firms
- Improved transport and better accessibility
- Government offices moved to unemployment areas
- Enterprise Zones and Development Areas
- Assistance from the European Union (EU)

Enterprise Zones (EZs)

The first Enterprise Zones came into operation in 1981. Their aim was to create conditions for industrial revival in areas of decay. Most Enterprise Zones are in old inner cities where factory closure had led to unemployment. Others are in towns that had relied upon one major industry which had closed, causing severe job losses.

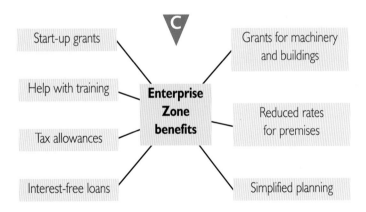

C

Start-up grants • Grants for machinery and buildings • Help with training • **Enterprise Zone benefits** • Tax allowances • Reduced rates for premises • Interest-free loans • Simplified planning

Urban Development Corporations (UDCs)

Urban Development Corporations were first set up by the government in 1981. There aims were to regenerate inner cities and so improve conditions for people living there. Funding for the schemes came from private sources, the British government and the EU. Four of their main tasks were to:

- reclaim and develop derelict and unused land
- provide land for industry, housing and leisure
- build roads and improve the environment
- protect existing jobs and create new ones.

B Development Areas in the UK, 2000

Key
- Development Areas
- Intermediate areas
- Special status for Northern Ireland
- • Urban Development Corporations

Trafford Park Development Corporation

During the early 1980s the Trafford Park area of Manchester was suffering severe decline. Houses were old and in need of repair, factories had closed, and there was high unemployment. Much of the area was derelict land and the environment was severely polluted.

In 1987 the Trafford Park Development Corporation was set up. Its aims were to improve the physical environment, bring jobs to the area and make Trafford Park an attractive place in which to live. Within 11 years the Corporation had exceeded all of its targets, and it was wound up in March 1998. A new organisation, called Midas, is now responsible for promoting the area.

TRAFFORD PARK

TRAFFORD PARK
DEVELOPMENT CORPORATION
MANCHESTER

- 1,825 companies and 55,000 jobs in year 2000
- New road, rail and canal network
- Access to motorways and international airport
- Good public transport, including rail-based Metrolink
- On-site business advice centre
- Training schemes available

- New shopping complex at Trafford Centre
- Newly built regional sports complex
- Clean and attractive environment
- Several pubs, restaurants and other leisure facilities
- Flats and houses available to rent or buy
- Hotel accommodation available

Wharfside
A commercial development alongside the Manchester Ship Canal. An attractive waterside location with offices, shops, pubs and restaurants.

Salford Quays
Once an area of derelict dockland, now the location for a spectacular new office block, a modern hotel and executive apartments.

Transnational corporations

Transnational corporations, or **multinational companies** as they are often called, are very large businesses that have offices and factories all over the world. The headquarters and main factory are usually located in developed countries, particularly the USA and Japan. Smaller offices and factories tend to be in the developing countries where labour is cheap and production costs are low.

In the past 30 years, transnationals have grown in size and influence. Some of the largest ones make more money in a year than all of the African countries put together. The world's 500 largest companies now control at least 70% of world trade and produce more than half of the world's manufactured goods. Being so large they also influence consumer tastes and lifestyles, and are responsible for many of today's scientific and technological breakthroughs.

Many people are concerned about the effects of transnationals. They argue that they locate in poorer countries just to make a profit, and pay low wages, particularly to women and young children. Others say that without transnationals the poorer countries would simply not be able to develop their own industries. People would have no jobs at all and their future would be very bleak.

 A The world's largest transnationals

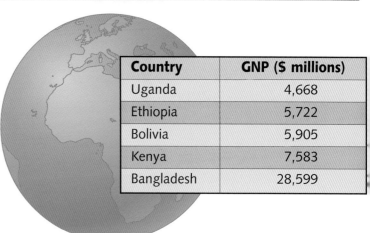

Company	Country	Sales ($ millions)
General Motors		133,622
Ford Motors	USA	108,521
Exxon		97,825
Royal Dutch/ Shell	UK/ Netherlands	95,134
Toyota Motors	Japan	85,283

Country	GNP ($ millions)
Uganda	4,668
Ethiopia	5,722
Bolivia	5,905
Kenya	7,583
Bangladesh	28,599

B Total GNP of selected countries

 C Transnationals in developing countries

Advantages
- Bring work and use local labour
- Improve education and work skills
- Provide money for industrial projects
- Help develop mineral wealth
- Improve energy production
- Improve roads, airports and services
- Provide technology and know-how
- Provide trade links with other countries

Disadvantages
- Local labour usually poorly paid
- Few local skilled workers employed
- Most of the profits go overseas
- Minerals are usually exported
- May need to import raw materials
- Products often of little value to local people
- Companies may pull out at any time
- Rarely consider the needs of the country

Transnationals in developing countries

The global car industry – Ford Motors

Car firms were amongst the first to realise the benefits of being a transnational company. They found that by locating in different parts of the world they could:

- access new local markets
- avoid import taxes
- reduce costs by using cheap labour
- create a world market.

Ford is an American company which was started by an engineer named Henry Ford, who lived in Detroit, Michigan. The history of Ford (**D**) shows how the company started manufacturing and selling cars in the local area and gradually expanded its business across the world.

Ford is a now a huge transnational company. Its operations are on a global scale, with component factories, assembly plants and sales in virtually every part of the world. Indeed the Ford Mondeo is the world's first truly global car: it is manufactured worldwide and sold in markets in many different countries.

Europe's version of the Mondeo is made in Belgium. As diagram **E** shows, however, it can hardly be described as a Belgian car, as its parts are from many different countries.

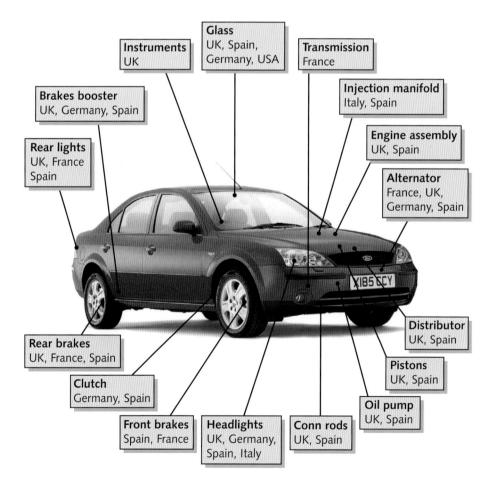

Instruments
UK

Glass
UK, Spain, Germany, USA

Transmission
France

Brakes booster
UK, Germany, Spain

Injection manifold
Italy, Spain

Rear lights
UK, France Spain

Engine assembly
UK, Spain

Alternator
France, UK, Germany, Spain

Rear brakes
UK, France, Spain

Distributor
UK, Spain

Clutch
Germany, Spain

Pistons
UK, Spain

Front brakes
Spain, France

Headlights
UK, Germany, Spain, Italy

Conn rods
UK, Spain

Oil pump
UK, Spain

 Ford's 'European' car

 D The history of Ford – a global car corporation

1896	Henry Ford builds his first car in his garden shed.
1903	Builds his first factory in Detroit, USA.
1911	First European factory opens at Trafford Park, Manchester.
1925	Factory opens in Berlin to serve large German market.
1931	Trafford Park too small, so factory moves to Dagenham which is close to London, the largest market for cars in the UK.
1931	Larger German factory opens at Cologne.
1962	New factory opens within a development area at Halewood, Liverpool.
1963	Rapid increase in demand requires new factories in Belgium and (in 1968) in Germany.
1968	Factory opens in Spain. Low wages and access to Africa and Middle East markets an advantage.
1970s	New factories open in South America, South Africa and Australia.
1980s	Factories open in East Asia, including Japan.
1989	Eastern European markets open up. Electrical components factory built in Hungary.
1990s	Company expands to India and China.
2000	Ford employs 380,000 people worldwide

The Pacific Rim

The Pacific Rim includes all those countries that surround the Pacific Ocean. Many of these countries have shown considerable economic growth in recent times.

In the past, most of the world's industries were located in Europe and North America. Today, the countries of the Pacific Rim, and particularly those of eastern Asia, are becoming more important. The first country to industrialise was Japan. This began in the 1950s – see opposite page.

The NICs in East Asia

The countries of eastern Asia have seen a dramatic increase in levels of industrialisation and wealth since the 1960s. They are now called **newly industrialised countries** or **NICs**.

The greatest increase in development has been in South Korea, Taiwan and Singapore, which became known as the three 'Tigers'. Hong Kong was known as the fourth Tiger, but is now part of China and no longer independent.

Like Japan, these Tiger countries lacked basic raw materials but each had a strong government and highly motivated workforce. The workforce were initially willing to work long hours for little pay. This helped their companies produce cheap goods and slowly take over world markets.

Since the 1980s Malaysia, Thailand and Indonesia have begun to join the list of NICs. The next to emerge, and certainly the largest, is likely to be China.

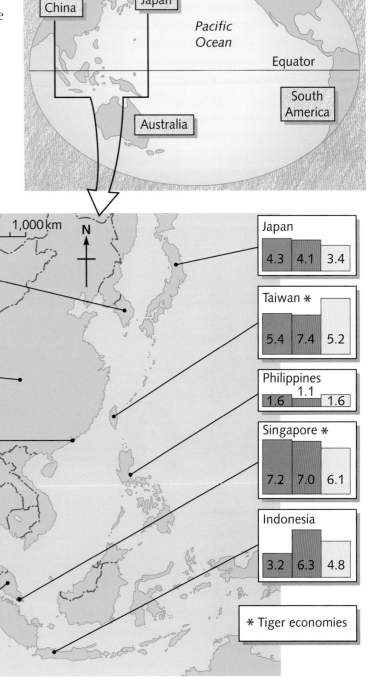

A The Pacific Rim

B Economic growth in East Asia

> Newly industrialised countries are mainly in eastern Asia and have undergone rapid and successful industrialisation since the 1960s.

> Tiger economies are based on industrial growth that is rapid and competitive.

South Korea * 6.8 | 10.1 | 8.7

China 5.5 | 9.5 | 8.0

Hong Kong * 6.3 | 7.1 | 5.1

Thailand 4.0 | 7.6 | 9.1

Malaysia 4.0 | 5.1 | 9.2

Japan 4.3 | 4.1 | 3.4

Taiwan * 5.4 | 7.4 | 5.2

Philippines 1.6 | 1.1 | 1.6

Singapore * 7.2 | 7.0 | 6.1

Indonesia 3.2 | 6.3 | 4.8

* Tiger economies

Key
Annual growth rate %

1965–1980	1981–1990	1991–2000

0   1,000 km

N

Japan

C Industry in Japan

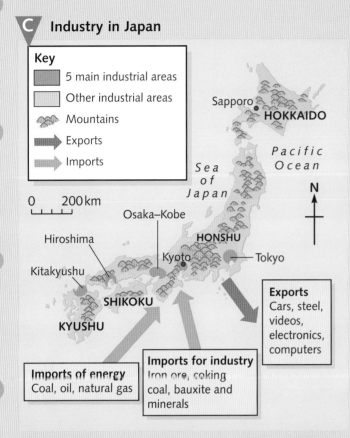

Key

- 5 main industrial areas
- Other industrial areas
- Mountains
- Exports
- Imports

0   200 km

Exports
Cars, steel, videos, electronics, computers

Imports for industry
Iron ore, coking coal, bauxite and minerals

Imports of energy
Coal, oil, natural gas

Sapporo • HOKKAIDO

Pacific Ocean

Sea of Japan

N

Osaka–Kobe

Hiroshima

HONSHU

Kyoto — Tokyo

Kitakyushu

SHIKOKU

KYUSHU

D Seto-Ohashi bridges, Inland Sea, Japan

In 1945 Japan's industry lay in ruins after the Second World War. By 1990 Japan had become, after the USA, the second most wealthy and industrialised country in the world.

How did it achieve this remarkable success? After all, it had been devastated by losing the war, and lacked most of the basic industrial needs.

 E

Problems

- Only 17% of the country is flat enough for development.
- Japan has few energy resources and has to import almost all of its oil, natural gas and coal.
- It lacks the basic raw materials needed for industry such as iron ore, coking coal and minerals.

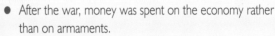

Solutions

- After the war, money was spent on the economy rather than on armaments.
- The country had a stable government that was committed to industrialisation.
- Modern machinery and technology were introduced.
- The workforce was hardworking, skilled and loyal.
- The country has good harbours for importing raw materials.
- An excellent transport system was developed.
- A large domestic market developed as the country became richer.
- Money was available to reclaim land from the sea.

Outcomes

- Five main industrial areas developed on coastal sites.
- Existing iron ore and coal were used to make steel.
- The steel was used to make ships.
- The ships were used to import raw materials.
- Car making became a major industry, with huge world markets.
- The electronics and high-tech industries became world leaders.
- Money made by selling goods abroad easily paid for imported raw materials and foodstuffs.

Places

Industry in less economically developed countries

Formal and informal sectors

Working in the poorer countries of the world can be very different from working in the UK. Most people work long hours and earn low wages. Few people have a proper full-time job, and there is little government support for those families with no money.

The situation in the cities is particularly bad. Here, there are many more people than jobs. With the rapid growth of these cities due to inward **migration** from the countryside, the job situation is continually worsening.

Some people manage to gain employment in the **formal sector**. These jobs provide a regular income and may be in an office, shop or organised factory. Most others, however, have to find work for themselves in the **informal sector**. Here they may work in jobs such as street-trading, shoe-shining or luggage carrying.

Many informal workers collect waste materials and, by the skill of the worker, recycle them into saleable products.

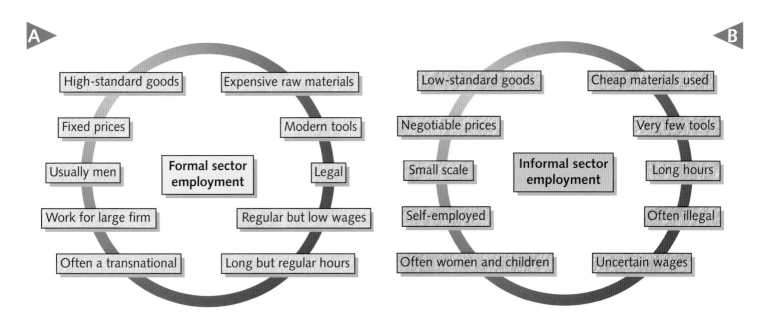

A

- High-standard goods
- Expensive raw materials
- Fixed prices
- Modern tools
- Usually men
- **Formal sector employment**
- Legal
- Work for large firm
- Regular but low wages
- Often a transnational
- Long but regular hours

B

- Low-standard goods
- Cheap materials used
- Negotiable prices
- Very few tools
- Small scale
- **Informal sector employment**
- Long hours
- Self-employed
- Often illegal
- Often women and children
- Uncertain wages

C Street traders on Copacabana beach, Rio de Janeiro, Brazil

D Ten-year-old boys shoe-cleaning in Ethiopia

124

There is little or no security in the informal sector. People live from day to day. As diagram **E** shows, they are trapped by a lack of opportunity to improve their position.

Estimates suggest that up to 90% of the working population of cities in the world's poorer countries are employed in the informal sector.

In some cities there are schemes to support informal sector workers. In Nairobi, for example, there are several small **Jua Kali** workshops. Scrap metal is collected and hammered into an assortment of products including locks, boxes and cooking utensils. These are sold cheaply and used locally.

The government supports the Jua Kali businesses by supplying electricity and providing roofs to protect the workers from the weather. Jua Kali means 'under the hot sun'.

Role of children

Children make up a large proportion of the informal sector workers. They may be as young as 10 years old, or even younger. Very few have schools to attend, and from an early age they go out on the streets to help earn money for their families. Visiting the local rubbish dump is a popular activity. Here they pick up anything that may be recycled and sold to make money.

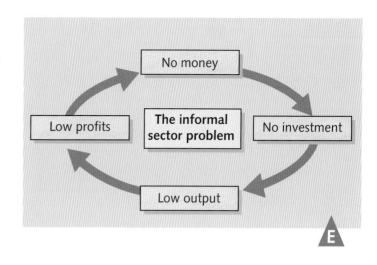

E

F Recycling metal products at a Jua Kali workshop, Nairobi, Kenya

Sustainable development in less economically developed countries

Improving standards of living and quality of life in poorer countries is very difficult. Some people think that big schemes like huge hydro-electric projects or new international airports are the wrong types of development. This is because they are too expensive, require the help of foreign companies and rarely give direct help to the poor. They are also unlikely to be **sustainable** as they tend to use up resources and can harm the environment.

In less economically developed countries, most people now favour smaller schemes which use **appropriate technology**. These schemes meet the needs of the local people and the environment in which they live. They are more likely to be sustainable and can help improve the quality of life for people today without damaging the future.

> Sustainable development improves people's standard of living and quality of life without wasting resources or harming the environment.

Appropriate technology...
- uses methods that are suited to the area where they are used
- is usually small-scale
- uses cheap and simple equipment
- has a small demand for energy
- uses local resources
- involves traditional skills
- helps ordinary people improve their quality of life.

A

B

Before

For women, most tasks are hard work, time-consuming and have to be done by hand. Separating grain from crops can take hours of hard work.

After

A simple machine can make tasks easier. Here, a small, water-driven turbine helps separate rice grains. It saves time and improves quality and productivity.

Before

Grinding enough corn to feed a family for a day takes five hard hours when done by hand.

After

By taking corn to the grinder in the mill-house – usually a popular meeting place for villagers – a day's worth of corn can be ground in just 5 minutes.

Intermediate Technology Development Group (ITDG)

The Intermediate Technology Development Group is a charitable organisation which works with people in developing countries. It is particularly active in rural areas where conditions are often most difficult and other help is rarely available.

The aim of the Intermediate Technology Development Group is to help people acquire the tools and techniques needed if they are to work themselves out of poverty.

C Intermediate technology ...

- helps people to meet their needs of food, clothing, housing, farm and industrial equipment, energy and employment
- uses and adds to local knowledge by providing advice, training, basic equipment and financial support so that people can become more self-sufficient and independent
- uses methods that are sustainable and appropriate.

The Intermediate Technology Development Group in northern Kenya

Until 1988 few villages in northern Kenya had safe drinking water. They relied on streams and pools, but these became badly polluted during the dry season. Water-borne diseases were widespread and people's health was poor.

Many of the streams and pools were far from the villages and difficult to get to. It was usually the women who had the tiring and time-consuming task of collecting the water.

A UK-funded project to provide water for the region began in 1988. Over 170 wells have been completed. The project has been very successful. The wells use simple technology, are easy to maintain, and have become a meeting place for villagers. Diseases in the area have been reduced, health has improved, and women no longer have to spend so much of the day carrying water.

The development project in northern Kenya is typical of many of the ITDG schemes around the world. It is small-scale, uses local labour and is suited to the environment. It is also cheap and, unlike many larger projects, directly benefits local people.

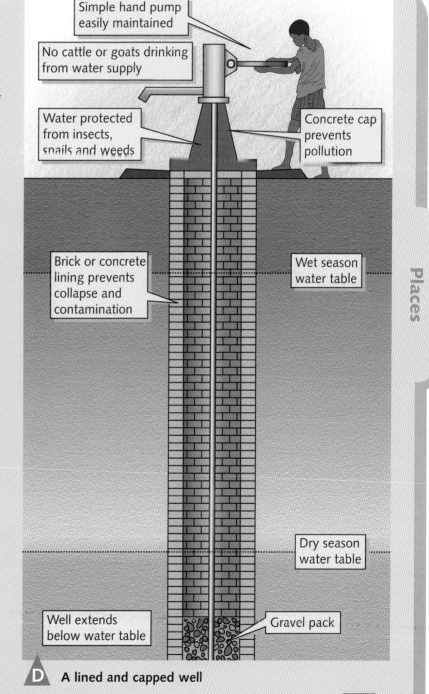

Simple hand pump easily maintained

No cattle or goats drinking from water supply

Water protected from insects, snails and weeds

Concrete cap prevents pollution

Brick or concrete lining prevents collapse and contamination

Wet season water table

Dry season water table

Well extends below water table

Gravel pack

D A lined and capped well

Places

127

Case Study 9

Industry in a developed city
Osaka–Kobe

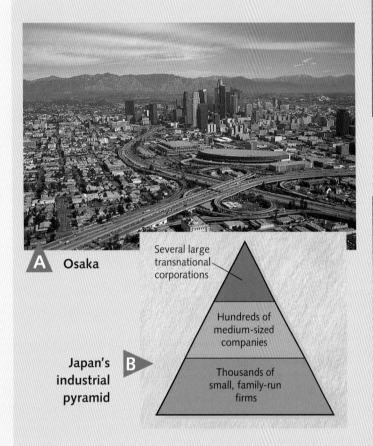

A Osaka

Japan's industrial pyramid **B**

- Several large transnational corporations
- Hundreds of medium-sized companies
- Thousands of small, family-run firms

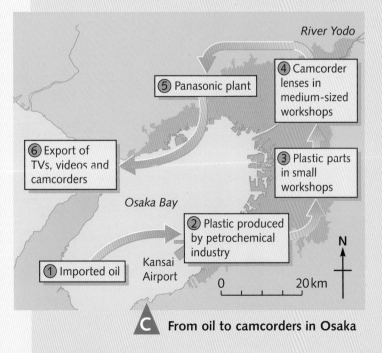

River Yodo

⑤ Panasonic plant

④ Camcorder lenses in medium-sized workshops

⑥ Export of TVs, videos and camcorders

③ Plastic parts in small workshops

Osaka Bay

② Plastic produced by petrochemical industry

① Imported oil

Kansai Airport

N

0   20 km

C From oil to camcorders in Osaka

Main features
- Located on Osaka Bay, a natural harbour providing good shelter from typhoons.
- Port facilities import raw materials and export finished products.
- The land around Osaka Bay is one of the few areas of flat land in Japan.
- Population of 9 million provides a skilled workforce and a large, wealthy domestic market.
- Major centre for modern high-tech industries.
- Japanese industry has a pyramid organisation. In Osaka there are many companies of different sizes.
- Industry is highly efficient and is based on hard work, loyalty and trust.

From oil to camcorders
1. Oil is imported into Osaka port.
2. The oil is processed into many by-products, including plastic.
3. Some of the plastic is taken to small work units and made into camcorder parts such as lenses, cases, control units and carrying bags.
4. The finished parts are then sent across the city to the huge Panasonic plant.
5. Panasonic assembles the component parts made by the many small and medium-sized firms.
6. The completed camcorders, along with other Panasonic products, are exported through Osaka port to 160 countries worldwide.

Problems
- Panasonic and other Japanese firms face competition from newly industrialised countries like Taiwan, Singapore and Malaysia.
- Low labour and production costs in those countries result in cheaper products than in Japan.

Solutions
To meet the challenge Panasonic has:
- set up factories in other countries
- invested in research and development to be ahead in technology
- developed new products.

Industry in a developing city

São Paulo

Brazil

Main features
- Located in cooler highland area some 50 km inland from Santos, the town's main port.
- Brazil's largest and most industrialised city.
- Coffee provided early wealth for region.
- Coffee profits invested in other industries.
- Rapid growth of city during so called 'economic miracle' of 1960s and 1970s.
- Present population an estimated 23 million.

 Iron and steel works in São Paulo

Industrial development
- Nearby iron ore and cheap energy led to development of iron and steel industry and manufacture of machinery, aircraft and cars.
- Ford, Volkswagen, Mercedes and General Motors now located in São Paulo.
- Brazil is world's ninth largest car producer.
- Brazilian car workers earn more than twice the average Brazilian wage.

Problems
- Heavy industry and traffic have caused air pollution.
- The great number of cars has led to serious traffic jams and gridlock conditions.
- A 'sky-scraper jungle' has developed in the city centre, with high land prices and little open space.

 Pepsi plant in Jundaia new town

Solutions
- Some industries have moved to new towns.
- These have a cleaner environment, better transport links and improved amenities.
- Several huge transnational companies, such as Pepsi, have already located in Jundaia new town.
- New companies provide better working conditions than old city centre industries.
- Run-down areas of São Paulo have been cleared and new businesses and leisure facilities built.
- Unfortunately, some of the redevelopment areas housed São Paulo's poor people. These people now have the problem of rebuilding flimsy shanty town homes and finding work.

REVISION QUESTIONS

1 (Page 112)
Write down the meaning of the following terms:
a) industry b) inputs
c) processes d) outputs.

2 (Page 112)
The systems diagram below is for the car industry. Copy and complete the diagram using the following terms:

- workforce
- car assembly
- profit
- money
- electricity
- finished cars
- car parts
- money back into company
- car testing.

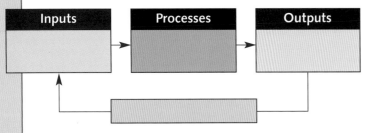

Inputs	Processes	Outputs

3 (Page 112)
a) List four physical factors and four human factors that affect the location of industry.
b) Explain how the following affect where industry should be located:
- raw materials
- labour
- government.

4 (Page 113)
List five reasons for job losses in the UK. Give an example for each one.

5 (Pages 114 and 115)
Copy and complete the table below to show the location factors for iron and steel works in South Wales.

Location factors	19th-century ironworks	1990s steelworks
Raw materials		
Power		
Capital		
Markets		
Transport		

6 (Pages 116 and 117)
a) What are high-tech industries?
b) What are footloose industries?
c) Describe the main features of a business park.
d) List what you think are the six most important attractions of Cambridge Science Park.

7 (Pages 122 and 123)
a) What are newly industrialised countries?
b) What are **Tiger economies**?
c) Name six Tiger countries in order of recent growth.
d) Draw a star diagram to show eight factors that have helped Japanese growth since the 1950s.

8 (Pages 118 and 119)
a) Describe what the UK government has done to try to reduce unemployment.
b) What were the aims of the Trafford Park Development Corporation?
c) List what you think are the six most important attractions of Trafford Park for locating industry.

9 (Pages 120 and 121)
a) What is a transnational company?
b) Give four bad points about transnationals.
c) What are the benefits to Ford of being a transnational company?
d) Which countries provide parts for Ford's 'European' car?

10 (Pages 124 and 125)
Copy and complete the table below to show the differences between formal and informal industries.

Features	Formal sector	Informal sector
Definition		
Wages		
Hours worked		
Quality of goods		
Price of goods		
Materials used		
Tools available		
Job examples		

EXAMINATION QUESTIONS

1 (Pages 112 to 115)

Look at map **A**.
a) Which site would have been best for an iron and steel works in 1820? Give four reasons for your choice. (4)
b) Which site would be best for a steelworks in the 21st century? Give four reasons for your choice. (4)
c) Give two ways that a government can influence the location of an industry. (2)

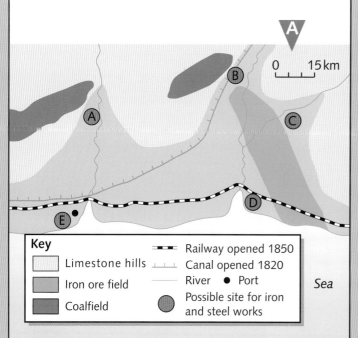

A

0   15 km

Key

Limestone hills	Railway opened 1850
Iron ore field	Canal opened 1820
Coalfield	River ● Port
	Possible site for iron and steel works

Sea

2 (Pages 116 and 117)

Look at map **B**.
a) What motorway links London with Bristol? (1)
b) How many electronic companies are shown on the map? (1)
c) Why has the presence of universities in this area attracted high-tech industry? (2)
d) Explain two other advantages that this area has for high-tech industries. (4)

3 (Pages 120 and 121)

a) How many Japanese car companies have factories in the UK? (1)
b) Name one country that has seven different Japanese car companies. (1)
c) Answer **true** or **false** to these statements:
- Japan only builds cars in rich countries.
- Nissan builds cars in the UK, Spain and India.
d) What is a transnational or multinational company? (1)
e) Give two possible reasons why foreign firms set up factories in other countries. (4)
f) Give two ways that countries benefit from having transnational companies. (4)

C **Countries in which Japanese vehicle manufacturers have factories**

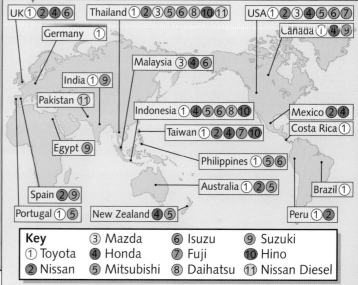

Key
① Toyota	④ Honda	⑨ Suzuki
② Nissan	⑤ Mitsubishi	⑩ Hino
③ Mazda	⑥ Isuzu	⑪ Nissan Diesel
	⑦ Fuji	
	⑧ Daihatsu	

B **The M4 Corridor: an area of high-technology industry**

0   15 km

Newport   M5   Swindon   Fast rail link   M40   M1   M25
Bristol   Reading   Slough   LONDON
River Severn   M4   M4   M3

Key
High-tech electronic company	Urban area
Research centre	Motorway
International airport	Railway (main line)
	Bridge

N

10 TOURISM

Recent trends and changing patterns

Tourism has become the world's fastest-growing industry and by the year 2000, employed more people worldwide than any other industry.

Graph **A** shows the increase in tourist numbers. At present, there are no signs of this increase slowing down. Indeed, as more places develop their tourist industries, and as travel becomes even easier, tourist numbers are expected to increase for many years to come.

Some of the largest increases in tourist numbers have been in the poorer countries of the world. For these places, tourism is seen as one of the few ways to make money and create jobs. For example, in 2003 Egypt had Africa's third largest tourist industry. More than 5 million tourists visited the country in that year. They spent an estimated £4 billion and provided employment for over 2 million local people.

Tourism has changed considerably in the last 40 years. Not only has there been a dramatic increase in tourist numbers, but there is a now a wider range of holiday destinations. People also seem to be travelling further, and more often than ever before. There are several reasons for these changes. Three of the main ones are shown in **C** below.

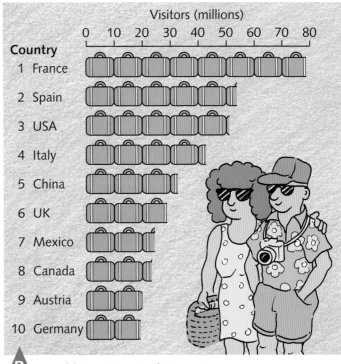

B World tourist arrivals, 2003

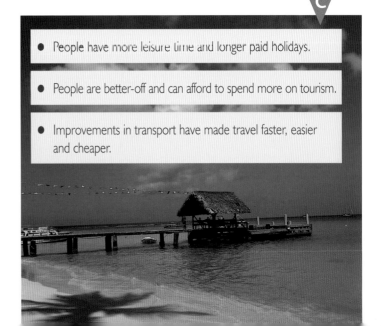

C

- People have more leisure time and longer paid holidays.
- People are better-off and can afford to spend more on tourism.
- Improvements in transport have made travel faster, easier and cheaper.

A World tourist arrivals, 1960–2005

The United Kingdom

The UK also has a large and profitable tourist industry. As graph **B** shows, the UK is now the world's sixth most popular tourist destination. In 2003, Britain received more than 28 million foreign visitors, who spent an estimated £19.6 billion. This provided work for some 2.1 million people employed in hotels, restaurants, cafés, pubs, travel agents, museums and other such places.

Mass tourism began in Britain about a hundred years ago. Resorts like Blackpool, Scarborough and Southend grew rapidly as industrial workers enjoyed a few days each year at the seaside.

Two things made this possible. First, the development of the railways provided cheap and rapid transport for thousands of day trippers and holiday-makers. Second, the introduction of paid holidays meant that workers could afford a week or two away from home each year.

Today, people travel much further than their nearest seaside resort, and often enjoy more than one holiday a year. The South West, with its warmer climate and wide range of attractive scenery, is the most popular tourist region in Britain for UK residents.

However, increasing numbers of British tourists now travel abroad, with Spain and France the most popular destinations. People are attracted to these places because they are easily accessible, and provide almost guaranteed sunshine throughout the summer months.

The latest trend is for long-haul holidays to far-off destinations like the USA, Thailand and Kenya. These have become popular as tourists have become more adventurous and price-wars between airlines have made fares even cheaper.

D Tourism in England and Wales

Key

Amount of tourist spending (£ million)

Foreign visitors | UK residents

6,000

0   150 km

N

Northumbria 485
Cumbria 475
Yorks & Humberside 1,330
North-west 490
East Midlands 1,025
Heart of England 1,430
Wales 1,320
East Anglia 1,480
London 6,485
South-east 1,550
West Country 2,865
Southern 1,745

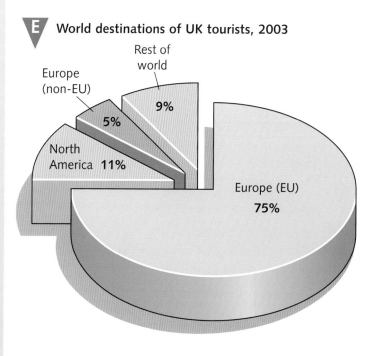

E World destinations of UK tourists, 2003

Rest of world 9%
Europe (non-EU) 5%
North America 11%
Europe (EU) 75%

National Parks in the UK

National Parks are large areas of beautiful countryside. Their scenery and wildlife are protected so that everyone can enjoy them. The world's first Park was opened as long ago as 1872 at Yellowstone in the USA. Since then many countries have set up similar Parks. Parks around the world vary in many ways but they all have the same two basic aims:

1 To preserve and care for the environment.
2 To provide a place for relaxation and outdoor recreation.

Britain's first National Parks were created in the 1950s. They are areas of attractive countryside but also places where people live and work. They include towns and villages as well as industries such as farming, forestry and mining.

The main idea of the Parks was to provide protection for the environment. It was also hoped, however, that they would be a way of looking after the way of life and livelihood of people already living there.

Who owns the National Parks?

The term 'National Park' can be misleading. They are not owned by the nation, and people do not have the right to wander where they like and do what they want. In fact most of the land belongs to private individuals, like farmers and house owners.

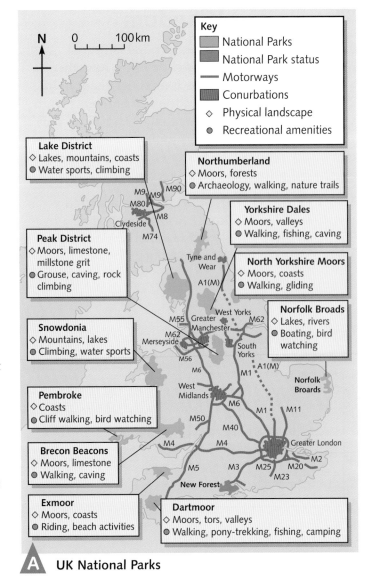

A UK National Parks

Key
- National Parks
- National Park status
- Motorways
- Conurbations
- ◇ Physical landscape
- ● Recreational amenities

Lake District
◇ Lakes, mountains, coasts
● Water sports, climbing

Northumberland
◇ Moors, forests
● Archaeology, walking, nature trails

Yorkshire Dales
◇ Moors, valleys
● Walking, fishing, caving

Peak District
◇ Moors, limestone, millstone grit
● Grouse, caving, rock climbing

North Yorkshire Moors
◇ Moors, coasts
● Walking, gliding

Norfolk Broads
◇ Lakes, rivers
● Boating, bird watching

Snowdonia
◇ Mountains, lakes
● Climbing, water sports

Pembroke
◇ Coasts
● Cliff walking, bird watching

Brecon Beacons
◇ Moors, limestone
● Walking, caving

Exmoor
◇ Moors, coasts
● Riding, beach activities

Dartmoor
◇ Moors, tors, valleys
● Walking, pony-trekking, fishing, camping

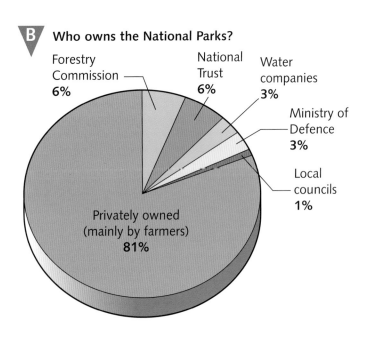

B Who owns the National Parks?

- Forestry Commission 6%
- National Trust 6%
- Water companies 3%
- Ministry of Defence 3%
- Local councils 1%
- Privately owned (mainly by farmers) 81%

C Yorkshire Dales National Park

Conflict in National Parks

The needs of different people can cause **conflict** in National Parks. Conflict is when there is disagreement over how something should be used. Conflict is often about land ownership. Farmers, for example, may not want tourists to walk across their land. Water companies may not allow water sports on their reservoirs. Other examples of conflict are shown in drawing **D**.

D Conflicts in the National Parks

> Wildlife may be frightened by large groups of walkers.

> The Army closes areas of the Park during firing practice.

> Farm animals can be at risk when gates are left open and walls damaged.

> Water companies have flooded valleys to create reservoirs.

> Tourists want wider roads, while locals want less traffic.

> Quiet places become busy and noisy from increased tourist use.

Should quarrying be allowed in National Parks?

There are 30 working quarries in the National Parks extracting 12 million tonnes of rock every year. The quarries are a major source of conflict, as they tend to destroy the very landscape that National Parks are supposed to protect (**E**).

National Park Authorities try to ensure that working quarries are landscaped and screened. They also insist that when a quarry closes, it should be restored to its original appearance.

E

Problems
- Quarries are dirty and dangerous.
- Noise is caused by blasting and heavy lorries.
- Wildlife is frightened away.
- Buildings and spoil heaps look ugly.
- Heavy lorries cause traffic congestion.

Benefits
- Quarries provide work and income for local people.
- A quarry is a source of money for the local council.
- Roads are improved for large lorries.
- Quarries provide important raw materials for the nation.
- Slate and limestone can be used locally.

Costa del Sol, Spain

A
FRANCE
PORTUGAL
SPAIN
Costa del Sol
Mediterranean Sea
AFRICA

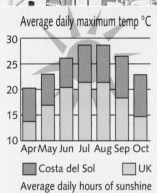

Average daily maximum temp °C

B

	Apr	May	Jun	Jul	Aug	Sep	Oct

Costa del Sol   UK

Average daily hours of sunshine

| 8 | 10 | 11 | 11 | 11 | 9 | 7 |

The Costa del Sol, or the sunshine coast, is the most southerly of Spain's tourist coasts. It faces the sun, the Mediterranean Sea and North Africa.

For holidaymakers, seeking sun, sand and excitement, it has just about everything.

Climate. Summers are hot, sunny and dry. Winters have some rain but it is mild.

Landscape. There are long sandy beaches beside the warm, blue Mediterranean Sea. Inland are spectacular mountains and steep-sided gorges.

Accommodation. Torremolinos and Fuengirola have high-rise hotels and apartments. Marbella has the most modern and luxurious hotels. The hills behind the town are dotted with fine villas and private apartments.

Nightlife and shopping. The area is alive after dark with numerous restaurants, cafés, bars and discos. Shops range from cheap local bazaars to expensive chic boutiques selling designer clothes.

Things to do. Many activities are linked to the sea, with a variety of water sports and several yachting harbours and marinas all along the coast. There are also many golf courses. Inland there are pretty whitewashed villages and the historic centres of Granada and Seville.

Changes in tourism and to the environment

Places with a pleasant climate and spectacular scenery like the Costa del Sol, attract tourists. Tourists demand amenities like hotels, restaurants and entertainments to make their visit more comfortable and enjoyable. As more amenities are added, however, the area gets crowded, congested and less attractive. Eventually tourists lose interest in the area and look for other places to visit. This is happening to the Costa del Sol.

Role of the Spanish government

The Spanish government saw tourism as one way to provide jobs and to raise the country's standard of living. It encouraged the construction of new hotels and leisure amenities. Now, though, it is concerned at the slow decline in tourism in the coastal resorts.

Some poor publicity, and competition from cheaper resorts elsewhere, are two reasons for this decline. Stricter controls on pollution, higher standards for hotels, and improved facilities, have been introduced in an attempt to attract tourists back.

C

Growth in tourism

1960s	1970s	1980s	1990s	2000s
Hardly any tourists Very few hotels Few amenities Poor roads Quiet, clean, unspoilt	**Rapid increase in number of tourists** Large hotels built Roads improved New bars, discos, shops Beaches less clean	**Too many tourists** More large hotels Towns congested Severe pollution Increase in crime	**Decline in tourism** Hotels looking old Bars/cafés closing New air terminal Pollution clean-up	**Growth or decline?**

D Changes in tourism

137

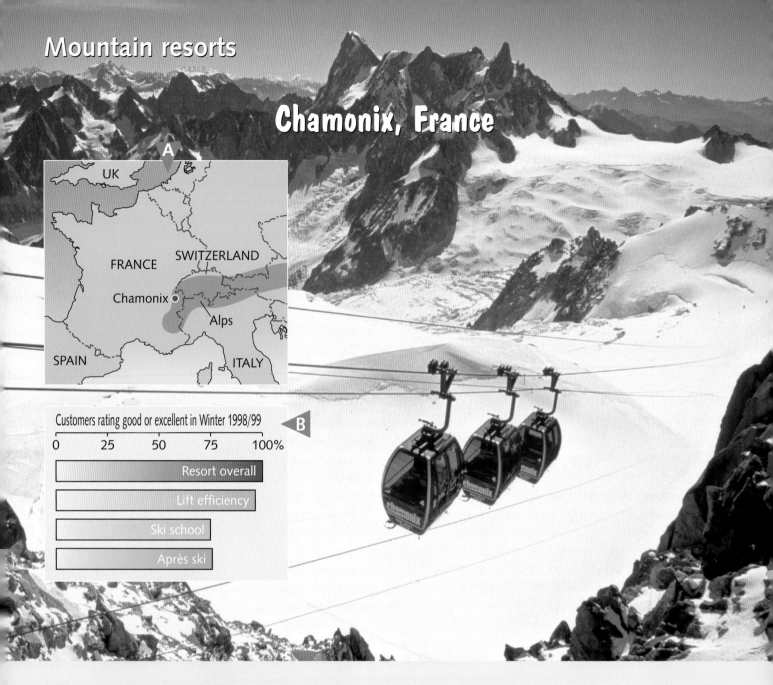

Chamonix, France

A

Customers rating good or excellent in Winter 1998/99 B

| | 0 | 25 | 50 | 75 | 100% |

- Resort overall
- Lift efficiency
- Ski school
- Après ski

The resort: Chamonix is a year-round resort with a fabulous range of attractions and facilities. It is located in the French Alps at the foot of Europe's highest mountain, the magnificent Mont Blanc.

The skiing is spectacular and a single lift pass is valid for all 62 lifts in the Mont Blanc area. After a hard day on the slopes, Chamonix is the perfect place to party the night away with a fantastic choice of fashionable bars and restaurants.

Skiing: Chamonix Valley has six main ski areas. There are steep, challenging slopes for experts, interesting runs for intermediates and easier areas for beginners. The famous Vallée Blanche descent may be followed with a guide and provides 24 km of unforgettable skiing in stunning scenery.

Après-ski: Chamonix is a very trendy resort and is popular with young people. The many bars stay open until the early hours and there is a good selection of restaurants and cafés. Why not check out the best bars – Jekyll and Hydes, Wild Wallabies, The Pub – then go dancing at one of the clubs, or even try the casino!

Activities: The town is bustling and lively. There is a sports centre, large heated swimming pool, ice skating and snowmobiling. Chamonix has a wide range of shops and smart boutiques, and day trips to Italy and Switzerland are available if you need a change.

C Extreme skiing

Winter sports: the good and the bad

Every year some 50 million people visit the Alps, two-thirds of them on winter skiing holidays. For many people, alpine resorts provide the best of everything. There is skiing, walking, climbing and sailing as well as dramatic scenery and clean, fresh air.

As may be expected, tourism has brought many benefits to the area. It has increased employment opportunities, raised living standards and generally improved the quality of life for most local people.

Unfortunately there have also been problems. Many people are concerned that winter sports facilities, in particular, are spoiling the countryside and permanently damaging the environment.

Chamonix, along with most other mountain resorts, is concerned about these problems. The town has introduced strict new planning controls, and the emphasis is now on improving existing facilities rather than developing new ones.

Ski resort map **D**

Chamonix

Good points
- Tourism has provided work for local people.
- Many of the jobs are suitable for young people.
- Jobs in tourism are better paid than those in traditional industries like farming and forestry.
- Roads, water supplies and sewerage have all been improved.
- New tourist facilities may be used by local people.
- Fewer people leave the area.

Bad points
- Many of the new jobs are seasonal.
- The better tourist jobs rarely go to local people.
- The traditional way of life may be lost.
- Ugly skiing facilities spoil the mountainside.
- New hotels are often unsightly.
- A huge increase in cars and buses causes congestion, traffic jams and parking problems.
- Plant life has been damaged and wildlife frightened away.
- Forest clearance for ski runs causes erosion and increases the chance of landslides and flooding.

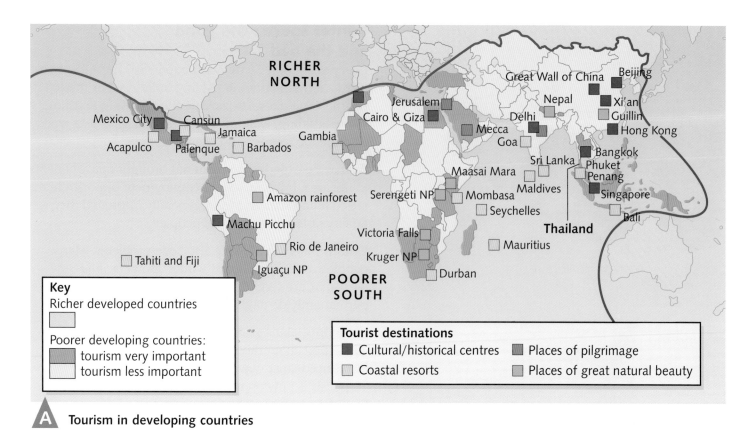

A Tourism in developing countries

Tourism in developing countries

Since the early 1980s, European tourists have become increasingly less satisfied with package tours to Mediterranean coastal resorts. They now look for holidays further afield where the environment and culture is very different from their own. The move to long-haul holidays has been helped by television travel programmes and by price wars between airlines which have reduced the cost of long-distance travel.

The countries that have benefited most from this change in holiday fashion have been the tropical, developing countries. These include places like Kenya, Egypt, Sri Lanka, Thailand, Malaysia and the West Indies. Indeed in Africa, tourism has become the continent's fastest-growing industry.

Tourism has brought many benefits to the poorer countries of the world. For most, it is the only way to earn money and increase living standards. Unfortunately, tourism can also be damaging. Without planning and sensitive management, it does little to benefit local people and is often harmful to their culture and environment.

Ecotourism

Mass tourism is the worst and most damaging type of tourism. It involves huge numbers of visitors, massive developments and crowded resorts. It is common to places like Florida, the Spanish costas and the Greek islands.

Some developing countries have tried to avoid mass tourism. Instead, they promote **ecotourism** or **green tourism**. Ecotourists usually travel in small groups and share special interests. They include wildlife enthusiasts, bird watchers and photographers. They often visit National Parks and game reserves where the wildlife and scenery is protected and managed.

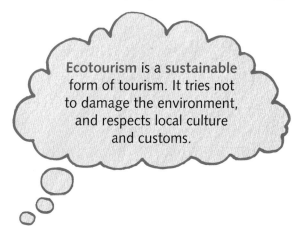

Ecotourism is a sustainable form of tourism. It tries not to damage the environment, and respects local culture and customs.

Thailand

Thailand is a developing country located in South-east Asia. Its tourist industry has grown rapidly in the last 20 years, and tourism is now the country's most important source of foreign income.

Thailand's attractions include hot sunny weather, tropical islands, clean sandy beaches and spectacular scenery. The country has an interesting history and an exotic way of life. Its towns are a paradise for shoppers, and there are numerous bars, restaurants and nightclubs.

Tourism has brought wealth and jobs to Thailand but has also caused problems. In recent years there has been a growth in ecotourism, particularly in the north where elephant trekking holidays are popular.

Advantages

- Tourism brings in more than £6 billion of foreign money a year.
- There are over 1.5 million jobs in the tourist industry.
- Income from tourism has helped develop other industries and provide jobs.
- Overseas investment has helped finance highways and sewerage systems.
- Local people can use tourist facilities.

B Tourism in Thailand

Disadvantages

- Many tourist developments are ugly and have spoilt the environment.
- Local culture and traditional ways of life have been destroyed.
- Farmland and homes have been lost to hotel developments and road building.
- Prostitution and disease have become problems in Bangkok and some other centres.
- Vegetation has been damaged and wildlife frightened away.

C Krabi Island, Thailand

D Royal Palace, Bangkok

Tourism and the environment

Few countries in the world can offer the traveller the variety of scenery that Kenya can. Inland there are snow-covered mountains, lakes, grassy plains and an abundance of wildlife. On the coast there are sandy beaches, coral islands and the warm, clean Indian Ocean.

These features attract large numbers of tourists to Kenya. Many go on organised tours called **safaris** where they view the animals in their natural surroundings. Kenya has over 50 National Parks and game reserves where animals are protected and tourism is encouraged.

On the safaris, tourists are usually taken around in mini-buses with open roofs for easier viewing. The drivers are expert guides who are able to track down wildlife and find the best places for taking photographs.

SAFARI

A

Day 1 Nairobi/Samburu (310 km)
After breakfast drive north, cross the Equator and pass Mount Kenya to Samburu Lodge. After lunch there will be a game drive where you should see elephant, buffalo, lion, giraffe, zebra, crocodile and many bird species.

Day 2 Samburu
Early morning game drive. Relax at midday around the pool or watch the Samburu perform traditional dances.

Day 3 Samburu/Lake Nakuru (200 km)
Drive to Thompson Falls and into the rift valley for lunch. A short drive will let you see vast flocks of pink flamingos by the lake.

Day 4 Nakuru/Maasai Mara (340 km)
Leisurely morning by the lakeside. After lunch drive to Keekorok Lodge in the Maasai Mara.

Day 5 Maasai Mara
The huge Mara plain provides some of the best game viewing in East Africa. During the early morning and late afternoon game drives you are likely to see huge herds of wildebeest and zebra as well as lion, elephant, cheetah, leopard, giraffe and hippo. An option is an early morning Balloon Safari.

Day 6 Maasai Mara/Nairobi (260 km)
Early morning departure arriving Nairobi for lunch. Afternoon flight to Mombasa to continue your holiday at a beach hotel.

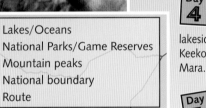

Lakes/Oceans
National Parks/Game Reserves
▲ Mountain peaks
— National boundary
— Route

N

Lake Turkana

Lake Victoria

Lake Nakuru

K E N Y A

Marsabit National Reserve

Samburu National Reserve

Meru National Park   Equator

▲ Mt Kenya 5,200 m

● Nairobi   Mt Kilimanjaro 5,895 m

Maasai Mara National Reserve

Amboseli National Park

Tsavo West   ▲

Tsavo East

Tsavo National Park

Indian Ocean

Mombasa

Shimba Hills National Reserve

0   200 km

Kenya realises the importance of its spectacular scenery and wildlife as a major tourist attraction. They are seen as a major source of income for a country that is desperately short of money. Money from tourism can be used to pay for improving services, building more houses and roads, and creating jobs.

Unfortunately, tourism can also cause problems. Large numbers of people going on holidays can damage the very environment which attracted them there in the first place. Tourism puts pressure upon **fragile environments**, wildlife and local people.

 B Problems caused by tourism

Land

The building of expensive new hotels and beach resorts has taken up much land. Natural vegetation has been cleared and good farmland lost. Many local people have lost their land, homes and jobs.

Wildlife

Mini-buses are not meant to go within 25 metres of animals. Drivers often ignore this rule as they are more likely to get good tips from the tourists if they can get close to the animals. This may prevent the animals from feeding, drinking and mating.

People

Apart from people working at safari lodges, nobody can live in the National Parks. Local tribes like the Maasai had to be moved away from their own grazing areas. Many now make a living by selling souvenirs or performing traditional dances for the tourists. Their way of life has been much changed.

Environment

Mini-buses are meant to keep to well-defined tracks. However, drivers often take new routes to get as near to the animals as possible. This can cause tracks to be widened, to turn dusty in the dry season and marshy in the wet season. Both damage vegetation and increase soil erosion.

The Lake District National Park

The Lake District is the largest and most popular National Park in Britain. Over 14 million people visit the Park each year. Most are attracted by the fine scenery, pretty villages and interesting history.

Many tourists like the area so much that they buy second-homes there. These people, together with the long-established permanent residents, give the National Park a total population of over 40,000. Most live in the larger towns of Windermere, Bowness, Ambleside and Keswick.

A Ashness Bridge, Lake District National Park

Attractions of the Lake District National Park

- Fell walking, climbing and scrambling in the hills
- Sailing, wind-surfing and cruising on the lakes
- Rambling, pony-trekking and sight-seeing in the valleys
- Fishing, canoeing and swimming in the rivers
- Visiting picturesque villages, each with its own architecture and character
- Investigating the past history of Neolithic sites, Roman remains and recent mining activities
- Visiting the homes of famous writers, poets and painters
- Enjoying the many restaurants, cafés, bars and coaching inns
- Staying overnight in one of the hotels, guest houses, cottages or campsites

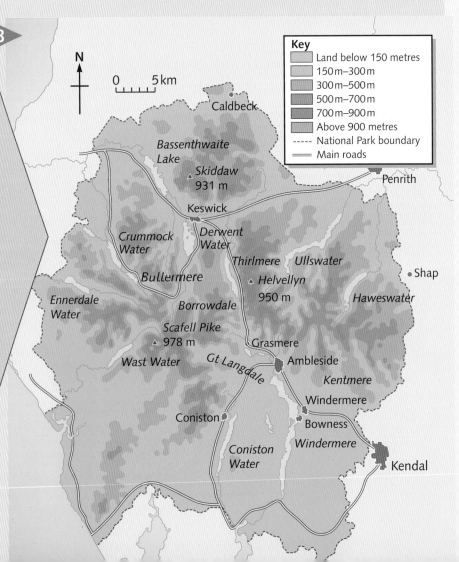

B

Key
	Land below 150 metres
	150 m–300 m
	300 m–500 m
	500 m–700 m
	700 m–900 m
	Above 900 metres
-----	National Park boundary
═══	Main roads

N

0   5 km

Caldbeck

Bassenthwaite Lake

Skiddaw 931 m

Penrith

Keswick

Crummock Water

Derwent Water

Thirlmere   Ullswater

Bullermere

Helvellyn 950 m

Shap

Ennerdale Water

Borrowdale

Haweswater

Scafell Pike 978 m

Grasmere

Wast Water

Gt Langdale

Ambleside

Kentmere

Windermere

Coniston

Bowness

Windermere

Coniston Water

Kendal

Problems of tourism

The 14 million annual visitors to the Lake District National Park are bound to cause problems, both to the environment and for the 42,000 local residents.

Some of the worst problems are in the **honeypot** areas. These are places that attract tourists in large numbers and are usually very busy and congested.

Traffic

Nearly 90% of visitors arrive by car. Congestion is heaviest on approach roads and in towns. Traffic congestion, parking difficulties, noise and air pollution are the main problems.

Second homes

One in six properties in the Lake District are either second homes or holiday cottages. This has forced house prices to rise beyond the reach of most local people.

Footpath erosion

More than 6 million visitors now take walks of 6 km or more. The most popular walking areas suffer badly from footpath erosion, creating ugly scars on the hills.

Conflict

Disagreement between people is common in the Park. Some, for example, like peace and quiet, while others may prefer noisier activities, such as driving speed boats.

Possible solutions to the problems

Solving the problems caused by increased tourism can be very difficult. Any schemes must balance the needs of local residents with those of visitors.

The schemes must also ensure that the environment is preserved and that the Lake District remains a beautiful place for all to use.

Traffic

A scheme has been proposed to reduce congestion by restricting visitor access by private car to the most popular areas, and closing other roads to traffic completely. Improved public transport, with more buses, ferries and trains, would be needed to make the plan work.

Footpath erosion

The National Park Authority and several volunteer groups work together to repair eroded footpaths. Alternative routes may be suggested in the busier and more damaged areas.

Conflict

Park Rangers are trained to talk to residents and tourists about issues that cause conflict. Many of the problems can be reduced after discussion and debate with concerned groups.

REVISION QUESTIONS

1 (Page 132)
a) Give three reasons why the tourist industry has increased in the last 40 years.
b) How many European countries are in the top 10 tourist nations? Name them.

2 (Pages 132 and 133)
a) Give two reasons why mass tourism started in Britain about a hundred years ago.
b) What attracts tourists to Britain's South West?
c) What attracts tourists to Spain and France?
d) Give three examples of long-haul holidays.

3 (Pages 134 and 135)
a) What are the main aims of National Parks?
b) How many National Parks are there in the UK?
c) Name the National Park nearest to where you live. Describe its main attractions.

4 (Pages 134 and 135)
a) What is conflict?
b) Give three examples of conflict.
c) Do you think quarrying should be allowed in National Parks? Give reasons for your answer.

5 (Pages 136 and 137)
Complete the star diagram below. Write between 10 and 20 words for each feature.

6 (Pages 136 and 137)
a) Give three reasons for the Costa del Sol's decline as a tourist area in the 1990s.
b) What has been done to attract tourists back?

7 (Pages 138 and 139)
a) Where is Chamonix located?
b) Why is it popular with a wide range of skiers?
c) Apart from skiing, what other attractions does Chamonix have for visitors?

8 (Pages 138 and 139)
a) What benefits can tourism bring to Chamonix?
b) List what you think are the six main problems caused by tourism in the Chamonix area.
c) What can be done to reduce the damaging effects of tourism in a resort like Chamonix?

9 (Pages 140 and 141)
Write down the meaning of the following terms:
a) mass tourism   b) ecotourism.

10 (Pages 140 and 141)
Briefly describe Thailand's tourist industry, using the headings shown below.
a) Location   b) Attractions
c) Advantages   d) Disadvantages
e) Recent developments

11 (Pages 142 and 143)
a) List five natural features that attract tourists to Kenya.
b) Many people go to Kenya for a safari holiday. What is a safari?

12 (Pages 142 and 143)
a) What benefits can tourism bring to an economically less developed country like Kenya?
b) Copy and complete the table below to show the problems caused by tourism in Kenya.

Problem	Cause	Effect
Environment		
Wildlife		
People		
Land		

13 (Pages 144 and 145)
a) List what you think are the six main attractions of the Lake District National Park.
b) Describe five problems of tourism in the Lake District National Park.
c) What has been done to reduce these problems?

146

EXAMINATION QUESTIONS

1

(Pages 134, 135, 144 and 145)

Look at map **A**.

a) How many National Parks are shown? **(1)**
b) Name one of the Parks in Wales. **(1)**
c) Which Park (A, B or C) is the Lake District? **(1)**
d) There has been an increase in tourist numbers in recent years. Suggest three reasons for this. **(3)**
e) Describe three problems caused by the increase in tourist numbers to National Parks. **(3)**
f) Describe two ways in which park planners can try to reduce these problems. **(2)**

A   **National Parks in England and Wales**

Northumberland

Ⓒ   Ⓑ   North York Moors

Ⓐ

N

0   150 km

Exmoor

Dartmoor

The Broads

Key

█ National Park

2

(Pages 136 and 137)

Look at map **B**.

a) How many visitors came from the UK? **(1)**
b) From which country were most visitors? **(1)**
c) Suggest why more visitors came from Portugal than from Italy. **(1)**
d) Suggest why places like the Costa del Sol attract tourists. Use the following headings:
  █ Climate █ Scenery █ Leisure facilities. **(6)**
e) The Costa del Sol has recently suffered a decline in popularity. Suggest reasons for this. **(2)**
f) Describe what has been done to attract tourists back to the Costa del Sol. **(2)**

B   **Number and origin of people visiting Spain**

Canada 0.1

UK 6.1

Netherlands 2.2

0   200 km

FRANCE

USA 0.7

France 12.1

PORTUGAL

Germany 7.7

Madrid

Barcelona

SPAIN

Mediterranean Sea

Portugal 10.5

Cordoba   Benidorm

Italy 1.8

N

Atlantic Ocean

Japan 0.2

Costa del Sol

Key

◁ Non-European country

◀ European country (visitors in millions)

3

(Pages 140, 141, 142 and 143)

Look at graph **C**.

a) How many tourists were there in 1990? **(1)**
b) During which years did tourism increase? **(1)**
c) When was the greatest fall in tourist numbers? **(1)**
d) Tourism can bring both advantages and disadvantages to developing countries (LEDCs) like Kenya and Thailand.
  █ Describe three advantages. **(3)**
  █ Describe three disadvantages. **(3)**
e) Some developing countries have tried ecotourism. What are the aims of ecotourism? **(2)**

C   **Number of tourists to Kenya**

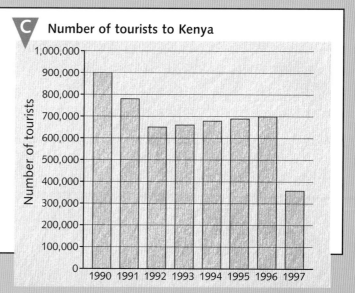

WORLD DEVELOPMENT AND INTERDEPENDENCE

All countries are different. Some are rich and have high standards of living and some are poor and have lower standards of living. **Development** is a measure of how rich or how poor a country is. Rich countries are said to be **economically more developed**. Poor countries are said to be **economically less developed**.

Development is not just about wealth, however. It is about growth and progress, and about using resources and technology to improve the **quality of life** for people.

Measuring development is not easy. The most commonly used method is to look at wealth. This is because many people consider that if a country is wealthy, the people living there will be happy and contented, and enjoy high living standards.

This is not always true. Sometimes a country's wealth does not go towards bettering people's lives, nor is it always spread evenly. So in measuring development, it is important to consider social factors as well as economic factors.

> **Quality of life** is a measure of how happy and content people are with their lives.

> **Economic development** aims to increase income and wealth through industrial growth.

> **Social development** is about providing essential services such as education, healthcare and housing.

Economic wealth

The easiest way of measuring a country's wealth is by its **Gross National Product (GNP) per capita**. This is the total amount of goods and services produced by a country in one year, divided by its population. To make comparisons between countries easy, GNP is given in US dollars (US$).

A The world's economic groups as defined by GNP

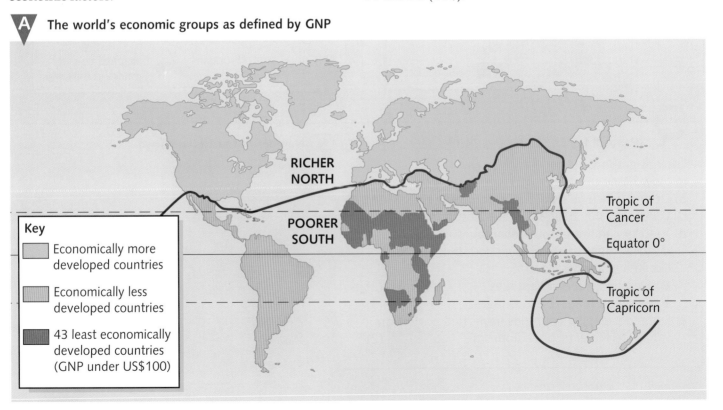

RICHER NORTH

POORER SOUTH

Tropic of Cancer

Equator 0°

Tropic of Capricorn

Key
- Economically more developed countries
- Economically less developed countries
- 43 least economically developed countries (GNP under US$100)

A disadvantage of using GNP is that it does not show differences in wealth within a country. This problem is greatest in developing countries where there is a huge gap between the rich and the poor. In other words, the rich are often very rich and the poor, very poor.

Social factors

Apart from wealth, there are many other ways of measuring the level of a country's development. Some of these are called social indicators because they are about people, about how they live, what they do and what quality of life they have.

However, many of these indicators are directly linked to the wealth of a country. For example, the more money a country earns, the more it can spend on improving education and healthcare, and therefore the better the quality of life its people will have.

Some of the social indicators used to measure development are shown in table **C** below.

B

Human Development Index (HDI)

The United Nations created its own measure of development in 1990. Called the **Human Development Index**, it combines information on health, education and wealth. It therefore measures social as well as economic progress.

The HDI has the advantage of being able to show differences in levels of development *within* a country as well as *between* countries.

C

Poorer, developing countries		Richer, developed countries
Most jobs are in the primary sector, especially farming. Relatively few people are employed in the secondary or tertiary sectors.	**Jobs**	Very few people have primary sector jobs. A larger number work in the secondary sector but the highest percentage are in tertiary employment.
Many children die at an early age, and life expectancy is short. Birth rates and death rates are high and there is rapid population growth.	**Population**	Few children die young and people have a long life expectancy. Birth rates and death rates are low and population growth is slow.
Healthcare is poor. There are few doctors, nurses or hospitals. There are often food shortages and many people have a poor diet.	**Healthcare**	Healthcare is good. There are many hospitals, trained nurses and doctors. Medicines are in good supply and most people have plenty to eat and a good diet.
There is a shortage of schools, teachers and resources. Not everyone has full-time education. Many adults are unable to read or write.	**Education**	Education is relatively well funded. Every child has the opportunity to attend school. Many go on to further education. Almost all adults can read and write.
Movement around the country and within cities is difficult. Rural transport is poor and urban transport is congested and old. Businesses and industries suffer.	**Transport**	Travel around the country is relatively easy. Most places have efficient transport links with cars, buses, planes and trains. Good accessibility helps industrial growth.

Sustainable development and appropriate technology

Sustainable development improves people's **standards of living** and **quality of life** without wasting resources or harming the environment. Sustainable development is sensible development because:

- it uses but does not waste resources
- it improves but does not threaten ways of life
- it looks after the needs of today, but does not damage the future.

Sustainable development may be achieved by:

- encouraging economic development at a pace a country can afford so that it does not run out of money and fall into debt
- developing technology that is appropriate to the skills, wealth and needs of the local people
- using natural resources carefully and remembering the three Rs: **R**enew, **R**ecycle, **R**eplace.

Drawing **A** shows some examples of sustainable development.

Sustainable development needs careful planning and management. As it involves world conservation, it must also have the support and co-operation of other countries. Experience has shown that schemes using **appropriate technology** (page 126) are likely to be most successful.

> Appropriate technology uses methods that are suited to the local people and the environment in which they live.

A

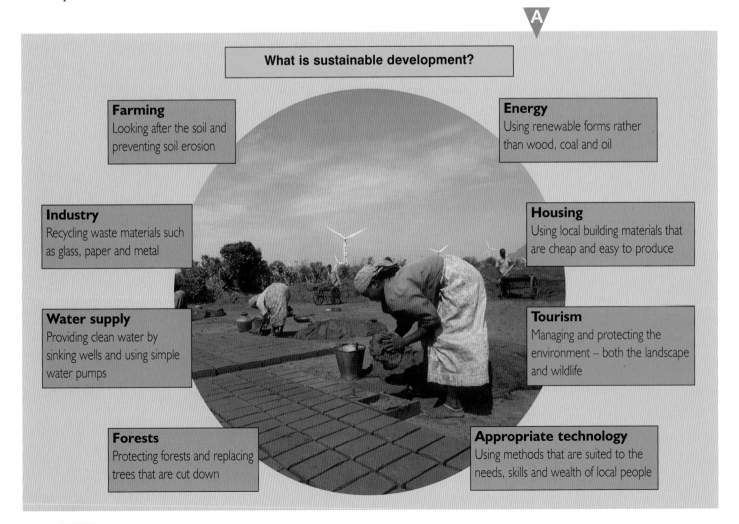

What is sustainable development?

Farming
Looking after the soil and preventing soil erosion

Energy
Using renewable forms rather than wood, coal and oil

Industry
Recycling waste materials such as glass, paper and metal

Housing
Using local building materials that are cheap and easy to produce

Water supply
Providing clean water by sinking wells and using simple water pumps

Tourism
Managing and protecting the environment – both the landscape and wildlife

Forests
Protecting forests and replacing trees that are cut down

Appropriate technology
Using methods that are suited to the needs, skills and wealth of local people

Sustainable development in LEDCs

Improving standards of living and quality of life in poorer countries is very difficult.

Large schemes like new port facilities or international airports are too expensive and rarely give direct help to the poor. Most people in less developed countries now favour smaller schemes which use appropriate technology.

Diagram **B** shows some of the ways in which appropriate technology has been used to help improve conditions in Ladakh.

Sustainable development in MEDCs

The richer, industrialised countries also need to develop sustainable methods of progress and use appropriate technology if they too are to limit resource use and reduce pollution.

The only difference is that for people living in developed countries, the appropriate technology is likely to involve more money, be high-tech and, in many cases, be large-scale.

Sustainable development in Ladakh (northern India)

Global Concerns is a British charitable organisation which supports sustainable development projects in Ladakh.

Ladakh is a mountainous area in the foothills of the Himalayas. It has an extreme climate, being very cold and very windy but dry and sunny for most of the year.

People in Ladakh are poor but do not want a Western style of development. They prefer progress to emphasise local conditions, resources and traditions which help protect the environment and preserve the local culture.

B

Ladakh

- Strong winds and sun are used as renewable energy resources.
- Water from snowmelt provides irrigation and hydro-electric power.
- Small hydro-electricity schemes provide power for lighting and grinding corn.
- Solar greenhouses allow vegetables to be grown throughout the year.
- Small hydraulic rams pump water to higher-level fields. This extends the area of cultivation and makes Ladakh self-sufficient in food.

Houses

- Solar power heats water and homes.
- The longest wall faces south to get most sunshine and heat.
- Solar cookers avoid using precious dung and fuelwood. They also make less smoke and are healthier.
- Cavity walls are filled with mud and stones to conserve heat.

Places

Trade and interdependence

No country has everything that it wants. All countries have to buy from and sell to each other. They buy things that they need or would like to have. They sell things to make money to pay for what they have bought. The exchanging of goods and services like this is called **trade**, and it is important in the development of a country.

Unfortunately not all countries gain equal benefit from world trade. As diagram **A** shows, the richer, developed countries earn more from trading than the poorer, developing countries.

One reason for this is that the poorer countries mainly export low-value primary goods while the richer countries mainly export expensive manufactured goods. The poorer countries therefore make much less money and develop a **trade deficit**.

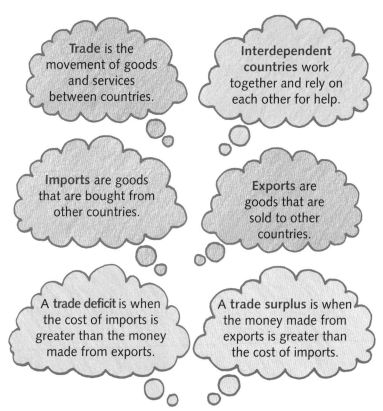

Trade is the movement of goods and services between countries.

Interdependent countries work together and rely on each other for help.

Imports are goods that are bought from other countries.

Exports are goods that are sold to other countries.

A **trade deficit** is when the cost of imports is greater than the money made from exports.

A **trade surplus** is when the money made from exports is greater than the cost of imports.

A

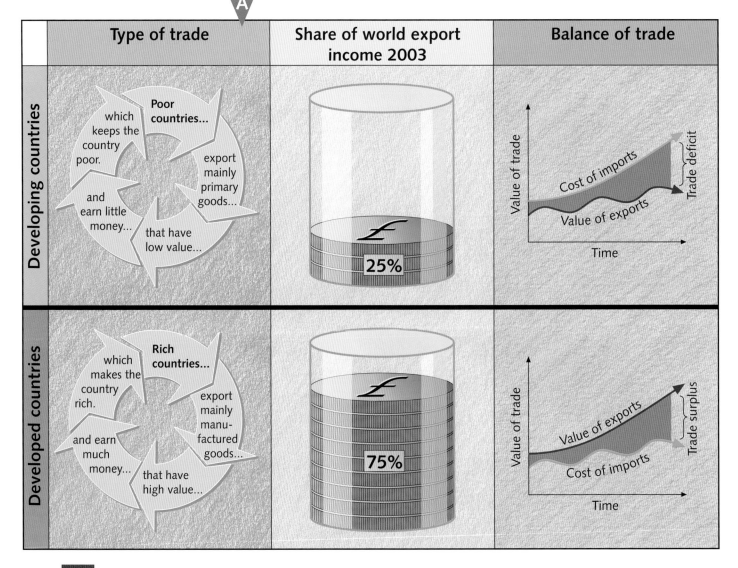

	Type of trade	Share of world export income 2003	Balance of trade
Developing countries	Poor countries... export mainly primary goods... that have low value... and earn little money... which keeps the country poor.	25%	Cost of imports / Value of exports → Trade deficit
Developed countries	Rich countries... export mainly manufactured goods... that have high value... and earn much money... which makes the country rich.	75%	Value of exports / Cost of imports → Trade surplus

Single product economies

Map **B** shows another problem faced by developing countries. Many of them rely on just one or two products to provide jobs at home and income from exports. When prices and demand for these products are high, then the income earned by exporting them is also high.

If, however, the price and demand for the product in the world market falls, the country will suffer job losses and receive less income from abroad. In this case the country may struggle to survive because of its dependence on that one export.

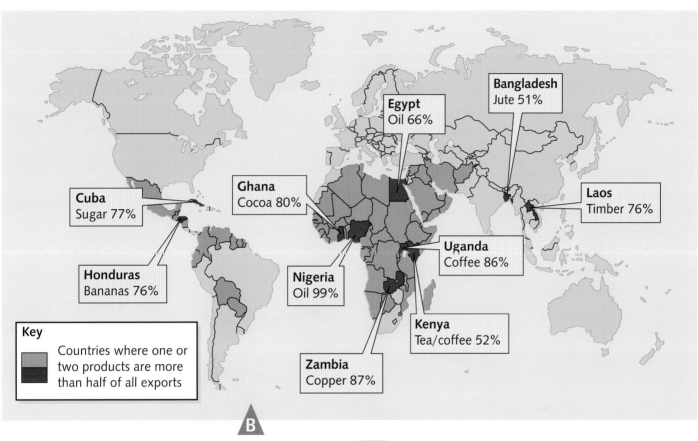

Egypt Oil 66%

Bangladesh Jute 51%

Ghana Cocoa 80%

Cuba Sugar 77%

Laos Timber 76%

Honduras Bananas 76%

Uganda Coffee 86%

Nigeria Oil 99%

Kenya Tea/coffee 52%

Zambia Copper 87%

Key
Countries where one or two products are more than half of all exports

B

Changes in Britain's trade

Britain has always been a trading nation. Over the centuries it has developed links with countries all around the world. This has helped Britain become **interdependent** and develop into one of the world's richer nations.

Until recently, most of the trade was with developing countries and nations of the British Commonwealth, like Australia, Canada, India and New Zealand. Nowadays, as the graphs **C** show, most of Britain's trading partners are countries of the European Union (EU).

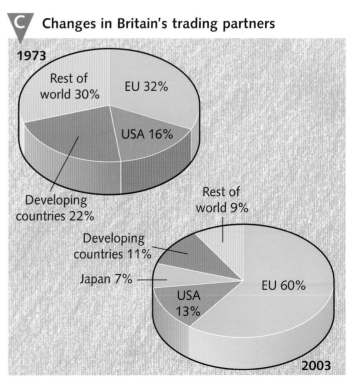

C Changes in Britain's trading partners

1973
Rest of world 30%
EU 32%
USA 16%
Developing countries 22%

Rest of world 9%
Developing countries 11%
Japan 7%
USA 13%
EU 60%
2003

Aid

One way of trying to help countries to develop and improve their standard of living and quality of life is to provide them with **aid**. Aid is a term used to describe any type of help given to a country. It can range from technical equipment and money to skilled workers and emergency supplies.

Most aid is given by governments of rich countries directly, or through international organisations, to poorer countries. Often, however, the most effective aid is provided by voluntary organisations, as this tends to go more directly to those in most need.

Countries may need aid to:

- provide money to buy goods from other countries and improve their standard of living
- help with large development schemes like hydro-electric projects and international airports
- help improve basic services and amenities, such as a reliable water supply, hospitals and schools, which help raise people's quality of life
- provide help after disasters such as earthquakes, flooding, famine or even war.

Types of aid

Bilateral aid is given by the government of one country directly to another. It can be in the form of money, food, equipment and technical assistance. The Pergau Dam in Malaysia was Britain's most costly aid project. Over half the cost of £415 million was paid for by the UK.

Multilateral aid is assistance given to poor countries through international organisations such as the World Bank, the International Monetary Fund or the EU Development Fund. Each organisation has its own aid programme and is funded by the world's richer, more developed countries.

Voluntary aid comes from charities such as Oxfam, Christian Aid, ActionAid and Intermediate Technology. These non-government organisations rely on private donations and gifts from businesses. Their emphasis is on low-cost schemes based on simple technology that benefit local people.

A

B Oxfam advertisement

How can just £2 a month help poor people to help themselves?

These days, £2 won't buy very much. But if you give £2 a month to Oxfam, your donation is stretched much further. We support people who are helping themselves, so they contribute their hard work, their time and energy to make every penny go further.

Plant 670 trees
Your £2 a month could supply 670 seedlings every year, which will be planted out by local Ethiopian farmers.

Fill in and return the form below within

Train 2 health workers
In Bangladesh, £2 a month would help pay to train 2 health workers, safeguarding HUNDREDS of people.

Clean water for a whole community

In Sudan, £2 a month will help provide enough tools for villagers to dig a well and give a permanent supply of clean, safe water.

http://www.oxfam.org.uk
a new window on the world

The disadvantages of aid

Unfortunately, foreign aid does not always benefit poor countries or reach the people who are most in need. All too often, aid finds its way into the pockets of politicians, government officials and those who are better-off.

There are arguments as to whether we should give aid at all. Some people think that aid can be damaging and that people should help themselves.

The advantages of aid

There are arguments both for and against aid. People who are in favour point out that we all live in the same world and all rely on each other for survival. We must therefore help each other and try, as far as possible, to improve the quality of life for everyone.

Aid can certainly bring many benefits, but it has become increasingly difficult to improve living standards for people living in poorer countries.

C

Disadvantages

- Big projects such as dams or airports often destroy people's homes.
- Provision of food aid often means that farmers no longer grow their own.
- Poor countries grow food to sell to rich countries rather than to use themselves.
- Countries can become dependent on aid and fail to progress themselves.
- Countries that are unable to pay back loans build up huge debts.
- Machinery or vehicles that have no spare parts cannot be repaired.

SHOULD WE GIVE AID?

Advantages

- Short-term aid like food, clothing and medicines can help people through a crisis.
- Providing a reliable supply of clean water can help improve health standards.
- Introducing high-yield crops and better farming methods can improve diet.
- Developing sustainable industries can provide jobs and increase wealth.
- Improving education and developing skills helps a country become self-sufficient.
- Advice on healthcare and family planning can improve the quality of life.

D Cabora Bassa Dam, Mozambique

E Using a simple borehole well with a handpump

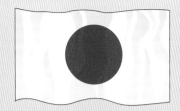

Japan

Levels of development

If development is measured by wealth, Japan is the fourth richest country in the world. Most of this wealth is due to rapid industrial growth since 1945, and the development of modern and very efficient manufacturing and service industries.

Very few Japanese work in low-income primary sector occupations. This is largely because farming is highly mechanised, there are few minerals to mine, and most forests are protected.

Japan's manufacturing industry is one of the best in the world. Workers are well educated, highly skilled and hard working, and the factories are modern and highly mechanised. Due to the country's wealth, many people work in the tertiary sector, in health, education, transport and leisure.

Trade and interdependence

Japan has a large population, little flat land for farming, and few natural resources of its own. For these reasons it has to import considerable amounts of foodstuffs and virtually all of its energy supplies and raw materials.

In order to pay for these expensive imports, Japan produces a range of goods noted for their high quality and reliability, which are exported to countries all around the world. This has resulted in Japan becoming the world's third largest trading nation. Since 1983 it has also had the world's largest trade surplus. Some of Japan's wealth has been used to build factories and finance aid programmes in developing countries.

The need to import raw materials and foodstuffs and to export manufactured goods has made Japan increasingly interdependent.

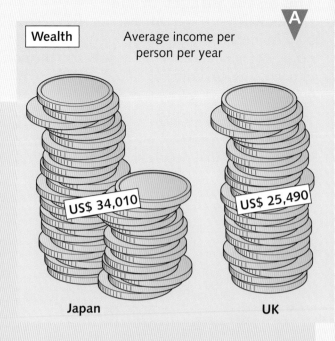

A

Wealth — Average income per person per year

US\$ 34,010 — Japan
US\$ 25,490 — UK

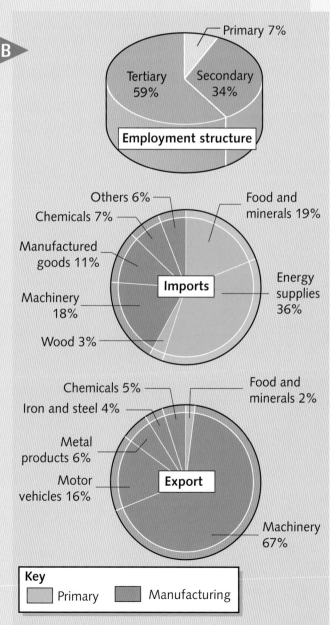

B

Employment structure
Primary 7%
Secondary 34%
Tertiary 59%

Imports
Others 6%
Chemicals 7%
Manufactured goods 11%
Machinery 18%
Wood 3%
Food and minerals 19%
Energy supplies 36%

Export
Chemicals 5%
Iron and steel 4%
Metal products 6%
Motor vehicles 16%
Food and minerals 2%
Machinery 67%

Key
☐ Primary   ☐ Manufacturing

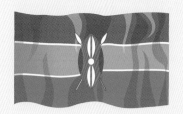

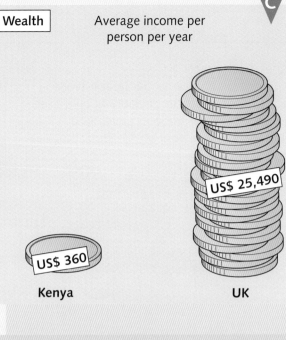

Wealth — Average income per person per year

US$ 25,490

US$ 360

Kenya   UK

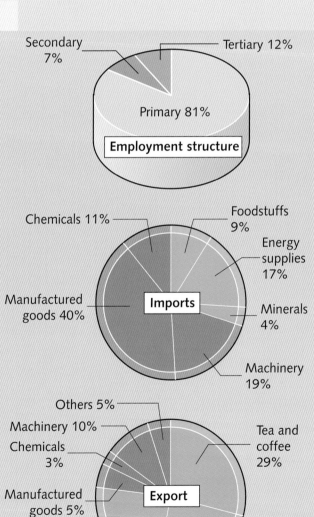

Secondary 7%

Tertiary 12%

Primary 81%

Employment structure

Chemicals 11%

Foodstuffs 9%

Energy supplies 17%

Manufactured goods 40%

Imports

Minerals 4%

Machinery 19%

Others 5%

Machinery 10%

Chemicals 3%

Tea and coffee 29%

Manufactured goods 5%

Export

Minerals 24%

Other foodstuffs 24%

Key

Primary   Manufacturing

D

Kenya

Levels of development

Measured by wealth, Kenya is one of the poorest and least developed countries in the world. This is largely due to limited economic progress and rapid population growth, which hinders development.

A high proportion of Kenyan people work in low-income primary sector occupations. Most are employed in farming, but there is a shortage of good fertile land, and 80% of the country is too dry to grow crops.

Few people are employed in the secondary sector. This is mainly due to a lack of capital, energy supplies and technical knowledge to establish industry. A limited education system and poor skill levels add to the problem. Because of the country's lack of wealth, few people work in the tertiary sector, although tourism is an important money earner.

Trade and interdependence

The south of Kenya is most suited to agriculture. Here, local farmers can produce enough food to be self-sufficient, and can grow crops such as tea, coffee and fruit for export. Unfortunately, foodstuffs are low-value exports and do not earn the country much money.

In contrast, Kenya has little formal industry and has to import most of its manufactured goods such as cars, machinery and equipment. These are all expensive to buy.

Because it spends more on imports than it gets back on exports, Kenya has a trade deficit. This has meant that the country has had to borrow money to buy its essential needs and has fallen into debt.

To help develop and make progress, Kenya receives large amounts of aid from around the world. This, and the country's need to trade with other countries, has increased its interdependence.

157

1 (Pages 148 and 149)
Write down the meaning of the following terms:
a) development   b) quality of life.

2 (Pages 148 and 149)
a) What is 'Gross National Product per capita'?
b) Why is GNP not always a good way of measuring development?
c) What is the 'Human Development Index', and why is it a good way of measuring development?

3 (Pages 148 and 149)
Draw a diagram like the one below to describe six features of an economically developing country.

4 (Page 150 and 151)
a) What is 'sustainable development'?
b) Give three ways that help achieve sustainable development.
c) Give four ways that sustainable energy and power sources have helped improve the quality of life in Ladakh.

5 (Pages 150 and 151)
a) What is appropriate technology?
b) What type of appropriate technology is most suited to:
▪ poorer, less developed countries
▪ richer, more developed countries?

6 (Pages 152 and 153)
Define the following terms:
a) trade   b) imports
c) exports   d) interdependence.

7 (Pages 152 and 153)
Write out the following paragraph twice – once to show trade in developing countries, and once to show trade in developed countries. Choose your words from those in the brackets.

> Countries that are (poor **or** rich) mainly export (manufactured **or** primary) goods which are of (high **or** low) value. These earn (little **or** a lot of) money, which keeps the country (wealthy **or** poor).

8 (Pages 152 and 153)
a) What is meant by a 'single product economy'?
b) Name six examples of single product countries.
c) Explain why relying on a single product may be bad for a country.

9 (Pages 154 and 155)
a) What is aid?
b) Why is aid needed by some countries?
c) What is the difference between bilateral aid, multilateral aid and voluntary aid?
d) Copy and complete the diagram below to show the advantages and disadvantages of giving aid. Give what you think are the four most important examples for each.

10 (Pages 156 and 157)
a) Copy and complete the table below.
b) Suggest reasons for each country's level of development.

	Japan	Kenya
Development	Developed	
Wealth		$360
Main employment		Primary
Main imports	Primary	
Main exports		
Trade		Deficit

EXAMINATION QUESTIONS

1

(Pages 150 and 151)

Study sketch **A** which shows people attempting to stop soil erosion (the removal of soil) in Kenya.

a) What have people done to the hillside to stop soil erosion? **(1)**

b) Which two of the following correctly describes the work being done in the sketch? Write out the two correct statements.
- Many people are involved in the work.
- The people are using expensive equipment.
- The people are using simple tools.
- The work is highly mechanised. **(2)**

c) Why can this form of soil erosion control be considered a good example of appropriate technology? **(4)**

A

2

(Pages 152 and 153)

Look at map **B**.

a) What are exports? **(1)**

b) Name the two countries that are very dependent on the crops they grow and export. **(2)**

c) Which country depends most on one export product? **(2)**

d) Countries that rely on one export product often have problems. Suggest a reason for this. **(2)**

e) Poorer countries earn less money from trade than richer countries. Suggest a reason for this. **(2)**

B Countries dependent on primary products for their exports

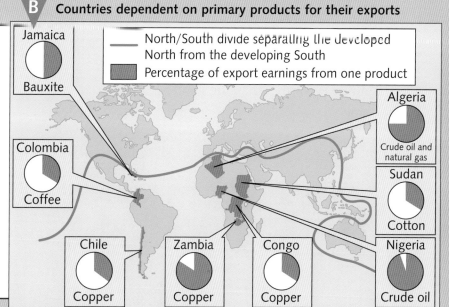

North/South divide separating the developed North from the developing South

Percentage of export earnings from one product

Jamaica — Bauxite
Colombia — Coffee
Algeria — Crude oil and natural gas
Sudan — Cotton
Chile — Copper
Zambia — Copper
Congo — Copper
Nigeria — Crude oil

3

(Pages 154 and 155)

Look at graph **C**.

a) Which country gave the highest percentage of its national wealth as aid? **(1)**

b) What percentage of national wealth is the United Nations target for countries to give as aid? **(1)**

c) How many of the countries met the United Nations target in 1992? **(1)**

d) Name two different types of aid. **(2)**

e) What are the disadvantages of some types of aid? **(2)**

C Percentage of national wealth given as aid

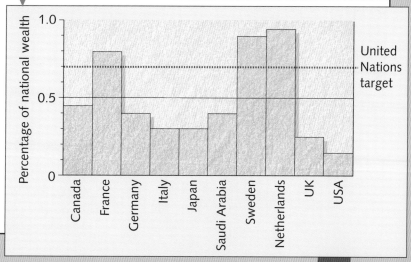

Percentage of national wealth

United Nations target

Canada, France, Germany, Italy, Japan, Saudi Arabia, Sweden, Netherlands, UK, USA

12 BRITAIN'S WEATHER AND CLIMATE

Britain's climate

Britain has a **variable** climate, which means that the weather changes from day to day. This makes it very difficult to forecast accurately. The climate can also be described as **equable**, which means that there are never any extremes. For example, it is never too hot or too cold. Nor is it too wet or too dry. Diagram **A** shows Britain's climate.

As diagram **B** shows, however, this climate varies from place to place and from season to season. The main differences are:

- the south is usually warmer and sunnier than the north in summer
- places in the west are milder and cloudier than places to the east in winter
- the summer is warmer than the winter.

Weather is the day-to-day condition of the atmosphere. It includes temperature, sunshine, rainfall and wind.

Climate is the average weather conditions of a place over many years.

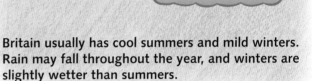

Britain's climate

Britain usually has cool summers and mild winters. Rain may fall throughout the year, and winters are slightly wetter than summers.

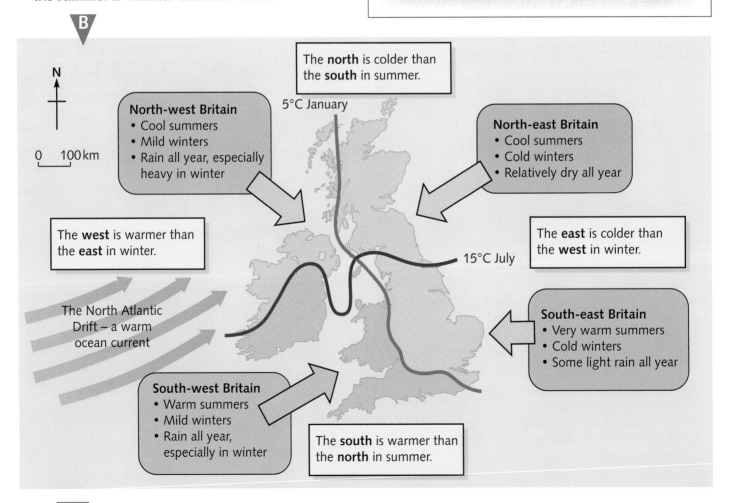

The **north** is colder than the **south** in summer.

5°C January

North-west Britain
- Cool summers
- Mild winters
- Rain all year, especially heavy in winter

North-east Britain
- Cool summers
- Cold winters
- Relatively dry all year

The **west** is warmer than the **east** in winter.

15°C July

The **east** is colder than the **west** in winter.

The North Atlantic Drift – a warm ocean current

South-east Britain
- Very warm summers
- Cold winters
- Some light rain all year

South-west Britain
- Warm summers
- Mild winters
- Rain all year, especially in winter

The **south** is warmer than the **north** in summer.

0   100 km

N

Factors affecting temperature

Latitude

Places nearer the Equator are much hotter than places near the poles. This is due mainly to the curvature of the Earth and the angle of the sun.

At the Equator the sun is always high in the sky. It shines straight down and its heat is concen-trated on a small area which gets very hot.

Towards the poles the sun shines more at an angle. Its heat is spread out over a larger area and temperatures are lower.

Notice that the sun's rays also have to pass through less atmosphere at the Equator than at the poles. As the atmosphere absorbs heat from the sun, this means that less heat is lost at the Equator than at the poles.

Ocean currents

Coastal areas are affected by ocean currents. The North Atlantic Drift is a warm current which originates in the Gulf of Mexico. It keeps Britain's west coast warm in winter. Cold currents such as the Labrador Current can lower temperatures by several degrees.

Prevailing winds

The prevailing wind is the direction from which the wind is likely to come. If it blows over a warm surface such as the land in summer or the sea in winter, it will raise temperatures. If it blows over a cold surface like the land in winter or sea in summer, it will lower temperatures. In Britain, winds from the south usually bring warm weather, whilst winds from the north bring cold weather.

Altitude (height of the land)

Temperatures decrease on average by 1°C for every 100 metres in height. As many mountains in Scotland are over 1,000 metres, their tops will be at least 10°C cooler than places on the coast. This is why many of the mountains are snow-covered in winter.

C Latitude

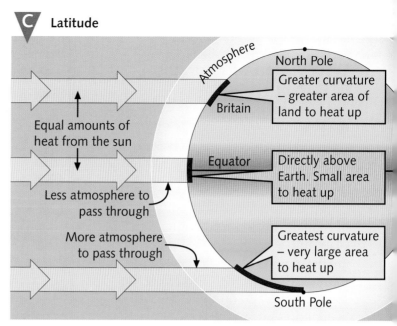

D Ocean currents

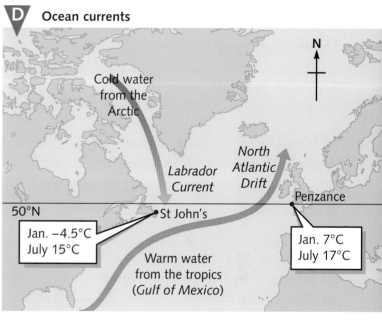

E Altitude

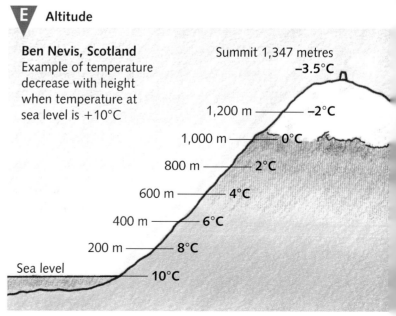

Rainfall

Distribution of rainfall in Britain

Britain can expect rain at any time of the year. Although winter is a little wetter than summer in the western areas, seasonal differences in rainfall are generally very small.

However, as map **A** shows, the amount of rainfall varies considerably from place to place. The greatest differences are between the west and east. For example, Fort William, located at the foot of Ben Nevis on the west coast of Scotland, is one of the wettest places in Britain. It has more than three times as much rainfall each year as Aberdeen, just 180 km away on the east coast.

Types of rainfall

The air around us contains moisture in the form of water vapour. Clouds are made up of very tiny drops of moisture called cloud droplets. They are only visible because there are billions of them crowded together in a cloud.

Clouds form when moist air rises, cools and changes into water droplets. This is **condensation**. A cloud gives rain after the tiny cloud droplets grow into larger raindrops. These eventually become heavy enough to fall to the ground as rain. Diagram **B** shows how rising air can cause rain to form.

In Britain, air can be forced to rise in three different ways. This gives the three main types of rainfall – these are **relief**, **frontal** and **convectional** rain.

A Annual rainfall in Britain

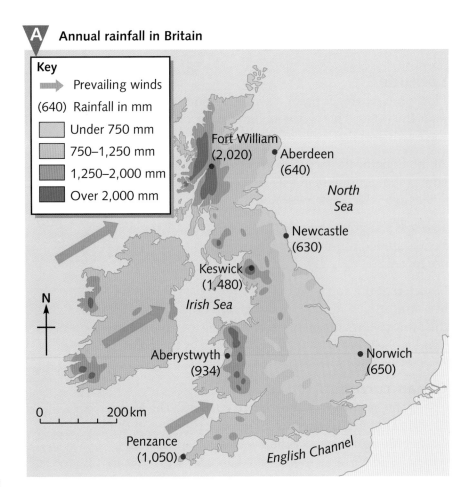

Key
→ Prevailing winds
(640) Rainfall in mm
⬜ Under 750 mm
⬜ 750–1,250 mm
⬜ 1,250–2,000 mm
⬜ Over 2,000 mm

Fort William (2,020)
Aberdeen (640)
North Sea
Newcastle (630)
Keswick (1,480)
Irish Sea
Aberystwyth (934)
Norwich (650)
Penzance (1,050)
English Channel

N

0   200 km

B How does it rain?

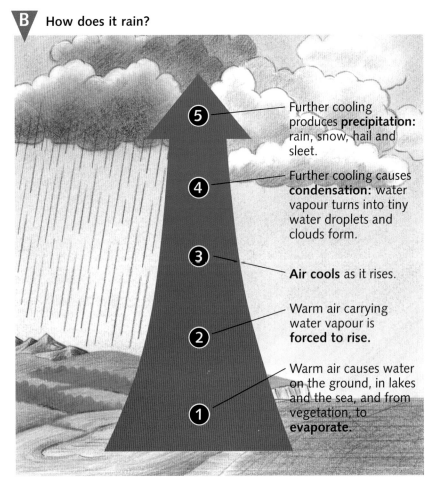

5 — Further cooling produces **precipitation**: rain, snow, hail and sleet.

4 — Further cooling causes **condensation**: water vapour turns into tiny water droplets and clouds form.

3 — **Air cools** as it rises.

2 — Warm air carrying water vapour is **forced to rise.**

1 — Warm air causes water on the ground, in lakes and the sea, and from vegetation, to **evaporate.**

Relief rainfall

Relief rainfall occurs when warm, moist air is forced to rise over mountains. As it rises it cools down, clouds form, and rain usually follows. This type of rainfall is quite common in Britain, especially in the west where most of the high mountains are located.

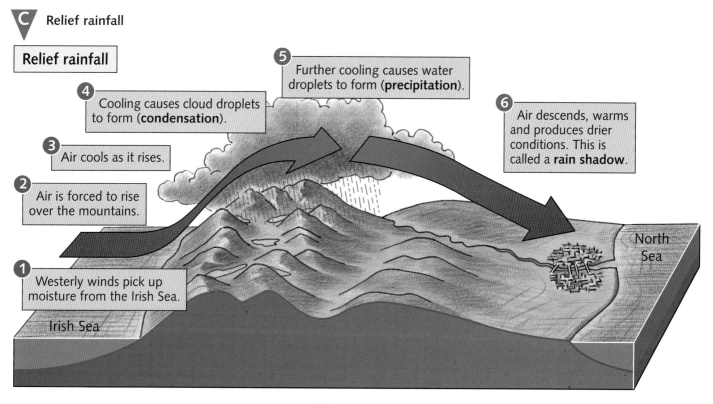

C Relief rainfall

Relief rainfall

5 Further cooling causes water droplets to form (**precipitation**).

4 Cooling causes cloud droplets to form (**condensation**).

3 Air cools as it rises.

2 Air is forced to rise over the mountains.

6 Air descends, warms and produces drier conditions. This is called a **rain shadow**.

1 Westerly winds pick up moisture from the Irish Sea.

North Sea

Irish Sea

Frontal rainfall

When a mass of warm air meets air at a lower temperature, it rises up and over the colder, heavier air. Once it is made to rise it cools down, clouds form and it begins to rain.

The place where warm air and cold air meet is called a **front**. Frontal rain is very common in Britain, especially in the winter.

Convectional rainfall

Convectional rainfall is caused by the sun heating the ground. The air above the ground is warmed up and begins to rise. If the ground surface is wet or vegetated there will be rapid evaporation and the rising air will be very moist. As the air rises it cools and can form huge clouds. Heavy rain and even thunderstorms may follow.

Convectional rain is most common in hot equatorial regions, where afternoon storms are common. It is less frequent in cooler Britain.

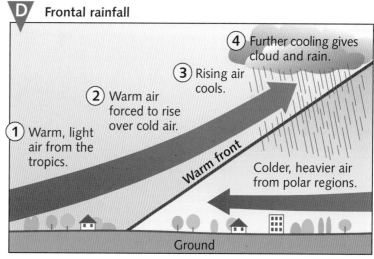

D Frontal rainfall

4 Further cooling gives cloud and rain.

3 Rising air cools.

2 Warm air forced to rise over cold air.

1 Warm, light air from the tropics.

Warm front

Colder, heavier air from polar regions.

Ground

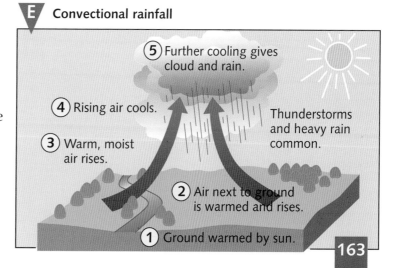

E Convectional rainfall

5 Further cooling gives cloud and rain.

4 Rising air cools.

3 Warm, moist air rises.

Thunderstorms and heavy rain common.

2 Air next to ground is warmed and rises.

1 Ground warmed by sun.

Depressions

For much of the year, Britain is affected by low pressure systems called **depressions**. These bring cloud, rain, wind and generally unsettled weather conditions to the country. Depressions form over the Atlantic Ocean and usually sweep across Britain from west to east.

Depressions form where warm air meets cold air. The boundary between these two different air masses is called a **front**. Along a front there will usually be thick cloud and heavy rain. Fronts are a common feature of Britain's weather.

Depressions develop as warm air is forced to rise over cold air. As the warm air rises it cools, condenses and forms cloud and rain. The rising air produces low pressure.

A

Cloud and rain

Low pressure

Warm air rises

B Features of a typical depression

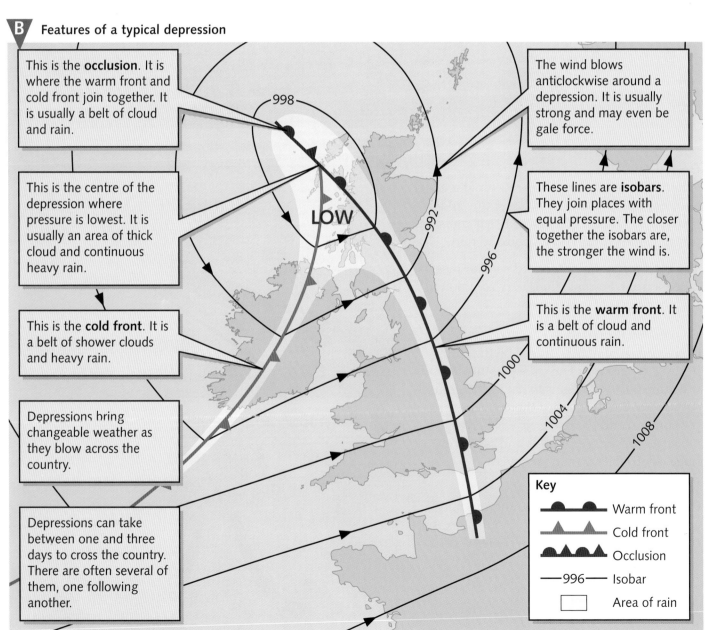

This is the **occlusion**. It is where the warm front and cold front join together. It is usually a belt of cloud and rain.

This is the centre of the depression where pressure is lowest. It is usually an area of thick cloud and continuous heavy rain.

This is the **cold front**. It is a belt of shower clouds and heavy rain.

Depressions bring changeable weather as they blow across the country.

Depressions can take between one and three days to cross the country. There are often several of them, one following another.

The wind blows anticlockwise around a depression. It is usually strong and may even be gale force.

These lines are **isobars**. They join places with equal pressure. The closer together the isobars are, the stronger the wind is.

This is the **warm front**. It is a belt of cloud and continuous rain.

998   992   996   1000   1004   1008

LOW

Key

⬤⬤ Warm front

▲▲ Cold front

⬤▲⬤▲ Occlusion

——996—— Isobar

▢ Area of rain

As a depression moves across Britain from west to east, it brings with it a particular pattern of weather.

Diagram **C** is a cross-section through a depression. It shows what the depression would look like if a slice was cut across it. Imagine that you are standing at point **X** on the cross-section with the depression coming towards you. As the depression passes through, your weather will change as described in the numbers **1** to **7**.

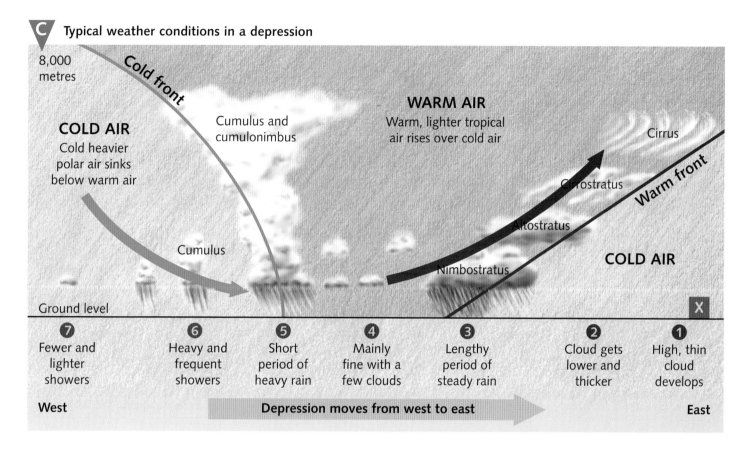

C Typical weather conditions in a depression

7	**6**	**5**	**4**	**3**	**2**	**1**
Fewer and lighter showers	Heavy and frequent showers	Short period of heavy rain	Mainly fine with a few clouds	Lengthy period of steady rain	Cloud gets lower and thicker	High, thin cloud develops

West → Depression moves from west to east → East

It is quite easy to forecast the weather in a depression because there is a regular pattern of cloud types and rain in depressions. The four weather maps in diagram **D** show a depression passing over Britain. The first map shows the depression approaching Britain from the west, and the second and third as it crosses the country. The fourth shows the depression as it finally heads out east across the North Sea. Notice how the weather changes at each stage. Can you forecast the weather for where you live?

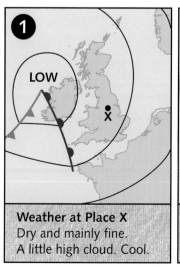

1

Weather at Place X
Dry and mainly fine. A little high cloud. Cool.

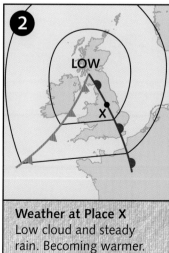

2

Weather at Place X
Low cloud and steady rain. Becoming warmer.

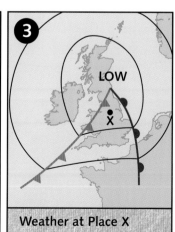

3

Weather at Place X
Rain clearing. Mainly fine with a few clouds. Warm.

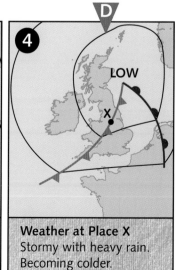

4

D

Weather at Place X
Stormy with heavy rain. Becoming colder.

Anticyclones

Anticyclones are areas of high pressure. They affect the British Isles far less often than depressions. However, once in position, an anticyclone may stay for several days. They usually bring fine weather and are most common in summer.

Anticyclones form in places where the air is descending. As more and more air descends, so the pressure increases and an area of high pressure develops.

When the air descends it also warms up and is able to pick up moisture. This usually results in settled conditions with clear skies and little chance of rain.

Sometimes, if the ground is cold, low cloud and fog may form when the moist air comes in to contact with the cold surface. This happens most often in winter, or on a summer's morning after a cloudless night.

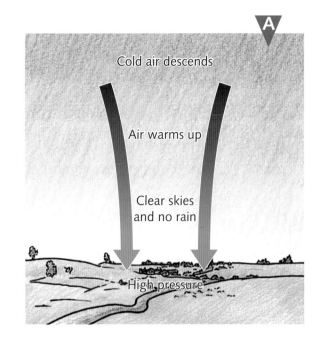

A

Cold air descends

Air warms up

Clear skies and no rain

High pressure

B **Features of a typical anticyclone**

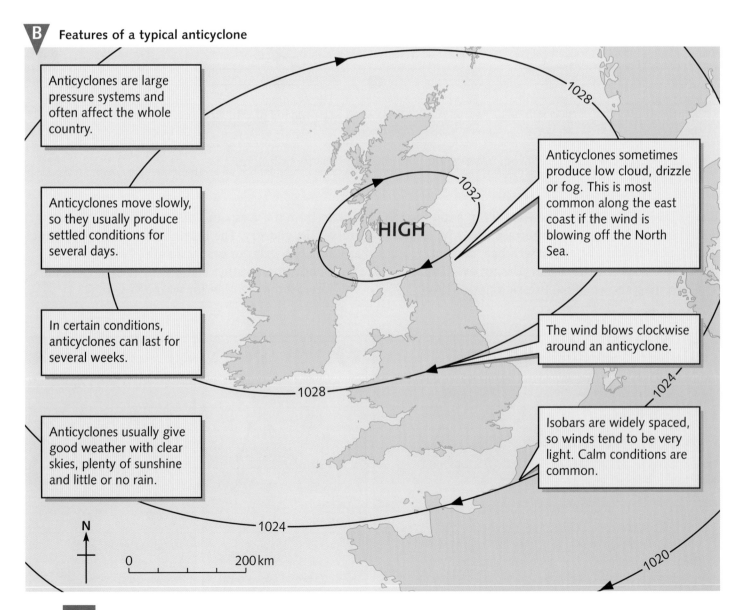

Anticyclones are large pressure systems and often affect the whole country.

Anticyclones move slowly, so they usually produce settled conditions for several days.

In certain conditions, anticyclones can last for several weeks.

Anticyclones usually give good weather with clear skies, plenty of sunshine and little or no rain.

Anticyclones sometimes produce low cloud, drizzle or fog. This is most common along the east coast if the wind is blowing off the North Sea.

The wind blows clockwise around an anticyclone.

Isobars are widely spaced, so winds tend to be very light. Calm conditions are common.

HIGH

1028
1032
1028
1024
1024
1020

N

0   200 km

In many respects, anticyclones are the opposite to depressions. They are high pressure systems, they move slowly and usually produce settled weather. They are also caused by descending air. This means that clouds are unlikely to develop and the weather is usually dry and sunny.

However, there are important seasonal differences in the weather associated with anticyclones. Photos **C** and **D** below show these differences. Both were taken at the same place in St Albans, Hertfordshire when an anticyclone extended over Britain. One was taken in the summer and the other in winter.

C

Summer conditions
- Very little cloud
- Dry with light winds
- Sun high in the sky, so hot and sunny
- Cloudless skies at night allow heat to escape, so nights can be cool
- Early morning dew and mist
- Risk of thunderstorms at end of 'heatwave' conditions

D

Winter conditions
- Dry and bright with very little cloud
- Sun low in the sky, so cold conditions
- Clear evening skies mean that nights can be very cold
- Early morning frost and fog may last all day
- Extensive low cloud or fog may produce overcast or 'gloomy' conditions

Air masses

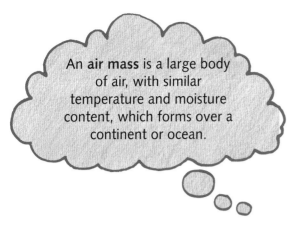

An **air mass** is a large body of air, with similar temperature and moisture content, which forms over a continent or ocean.

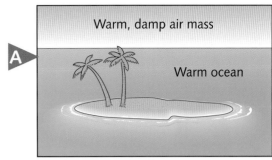

An air mass coming from a warm ocean will be warm and damp.

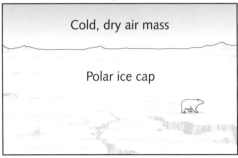

An air mass coming from the North Pole will be cold and dry.

Britain's weather and climate are controlled by different **air masses**. An air mass forms when air stays in the same place for several days. During this time the air takes the temperature and humidity of that area.

Air masses can be continental (dry) or maritime (moist), depending on whether they formed over the land or the sea. They can also be either tropical (warm) or polar (cold), depending on whether they formed near the Equator or near the North Pole.

When these different air masses move towards the British Isles, they bring with them their own characteristic type of weather. Map **B** shows the four main air masses affecting Britain.

B Air masses and their associated weather

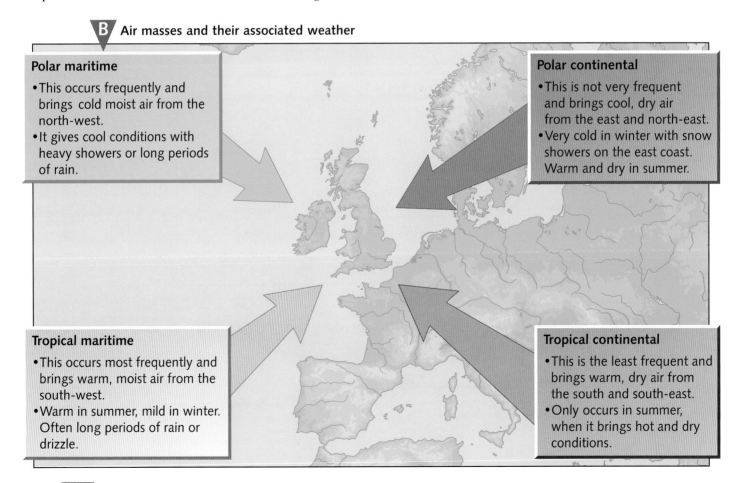

Polar maritime
- This occurs frequently and brings cold moist air from the north-west.
- It gives cool conditions with heavy showers or long periods of rain.

Polar continental
- This is not very frequent and brings cool, dry air from the east and north-east.
- Very cold in winter with snow showers on the east coast. Warm and dry in summer.

Tropical maritime
- This occurs most frequently and brings warm, moist air from the south-west.
- Warm in summer, mild in winter. Often long periods of rain or drizzle.

Tropical continental
- This is the least frequent and brings warm, dry air from the south and south-east.
- Only occurs in summer, when it brings hot and dry conditions.

1 (Pages 160 and 161)
   a) Why is the Equator hotter than the poles?
   b) How is Britain's west coast warmed in winter?
   c) Which winds bring warm weather to Britain?
   d) What effect does altitude have on temperature?

2 (Pages 162 and 163)
   Put the following into the correct order to describe how it rains:
   ■ Condensation   ■ Water evaporates
   ■ Precipitation   ■ Air forced to rise
   ■ Air cools as it rises

3 (Pages 162 and 163)
   Name and describe the three types of rainfall shown in these diagrams:

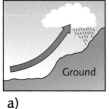 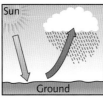 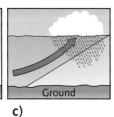

   a)   b)   c)

4 (Pages 164 and 165)
   a) What are isobars, and what do they measure?
   b) Draw a simple isobar pattern for a depression.
   c) Give two facts about the wind in a depression.
   d) Describe the weather as a depression passes over a particular place.

5 (Pages 166 and 167)
   a) What is an anticyclone, and how does it form?
   b) Draw a simple isobar pattern for an anticyclone.
   c) Give two facts about the wind in an anticyclone.
   d) Describe the seasonal differences in anticyclone weather, using a copy of the table below:

Summer weather	Winter weather
*	*
*	*
*	

(Pages 166 and 167)
a) Look at weather map **A** and complete the following sentences. Choose your answers from the brackets.
   ■ The pressure system is a (depression **or** anticyclone). **(1)**
   ■ The pressure over Britain is (high **or** low). **(1)**
   ■ The pressure at place **X** is (1016 **or** 1025). **(1)**
   ■ The wind is blowing in a (clockwise **or** anticlockwise direction). **(1)**
b) Give a simple weather forecast for London. **(4)**
c) Describe the weather that this same system may bring to London on a winter's day. **(4)**

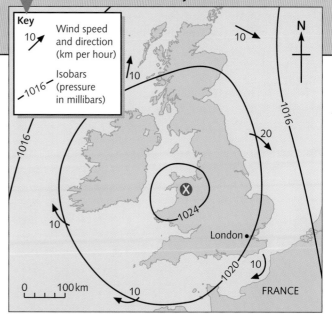

A Weather chart on 6 July at 1200 hrs

Key
10 ↗ Wind speed and direction (km per hour)
1016 Isobars (pressure in millibars)

13 WORLD CLIMATE

The equatorial climate

Graph **A** shows the equatorial type of climate. It is for a place called Manaus, which is located in the centre of the Amazon Basin in Brazil. It is typical of an equatorial climate in that it is hot, wet and humid throughout the year. Rainfall is heavy and falls during most afternoons as torrential rainstorms. There are no seasons in the equatorial regions, so there are no winters or summers as there are in Britain.

 A Climate graph for Manaus

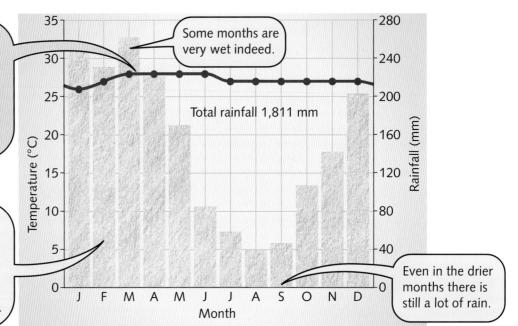

Temperature
- It is always hot with little difference in temperature from month to month.
- This is due to the sun being overhead, or at a high angle, all through the year.

Some months are very wet indeed.

Total rainfall 1,811 mm

Rainfall
- Rainfall totals can be greater than 2,000 mm a year (London has 610 mm).
- The rainfall is mainly due to **convectional** thunderstorms.

Even in the drier months there is still a lot of rain.

B A thunderstorm in the Amazon Basin

170

Convectional rainfall occurs when moist air is made to rise by heat from the sun. As the air rises it cools, condenses and forms huge storm clouds. These give heavy rain.

The daily pattern

The weather in Britain changes from day to day. In equatorial areas almost every day is exactly the same: it is fine in the morning, cloudy and wet in the afternoon, with clear skies again in the evening.

Every day is about the same length, with 12 hours of daylight and 12 hours of darkness.

The weather pattern described in table **C** is likely to be repeated day after day for most of the year.

C The daily pattern

	Time	Weather conditions
	6.00 am	Sun always rises at the same time. Morning mist quickly clears.
	8.00 am	Clear sky, no clouds, very warm (25°C), little wind.
	10.00 am	Hot air rises. Water vapour from rivers, swamps and forest carried high into the sky.
	Midday	Sun overhead, very hot (33°C). Small patches of cloud start to form.
	2.00 pm	Clouds increase in size and height. Huge cumulonimbus clouds develop.
	3.00 pm	Torrential rainstorms with thunder and lightning. Wind increases.
	4.00 pm	Storms continue. Sky is dark with thick cloud.
	5.00 pm	Storms end. Clouds begin to break up. Wind dies down.
	6.00 pm	Skies clear. Sun sets at same time each evening.
	8.00 pm	Nights are clear, warm (23°C) and very humid.

Location

Map **D** shows the location of the world's major equatorial regions. They mainly lie in a narrow zone which extends roughly 1,500 km either side of the Equator. The zone is not continuous, though. It is broken by the Andes Mountains in South America, and the East Africa Plateau in Africa.

The two main equatorial regions are the huge river basins of the Amazon in South America and the Congo in Africa.

The major factor that affects this climate is its latitude. At the Equator the sun is overhead throughout the year. This gives high temperatures and is responsible for the convectional rainfall.

The vegetation of the equatorial rainforest is described on pages 190 and 191.

D Equatorial climates

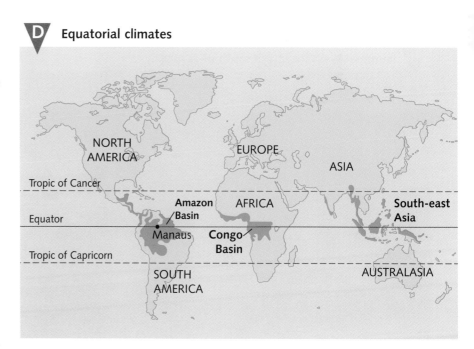

The Mediterranean climate

Graph **A** shows the Mediterranean type of climate. It is for Athens, the capital city of Greece. It is typical of a Mediterranean climate, and shows two very different seasons. The weather in summer is hot and dry, while in winter it is warm and wet.

Places with a Mediterranean climate are often popular holiday destinations. The rain in winter enables trees and plants to flourish and helps make the area attractive. The hot sun and blue skies of summer provide a welcome change for tourists who come from cloudier and cooler locations like Britain.

A **Climate graph for Athens**

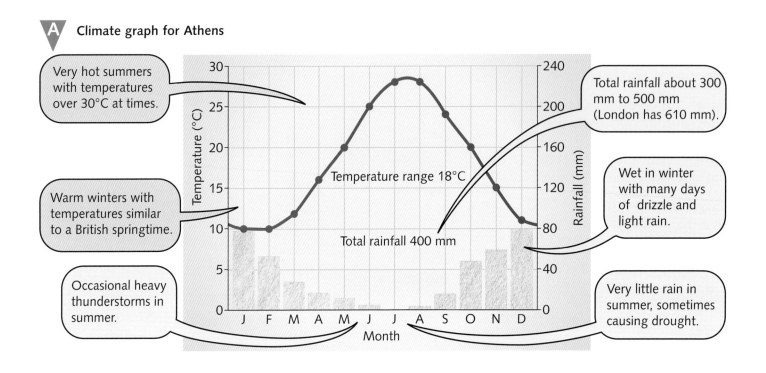

Very hot summers with temperatures over 30°C at times.

Warm winters with temperatures similar to a British springtime.

Occasional heavy thunderstorms in summer.

Temperature range 18°C

Total rainfall 400 mm

Total rainfall about 300 mm to 500 mm (London has 610 mm).

Wet in winter with many days of drizzle and light rain.

Very little rain in summer, sometimes causing drought.

B **Summer weather in the south of France**

Summers are hot because although it is never overhead, the sun is at a high enough angle in the sky to give plenty of heat. The wind is easterly and blows from the land. As the land is hot at this time of year, then the wind blowing from it will bring hot weather.

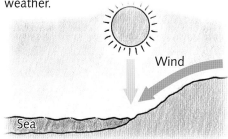

Summers are dry because the wind blows over a warm, dry land surface and cannot pick up moisture. This means that most places have very little rain. When rain does fall, it comes in heavy **convectional** thunderstorms.

Mediterranean climate

Hot dry summers and warm wet winters

Winters are warm because although the sun is lower in the sky, it is still high enough to give warm days. The nearby sea which was warmed up in summer only loses its heat slowly. The wind changes direction in winter and blows from this warm sea, keeping temperatures high.

Winters are wet because the wind blows off the sea and brings in warm, moist air which gives **relief rain**. **Depressions** are also common in winter and bring **frontal rain**. However, wet days are usually followed by two or three days that are warm and sunny.

Location

The name 'Mediterranean' is given to climates in several different parts of the world. Map **D** shows the location of these climatic regions.

Apart from the Mediterranean Sea area, all of the regions are located on the west coast of continents. They are also all found between latitudes 30° and 40° both north and south of the Equator.

In these latitudes the sun is at a high enough angle in the sky to bring warmth all year round.

The vegetation of places with a Mediterranean climate is described on page 192.

D Mediterranean climates

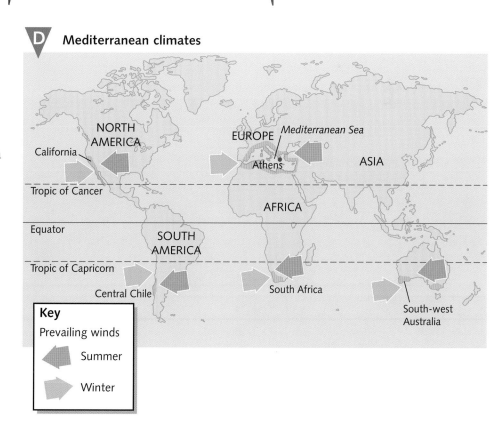

NORTH AMERICA
California
EUROPE *Mediterranean Sea*
Athens
ASIA
Tropic of Cancer
AFRICA
Equator
SOUTH AMERICA
Tropic of Capricorn
Central Chile
South Africa
South-west Australia

Key
Prevailing winds
Summer
Winter

The hot desert climate

Graph **A** shows the hot desert type of climate. It is for a place called Ain Salah, which is in the Sahara Desert. The hot deserts are very hot during the day and in summer. They have cooler winters and cold nights. Clouds are few, and there is very little rain.

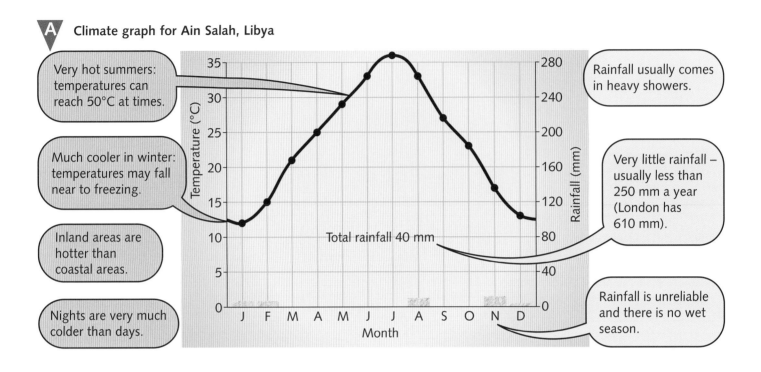

A Climate graph for Ain Salah, Libya

Very hot summers: temperatures can reach 50°C at times.

Much cooler in winter: temperatures may fall near to freezing.

Inland areas are hotter than coastal areas.

Nights are very much colder than days.

Rainfall usually comes in heavy showers.

Very little rainfall – usually less than 250 mm a year (London has 610 mm).

Rainfall is unreliable and there is no wet season.

Total rainfall 40 mm

B Sand dunes near Ain Salah in the Sahara Desert

Effects

Tropical storms are extremely destructive. They claim an average of 20,000 lives each year and cause immense damage to property, vegetation, shipping, and a country's economy.

- **High winds** often exceed 160 km/hr and in extreme cases reach 250 km/hr. They uproot trees, ruin crops, blow down power lines and severely damage buildings. In poorer countries whole villages may be destroyed.

- **Storm** or **tidal surges**, sometimes up to 5 m in height, can flood low-lying coastal areas. These destroy property and cause loss of life. Over 40,000 people were drowned in Bangladesh during the 1985 cyclone disaster.

- **Flooding** can also result from rivers swollen by torrential rain. In the year 2000, over 300,000 people in Mozambique lost their homes as the Limpopo and Save Rivers burst their banks after a cyclone and heavy rain hit the country.

- **Landslides** may occur, when heavy rainfall washes away buildings erected on steep, unstable slopes.

Predictions and precautions

The poster in **D** shows the advice given to people in Florida on what to do before, during and after a hurricane. Nowadays, modern technology can track hurricanes and tell us when and where they may strike. This gives people more time to prepare and perhaps evacuate an area.

Richer countries like the USA give different levels of warning and have detailed storm management plans in place. They are also able provide emergency help to those in need, and quickly repair damage once the storm is over.

Poorer countries are rarely able to afford or organise efficient disaster plans. They suffer most from tropical storms, and usually have to seek emergency help from other countries and international organisations.

C Cyclone damage in Bangladesh

D Hurricane warning

WHEN A **HURRICANE** THREATENS

KEEP YOUR RADIO OR TV ON...AND LISTEN TO LATEST WEATHER BUREAU ADVICE TO SAVE YOUR **LIFE** AND POSSESSIONS

BEFORE THE WIND AND FLOOD	Have gas tank filled . . . check battery and tires.	Have supply of drinking water. Stock up on foods that need no cooking or refrigeration.
	Have on hand flashlight, first aid kit, fire extinguisher, battery-powered radio.	Store all loose objects: toys, tools, trash cans, awnings, etc. Board or tape up all windows.	Get away from low areas that may be swept by storm tides or floods.
DURING THE STORM	Stay indoors. Don't be fooled if the calm 'eye' passes directly over, and don't be caught in the open when the hurricane winds resume from the opposite direction.	Listen to your radio or TV for information from the Weather Bureau, civil defense, Red Cross, and other authorities..
AFTER THE STORM HAS PASSED	Do not drive unless necessary. Watch out for undermined pavement and broken power lines.	Report downed power wires, broken water or sewer pipes to proper authorities or nearest policeman.
	Use extreme caution to prevent outbreak of fire, or injuries from falling objects.	Use phone for emergencies only. Jammed switchboards prevent emergency calls from getting through.

YOUR ABILITY TO MEET EMERGENCIES WILL INSPIRE AND HELP OTHERS

US DEPARTMENT OF COMMERCE • WEATHER BUREAU

Acid rain

Acid rain was first noticed in Scandinavia in the late 1950s, when scientists reported that large numbers of fish were dying in lakes and rivers. They discovered that the water had become very acid and had been carried there by rain. They called the problem **acid rain**.

Acid rain is a kind of air pollution. It is caused mainly by power stations and industries burning **fossil fuels** which give off sulphur dioxide and nitrogen oxide. Nitrous oxide from car exhausts also adds to the problem.

The chemicals in acid rain are carried up into the atmosphere and then spread over wide areas by the prevailing wind. Acid rain can be very damaging to the environment, and causes serious harm to forests, lakes, rivers and the stonework of buildings.

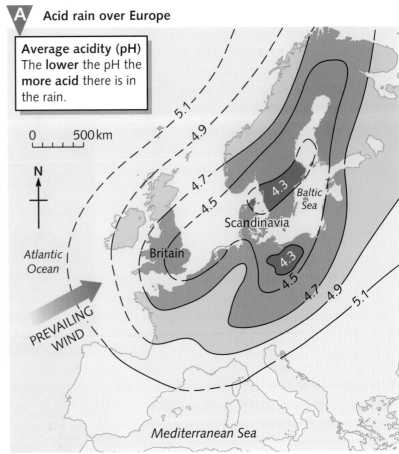

A Acid rain over Europe

Average acidity (pH)
The **lower** the pH the **more acid** there is in the rain.

B Acid rain

Causes

Effects

4 Acid-polluted air is blown by the wind.

3 Chemical changes produce acids.

5 Water droplets in the clouds become polluted.

2 Chemicals like sulphur dioxide and nitrogen oxide rise into the air.

6 Acid rain falls to the ground.

1 Power stations, factories and cars cause pollution.

7 Trees and vegetation polluted and may die.

8 Water and soil polluted with acid.

Leaves damaged, weakened trees die

Stonework damaged

Crops affected, yields reduced

Groundwater polluted

Acid water kills insects and fish

Acid rain in Europe

Most European countries add acids to the air. Britain is one of the major culprits, but only about one-third of its acid rain actually falls back on British soil: some falls in the North Sea but most is blown towards Scandinavia. Despite being one of the least offenders, Scandinavia is one of the main sufferers of acid rain.

Because acid rain is blown from country to country, it is an international problem. Problems like these are difficult to solve because dealing with them is expensive and international co-operation and management are needed.

Prevention or cure?

There are two main options when it comes to tackling the acid rain problem. One way is to try to cure the problem by repairing the damage done, by washing away the acid or adding chemicals to reduce its effects. The other is to prevent the damage in the first place. Prevention is better than cure, and this is done by reducing the use of processes that produce acid rain.

A European Union (EU) directive in 1988 called for a 71% reduction in sulphur dioxide emissions by 2005. This has been a difficult and expensive task. So far, Britain's emissions are down by just 42%.

C Some ways of reducing acid rain

	Method	Problem
Cure	Spray trees to wash off acid.	Costly and needs to be repeated.
	Add lime to soils to reduce acidity.	Difficult, expensive and short-term solution.
Prevention	Burn less fossil fuels by conserving energy.	Difficult to implement.
	Use non-fossil fuels such as nuclear energy.	Would mean closure of coalmines and loss of jobs.
	Remove sulphur from coal before burning.	Extra process means extra time and costs.
	Use new, more efficient boilers.	Expensive and still need to dispose of waste.
	Remove sulphur from waste gases.	Very expensive, which will increase customer costs.

D Trees killed by acid rain in Scandinavia

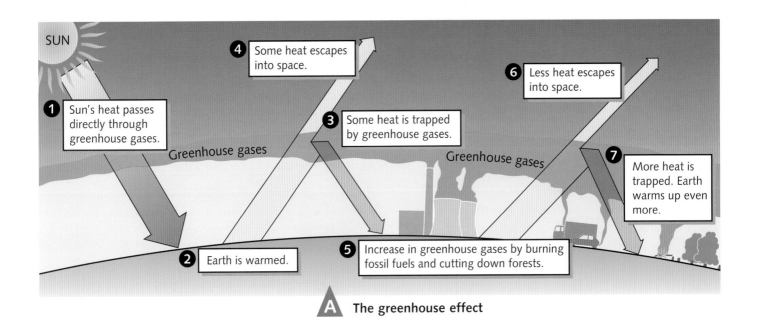

1 Sun's heat passes directly through greenhouse gases.

4 Some heat escapes into space.

3 Some heat is trapped by greenhouse gases.

6 Less heat escapes into space.

Greenhouse gases

Greenhouse gases

7 More heat is trapped. Earth warms up even more.

2 Earth is warmed.

5 Increase in greenhouse gases by burning fossil fuels and cutting down forests.

A The greenhouse effect

Global warming

The world is now warmer than it has been for many thousands of years. In the 20th century, average temperatures rose by 0.6°C, and most of this increase was in the last 40 years. The warmest years ever recorded were in 1990 and 1995.

Some scientists believe that the Earth's climate is going to get even warmer. They predict that by 2100 the average global temperature could be between 1.6°C and 4.2°C higher than it is today. This heating up of our planet is called **global warming**, and it may cause serious problems in the future.

Causes of global warming

Global warming is thought to be due to the **greenhouse effect**. The Earth is surrounded by a layer of gases, including carbon dioxide. This keeps the Earth warm by preventing the escape of heat that would normally be lost from the atmosphere.

The gases act rather like the glass in a greenhouse. They let heat in but prevent most of it from getting out. The burning of fossil fuels such as oil, coal and natural gas produces large amounts of carbon dioxide. As the amount of this gas increases, the Earth becomes warmer.

B Greenhouse gases

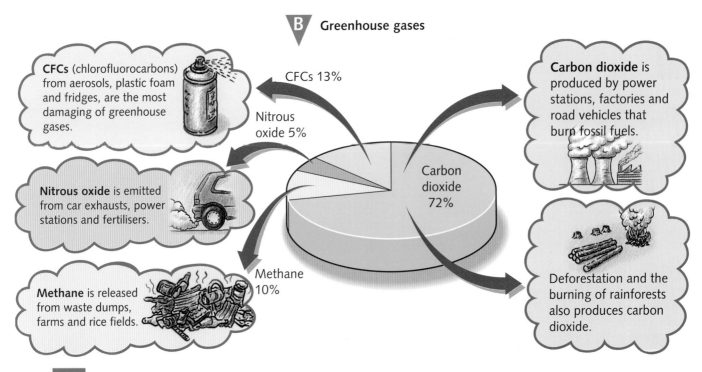

CFCs (chlorofluorocarbons) from aerosols, plastic foam and fridges, are the most damaging of greenhouse gases.

CFCs 13%

Nitrous oxide 5%

Nitrous oxide is emitted from car exhausts, power stations and fertilisers.

Methane 10%

Methane is released from waste dumps, farms and rice fields.

Carbon dioxide 72%

Carbon dioxide is produced by power stations, factories and road vehicles that burn fossil fuels.

Deforestation and the burning of rainforests also produces carbon dioxide.

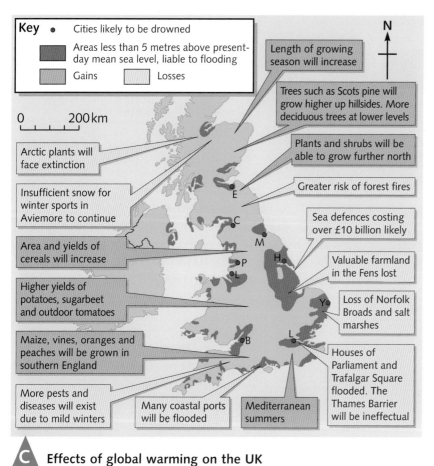

Key
- • Cities likely to be drowned
- ▨ Areas less than 5 metres above present-day mean sea level, liable to flooding
- ▨ Gains
- ☐ Losses

0   200km

- Arctic plants will face extinction
- Insufficient snow for winter sports in Aviemore to continue
- Area and yields of cereals will increase
- Higher yields of potatoes, sugarbeet and outdoor tomatoes
- Maize, vines, oranges and peaches will be grown in southern England
- More pests and diseases will exist due to mild winters
- Many coastal ports will be flooded
- Mediterranean summers
- Length of growing season will increase
- Trees such as Scots pine will grow higher up hillsides. More deciduous trees at lower levels
- Plants and shrubs will be able to grow further north
- Greater risk of forest fires
- Sea defences costing over £10 billion likely
- Valuable farmland in the Fens lost
- Loss of Norfolk Broads and salt marshes
- Houses of Parliament and Trafalgar Square flooded. The Thames Barrier will be ineffectual

E C M P L H Y B L

C **Effects of global warming on the UK**

Effects of global warming

Nobody knows exactly what the effects of global warming will be. Some of the effects will, no doubt, be harmful, but others may bring some benefits.

- Sea temperatures would rise, the water would expand and sea levels rise.
- Ice caps and glaciers would start to melt, causing sea levels to rise even further.
- Low-lying areas would be flooded. Some islands would disappear altogether.
- There might be more violent storms and extreme weather.
- Hot regions could become hotter and deserts would spread.
- Climatic belts and vegetation types would move.
- Some plants and animals would become extinct.
- There could be an increase in insect pests like aphids and fleas.
- Tropical diseases may spread to temperate regions such as the UK.

D **Effects of global warming on the world**

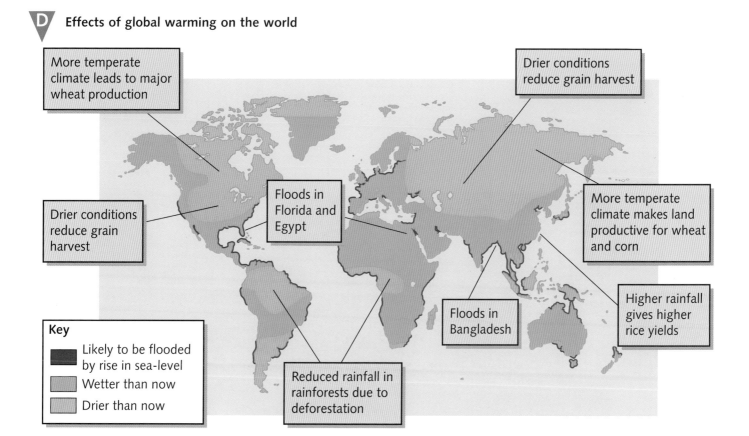

- More temperate climate leads to major wheat production
- Drier conditions reduce grain harvest
- Drier conditions reduce grain harvest
- Floods in Florida and Egypt
- More temperate climate makes land productive for wheat and corn
- Floods in Bangladesh
- Higher rainfall gives higher rice yields
- Reduced rainfall in rainforests due to deforestation

Key
- ▨ Likely to be flooded by rise in sea-level
- ▨ Wetter than now
- ☐ Drier than now

Drought and water supply in the UK

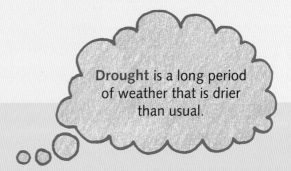

Drought is a long period of weather that is drier than usual.

The UK has a temperate climate which is described as being not too hot, not too cold, not too wet and not too dry. It can expect to have rain throughout the year – not in any great amounts, but certainly enough to provide for the country's needs.

Perhaps it is because drought is less frequent in Britain than in other places, that the country seems unable to cope with water shortages. Two major droughts occurred in the UK in the last part of the 20th century, and both caused unexpected problems for the country.

A

Causes

Summer 1975
- Depressions, which usually bring cloud and rain, were diverted to the north of Britain.
- The weather was hot, with very little rain.
- Water supplies gradually ran dry.

Winter 1975–76
- Fewer depressions than usual.
- Mild and dry conditions.
- Water supplies (usually replenished in winter) remained very low.

Spring and summer 1976
- Anticyclones common.
- Dry, sunny weather continued. There was 50% less rain than usual in the south.
- Drought conditions developed.

Drought in the UK, 1975–76

Effects
- Reservoirs dried up and fell to lowest ever levels. Underground water supplies ran low.
- Garden hosepipes were banned and water rationing was introduced in some places.
- Clay soils dried out and shrank. Buildings were damaged as their foundations moved.
- Grass stopped growing, leaving a shortage of cattle feed. Farmers' crops wilted and died in the hot, dry conditions.
- Heathland and forest areas became tinder-dry. Large areas were destroyed by fire.
- Many recreational activities had to be cancelled.

B

Dried-up feeder river

Remains of bridge

Normal level of water

Old course of river

Remains of drowned village (Mardale)

Remains of cleared woodland

Drought in the UK 1995–96

Despite the problems of 1975–76, water authorities seemed unprepared for the hot, dry summer of 1995.

By late August, after six months of below average rainfall, rivers were flowing at less than half their average for that time of year. Reservoirs were rapidly emptying, and by November some reservoirs in Yorkshire were less than 10% full. The situation was becoming desperate.

Eventually, Yorkshire Water had to buy and transport surplus water from Kielder in Northumberland. This water had first to be pumped from the River Tees to a reservoir in Cleveland. It was then transported by road by a fleet of 200 tankers working 24 hours a day, seven days a week.

The transfer was nicknamed 'Drought Aid', and is shown in map **C**.

Water supplies and transfers

The UK receives more than enough rainfall in an average year to meet its needs. Unfortunately this rainfall does not always fall where and when it is needed.

Map **D** shows that the north and west of Britain usually has more water than it needs. This is called a **surplus**. The south and east tends to have less than it needs, which is called a **deficit**.

To ensure that all of the country has a reliable supply of water, the water authorities store surplus water in reservoirs and transfer it, when needed, to areas that have a deficit.

The future

The above average rainfall of 2001, 2002 and 2004 more than filled reservoirs and underground supplies. Despite this, the increasing demand for water, especially in the south-east, has led five water authorities to predict a significant water shortage by the year 2021.

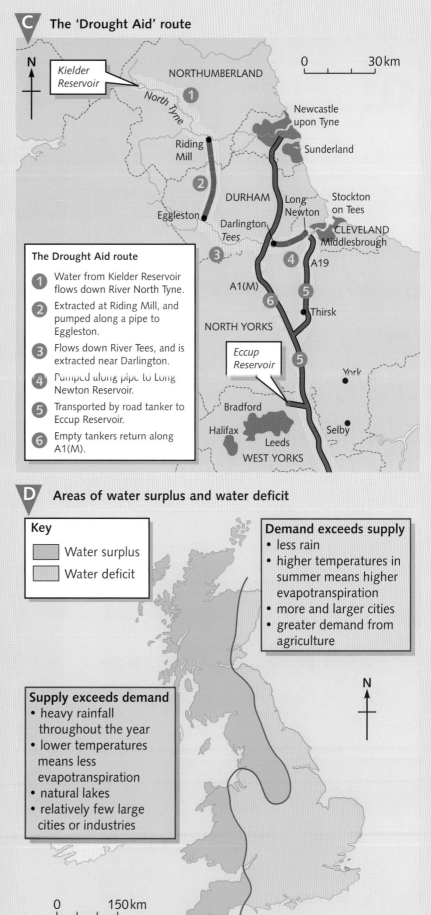

C The 'Drought Aid' route

0   30 km

The Drought Aid route

1. Water from Kielder Reservoir flows down River North Tyne.
2. Extracted at Riding Mill, and pumped along a pipe to Eggleston.
3. Flows down River Tees, and is extracted near Darlington.
4. Pumped along pipe to Long Newton Reservoir.
5. Transported by road tanker to Eccup Reservoir.
6. Empty tankers return along A1(M).

D Areas of water surplus and water deficit

Key

Water surplus

Water deficit

Demand exceeds supply
- less rain
- higher temperatures in summer means higher evapotranspiration
- more and larger cities
- greater demand from agriculture

Supply exceeds demand
- heavy rainfall throughout the year
- lower temperatures means less evapotranspiration
- natural lakes
- relatively few large cities or industries

0   150 km

REVISION QUESTIONS

 (Pages 170 and 171)
a) List the main features of an equatorial climate.
b) Name three places with an equatorial climate.
c) What is convectional rainfall?
d) Describe the daily pattern of weather in equatorial areas, using the drawings below:

 (Pages 172 and 173)
a) Describe the Mediterranean climate.
b) Why are the summers different from the winters?
c) Name five places with a Mediterranean climate.

3 **(Pages 174 and 175)**
Explain hot desert climates as follows:
a) Why are they very dry? Give three reasons.
b) Why are they hotter in summer than in winter?
c) Why are they cooler inland than on the coast?
d) Why are days very much hotter than nights?
e) Name six hot deserts.

4 **(Pages 170 to 175)**
Look at the climate map below.
a) Name the climate types A, B and C in the key.
b) Name the climate type and locations of the numbered areas.

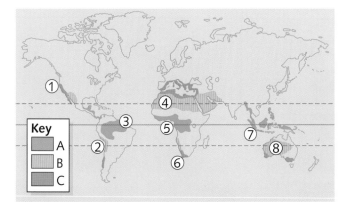

 (Pages 176 and 177)
Complete the diagram below by writing about 10 to 20 words for each heading.

Effects
- High winds
- Storm surges
- Flooding
- Landslides

Hurricanes

Precautions
- Before
- During
- After

 (Pages 178 and 179)
a) What are two main causes of acid rain?
b) Give four effects of acid rain.
c) Which parts of Europe are most affected by acid rain? Suggest reasons for this.
d) Describe how acid rain may be reduced.

 (Pages 180 and 181)
a) What is global warming?
b) What causes the greenhouse effect?
c) Make a larger copy of the drawing below and complete it using the following labels.

- Burning fossil fuels
- Earth warms up
- Heat trapped
- Heat from sun
- Temperature rises
- Greenhouse gases

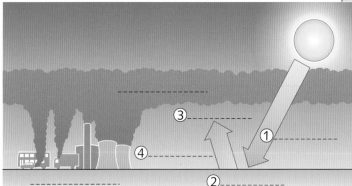

 (Pages 182 and 183)
a) What is drought?
b) For a drought that you have studied:
- list the main causes
- describe the effects on the local people.
c) How do water authorities try to overcome the problem of water shortage?

1

(Pages 178 and 179)

a) What are the two main sources of acid rain? **(2)**
b) Look at the map below.
 ■ Which four countries have most sulphur deposited? **(2)**
 ■ Which countries receive more than half their deposits from elsewhere? **(3)**
c) Why is acid rain an international problem? **(2)**
d) How could the problem of acid rain be reduced? **(2)**

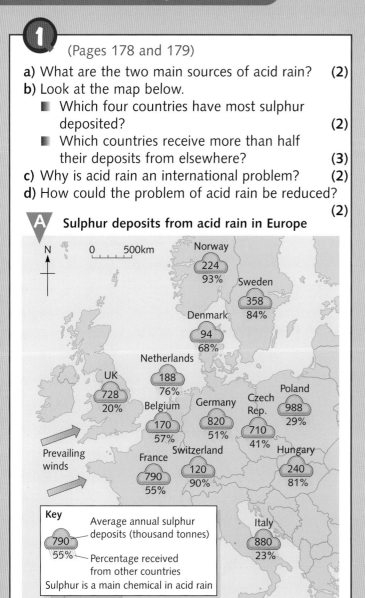

A Sulphur deposits from acid rain in Europe

2

(Pages 176 and 177)

Look at map **B**.
a) What is a hurricane? **(1)**
b) Name two land areas crossed by Hurricane Hugo. **(2)**
c) How was the track of Hurricane Gilbert different from the track of Hurricane Joan? **(2)**
d) Name a town likely to have been severely damaged by Hurricane Joan. **(1)**
e) Describe three effects of a hurricane on the landscape and people. **(3)**
f) Describe two ways that a government might try to reduce the effects of a hurricane. **(2)**

3

(Pages 180 and 181)

a) What is global warming? **(2)**
b) What causes global warming? **(2)**
c) Three effects of global warming are shown below. Using diagram **C**, give two of the problems caused by each of these effects:
 ■ increase in temperature
 ■ decrease in rainfall
 ■ rise in sea level. **(6)**
d) List four effects of global warming on the UK. **(4)**

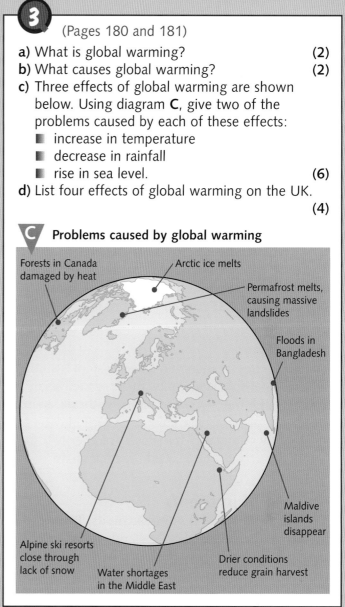

C Problems caused by global warming

B Tracks of two Caribbean hurricanes

Ecosystems

An **ecosystem** is a natural system which links together all the elements of the environment. In it, thousands of different plants, insects and animals all live together and depend on each other for food and shelter. They also have close links with non-living elements of the environment, such as the local relief, climate and soil.

Ecosystems vary in size, from vast rainforests to small areas of woodland and tiny ponds. There are also many different types of ecosystem. These include tropical rainforests, hot, dry deserts, and deciduous woodlands which are common to Britain.

Energy flows

The main source of energy in an ecosystem is sunlight. The sun's energy is taken in by the green leaves of plants through the process of **photosynthesis**. Animals then eat the plants. These animals in turn may then be eaten by other animals. This process of energy transfer through the ecosystem is called the **food chain**.

Recycling of nutrients

All plants and animals require **nutrients**. These are minerals that come from the soil and are taken up by the roots of plants. They are then transferred to animals through the food chain. Eventually when the plants or animals die, they rot away and decompose due to the action of fungi and bacteria. In this way the nurients are returned to the soil and re-used. This is called **nutrient recycling**.

> An **ecosystem** is a system where plants and animals interact with each other and with their natural surroundings.

> **Nutrients** are chemicals used in the growth of plants.

> **Photosynthesis** is a process by which green plants turn sunlight into plant growth.

A A simple ecosystem

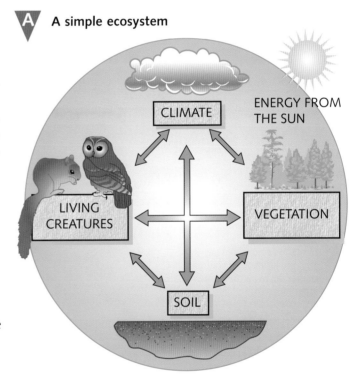

B The food chain and nutrient recycling

| **Non-living environment** This includes heat and light from the sun, air, rain, soil, rock and water from the ground. | → | **Producers** Plants use energy from the sun through photosynthesis, e.g. grass and leaves. | Eaten by | **Consumers** Herbivores are plant eaters, e.g. insects, mice, rabbits. | Eaten by | **Consumers** Carnivores are meat eaters, e.g. birds, foxes, people. |

Die ... Die ... Die

Recycled

Decomposers Bacteria which break down dead material. Also include worms and mushrooms.

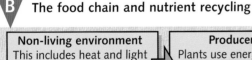

A deciduous woodland ecosystem in Britain

Britain was once covered in dense forest. The climate was colder than it is today and coniferous trees such as Scots pine were most common. As the climate gradually became warmer, so the type of vegetation and wildlife gradually changed to suit the new conditions.

Today, Britain's natural woodland consists mainly of **deciduous** trees such as oak, ash, beech and elm. Most deciduous trees lose their leaves in winter.

Diagrams **C** and **D** show the main features of this type of ecosystem.

Tallest layer between 30 and 40 metres
Mainly trees such as oak, ash, elm and beech

Ash

Oak

Insects and birds

Middle layer between 5 and 15 metres
Smaller trees such as birch, holly and hawthorn

Birch

Lower or ground layer
May include bracken, brambles, shrubs, ferns, wild flowers and grasses

Rabbits, mice, hedgehogs, deer, squirrels, etc.

Weathered rock releases nutrients

Worms and insects

Fungi and bacteria feed on dead material

C

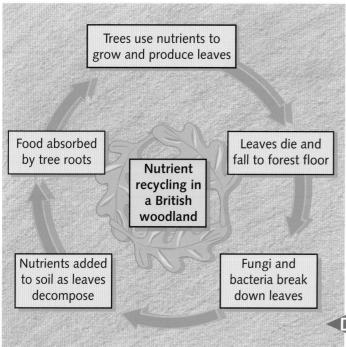

Trees use nutrients to grow and produce leaves

Food absorbed by tree roots

Nutrient recycling in a British woodland

Leaves die and fall to forest floor

Nutrients added to soil as leaves decompose

Fungi and bacteria break down leaves

D

The woodland ecosystem shown in diagram **C** is said to be in balance with nature. Unfortunately, human activities can very easily alter, or even destroy, delicate ecosystems.

For example, the clearing of trees for house building may result in the loss of food and shelter for plants and animals living there. Similarly, water pollution, and the use of fertilisers, can poison food sources and affect other elements of the ecosystem.

It is important that people today learn how to use the environment without damaging or destroying it. This is called **sustainable development**.

Wetlands – an ecosystem under threat

Places

The Everglades, Florida

One of the main roads crossing southern Florida has the name of 'Alligator Alley'. It takes visitors across the Everglades, an area of wetland that is a haven for special kinds of plants, birds and animals.

Among those animals are thousands of alligators. Visitors can join organised tours to watch the alligators feeding, swimming and sunning themselves in their natural environment.

The wetlands are a very special type of ecosystem. The land is usually waterlogged and shallow lakes and ponds cover much of the land surface. Unfortunately, they are fragile places whose existence has become threatened by development programmes and a variety of human activities.

Large areas of the Everglades have already been damaged, and numerous plants and animals lost. Alligator numbers have dropped from 200,000 to just 20,000 in the last 50 years.

A Alligators in the Everglades National Park

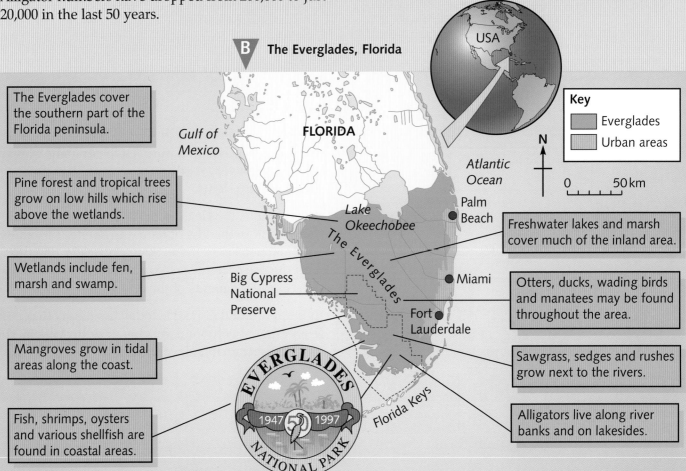

B The Everglades, Florida

The Everglades cover the southern part of the Florida peninsula.

Pine forest and tropical trees grow on low hills which rise above the wetlands.

Wetlands include fen, marsh and swamp.

Mangroves grow in tidal areas along the coast.

Fish, shrimps, oysters and various shellfish are found in coastal areas.

Freshwater lakes and marsh cover much of the inland area.

Otters, ducks, wading birds and manatees may be found throughout the area.

Sawgrass, sedges and rushes grow next to the rivers.

Alligators live along river banks and on lakesides.

Key
Everglades
Urban areas

Gulf of Mexico

FLORIDA

Atlantic Ocean

Lake Okeechobee

The Everglades

Palm Beach

Miami

Big Cypress National Preserve

Fort Lauderdale

Florida Keys

EVERGLADES NATIONAL PARK 1947 50 1997

N

0   50km

The Everglades once covered 10,000 km² of southern Florida, and was one of the largest freshwater marshes in the world. Today less than half of that wetland remains. The rest has been drained and the land built upon or used for farming.

Sadly, even the wetland that still remains is slowly being poisoned by water pollution and agricultural fertilisers.

In the 1980s, the state of Florida was sued for its failure to protect the Everglades area. After several years of argument, the Everglades Forever Act was eventually passed in 1994.

This Act set standards for the future and started a massive clean-up scheme. Its aims were to protect the fragile environment while also sustaining the local economy. In 1997, Congress set aside $200 million to help with the scheme.

C Problems of the Everglades

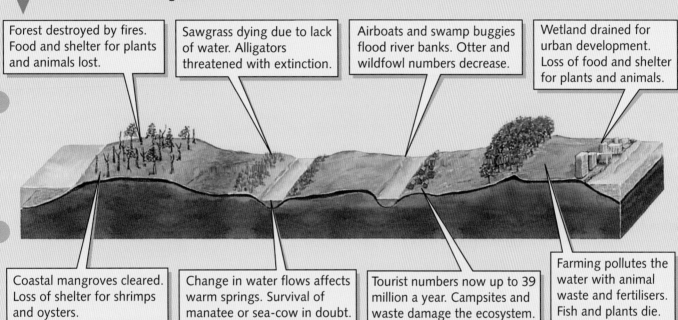

Forest destroyed by fires. Food and shelter for plants and animals lost.

Sawgrass dying due to lack of water. Alligators threatened with extinction.

Airboats and swamp buggies flood river banks. Otter and wildfowl numbers decrease.

Wetland drained for urban development. Loss of food and shelter for plants and animals.

Coastal mangroves cleared. Loss of shelter for shrimps and oysters.

Change in water flows affects warm springs. Survival of manatee or sea-cow in doubt.

Tourist numbers now up to 39 million a year. Campsites and waste damage the ecosystem.

Farming pollutes the water with animal waste and fertilisers. Fish and plants die.

D Coastal mangroves

Tropical rainforest ecosystem

Tropical rainforest is the natural vegetation of places with an **equatorial climate**. This climate is hot, wet and humid throughout the year (see pages 170 and 171). The rainforests provide the most luxuriant vegetation found on Earth.

One-third of all the world's trees grow here. There are thousands of different species, with many still to be identified and studied. The rainforest is also the home of a huge number of animals and insects. Each plant, animal and insect plays an important role in the forest **ecosystem**.

Despite its dense and lush appearance, the rainforest is a fragile environment. Recently, large areas of forest have been cleared for development. This has permanently destroyed the ecosystem, and large numbers of plants and animals have been lost for ever.

Photo **D** opposite shows what it is like in the tropical rainforest. Notice that there are three separate layers. The lowest is the forest floor where there is a layer of shrubs. Above this is a layer of mainly new trees. The top layer is the main canopy which is like an umbrella sheltering the forest below.

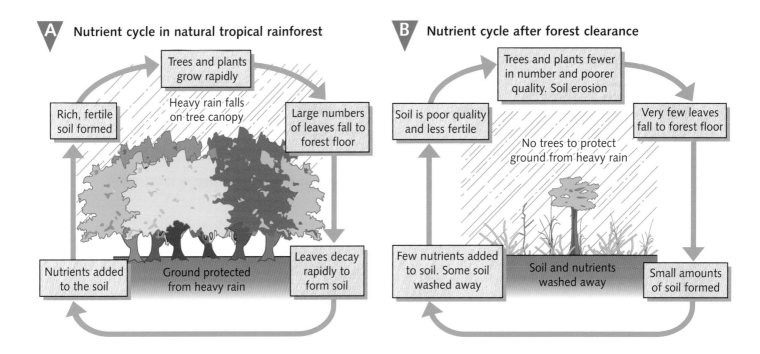

A Nutrient cycle in natural tropical rainforest

Trees and plants grow rapidly

Heavy rain falls on tree canopy

Rich, fertile soil formed

Large numbers of leaves fall to forest floor

Nutrients added to the soil

Ground protected from heavy rain

Leaves decay rapidly to form soil

B Nutrient cycle after forest clearance

Trees and plants fewer in number and poorer quality. Soil erosion

Soil is poor quality and less fertile

No trees to protect ground from heavy rain

Very few leaves fall to forest floor

Few nutrients added to soil. Some soil washed away

Soil and nutrients washed away

Small amounts of soil formed

C The Amazon rainforest, Brazil

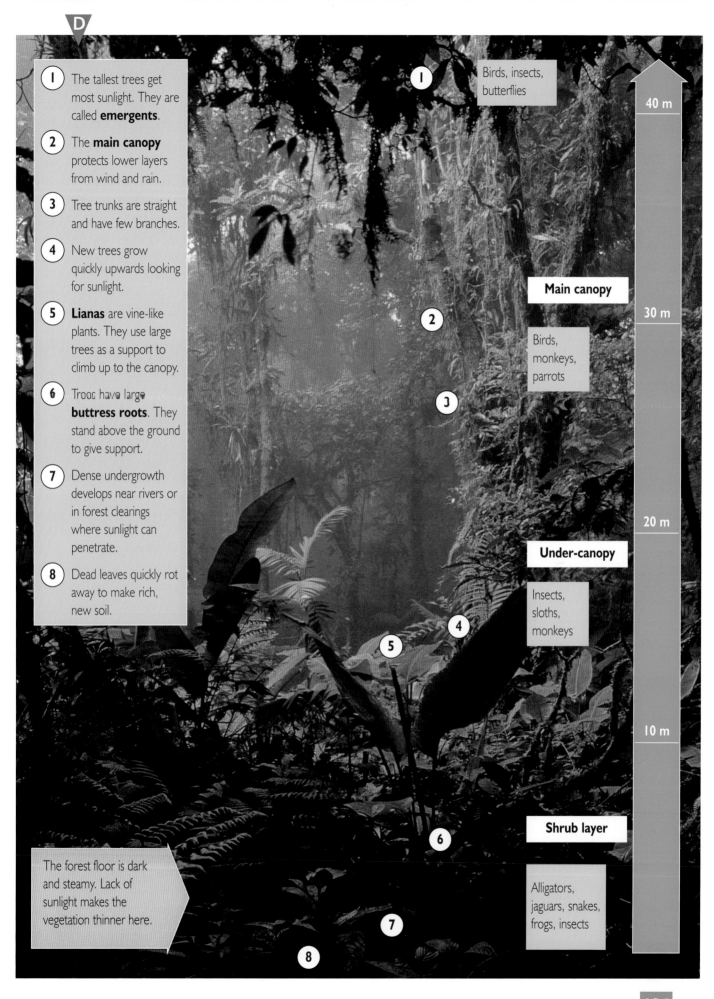

1. The tallest trees get most sunlight. They are called **emergents**.

2. The **main canopy** protects lower layers from wind and rain.

3. Tree trunks are straight and have few branches.

4. New trees grow quickly upwards looking for sunlight.

5. **Lianas** are vine-like plants. They use large trees as a support to climb up to the canopy.

6. Trees have large **buttress roots**. They stand above the ground to give support.

7. Dense undergrowth develops near rivers or in forest clearings where sunlight can penetrate.

8. Dead leaves quickly rot away to make rich, new soil.

Birds, insects, butterflies

Main canopy

Birds, monkeys, parrots

Under-canopy

Insects, sloths, monkeys

Shrub layer

Alligators, jaguars, snakes, frogs, insects

40 m

30 m

20 m

10 m

The forest floor is dark and steamy. Lack of sunlight makes the vegetation thinner here.

Mediterranean ecosystems

The natural vegetation of the Mediterranean lands is woodland and scrub. These areas have hot dry summers and warm, wet winters. Pages 172 and 173 describe the Mediterranean climate.

At one time, Mediterranean hillsides were densely wooded. Where the woodland still exists the main trees are often evergreen oaks, pines and several types of conifer. Where woodland has been destroyed by forest fires or cut down for human needs, a scrub vegetation has developed. **Scrub** is a mixture of small trees, bushes and undergrowth.

Due to human activities, little of the natural Mediterranean vegetation survives today. It has been changed as a result of several factors.

- **Deforestation.** Trees have been cut down to create space for farming and settlement. Wood was also used for building and as a fuel for heat and cooking.
- **Grazing animals.** Herds of sheep and goats eat leaves of young plants and kill them off.
- **Fire.** Most forest fires start naturally during the long dry summer. They destroy the vegetation and, in many cases, permanently change the ecosystem.

A Mediterranean vegetation

Woodland
- Includes pine, cork, oak and cypress
- Most have thick bark as protection against the heat
- Many have small leathery leaves to reduce moisture loss

Scrub
- Mainly small, low shrubs
- Includes sweet-smelling herbs like lavender and thyme
- Very little grass – too hot and dry
- Plants often prickly or with waxy leaves to hold moisture
- Quick life cycle for short growing season

Plants and trees have long roots to reach underground water

Hot desert ecosystems

Hot deserts are places where rain rarely falls. Most are also very hot, but temperatures may fall below freezing point at night. Many are sandy but some are just vast areas of bare rock.

These conditions make it very difficult for plants and wildlife to survive. Most plants that do survive have to grow a long way from other plants. This is so that they can make the most of the little moisture available.

Many desert plants lie **dormant** in the desert for long periods of time. Dormant means a plant is resting and inactive. A sudden rare rainstorm will bring these plants to life and they will burst into flower. After a short time they dry up and once again become dormant.

A few animals live in the desert. Many only come out in the cool of the night to sip the dew that forms on rocks and plants. Kangaroos, rats and gerbils get much of their moisture by gnawing seeds and plant roots. Their droppings help fertilise the ground and so form an important part of the ecosystem.

B | **Hot desert vegetation**

Other plants
- Most have thin, spiky or glossy leaves to reduce loss of moisture.
- Some have long tap roots to reach water that may be deep underground.
- Others have shallow roots to make full use of any surface moisture.
- Some plants can store moisture in bulbs on their roots.

Saguaro cactus
- Thick, waxy skin to reflect heat and reduce moisture loss.
- Can live for up to 200 years, store 8,000 litres of water and grow to a height of 15 metres.
- Spikes instead of leaves stop animals from eating the plant.
- Cacti seeds can lie dormant for several years until it rains.

Tropical savanna grassland

The savanna grassland, which often includes scattered trees, is the natural vegetation of places with a **tropical continental climate**. This may be found in places like Kenya, Tanzania and parts of Brazil. The climate has two distinct seasons. One is very warm and dry, the other is hot and wet.

The plants growing here have to adapt to the local environment. This means that they have to survive months of very warm conditions with occasional heavy rainfall in the wet season, followed by a very long period without any rain at all, in the dry season.

Some of the ways in which the grass and trees have adapted to these conditions are shown in drawing **A**.

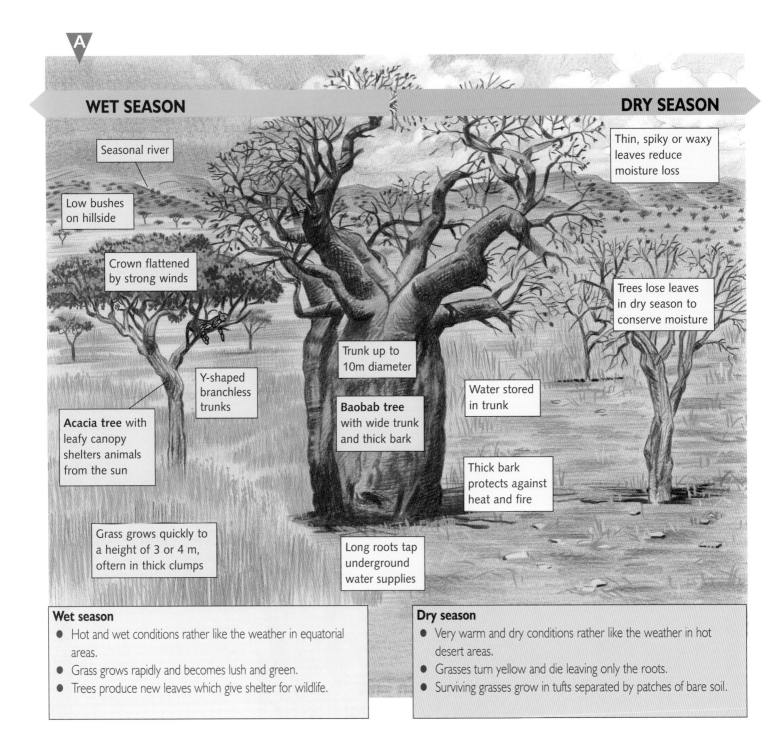

A

WET SEASON

DRY SEASON

Seasonal river

Low bushes on hillside

Crown flattened by strong winds

Thin, spiky or waxy leaves reduce moisture loss

Trees lose leaves in dry season to conserve moisture

Trunk up to 10m diameter

Y-shaped branchless trunks

Acacia tree with leafy canopy shelters animals from the sun

Baobab tree with wide trunk and thick bark

Water stored in trunk

Thick bark protects against heat and fire

Grass grows quickly to a height of 3 or 4 m, oftern in thick clumps

Long roots tap underground water supplies

Wet season
- Hot and wet conditions rather like the weather in equatorial areas.
- Grass grows rapidly and becomes lush and green.
- Trees produce new leaves which give shelter for wildlife.

Dry season
- Very warm and dry conditions rather like the weather in hot desert areas.
- Grasses turn yellow and die leaving only the roots.
- Surviving grasses grow in tufts separated by patches of bare soil.

Coniferous forests

Coniferous forest is the natural vegetation of places that have a cold climate. In the northern hemisphere they stretch in a great belt from Scandinavia, through Siberia and across the Bering Straits to Alaska and Canada.

The trees growing here have had to adapt to a harsh local environment with short cool summers and long, very cold winters. Precipitation is low and falls mainly in the summer. Snow is common in winter. Some of the ways in which the trees have adapted to these conditions are shown in drawing **C**.

B Coniferous forest in Canada

The most common trees in coniferous forests are fir, pine and spruce. They are evergreens and grow very tall, perhaps up to 30 or 40 metres. Coniferous trees are softwoods which makes them valuable for timber as well as pulp and paper.

Coniferous forests have been little affected by human activity. This is mainly because they are located in inhospitable areas where few people live.

C

Whirls

Spruce can grow 30 metres high

Distance between whirls indicates 1 year

Evergreen – no need to renew leaves for the short growing season

Compact conical shape gives stability in the wind

Needles to reduce moisture loss

Trunk is usually straight and tall in attempt to reach the sunlight

Thick, resinous bark gives protection against cold winds. Trunk is thin due to rapid upward growth.

Cones protect the seeds during very cold winters

Downward-sloping and springy branches allow snow to slide off

Very little undergrowth, as trees are closely spaced and branches cut out sunlight

Cold climate discourages decay so ground is covered with dead pine needles

Shallow roots because:
• soils are thin, or
• subsoil is frozen for much of the year, or
• cold boulder clay soil discourages deep root growth

Long roots for anchorage against strong winds

Deforestation – the destruction of the ecosystem

Amazon rainforest

Brazil

The Amazon Basin

> Deforestation is the complete clearance of forested land.

> Subsistence farming is when just enough food is grown for the farmer's own needs.

The world is in great danger of losing its rainforests. More than half have been lost in the last 50 years.

The Amazon forest is most at risk. Every year more and more of it is burnt down and cleared. The forest is huge, and millions of years old. At the present rate of destruction it could all be gone in just 40 years.

Rates of forest clearance

No one knows exactly how much of the Amazon rainforest has been lost since clearances began in the early 1960s. Some estimates suggest that up to 40% may have been lost already. If this is accurate, it would mean that some 15 hectares have been cleared every minute. That is the same area as about 15 football pitches!

A   Why is Brazil's rainforest being cleared?

Subsistence farming has increased as the government has given free land to millions of settlers willing to move into the Amazon region. The settlers clear the forest to grow crops.

Cattle ranching. Large areas of the forest have been bought by transnational companies. They clear the forest to graze cattle for beef.

Hydro-electricity is an important renewable energy source. The building of dams and creation of lakes has led to the flooding of large areas of forest.

New roads have been built across the rainforest to develop the region and transport timber. The largest is the 5,300 km Trans-Amazonia highway.

Mining companies found rich deposits of iron ore, bauxite, gold, diamonds and other minerals in the forest. They have felled trees and built roads to reach these deposits.

Logging companies fell trees to sell to developed countries. Little attempt has been made to replant deforested areas.

Settlement. The population of Amazonia has increased by over 30 million in the last 40 years. Large areas of forest have been cleared so that new towns can be built to house these people.

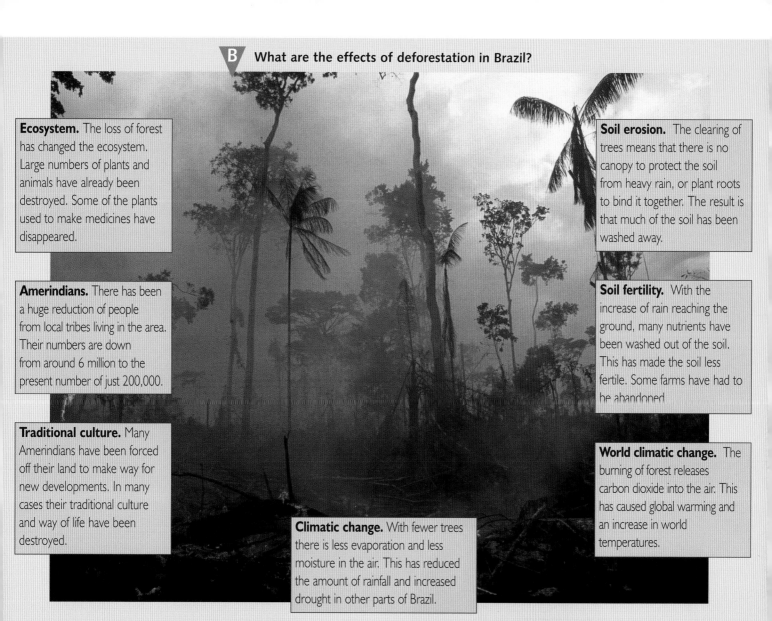

Ecosystem. The loss of forest has changed the ecosystem. Large numbers of plants and animals have already been destroyed. Some of the plants used to make medicines have disappeared.

Amerindians. There has been a huge reduction of people from local tribes living in the area. Their numbers are down from around 6 million to the present number of just 200,000.

Traditional culture. Many Amerindians have been forced off their land to make way for new developments. In many cases their traditional culture and way of life have been destroyed.

Climatic change. With fewer trees there is less evaporation and less moisture in the air. This has reduced the amount of rainfall and increased drought in other parts of Brazil.

Soil erosion. The clearing of trees means that there is no canopy to protect the soil from heavy rain, or plant roots to bind it together. The result is that much of the soil has been washed away.

Soil fertility. With the increase of rain reaching the ground, many nutrients have been washed out of the soil. This has made the soil less fertile. Some farms have had to be abandoned.

World climatic change. The burning of forest releases carbon dioxide into the air. This has caused global warming and an increase in world temperatures.

What can be done to save the forest?

The clearing of the forest would be tragic. Almost a million Indian people live in the forest, and their way of life would end. The forest ecosystem would also change, and the plants and animals living there could be destroyed and perhaps lost for ever. It could also damage our world in many other ways.

Drawing C shows a plan to protect an area of forest in Brazil. The area is divided into three sections, each with a particular use. The largest section is the core where access is severely restricted. Local people live in the buffer area.

This plan has the advantage of satisfying the needs of different users whilst at the same time protecting the forest from overdevelopment.

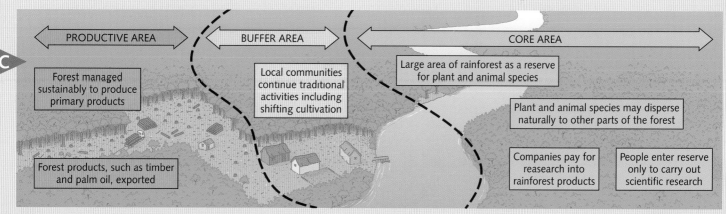

C

PRODUCTIVE AREA | BUFFER AREA | CORE AREA

Forest managed sustainably to produce primary products

Local communities continue traditional activities including shifting cultivation

Large area of rainforest as a reserve for plant and animal species

Plant and animal species may disperse naturally to other parts of the forest

Forest products, such as timber and palm oil, exported

Companies pay for research into rainforest products

People enter reserve only to carry out scientific research

REVISION QUESTIONS

1 (Page 186 and 187)
Write down the meaning of the following terms:
a) ecosystem   b) photosynthesis
c) nutrients   d) food chain.

2 (Pages 186 and 187)
Draw a diagram of a simple ecosystem to show the links between energy from the sun, climate, living creatures, soil and vegetation.

3 (Pages 186 and 187)
a) What is a food chain?
b) What is the difference between a herbivore and a carnivore?
c) What are decomposers?
d) Copy and complete this diagram of a simple food chain by adding two examples to each of the boxes:

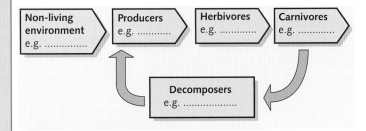

4 (Pages 186 and 187)
a) What is nutrient recycling?
b) Draw a simple diagram to show nutrient recycling in a British woodland.

5 (Pages 188 and 189)
Describe the main features of the Everglades by answering the questions below.

The Everglades – a wetland ecosystem under threat
- Where are the Everglades?
- What are they?
- What are the problems?
- What has been done to reduce these problems?

6 (Pages 170, 171, 190 and 191)
Tropical rainforests are found in places with an equatorial climate.
a) List the main features of an equatorial climate.
b) Name three places with this type of climate.
c) Describe the tropical rainforest by adding 10 facts to a copy of the drawing below.

d) Draw a simple diagram to show the nutrient cycle after clearance of tropical rainforest.

7 (Pages 172, 173 and 192)
a) Describe the Mediterranean climate.
b) Name five places with this type of climate.
c) Give three ways by which Mediterranean vegetation can survive the hot, dry summers.
d) Explain why little of the original Mediterranean vegetation survives today.

8 (Pages 174, 175 and 193)
a) Describe the hot desert climate.
b) Name six places with this type of climate.
c) Describe the hot desert vegetation by adding eight facts to a copy of this drawing:

Saguaro cactus   Other plants

9 (Pages 196 and 197)
a) What is deforestation?
b) Describe how the following cause deforestation:
 ■ farming   ■ hydro-electric schemes
 ■ mining.
c) How could logging be made less damaging?

EXAMINATION QUESTIONS

1

(Pages 186 and 187)

Look at diagram **A**.

a) Five of the following statements are true. Write them out.
- Rabbits eat heather.
- Aphids eat spiders.
- Kestrels eat rabbits.
- Kestrels are carnivores.
- All the birds and animals eat heather.
- The energy for the ecosystem comes from the sun.
- The heather is the producer of the system. **(5)**

b) Foxes eat sheep. If the farmer took all the sheep away, would the foxes starve? Explain your answer. **(3)**

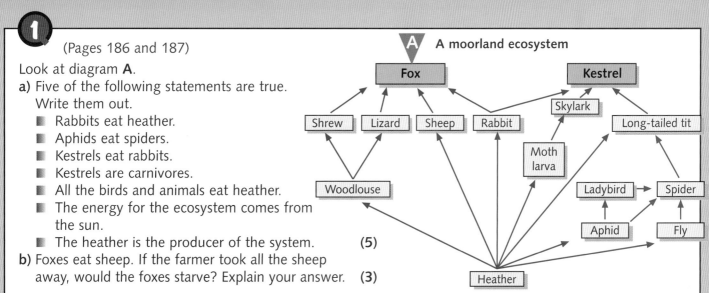

A A moorland ecosystem

2

(Pages 190 and 191)

Study diagram **B**.

a) Name the features at A, B, C, D, E and F. Choose from the following list.
- buttress root
- branchless trunk
- drip tip
- emergent
- shrub layer
- under-canopy. **(6)**

b) How tall are the tallest trees? **(1)**

c) Copy and complete the following sentences to show how the trees have adapted to conditions in the rainforest. **(3)**
- There are buttress roots because ....
- There are drip tips because ...
- New trees grow quickly upwards because ...

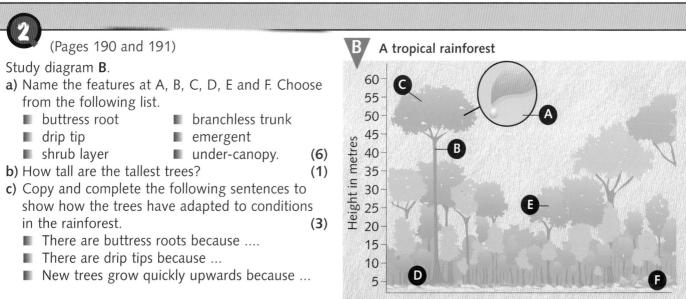

B A tropical rainforest

3

(Pages 196 and 197)

Look at drawing **C**.

a) Describe five changes that have taken place between 1950 and 1990. **(5)**

b) What effects might these changes to the Amazon rainforest have on:
- the local people? **(3)**
- the local environment? **(3)**
- the global environment? **(3)**

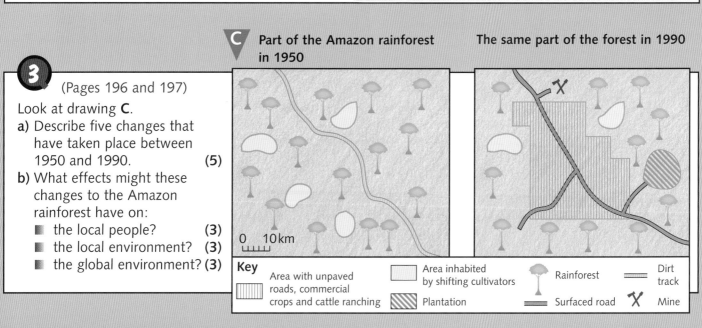

C Part of the Amazon rainforest in 1950

The same part of the forest in 1990

Key

Area with unpaved roads, commercial crops and cattle ranching

Area inhabited by shifting cultivators

Plantation

Rainforest

Surfaced road

Dirt track

Mine

ROCKS AND SOILS

Rock types

Although there are hundreds of different kinds of rock, we can group them all into three main types.

These are **igneous**, **sedimentary** and **metamorphic**. This simple classification is based on how each type of rock was formed.

A Granite

Igneous rocks result from volcanic activity. They consist of tiny crystals which formed as the volcanic rock cooled down.

Granite forms when magma cools down below ground level. Basalt forms when lava cools on the Earth's surface.

B Limestone

Sedimentary rocks are usually found in layers. They are made from small particles of other rocks, from the remains of plants and animals, or from chemicals that have built up in layers.

Sandstone is made from grains of sand. Limestone is made from shells and skeletons of sea creatures.

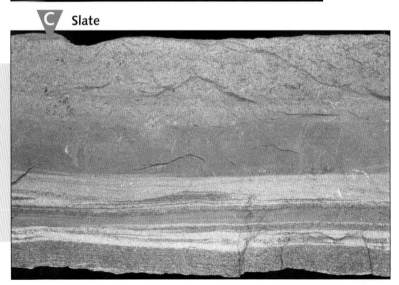

C Slate

Metamorphic rocks have been changed by great heat or pressure.

Marble is made when limestone is heated to great temperatures. Slate is made when soft mudstone is put under great pressure, perhaps in an earthquake.

Rock structure

Rocks are made of different materials and put together in different ways. This is called **rock structure**. The structure of a rock affects its resistance to erosion and permeability to water. Different landforms are produced in this way.

Resistance

Some rocks are more resistant to erosion than others. Hard rocks are difficult to wear away and break down. They are usually found as hills, mountains or coastal headlands. Soft rocks are less resistant to erosion and are easily worn away. Valleys and coastal bays are formed in softer rocks.

Permeability

Rocks are also affected in different ways by water. They can be **permeable**, **impermeable** or **porous**.

Because water soaks through them, permeable rocks often produce landscapes without any surface rivers or streams. Impermeable areas have many rivers and streams. They easily flood.

Use of rocks

Rocks have many uses. They affect farming and may be used for building, as a source of chemicals, and even as a fuel. Those rocks that are useful to us are usually extracted from the ground by quarrying or mining.

D Hard granite rock at Hound Tor, Dartmoor

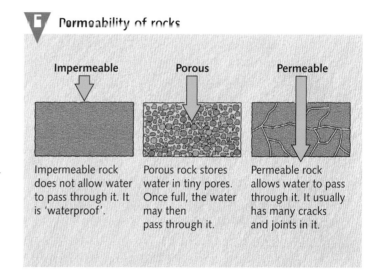

E Permeability of rocks

Impermeable	Porous	Permeable
Impermeable rock does not allow water to pass through it. It is 'waterproof'.	Porous rock stores water in tiny pores. Once full, the water may then pass through it.	Permeable rock allows water to pass through it. It usually has many cracks and joints in it.

F

Rock type	Description	Where it can be found	Landscape	Human use
Granite (igneous)	Very hard, sparkles, crystals visible	Scottish Highlands, Dartmoor	High mountains, steep cliffs, headlands	Buildings, roads, pottery
Limestone (sedimentary)	Shells and skeletons of marine life; coral	Yorkshire, Derbyshire	Limestone cliffs, caves	Buildings, cement, tourism (to caves)
Coal (sedimentary)	Fossilised remains of trees and plants	Northumberland, Durham, Midlands	Underground and opencast mining	Heating, electricity for homes, power stations, factories
Slate (metamorphic)	Hard, grey, splits into thin, flat sheets	Welsh mountains, Cumbria	High hills, many quarries	Roofing tiles, snooker tables

Weathering and mass movement

Weathering

Rocks are exposed to air, water, changing temperatures, plants and animals. All of these attack the rocks, causing them to break down and rot away. This process is known as **weathering**. There are three main types of weathering. These are **physical**, **chemical** and **biological**.

1 **Physical weathering**

   a) **Freeze–thaw** or **frost shattering**. This occurs when water gets into a crack in a rock and freezes. As the water turns to ice it expands and causes the crack to open up. Repeated freezing and thawing weakens the rock and eventually splits it into pieces.

   This type of weathering is most common in places where temperatures are around freezing point.

   b) **Exfoliation** or **onion-skin weathering.** This occurs in very warm climates where rock is repeatedly heated and cooled. As it is heated during the day, the outer layers of the rock expand. When it cools at night, the layers then contract. This puts a strain on the rock, and its surface layers peel off like the skin of an onion.

2 **Chemical weathering.** This is caused by the action of water. Ordinary rainwater is slightly acidic. When it comes into contact with rock the acid attacks it and causes it to rot and crumble away. Water and heat make chemical weathering happen faster, so its effects are greatest in places that are warm and wet.

3 **Biological weathering** is when plants and animals help to break down rocks. The roots of plants and trees can get into cracks in a rock. As they grow, they put pressure on the rock, which can be enough to split it. Burrowing animals such as rabbits, moles and even earthworms can also help break down weaker rocks.

A Scree at Wasdale in the Lake District

Scree is weathered rock that collects at the foot of a cliff

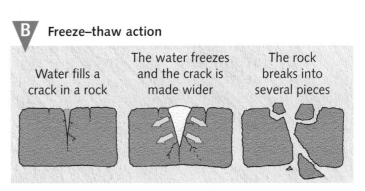

B Freeze–thaw action

Water fills a crack in a rock | The water freezes and the crack is made wider | The rock breaks into several pieces

C Sierra Nevada, California

Steep cliffs are created by freeze–thaw action. Rounded boulders are shaped by onion–skin weathering

Mass movement

Weathering leaves large amounts of loose material on the Earth's surface. On sloping ground, this material, which includes soil, stones and larger pieces of rock, is slowly moved down the slope under the force of gravity. The downhill movement of weathered material is called **mass movement**.

The speed of downward movement can vary considerably. With soil creep, the movement is barely noticeable. In the case of landslides, mudflows and avalanches, however, movement can be very rapid indeed.

Soil creep. This is the slowest and most common way in which material moves down a slope. It occurs on very gentle and well-vegetated slopes, and movement may be less than 1 cm a year.

Despite the very slow pace, the whole surface of a slope is on the move. Over a long period of time, very large amounts of material can change position. Diagram **E** shows some of the effects of soil creep.

Landslides. These take place when large quantities of loosened rock and soil suddenly slip down a steep slope. The movement is very rapid and often occur with little warning. There are many reasons for landslides. For example:

- Heavy rain can make soil heavier and cause it to move downhill.
- A river may undercut the bottom of a slope, causing it to collapse.
- Earthquakes or volcanic eruptions shake the ground and can loosen material.

Mudflows. These often occur on slopes with little or no vegetation. Heavy rainfall is easily soaked up by the bare soil. This makes the soil heavier and at the same time lubricates it. Eventually, gravity causes the mud to flow rapidly downhill rather like thick porridge.

D Terracettes in the Yorkshire Dales

E The effects of soil creep

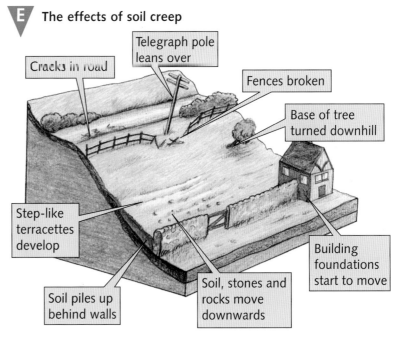

Telegraph pole leans over

Cracks in road

Fences broken

Base of tree turned downhill

Step-like terracettes develop

Building foundations start to move

Soil piles up behind walls

Soil, stones and rocks move downwards

F A mudflow near Armero, Colombia

Limestone

Limestone is a rock consisting mainly of calcium carbonate. Calcium carbonate comes from the remains of sea shells and coral. This means that limestone was formed on the sea bed. There are several types of limestone each producing its own type of scenery.

Carboniferous limestone

Carboniferous limestone produces a special type of scenery called **karst**. There are three main reasons for this distinctive type of landform. These are structure, permeability and chemical weathering.

Structure. Limestone is a sedimentary rock, which means it was laid down in layers. Each layer is separated by a bedding plane. At right-angles to bedding planes are joints. Bedding planes and joints are areas of weakness.

Permeability. Carboniferous limestone is a permeable rock. It allows water to flow along the bedding planes and down the joints.

Chemical weathering. Rainwater contains weak carbonic acid and reacts with the calcium carbonate in limestone. The limestone is slowly dissolved and is removed in solution by running water.

Chemical weathering is very active in limestone areas. It attacks the rock surface as well as the bedding planes and joints.

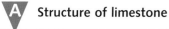
A Structure of limestone

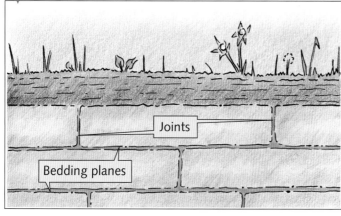

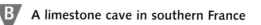
B A limestone cave in southern France

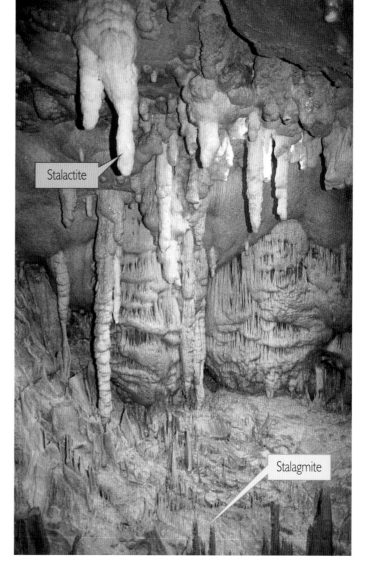

Stalactite

Stalagmite

C Limestone pavement, Malham

Clint

Gryke

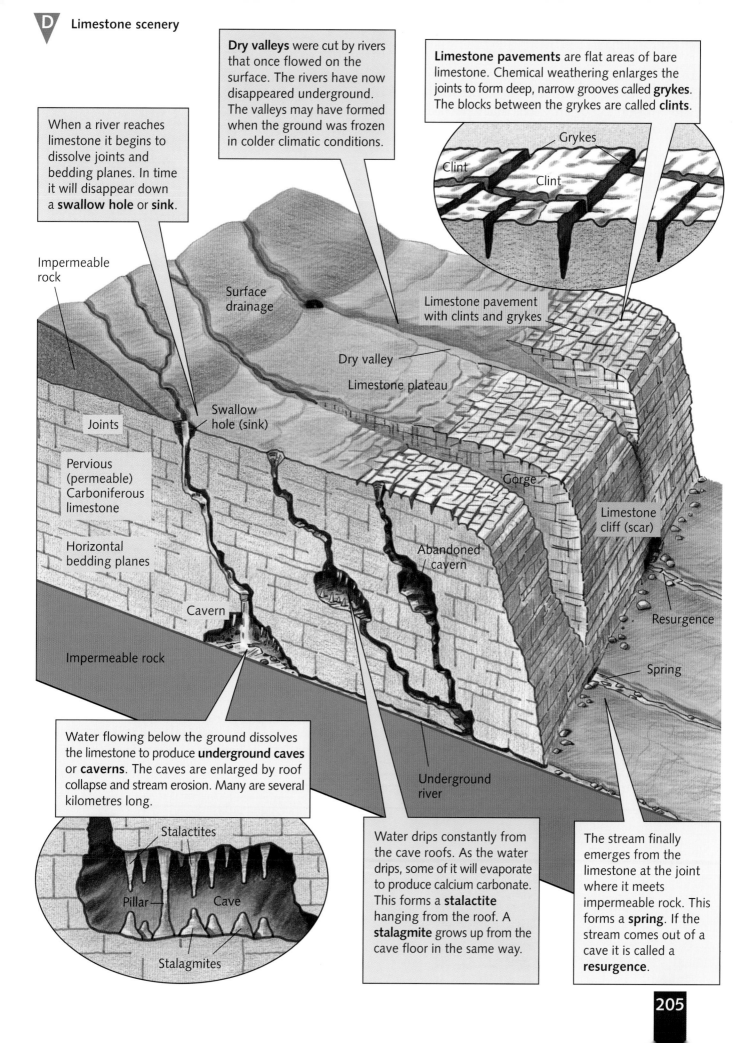

Dry valleys were cut by rivers that once flowed on the surface. The rivers have now disappeared underground. The valleys may have formed when the ground was frozen in colder climatic conditions.

Limestone pavements are flat areas of bare limestone. Chemical weathering enlarges the joints to form deep, narrow grooves called **grykes**. The blocks between the grykes are called **clints**.

Grykes

Clint

Clint

When a river reaches limestone it begins to dissolve joints and bedding planes. In time it will disappear down a **swallow hole** or **sink**.

Impermeable rock

Surface drainage

Limestone pavement with clints and grykes

Dry valley

Limestone plateau

Joints

Swallow hole (sink)

Pervious (permeable) Carboniferous limestone

Gorge

Limestone cliff (scar)

Horizontal bedding planes

Abandoned cavern

Cavern

Impermeable rock

Resurgence

Spring

Water flowing below the ground dissolves the limestone to produce **underground caves** or **caverns**. The caves are enlarged by roof collapse and stream erosion. Many are several kilometres long.

Underground river

Stalactites

Pillar

Cave

Stalagmites

Water drips constantly from the cave roofs. As the water drips, some of it will evaporate to produce calcium carbonate. This forms a **stalactite** hanging from the roof. A **stalagmite** grows up from the cave floor in the same way.

The stream finally emerges from the limestone at the joint where it meets impermeable rock. This forms a **spring**. If the stream comes out of a cave it is called a **resurgence**.

Soil erosion

Soil erosion is a serious problem. Each year, some 75 million tonnes are lost around the world. In just a few years, erosion can destroy soils that have taken thousands of years to develop.

Erosion is greatest on steep slopes and when the soil is bare. It is least when there is a thick cover of vegetation. This is because plants and trees provide shelter from rain and wind, and their root systems hold together the soil particles, making them difficult to remove.

Soil erosion is a natural process, but in some places it has been increased by poor land management and bad farming methods. The four main causes of soil erosion are shown in diagram **A** below.

> Soil erosion is the wearing away and loss of topsoil, mainly due to wind, rain and running water.

> Deforestation is the complete clearance of forested land.

Overcultivation is when crops are grown on the same piece of land year after year. Eventually the soil loses its goodness and crops can no longer grow. This leaves bare soil which is quickly removed by the action of wind and rain.

Overgrazing is when there are too many animals for the amount of food available. The animals eat all the vegetation and it dies off. This leaves the ground bare and unprotected. Wind and rain can then carry off the loose soil.

Some causes of soil erosion

Removal of vegetation causes most soil erosion, with **deforestation** the main problem. Once the vegetation or trees have gone, there is nothing to protect the land from rainfall, and no roots to hold the soil in place. This makes it easy for the soil to be washed or blown away.

Wrong ploughing. Farmers find it easier to plough up and down a slope rather than across it. When it rains, water flows straight down the furrows and washes away the soil. Fields may also be ploughed in winter, which leaves the land bare and exposed to winter winds.

Soil management

Soil is one of our most important resources. We depend on it for most of the food that we eat, and without it we would be unable to survive. Soil is a **sustainable resource** that can be used over and over again – as long as the land is managed carefully.

There are two main ways of looking after soil:

- The first is to keep the soil fertile by replacing **nutrients** and **organic matter** which crops take out.
- The second is to protect the soil from being exposed to rain and wind. This can be done by retaining vegetation at all times, and planting bushes and trees to act as wind breaks.

Some methods of preventing, or at least limiting, soil erosion, are shown in diagram **C** below.

B Contour ploughing

C Some ways to reduce soil erosion

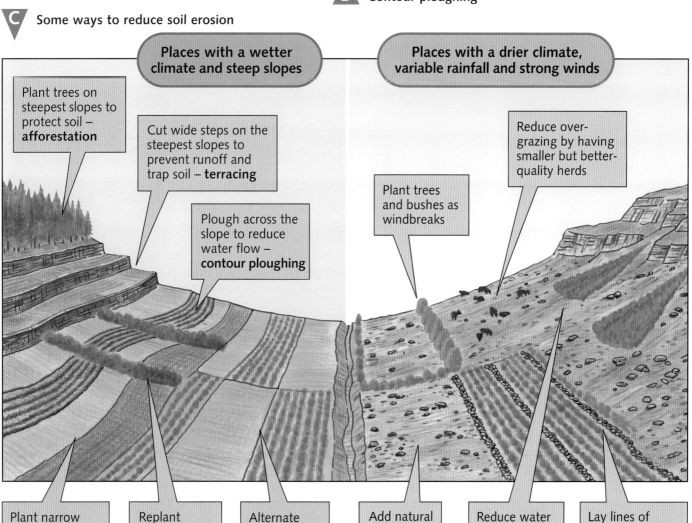

Places with a wetter climate and steep slopes

Places with a drier climate, variable rainfall and strong winds

Plant trees on steepest slopes to protect soil – **afforestation**

Cut wide steps on the steepest slopes to prevent runoff and trap soil – **terracing**

Plough across the slope to reduce water flow – **contour ploughing**

Plant trees and bushes as windbreaks

Reduce over-grazing by having smaller but better-quality herds

Plant narrow strips of different crops to retain nutrients

Replant hedgerows to reduce wind damage

Alternate crops with grass to keep soil fertile

Add natural manure to replace nutrients

Reduce water flow by filling in gullies and replanting

Lay lines of stones to reduce water runoff and trap soil

Desertification is the gradual change of land into desert.

Desertification in the Sahel

Over 900 million people are affected by **desertification**. They live in countries that are amongst the poorest in the world.

In these countries people have to rely on the land for their food, income and employment. Traditionally, they were subsistence farmers and nomadic herders who could produce just about enough food for their own needs.

With the spread of desert conditions to their land, this has become increasingly difficult.

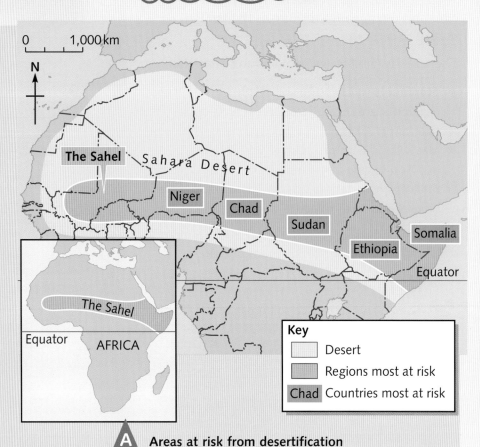

The Sahel · Sahara Desert · Niger · Chad · Sudan · Somalia · Ethiopia · Equator

The Sahel · Equator · AFRICA

Key
- Desert
- Regions most at risk
- Chad Countries most at risk

A Areas at risk from desertification

The Sahel

The effects of desertification are greatest in the Sahel. The Sahel is a belt of land to the south of the Sahara where the desert is advancing in places by up to 6 km every year.

The climate here has become much drier. In some years there is no rain at all. In others, the total rainfall may come in several downpours, when the water is immediately lost through surface runoff. Each year of dry weather means less grazing land, fewer crops and less food.

Unfortunately the countries of the Sahel have some of the highest population growth rates in the world. This makes the problem even greater.

B Rainfall in the Sahel, 1945–2003

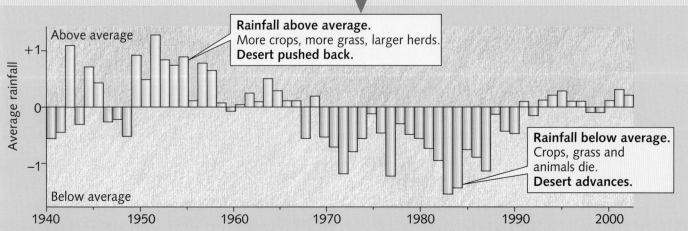

Rainfall above average.
More crops, more grass, larger herds.
Desert pushed back.

Rainfall below average.
Crops, grass and animals die.
Desert advances.

Above average
Average rainfall
+1
0
−1
Below average
1940 1950 1960 1970 1980 1990 2000

Causes of desertification

The causes of the problem are complex and far from clear. Most people agree, however, that climatic change, overgrazing and population growth are the main causes.

Climatic change

There is some evidence of a change towards a drier climate in the Sahel. Graph **B** shows that average rainfall has decreased since the mid-1960s. One suggestion is that global warming has caused temperatures to rise. This in turn has resulted in less rainfall.

Overgrazing

Changes in farming may also have helped cause desertification. Animal grazing increased by up to 40% in the wetter years of the 1950s. When the drought began in the 1960s, there were just too many animals for the grass available. All vegetation was quickly stripped off and the land turned to desert.

Population growth

The population of most Sahel countries has increased rapidly since 1950. Farmers have had to produce more food, and the land has become exhausted and infertile. There has also been a greater need for wood for cooking and building. This has led to deforestation, and has further increased desertification.

The results of desertification

Desertification has led to a loss of vegetation cover in the Sahel. This has exposed the soil to the wind and the occasional heavy downpour. Soil erosion has become a serious problem in the region.

The people are also badly affected. Drought and food shortages have led to famine and starvation. Many people have had to move away from their homelands, and their traditional way of life has been lost.

The Sahel's fragile environment requires very careful management if it is to be farmed successfully and soil erosion reduced.

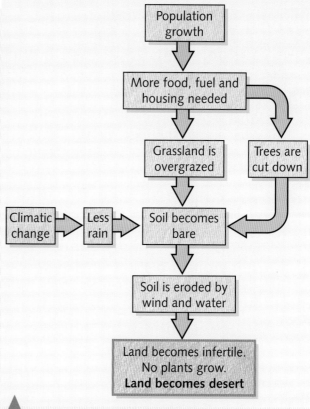

 The process of desertification

D The effects of drought on people

209

1 (Pages 200 and 201)
a) What are the three main types of rock?
b) What are igneous rocks formed from?
c) What is the difference between granite and basalt?

2 (Pages 200 and 201)
a) What are sedimentary rocks formed from?
b) What is the difference between sandstone and limestone?
c) How are metamorphic rocks formed?
d) Name two metamorphic rocks. What were they originally?

3 (Pages 200 and 201)
Draw labelled diagrams to show the differences between impermeable, permeable and porous rocks.

4 (Pages 204 and 205)
a) What evidence is there to suggest that limestone was formed on the sea bed?
b) What name is given to limestone scenery?
c) What is chemical weathering?

5 (Pages 204 and 205)
Look at the drawing below, which shows an area of limestone scenery.
a) What are clints and grykes?
b) What are stalactites and stalagmites?
c) What is a swallow hole and a resurgence?
d) How do dry valleys form?

6 (Page 202)
a) What is weathering?
b) Describe two types of physical weathering.
c) When does chemical weathering happen most?
d) Show how root action can break up rocks by putting the following in the correct order.

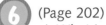

- Roots develop
- Crack gives moisture and shelter
- Seeds blow into crack
- Tree grows
- Roots break up soil

7 (Page 203)
a) What is mass movement?
b) Give three causes of landslides.
c) How do mudflows happen?
d) Name the six effects of soil creep shown below:

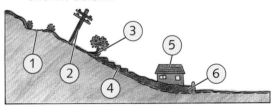

8 (Pages 206 and 207)
Write down the meaning of the following terms:
a) soil erosion
b) overcultivation
c) overgrazing
d) deforestation.

9 (Pages 206 and 207)
Explain how each of the following may help reduce soil erosion:
a) contour planning
b) nutrient replacement
c) terracing
d) tree and hedgerow planting.

10 (Pages 208 and 209)
a) What is desertification?
b) Describe three possible causes of desertification.

11 (Pages 208 and 209)
a) Where is the Sahel?
b) Name six Sahel countries.
c) When did the Sahel become drier?
d) Give two problems caused by desertification in the Sahel.

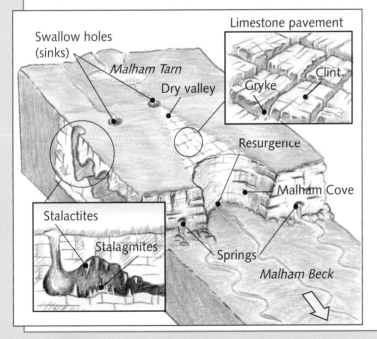

Swallow holes (sinks)

Malham Tarn

Dry valley

Limestone pavement

Clint

Gryke

Resurgence

Malham Cove

Stalactites

Stalagmites

Springs

Malham Beck

EXAMINATION QUESTIONS

1

(Pages 204 and 205)

Look at diagram **A**.

a) Name the features at A, B, C, D and E on the diagram. Choose from the following list:
- stalagmite
- stalactite
- swallow hole
- resurgence
- underground cave. (5)

b) The feature at **X** is a limestone pavement. Describe the feature and explain how it formed. (2)

c) Name a place in Britain where limestone pavement may be found. (1)

A

2

(Pages 206 and 207)

a) What is soil erosion? (1)

b) What is deforestation? (1)

c) Use diagram **B** to explain how forested areas can reduce soil erosion. (3)

d) Use diagram **C** to explain why soil is eroded by wind and rain when forested areas are cleared. (3)

e) Explain how overgrazing and overcultivation can cause soil erosion. (2)

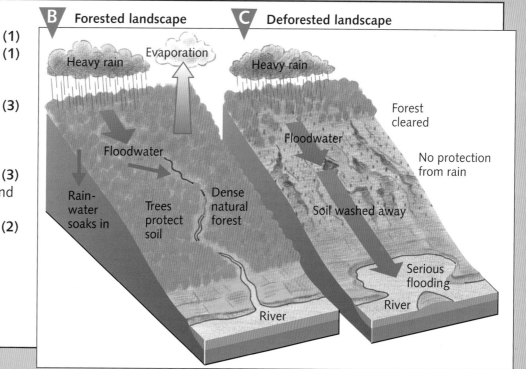

B **Forested landscape**

C **Deforested landscape**

3

(Pages 208 and 209)

a) Look at diagram **D**. Match each of the following statements with a letter from the diagram:
- More land needed for crops
- Rivers and water holes dry up
- Soil exposed to rain and wind
- Overgrazing
- Less rainfall
- Vegetation dies. (6)

b) What is desertification? (1)

c) Describe three effects of desertification. (3)

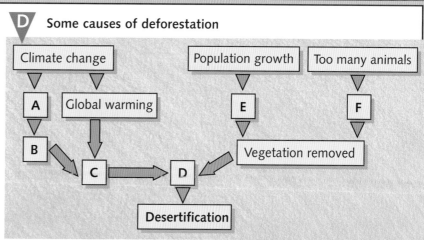

D **Some causes of deforestation**

211

16

PLATE TECTONICS

Earthquakes and volcanic eruptions are caused by movements within the Earth. They happen all the time, and scientists continuously record and measure them. We only hear about the ones that cause most damage, but in 1997 over 820 strong earthquakes and 320 different volcanic eruptions were recorded.

Earth movements cannot yet be predicted but scientists now know which parts of the world are most likely to be affected. However, they are unable to say when the movement will occur or how strong it will be.

Earthquakes

Earthquakes can occur anywhere, but they are more common in some places than others. Map **A** shows where earthquakes are strongest and most frequent. Notice that they tend to occur in long narrow belts. These belts include those that:

- circle the whole of the Pacific Ocean
- extend down the middle of the Atlantic Ocean
- stretch across Europe and Asia between the Atlantic and Pacific Oceans.

A Earthquake activity

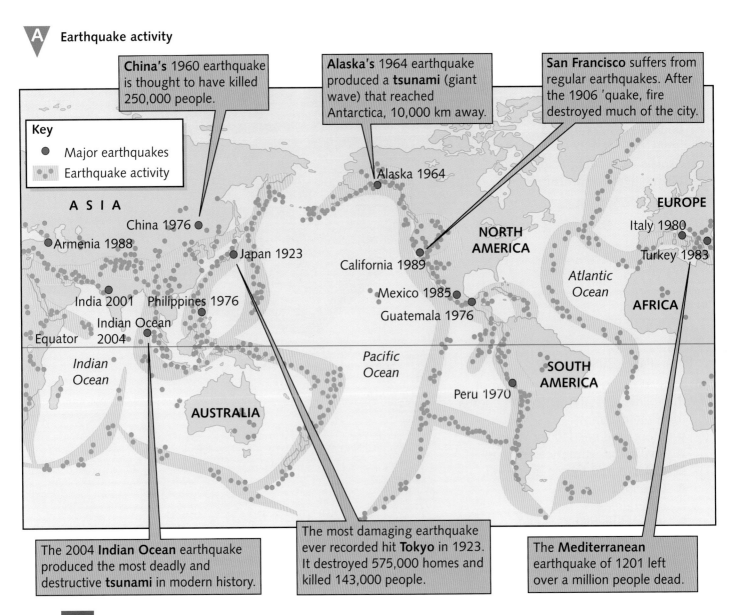

China's 1960 earthquake is thought to have killed 250,000 people.

Alaska's 1964 earthquake produced a **tsunami** (giant wave) that reached Antarctica, 10,000 km away.

San Francisco suffers from regular earthquakes. After the 1906 'quake, fire destroyed much of the city.

Key
- Major earthquakes
- Earthquake activity

ASIA

China 1976
Armenia 1988
Japan 1923
India 2001   Philippines 1976
Indian Ocean
Equator   2004
Indian Ocean

AUSTRALIA

Alaska 1964

California 1989
Mexico 1985
Guatemala 1976

Pacific Ocean

Peru 1970

NORTH AMERICA

SOUTH AMERICA

EUROPE
Italy 1980
Turkey 1983
Atlantic Ocean
AFRICA

The 2004 **Indian Ocean** earthquake produced the most deadly and destructive **tsunami** in modern history.

The most damaging earthquake ever recorded hit **Tokyo** in 1923. It destroyed 575,000 homes and killed 143,000 people.

The **Mediterranean** earthquake of 1201 left over a million people dead.

Volcanoes

Scientists now know a lot about volcanoes, but they still find it difficult to predict exactly where and when an eruption will actually happen. What we do know, however, is that volcanic eruptions do not occur just anywhere on the Earth's surface, but are confined to certain areas.

Map **B** shows the major centres of volcanic activity and some of the most recent eruptions. The map also shows that volcanoes occur in long narrow belts. These belts include:

- the so-called 'Ring of Fire' which circles the whole of the Pacific Ocean
- the one that extends down the entire length of the Atlantic Ocean
- smaller areas in southern Europe, the Caribbean, East Africa and the mid-Pacific Ocean.

Notice that both maps **A** and **B** are centred on the Pacific Ocean. This makes it easier to identify the belts of activity, particularly the Ring of Fire.

Look carefully at map **A** showing earthquakes and map **B** showing volcanic activity. Can you see how similar they are? From studying maps like these, scientists have concluded that earthquakes and volcanoes often occur in the same places and in long narrow belts. These narrow belts are called **zones of activity** – they can be the most dangerous areas on Earth.

B ▽ Volcanic activity

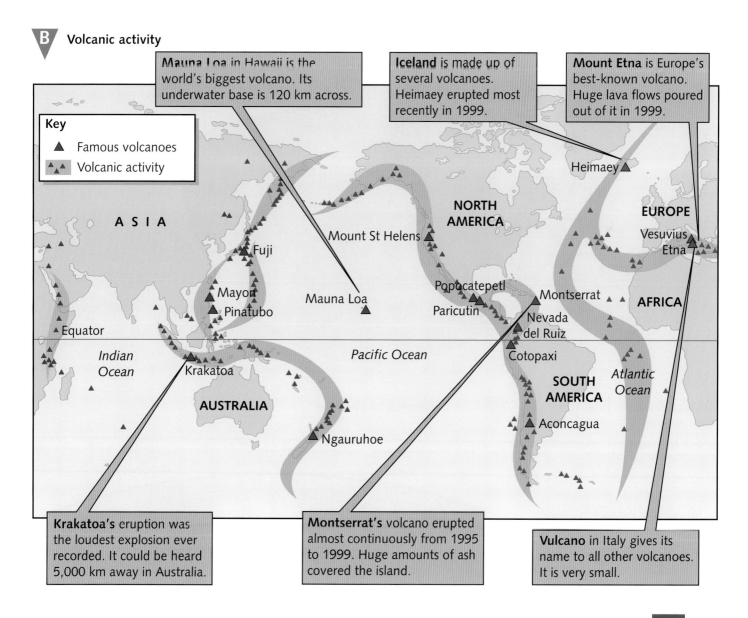

Mauna Loa in Hawaii is the world's biggest volcano. Its underwater base is 120 km across.

Iceland is made up of several volcanoes. Heimaey erupted most recently in 1999.

Mount Etna is Europe's best-known volcano. Huge lava flows poured out of it in 1999.

Key
- ▲ Famous volcanoes
- ▲▲ Volcanic activity

Krakatoa's eruption was the loudest explosion ever recorded. It could be heard 5,000 km away in Australia.

Montserrat's volcano erupted almost continuously from 1995 to 1999. Huge amounts of ash covered the island.

Vulcano in Italy gives its name to all other volcanoes. It is very small.

Plate tectonics

We now know that earthquakes and volcanic activity often occur in the same places. They are usually found in long narrow belts called **zones of activity**. So why does this happen?

The Earth was formed some 4,600 million years ago. Since then it has been slowly cooling down, and a thin, hard **crust** has formed around the outside. This crust is not in one piece but has been broken into several enormous sections called **plates**. Some of the plates are as large as continents while others are much smaller.

Underneath the crust is the **mantle**. The mantle is so hot it remains molten and flows like treacle. The plates float on this layer and move about very slowly – perhaps just a few centimetres a year.

The place where two plates meet is called a **plate boundary**. Most earthquakes and volcanoes happen here.

The Earth is rather like an enormous apple. It has a thin, tough skin called the **crust**, a softer inside called the **mantle**, and a centre part called the **core**.

A Inside the Earth

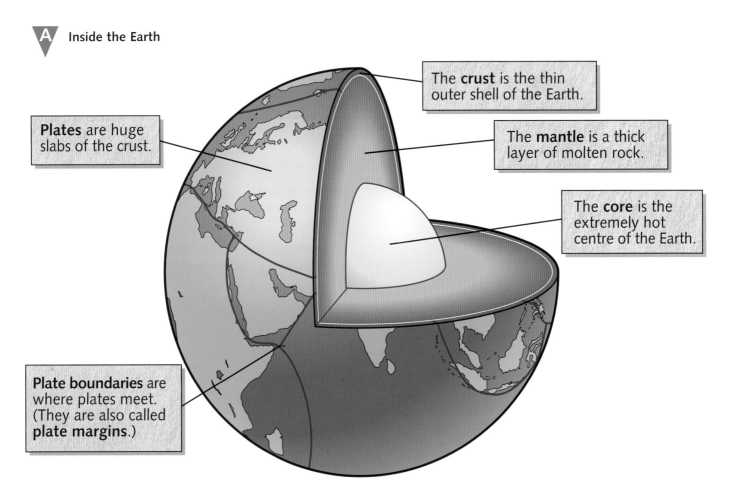

Plates are huge slabs of the crust.

The **crust** is the thin outer shell of the Earth.

The **mantle** is a thick layer of molten rock.

The **core** is the extremely hot centre of the Earth.

Plate boundaries are where plates meet. (They are also called **plate margins**.)

Diagram **B** shows how the plates are made to move. Notice that in some places the plates move towards each other, and in others they move apart. Sometimes the plates just scrape slowly past each other.

B The movement of plates

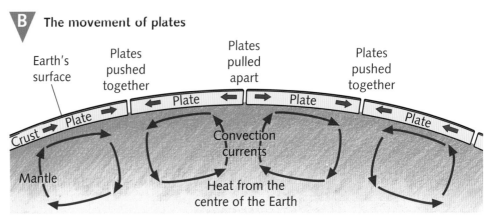

Earth's surface

Plates pushed together

Plates pulled apart

Plates pushed together

Crust → Plate →

← Plate ←

→ Plate →

Plate ←

Convection currents

Heat from the centre of the Earth

Mantle

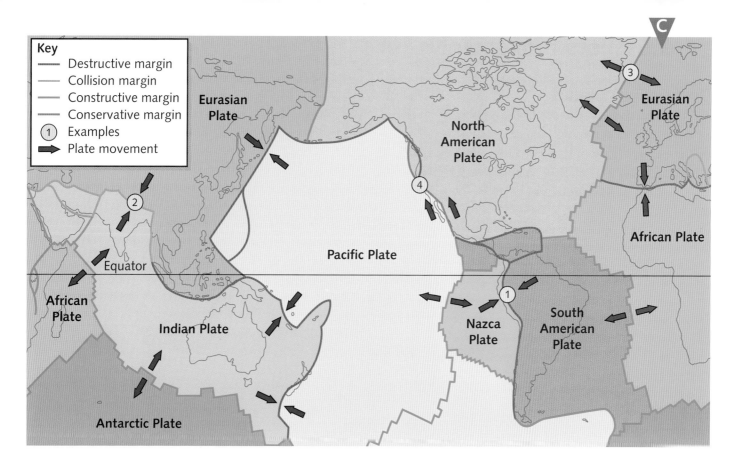

Key
— Destructive margin
— Collision margin
— Constructive margin
— Conservative margin
① Examples
➜ Plate movement

Eurasian Plate

North American Plate

Eurasian Plate

African Plate

Equator

African Plate

Pacific Plate

Indian Plate

Nazca Plate

South American Plate

Antarctic Plate

Map **C** show the major plates and their boundaries or margins. It also shows where the plates come together, move apart, or scrape alongside each other.

There are four different types of plate boundary. These are **destructive**, **collision**, **constructive** or **conservative**. Earthquakes occur at all four types of boundary. Volcanic eruptions tend to occur only at destructive and constructive margins.

Plates consist of two types of crust. These are **continental** and **oceanic**.

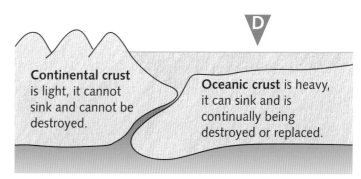

Continental crust is light, it cannot sink and cannot be destroyed.

Oceanic crust is heavy, it can sink and is continually being destroyed or replaced.

Type of plate boundary	Description	Features	Example
① Destructive	Two plates move towards each other. One is oceanic, the other is continental.	Violent volcanic and earthquake activity.	South America, e.g. Peru
② Collision	Two plates move towards each other. Both are continental.	Earthquake activity. No volcanic activity.	Northern India, e.g. Himalayas
③ Constructive	Two plates move away from each other.	Gentle volcanic and earthquake activity.	Mid-Atlantic Ridge, e.g. Iceland
④ Conservative	Two plates move sideways past each other.	Can be violent earthquakes. No volcanic activity.	North America, e.g. San Francisco

Types of plate movement

Destructive margins

- A **destructive margin** is a boundary between two plates that are moving towards each other.
- One plate slides underneath the other and is destroyed in the mantle. Where this happens is called the **subduction zone**.

Most of the Pacific Ocean is surrounded by destructive plate margins. Violent earthquakes and volcanic eruptions are common here. One of the worst-affected areas is off the west coast of South America. This example is shown in diagram **A**.

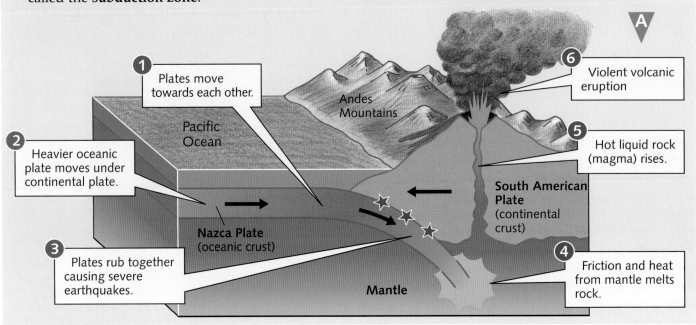

A

① Plates move towards each other.

② Heavier oceanic plate moves under continental plate.

③ Plates rub together causing severe earthquakes.

④ Friction and heat from mantle melts rock.

⑤ Hot liquid rock (magma) rises.

⑥ Violent volcanic eruption

Andes Mountains

Pacific Ocean

Nazca Plate (oceanic crust)

South American Plate (continental crust)

Mantle

Collision margins

- A **collision margin** is a type of destructive margin.
- In the collision margin the two plates moving towards each other are both continental crust.

The Himalayan mountains in northern India are located on a collision margin. Here, the rock has been pushed up in great folds to form the highest mountains in the world. Evidence suggests that Mount Everest is still increasing in height as plate movement continues.

The area also suffers from violent earthquakes. In 1993, 10,000 people died and a further 150,000 were left homeless when an earthquake hit central India.

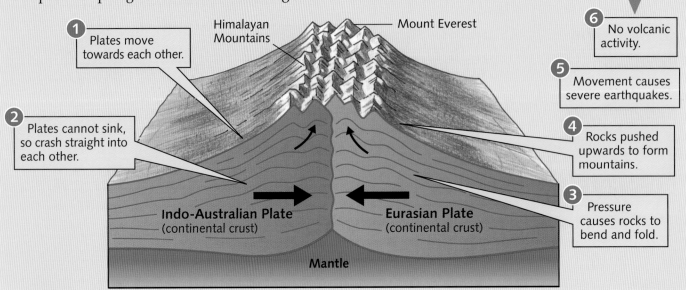

B

① Plates move towards each other.

② Plates cannot sink, so crash straight into each other.

③ Pressure causes rocks to bend and fold.

④ Rocks pushed upwards to form mountains.

⑤ Movement causes severe earthquakes.

⑥ No volcanic activity.

Himalayan Mountains

Mount Everest

Indo-Australian Plate (continental crust)

Eurasian Plate (continental crust)

Mantle

Constructive margins

- A **constructive margin** is a boundary between two plates that are moving apart.
- New crust is formed at this margin.

The best example of a constructive margin is the Mid-Atlantic Ridge. The Atlantic Ocean is widening by 3 cm a year, which means that the Americas are moving away from Europe and Africa. This movement has caused a long ridge of mountains to form under the ocean. The tops of some of these mountains break the surface to form islands such as Iceland and the Azores.

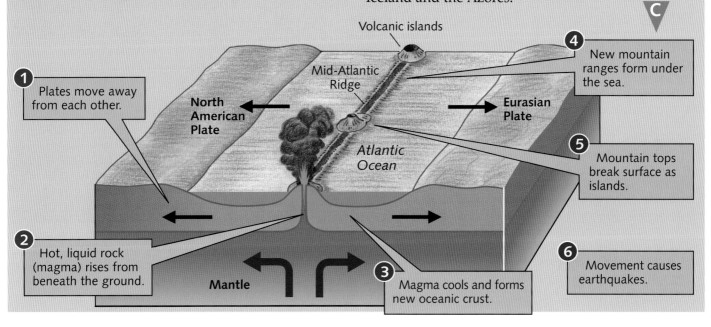

C

Volcanic islands

Mid-Atlantic Ridge

North American Plate

Eurasian Plate

Atlantic Ocean

Mantle

1 Plates move away from each other.

2 Hot, liquid rock (magma) rises from beneath the ground.

3 Magma cools and forms new oceanic crust.

4 New mountain ranges form under the sea.

5 Mountain tops break surface as islands.

6 Movement causes earthquakes.

Conservative margins

- A **conservative margin** is a boundary between two plates that are sliding past each other.
- No new crust is being formed.

The best example of a conservative plate boundary may be found in California. Here two plates meet and scrape alongside each other at the famous San Andreas Fault. Over 40,000 earth tremors are recorded in California every year. In 1906 one of the most powerful earthquakes of the century hit San Francisco. It caused 52 fires, destroyed 28,000 buildings and killed nearly 1,000 people.

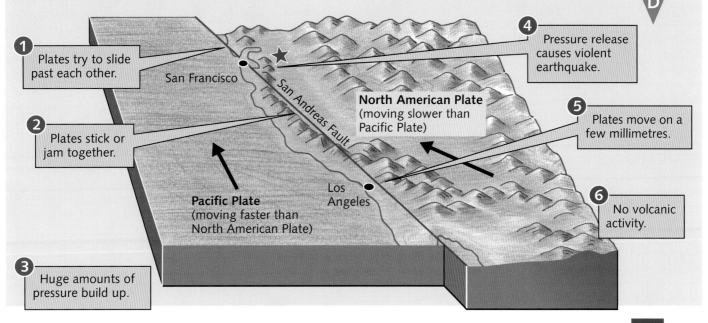

D

San Francisco

San Andreas Fault

North American Plate (moving slower than Pacific Plate)

Pacific Plate (moving faster than North American Plate)

Los Angeles

1 Plates try to slide past each other.

2 Plates stick or jam together.

3 Huge amounts of pressure build up.

4 Pressure release causes violent earthquake.

5 Plates move on a few millimetres.

6 No volcanic activity.

Causes and effects of a volcanic eruption: Mount St Helens, USA

What happened

Mount St Helens is located close to Seattle in the state of Washington, USA. It is one of several volcanoes in the Cascades mountains, and had last erupted in 1857.

In May 1980 the volcano erupted again, with devastating force. Scientists had been predicting the eruption for some time and were well prepared. Even so, the fury of the eruption took the scientists by surprise.

For several months the volcano had steamed and smoked. In early May a huge bulge built up on its north side. Eventually the volcano exploded and a deadly cloud of hot ash, dust and rock was blasted into the air, destroying everything before it. The shape of the mountain changed completely.

Causes of the eruption

Mount St Helens is located on a destructive plate margin where there are many volcanoes. The eruption was particularly violent because pressure built up in the volcano for a long period of time. When it finally exploded it did so with immense force.

A The Mount St Helens ashcloud

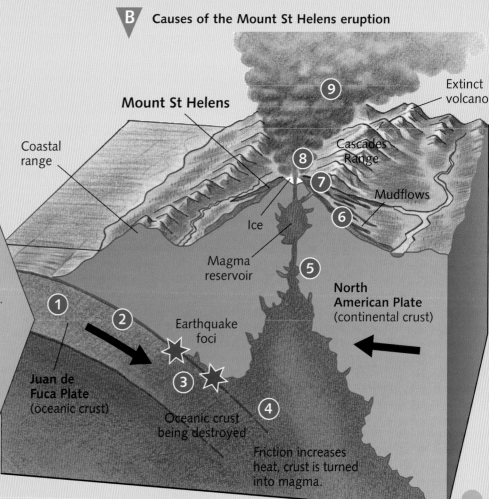

B Causes of the Mount St Helens eruption

1. Juan de Fuca Plate moves towards the North American Plate.
2. Juan de Fuca Plate forced down as it is oceanic crust.
3. Friction produces earthquakes.
4. Friction and heat from mantle melts rock.
5. Hot liquid rock rises.
6. Huge bulge appears on mountain side.
7. Earthquake triggers violent eruption.
8. Top and side of mountain removed by explosion.
9. Rock, dust and gas blasted out at 120 km per hour.

Effects of the eruption

The 1980 eruption changed the environment and affected the lives of many people over a wide area. The main problem was the enormous ash cloud which billowed north-eastwards. It turned day into night, and covered vast areas with ash. The ash crossed the USA in three days and travelled right around the world in just 17 days.

C Effects of the Mount St Helens eruption

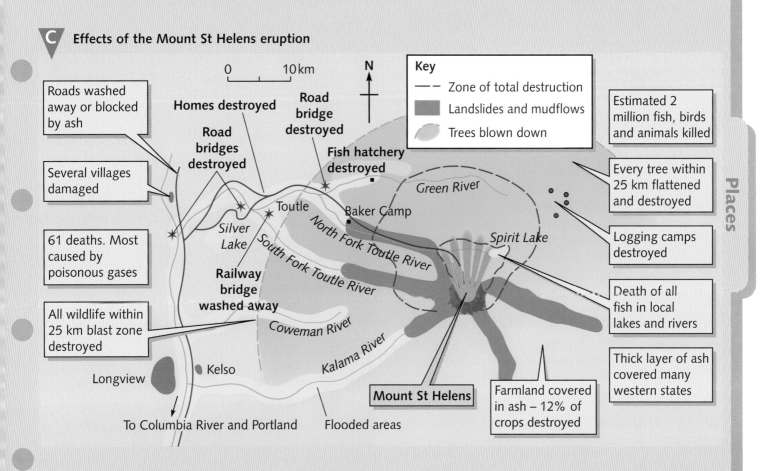

0   10km

N

Key
- – – Zone of total destruction
- Landslides and mudflows
- Trees blown down

Roads washed away or blocked by ash

Several villages damaged

61 deaths. Most caused by poisonous gases

All wildlife within 25 km blast zone destroyed

Homes destroyed

Road bridges destroyed

Road bridge destroyed

Fish hatchery destroyed

Green River

Toutle

Baker Camp

Silver Lake

North Fork Toutle River

South Fork Toutle River

Railway bridge washed away

Spirit Lake

Coweman River

Kalama River

Longview

Kelso

Mount St Helens

To Columbia River and Portland

Flooded areas

Farmland covered in ash – 12% of crops destroyed

Estimated 2 million fish, birds and animals killed

Every tree within 25 km flattened and destroyed

Logging camps destroyed

Death of all fish in local lakes and rivers

Thick layer of ash covered many western states

D Destruction of forest by the Mount St Helens eruption

Kobe, Japan

Causes and effects of an earthquake in an MEDC

Measuring an earthquake

The strength of an earthquake is usually measured on the **Richter scale**. Each level on the scale is 10 times greater than the level below it. This means that an earthquake with a score of 8 is 10 times more powerful than one with a score of 7.

The most powerful earthquake officially recorded struck Chile in 1960. It measured 9.5 on the Richter scale. The Indian Ocean earthquake of 2004 measured 9.0 and produced the world's biggest **tsunami** in recorded history

What happened

Kobe is a large city located on the west coast of Japan. At 5.46 a.m. on 17 January 1995, an earthquake measuring 7.2 on the Richter scale shook the city.

By Japanese standards, the earthquake was not large, yet the damage was enormous. Buildings were destroyed, elevated roads collapsed and gas and water supplies were damaged.

More than 5,000 people were killed, but the death toll would probably have been much higher if the earthquake had struck during the daytime. Most people died in the fire storms that swept through the city in the 24 hours after the earthquake.

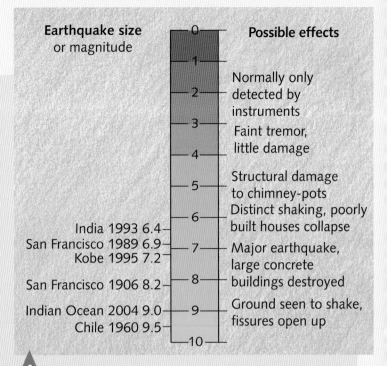

Earthquake size or magnitude		Possible effects
	0	
	1	
	2	Normally only detected by instruments
	3	Faint tremor, little damage
	4	
	5	Structural damage to chimney-pots
	6	Distinct shaking, poorly built houses collapse
India 1993 6.4		
San Francisco 1989 6.9	7	Major earthquake, large concrete buildings destroyed
Kobe 1995 7.2		
San Francisco 1906 8.2	8	
Indian Ocean 2004 9.0	9	Ground seen to shake, fissures open up
Chile 1960 9.5		
	10	

A The Richter scale

B Earthquake damage: collapse of a motorway

Causes of the earthquake

Japan is located on a destructive plate margin. The country has many volcanoes and is constantly affected by earthquakes. Of the 10,000 major earthquakes in the world each year, over 1,000 occur in Japan.

The Kobe earthquake was caused by the Philippines Plate being forced downwards and below the Eurasian Plate. Plates are not pushed downwards easily or smoothly. The pushing down often needs considerable force. This force comes from a build-up of pressure. If this pressure is released suddenly, then the plate may jerk forwards in a violent movement. This is what caused the Kobe earthquake.

The damage was much greater than might be expected of an earthquake measuring just 7.2 on the Richter scale. There were two main reasons for this. First, the 'quake was shallow, with its **focus** just below the Earth's surface. Second, its **epicentre** was very close to Kobe.

The **focus** is the point where the earthquake starts.

The **epicentre** is the point on the Earth's surface immediately above the focus.

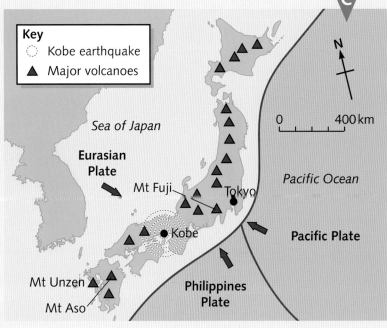

C

Key
- ⬚ Kobe earthquake
- ▲ Major volcanoes

Sea of Japan

Eurasian Plate

Mt Fuji

Tokyo

Pacific Ocean

Kobe

0   400 km

Pacific Plate

Mt Unzen

Mt Aso

Philippines Plate

D Causes of Kobe earthquake

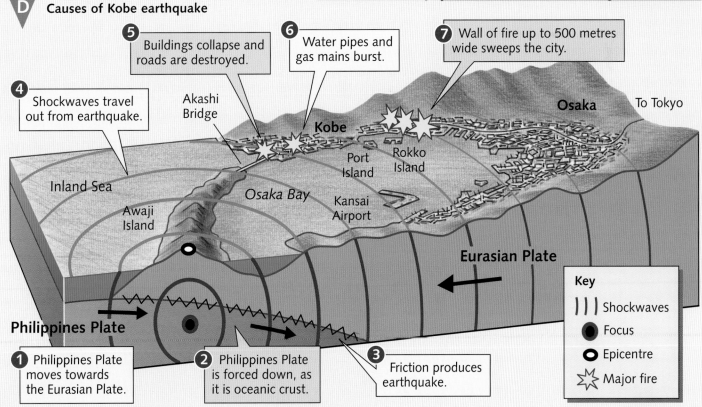

5 Buildings collapse and roads are destroyed.

6 Water pipes and gas mains burst.

7 Wall of fire up to 500 metres wide sweeps the city.

4 Shockwaves travel out from earthquake.

Akashi Bridge

Kobe

Osaka

To Tokyo

Port Island

Rokko Island

Inland Sea

Awaji Island

Osaka Bay

Kansai Airport

Eurasian Plate

Philippines Plate

1 Philippines Plate moves towards the Eurasian Plate.

2 Philippines Plate is forced down, as it is oceanic crust.

3 Friction produces earthquake.

Key
-))) Shockwaves
- ● Focus
- ◉ Epicentre
- ✦ Major fire

Kobe, Japan

Effects of the earthquake

Kobe is a wealthy city with a population of 1.5 million. A further 10 million people live in nearby Osaka. The region is the second largest centre of industry and population in Japan.

Kobe normally escapes any severe earth movements. Most people were surprised and not well prepared for the huge one that wrecked the city in 1995. It was the most devastating earthquake to hit Japan since the one that flattened Tokyo in 1923.

A Fires following the earthquake

B Effects of the Kobe earthquake

Kobe earthquake
- 5,390 people killed and 23,600 injured
- 180,000 houses totally destroyed
- 230,000 people made homeless
- 849,500 lost their gas and electricity supply
- Aftershocks felt for 10 more days

Major industries at Mitsubishi and Panasonic forced to close.

Hanshin elevated expressway collapses.

Temples in Kyoto damaged.

Several bridges damaged on high-speed bullet train route.

Ten trains derailed on local commuter line.

Wall of fire up to 500 metres wide sweeps the town.

Damage extends to 90 km radius around Kobe.

New Kansai airport largely unaffected

5.46 a.m. local time. Tremors spread from island epicentre.

Tarumi

Kobe

Akashi Bridge

Osaka

Nara

Osaka Bay

Awaji Island

Kyoto

Wakayama

N

0   15 km

Reducing the effects of earthquakes

Although we are not able to prevent earthquakes, much can now be done to reduce the damage caused by them. Kobe, for example, had largely recovered from the worst effects of the 1995 'quake within a few months.

There are two main reasons for this. The first is that Kobe had a well planned and effective Earthquake Emergency Plan. The second is that Japan is a rich country and has the money, resources and ability to deal with large-scale disasters. For this reason, poorer countries are usually more affected by earthquakes than rich countries.

However, most towns and cities that have been built in active earthquake zones do have some form of emergency earthquake plan. Usually these are in two parts. The first prepares the area for the earthquake. The second tries to save lives, look after the people who are worst affected, and then bring the city back to normal as quickly as possible.

C ▷ **Emergency Planning: an earthquake disaster plan**

Before
- Scientists identify danger areas and monitor earth movements.
- Design buildings to resist earthquakes.
- Train emergency services such as fire and ambulance crews.
- Educate people on what to expect.
- Practise emergency drills.

After
- Emergency services quickly reach problem areas.
- Immediate aid given to those most in need.
- Monitor and prepare for aftershocks.
- Remove debris and clear highways.
- Provide medical care, food and shelter.
- Restore gas, electricity and water services.
- Repair or rebuild damaged buildings, bridges and roads.

Earthquake in Japan

Ten steps to take when a big earthquake strikes

1 Extinguish all fires.
2 Keep yourself and family safe.
3 Don't rush outside.
   It is more dangerous there.
4 Keep the door open for later escape.
5 Protect your head from falling objects.
6 Follow instructions from people in charge.
7 If driving, stop immediately.
8 Be prepared for landslides or tidal waves.
9 Leave for a safe area on foot.
10 Don't listen to rumours.

D ▷ A poster from Japan's Earthquake Information Service

E ▷ **Building to resist earthquakes**

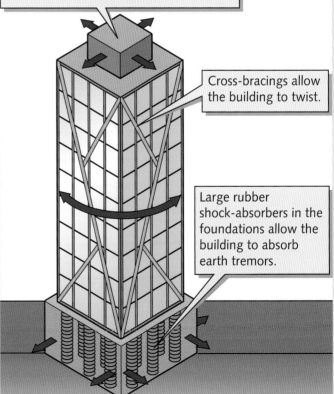

A heavy concrete weight on top of the building is controlled by a computer. It moves the building in opposite directions to the earthquake forces.

Cross-bracings allow the building to twist.

Large rubber shock-absorbers in the foundations allow the building to absorb earth tremors.

Indian Ocean earthquake and tsunami

Causes and effects on LEDCs

A The tsunami hits Phi Phi island, Thailand

What happened

On 26 December 2004, an earthquake measuring 9.0 on the Richter scale was recorded in the Indian Ocean off the north-western coast of Sumatra, Indonesia. The earthquake produced a **tsunami**, a huge wave, that devastated the coastal areas of Indonesia, Sri Lanka, India, Thailand and several other countries with waves up to 15 metres in height.

The earthquake was the fourth most powerful since 1900. Tremors were felt some 2,100 km (1,300 miles) away in India. The tsunami caused damage as far away as Somalia in East Africa, 4,500 km (2,800 miles) west of the earthquake **epicentre**

Causes of the earthquake and tsunami

The earthquake occurred on a destructive margin (page 216) just west of Sumatra. Here, the Indian and Eurasian plates collide with each other at the rate of about 6 cm a year. As the two plates move towards each other, pressure builds up. Eventually the pressure is released. This caused the Indian Ocean earthquake.

The movement of plates was both sudden and massive. It caused water above the earthquake to be pushed upwards causing a tsunami. The tsunami waves then spread rapidly out from the epicentre in all directions.

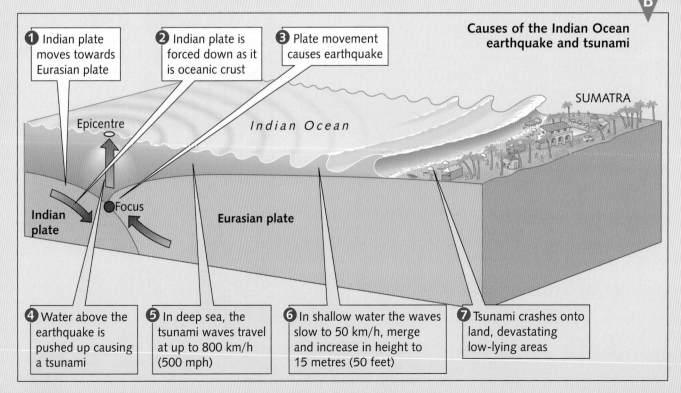

B Causes of the Indian Ocean earthquake and tsunami

1 Indian plate moves towards Eurasian plate

2 Indian plate is forced down as it is oceanic crust

3 Plate movement causes earthquake

Epicentre

Indian Ocean

SUMATRA

Focus

Indian plate

Eurasian plate

4 Water above the earthquake is pushed up causing a tsunami

5 In deep sea, the tsunami waves travel at up to 800 km/h (500 mph)

6 In shallow water the waves slow to 50 km/h, merge and increase in height to 15 metres (50 feet)

7 Tsunami crashes onto land, devastating low-lying areas

Effects

The Indian Ocean tsunami was the most deadly and destructive in recorded history. No one will ever know the exact number of people killed, but it is believed to be over 310,000. A third of these were children, most of them washed away by the surging water. More than 650,000 people were severely injured and 1.7 million made homeless as whole towns and villages were flattened. Livelihoods were also lost as fishing, farming, forestry and tourist industries were literally washed away. Estimates put the cost of the disaster at over £6 billion.

Why were the effects so serious?

The effects were serious simply because the tsunami was so powerful and affected such a large area. In most cases, nothing could withstand the destructive force of the giant waves as they hit shorelines around the Indian Ocean.

The situation was made worse by the fact that the countries affected by the disaster are poor. These countries therefore do not have the money, organisation or technology to predict, plan for or cope with major natural disasters. For example, there is no tsunami warning system in place for the region. If people had known that the wave was on its way, many thousands of lives may have been saved.

D The town of Banda Aceh after the tsunami hit

C The Indian Ocean earthquake and tsunami

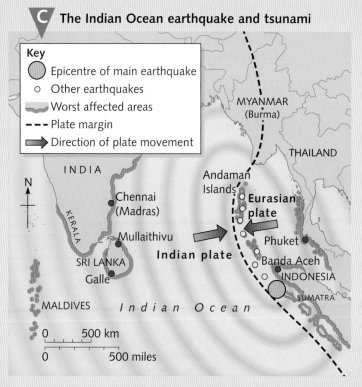

Key
- ⬤ Epicentre of main earthquake
- ○ Other earthquakes
- Worst affected areas
- - - - Plate margin
- ⇒ Direction of plate movement

INDIA
N
KERALA
Chennai (Madras)
Mullaithivu
SRI LANKA
Galle
MALDIVES
Indian Ocean
MYANMAR (Burma)
THAILAND
Andaman Islands
Eurasian plate
Indian plate
Phuket
Banda Aceh
INDONESIA
SUMATRA

0 _____ 500 km
0 _____ 500 miles

E

Problems in poorer, less developed countries

- There is not the technology available to predict when a disaster might occur.
- Local rescue workers are poorly prepared and equipped.
- There are too few ambulances, hospital spaces, nurses and doctors.
- Buildings are often poorly constructed and easily damaged.
- Poor roads and unreliable transport hinder emergency aid.
- There is a shortage of emergency clothing, shelter and medical supplies.
- Lack of food and unhealthy living conditions may lead to further deaths.

The world's response

Help came to the stricken countries from all around the world. It included food, clean water, medical supplies, machinery, expert assistance and money. The beginnings of a tsunami warning system for the Indian Ocean region have also been put in place and will be completed in stages during the next few years.

225

1 (Pages 212 and 213)
a) Give three facts about where earthquakes occur.
b) Describe three recent earthquakes.
c) Name five earthquakes that have happened on the west coast of North and South America.

2 (Pages 212 and 213)
a) Give three facts about where volcanoes may be found.
b) Name six volcanoes located on the west coast of North and South America.
c) What is the 'Ring of Fire'?

3 (Pages 214 and 215)
a) What are zones of activity?
b) When was the Earth formed?
c) What are the three main layers of the Earth?

4 (Pages 214 and 215)
a) What are plates?
b) Why do plates move over the surface of the Earth?
c) On which plate does Britain lie?
d) Name and describe the four plate boundaries shown below. Give an example of each.

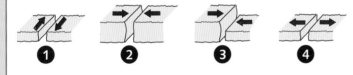

5 (Pages 216 and 217)
The drawing below shows a destructive margin off the west coast of South America.
a) Name the two plates A and B.
b) Name the ocean C and mountains D.
c) Draw arrows to show plate movement.
d) Explain why earthquakes and volcanoes happen here.

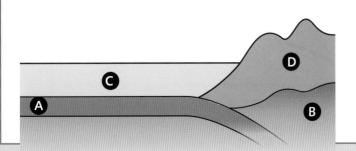

6 (Pages 216 and 217)
a) What is the difference between a **constructive** margin and a **destructive** margin?
b) With the help of a labelled diagram, explain what happens at the collision margin in northern India.

7 (Pages 216 and 217)
The drawing below shows a conservative margin off the west coast of the USA.
a) Name the plates A and B.
b) Name the cities at C and D.
c) Name the fault line at E.
d) Explain how earthquakes happen here.

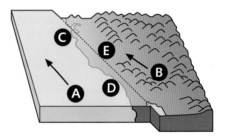

8 (Pages 218 and 219)
a) Where is Mount St Helens?
b) On what type of plate boundary is this volcano?
c) Put the following into the correct order to show how Mount St Helens erupted:
   ▪ Molten rock rises
   ▪ Friction melts the rock
   ▪ Plates rub together
   ▪ Volcano erupts on the surface
   ▪ Plates move towards each other
d) Give six effects of the Mount St Helens eruption.

9 (Pages 220 and 221)
a) What is the Richter scale?
b) What is the difference between the **focus** and **epicentre** of an earthquake?

10 (Pages 220 to 223)
a) Describe the Kobe earthquake as follows:
   ▪ What happened?
   ▪ What caused the earthquake?
   ▪ What were the main effects?
b) Describe what can be done to reduce the effects of an earthquake.

EXAMINATION QUESTIONS

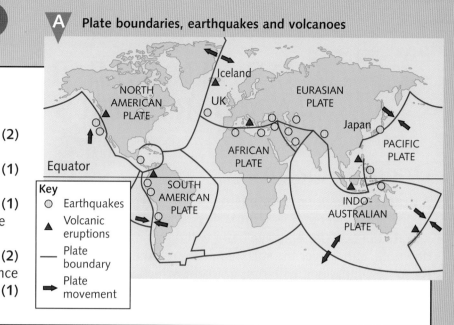

A Plate boundaries, earthquakes and volcanoes

1 (Pages 212 and 213)

Look at map **A**.
a) Name the two plates that meet
   near Japan. (2)
b) Describe the plate movement
   near Japan. (1)
c) Name a place where two plates
   are moving apart. (1)
d) What does the map show about where
   volcanoes and earthquakes may
   be found? (2)
e) Suggest why the UK does not experience
   serious earthquakes. (1)

Key
○ Earthquakes
▲ Volcanic eruptions
— Plate boundary
→ Plate movement

2 (Pages 214, 215 and 217)

Look at diagram **B**.
a) Give the meaning of the following terms:
   ■ magma   ■ convection currents
   ■ tectonic plates. (3)
b) The island is located on a constructive
   plate boundary. What is happening to
   the plates here? (1)
c) Use the information on the diagram to
   explain how the volcanic island has
   been formed. (3)
d) Name a place where volcanic islands like
   this may form. (1)

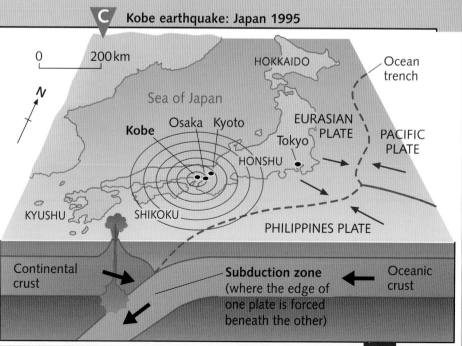

B

Volcanic island

Lava flow

Ocean

Plate movement

Plate movement

Ocean

Convection currents

Magma

3 (Pages 214, 215, 216, 220 and 221)

Look at drawing **C**.
a) Which three plates are shown
   on the diagram? (3)
b) What is an ocean trench? (2)
c) What is happening to the
   Philippines Plate? (2)
d) What type of plate boundary is
   shown here? Is it constructive,
   destructive or conservative? Give
   a reason for your answer. (2)
e) Use the diagram to help explain
   how the Kobe earthquake
   happened. (4)

C Kobe earthquake: Japan 1995

0   200 km

N

Sea of Japan

HOKKAIDO

Ocean trench

Kobe   Osaka Kyoto

EURASIAN PLATE

PACIFIC PLATE

Tokyo

HONSHU

KYUSHU   SHIKOKU

PHILIPPINES PLATE

Continental crust

Subduction zone
(where the edge of
one plate is forced
beneath the other)

Oceanic crust

17 DRAINAGE BASINS AND RIVERS

Drainage basins

A **drainage basin** or **river basin** is an area of land drained by a river and its **tributaries**. Most of the rain that falls in the drainage basin will flow slowly downhill, either over the surface or through the topsoil. Eventually it will form a stream, which will gradually increase in size to eventually flow into a lake or the sea. The main features of a drainage basin are shown in diagram **A**.

Hydrological cycle

Water is a **non-renewable resource** – one that cannot be replaced – and the world would run out of it in about four weeks if it could not be re-used. Fortunately, nature recycles water so that it can be used over and over again.

The constant movement, or **transfer**, of water between the sea, land and atmosphere is called the **hydrological cycle** or, more simply, the **water cycle**. The main features of this cycle are shown in diagram **B** below.

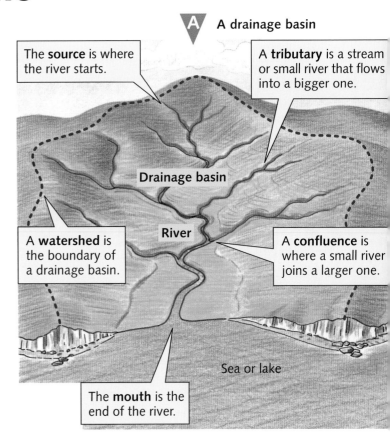

A A drainage basin

The **source** is where the river starts.

A **tributary** is a stream or small river that flows into a bigger one.

Drainage basin

River

A **watershed** is the boundary of a drainage basin.

A **confluence** is where a small river joins a larger one.

Sea or lake

The **mouth** is the end of the river.

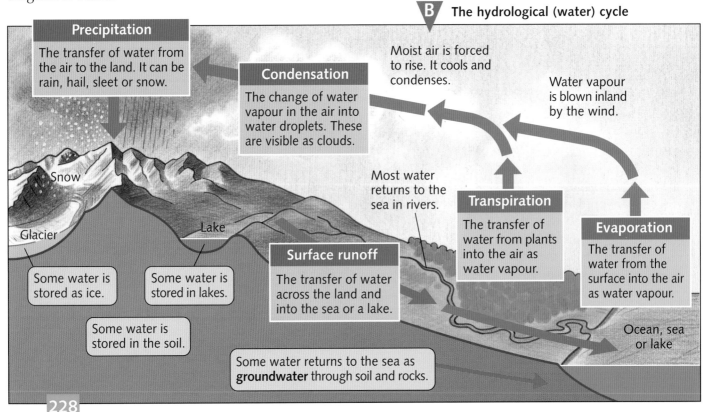

B The hydrological (water) cycle

Precipitation
The transfer of water from the air to the land. It can be rain, hail, sleet or snow.

Condensation
The change of water vapour in the air into water droplets. These are visible as clouds.

Moist air is forced to rise. It cools and condenses.

Water vapour is blown inland by the wind.

Snow

Glacier

Lake

Most water returns to the sea in rivers.

Transpiration
The transfer of water from plants into the air as water vapour.

Evaporation
The transfer of water from the surface into the air as water vapour.

Surface runoff
The transfer of water across the land and into the sea or a lake.

Some water is stored as ice.

Some water is stored in lakes.

Some water is stored in the soil.

Some water returns to the sea as **groundwater** through soil and rocks.

Ocean, sea or lake

The drainage basin system

The part of the hydrological cycle that operates on land is called the **drainage basin system** or **river basin system**.

This system is made up of inputs, flows or transfers, stores and outputs. Diagrams **C** and **E** are **systems diagrams**. A systems diagram simplifies something that is complicated.

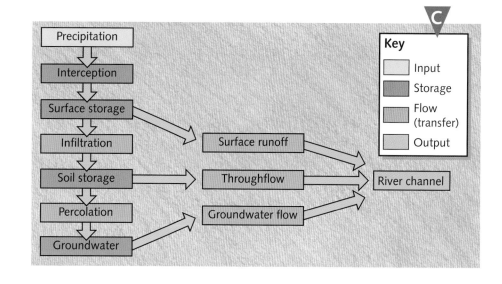

C

Key
- Input
- Storage
- Flow (transfer)
- Output

Precipitation → Interception → Surface storage → Infiltration → Soil storage → Percolation → Groundwater

Surface runoff, Throughflow, Groundwater flow → River channel

D

DEFINITIONS

Inputs enter the system

Precipitation – rain, hail, sleet or snow

Storage (water held within the system)

Interception – when water droplets collect on trees and plants

Surface storage – when water lies on the ground as puddles or lakes

Soil moisture – water stored in the soil and broken rocks near the surface

Groundwater – water stored in porous rocks deep below the ground

Flows or transfers movement of water

Surface runoff – water moving across the ground as a stream or river

Throughflow – water flowing downhill through the soil

Infiltration – when surface water soaks into the soil

Percolation – water moving downwards through the soil into rocks below

Groundwater flow – very slow water movement deep below the ground

Outputs leave the system

Transpiration – water vapour released by trees and plants

Evaporation – when water heated by the sun changes to water vapour

E The drainage basin system

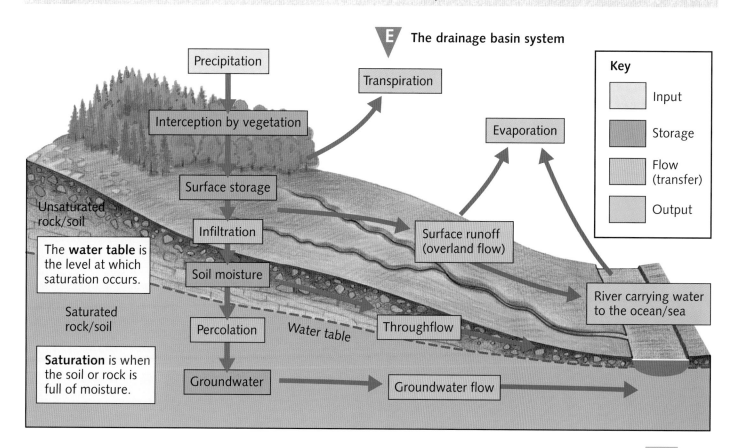

The **water table** is the level at which saturation occurs.

Saturation is when the soil or rock is full of moisture.

Key
- Input
- Storage
- Flow (transfer)
- Output

River discharge and flood hydrographs

River discharge

The water level in rivers is not always the same. It varies from month to month and even from day to day. So why does this happen?

Rivers are affected mainly by the weather. When there is heavy rain, river levels usually rise. When it is warm and temperatures are high, water evaporates into the air and levels fall.

As we have seen, however, water is also stored in the soil or rock itself. Eventually it finds its way back to the surface and into the river. In this way the river is able to gain water even though it may not be raining.

The amount of water in a river is called the **runoff** or **discharge**. The amount of runoff depends on **precipitation**, the amount of water stored, and how much is lost through **evapotranspiration**. This is called the **water balance**.

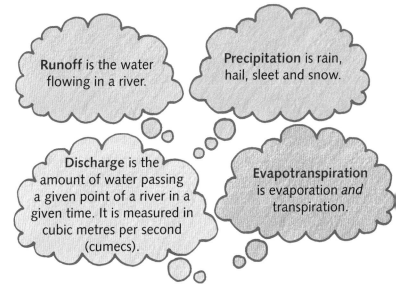

> **Runoff** is the water flowing in a river.

> **Precipitation** is rain, hail, sleet and snow.

> **Discharge** is the amount of water passing a given point of a river in a given time. It is measured in cubic metres per second (cumecs).

> **Evapotranspiration** is evaporation *and* transpiration.

Flood hydrographs

A **hydrograph** is a line that shows river discharge over a period of time. Flood hydrographs show a river's discharge after a period of heavy rain.

Flood hydrographs help identify the link between rainfall and the level of a river. This helps people to forecast river levels and predict possible floods.

The water balance: Runoff = precipitation + water from storage – evapotranspiration

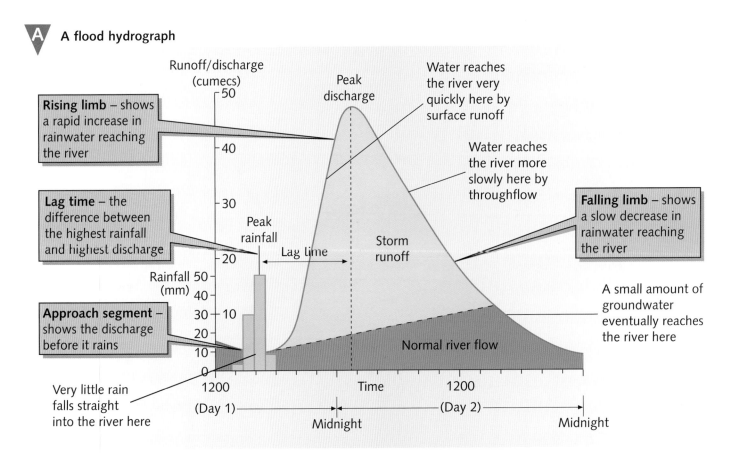

A A flood hydrograph

Differences in flood hydrographs

When it rains, some water soaks into the ground and some stays on the surface. The surface water runs downhill and eventually reaches the river. It takes time to do this, so there is a delay or **lag time** between the time when the rain falls and when it reaches the river.

As drainage basins are all very different, the lag times for each basin also vary. This produces differences in the shape of hydrographs. In some rivers, the discharge rises and falls very quickly. These rivers are liable to flooding or drought as the weather changes. Rivers fed by underground water or a reservoir have more even patterns of discharge.

B Reasons for differences in flood hydrographs

Size

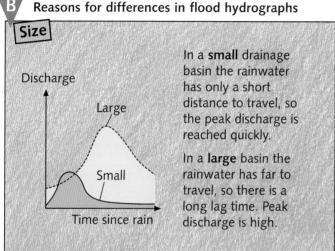

In a **small** drainage basin the rainwater has only a short distance to travel, so the peak discharge is reached quickly.

In a **large** basin the rainwater has far to travel, so there is a long lag time. Peak discharge is high.

Steepness

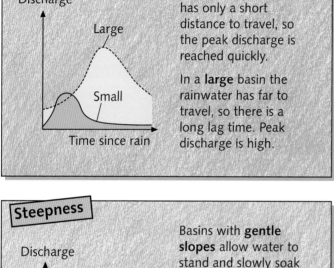

Basins with **gentle slopes** allow water to stand and slowly soak into the ground. Rainwater takes a long time to reach the river.

On **steep slopes**, the rainwater runs quickly down to the river. Lag times are short.

Rock or soil type

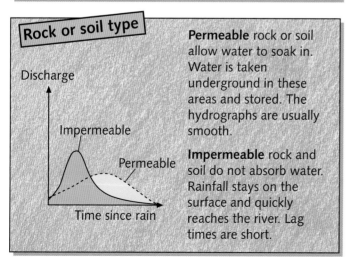

Permeable rock or soil allow water to soak in. Water is taken underground in these areas and stored. The hydrographs are usually smooth.

Impermeable rock and soil do not absorb water. Rainfall stays on the surface and quickly reaches the river. Lag times are short.

Stream density

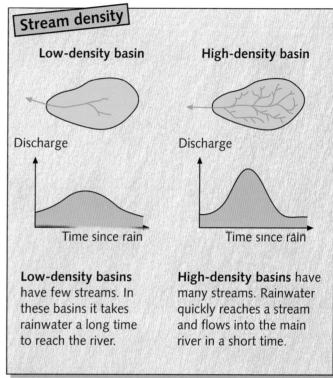

Low-density basins have few streams. In these basins it takes rainwater a long time to reach the river.

High-density basins have many streams. Rainwater quickly reaches a stream and flows into the main river in a short time.

Vegetation

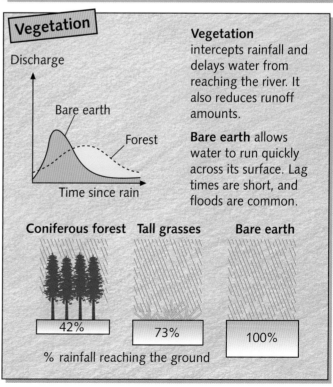

Vegetation intercepts rainfall and delays water from reaching the river. It also reduces runoff amounts.

Bare earth allows water to run quickly across its surface. Lag times are short, and floods are common.

231

River processes

Rivers do more than carry water across the land. They help shape the landscape, affect human activity and are a valuable resource.

Rivers shape the land through processes of **erosion**, **transportation** and **deposition**. These processes are greatest in large rivers or at times of flood.

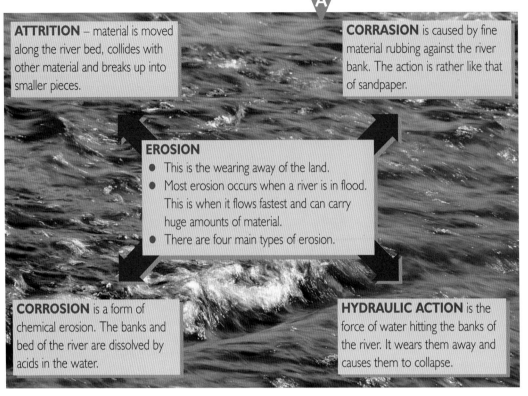

A

ATTRITION – material is moved along the river bed, collides with other material and breaks up into smaller pieces.

CORRASION is caused by fine material rubbing against the river bank. The action is rather like that of sandpaper.

EROSION
- This is the wearing away of the land.
- Most erosion occurs when a river is in flood. This is when it flows fastest and can carry huge amounts of material.
- There are four main types of erosion.

DEPOSITION
- This is the laying down or dumping of material.
- It happens when a river slows and loses energy.
- This may be during a dry spell, on the inside of a river bend, or when the river reaches the sea.

CORROSION is a form of chemical erosion. The banks and bed of the river are dissolved by acids in the water.

HYDRAULIC ACTION is the force of water hitting the banks of the river. It wears them away and causes them to collapse.

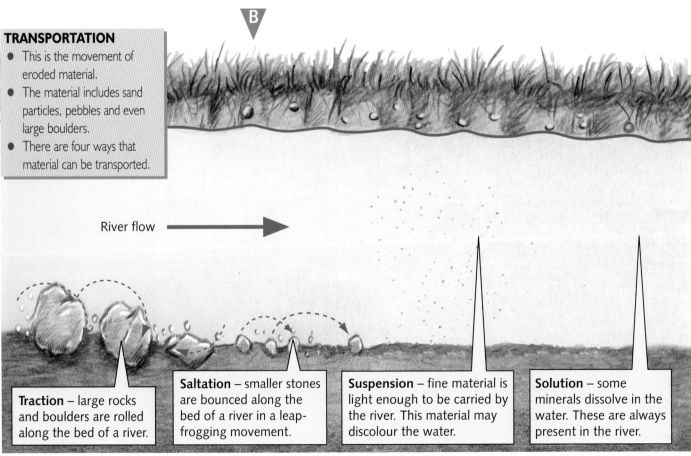

B

TRANSPORTATION
- This is the movement of eroded material.
- The material includes sand particles, pebbles and even large boulders.
- There are four ways that material can be transported.

River flow →

Traction – large rocks and boulders are rolled along the bed of a river.

Saltation – smaller stones are bounced along the bed of a river in a leap-frogging movement.

Suspension – fine material is light enough to be carried by the river. This material may discolour the water.

Solution – some minerals dissolve in the water. These are always present in the river.

River landforms in a highland area

V-shaped valleys and interlocking spurs

A river, especially when in flood, transports material along its bed. This material cuts downwards and deepens the bed of the river. After periods of heavy rain, soil on the valley sides slowly moves downhill under gravity. The valley becomes steep sided and V-shaped. This is because erosion deepens the valley faster than it widens it.

The river winds its way around ridges called **interlocking spurs**. These are like the teeth of a zip-fastener.

3 Slopes attacked by heavy rain

4 Valley sides slowly move downhill

5 Valley forms a V-shape

1 Rocks and pebbles moved along river bed

2 River erodes downwards – valley deepened

Waterfalls

Waterfalls usually occur where a band of hard rock lies next to soft rock. The soft rock is worn away more quickly than the hard rock, and a step develops over which the river falls.

Sometimes the softer rock lies underneath the hard rock. In this case the softer rock may be worn away and the hard rock left unsupported, and this will collapse. This process is likely to be repeated many times, causing the waterfall to move upstream. A steep-sided gorge will be left behind.

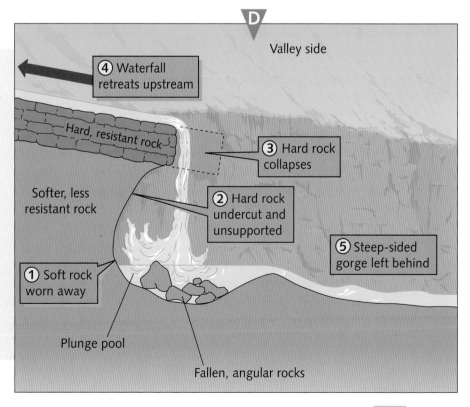

Valley side

4 Waterfall retreats upstream

Hard, resistant rock

3 Hard rock collapses

Softer, less resistant rock

2 Hard rock undercut and unsupported

5 Steep-sided gorge left behind

1 Soft rock worn away

Plunge pool

Fallen, angular rocks

233

River landforms in a lowland area

Meanders and ox-bow lakes

As a river approaches its mouth it usually flows over flatter land and develops large bends called **meanders**. Meanders constantly change their shape and position.

When a river goes around a bend most of the water is pushed towards the outside causing **erosion**. This deepens the channel and wears away the bank. On the inside of the bend water movement is slower. Material builds up here due to **deposition**. This makes the bank gently sloping and the river channel shallow.

As erosion continues, the neck of the meander becomes narrower. Eventually the river cuts right through the neck and shortens its course. Deposition then blocks off the old bend to leave an **ox-bow lake**. The ox-bow lake will dry up, only refilling after heavy rain or in a flood.

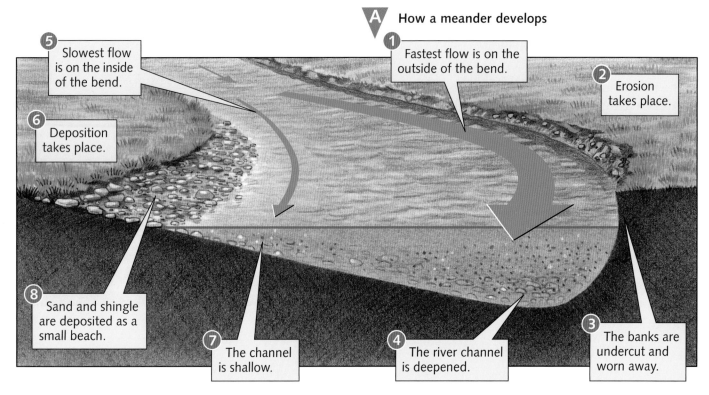

A How a meander develops

⑤ Slowest flow is on the inside of the bend.

⑥ Deposition takes place.

⑧ Sand and shingle are deposited as a small beach.

① Fastest flow is on the outside of the bend.

② Erosion takes place.

⑦ The channel is shallow.

④ The river channel is deepened.

③ The banks are undercut and worn away.

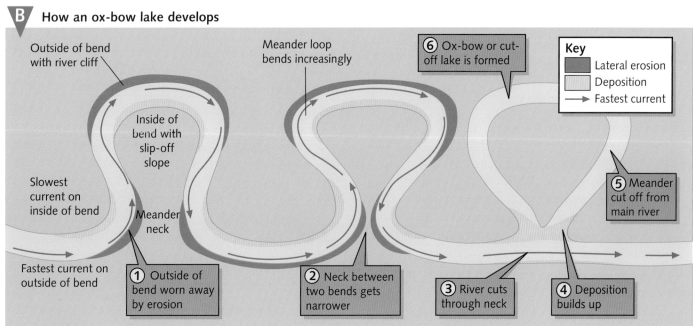

B How an ox-bow lake develops

Outside of bend with river cliff

Inside of bend with slip-off slope

Slowest current on inside of bend

Meander neck

Fastest current on outside of bend

① Outside of bend worn away by erosion

Meander loop bends increasingly

② Neck between two bends gets narrower

③ River cuts through neck

④ Deposition builds up

⑥ Ox-bow or cut-off lake is formed

⑤ Meander cut off from main river

Key
- Lateral erosion
- Deposition
- → Fastest current

Floodplains and levées

The flat area of land over which a river meanders is called a **floodplain**. During times of flood, a river will overflow its banks and cover any surrounding flat land. Each time the river floods, a thin layer of material called **silt** is spread over the floodplain. Silt is a fertile soil that is good for farming. Larger material, such as sand and gravel, is deposited along the banks of the river. This builds up to form a natural embankment called a **levée**. Sometimes levées are strengthed to protect the surrounding area from floods.

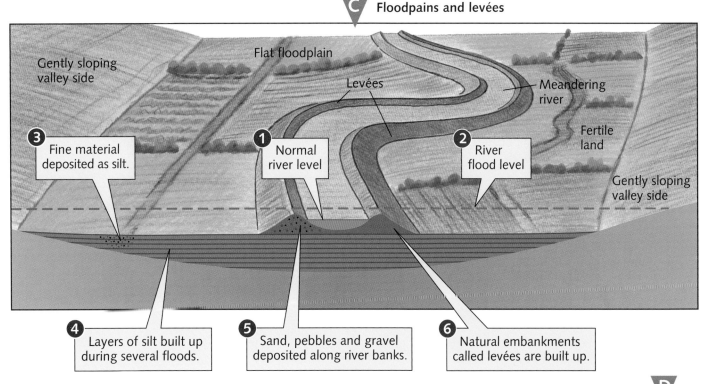

C Floodpains and levées

Gently sloping valley side

Flat floodplain

Levées

Meandering river

Fertile land

Gently sloping valley side

3 Fine material deposited as silt.

1 Normal river level

2 River flood level

4 Layers of silt built up during several floods.

5 Sand, pebbles and gravel deposited along river banks.

6 Natural embankments called levées are built up.

Deltas

Large rivers transport huge amounts of material down to their mouths. If a river flows into a relatively calm sea or lake, then it slows down and the material is deposited. Gradually this builds upwards and outwards to form a delta.

Deltas only form when a river deposits material too fast for the sea to remove it. This happens:

- where the river carries large amounts of material
- when the sea has weak currents or is tideless.

The largest deltas in the world are at the mouth of the Rivers Nile, Ganges and Mississippi. They provide some of the best farming in the world, because of the rich soils and flat land there. However, they are always in danger of serious flooding because the land is so flat.

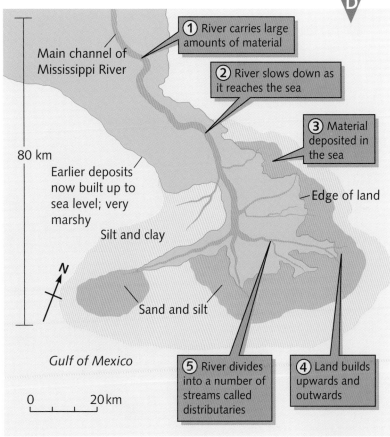

D

Main channel of Mississippi River

1 River carries large amounts of material

2 River slows down as it reaches the sea

3 Material deposited in the sea

Edge of land

80 km

Earlier deposits now built up to sea level; very marshy

Silt and clay

N

Sand and silt

Gulf of Mexico

5 River divides into a number of streams called distributaries

4 Land builds upwards and outwards

0   20km

River floods

Rivers are useful to people. They can provide water for domestic use and supply the needs of industry and agriculture. They may also be used for transport, for the generation of power and, more recently, for recreational purposes. For these reasons rivers have long been good places to locate towns and cities.

However, rivers can also cause problems. In recent times serious floods have caused death and widespread damage. Evidence suggests that much of this flooding has been caused by human mismanagement.

Boscastle 2004

One of Britain's worst ever floods devastated the North Devon village of Lynmouth in 1952. The flood destroyed 90 buildings, killed 34 people and made over 1,000 homeless. On exactly the same day, 52 years later, a similar disaster hit Boscastle in North Cornwall. The causes of the two floods were almost identical.

On the morning of 16 August 2004, extremely heavy rain fell over the Boscastle area. The rain caused the rivers flowing though the village to burst their banks and flood the narrow valley. Much of the lower part of the village down to the harbour was virtually wiped out.

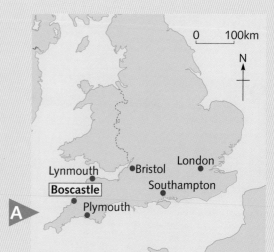

A

B Causes of the flood

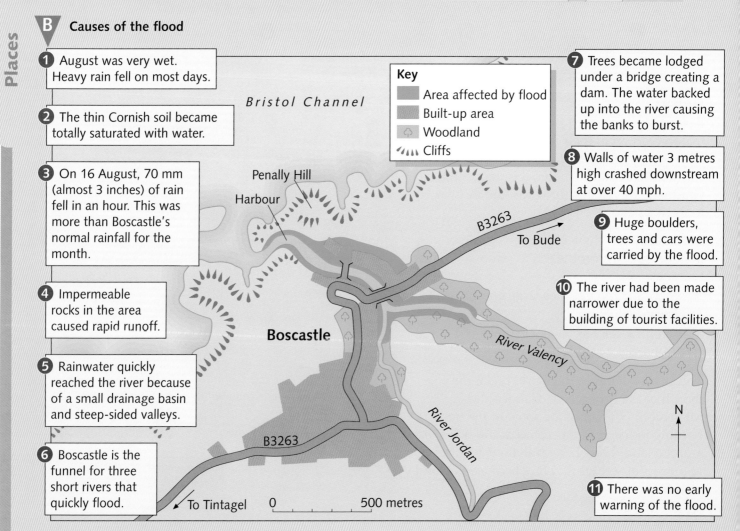

1 August was very wet. Heavy rain fell on most days.

2 The thin Cornish soil became totally saturated with water.

3 On 16 August, 70 mm (almost 3 inches) of rain fell in an hour. This was more than Boscastle's normal rainfall for the month.

4 Impermeable rocks in the area caused rapid runoff.

5 Rainwater quickly reached the river because of a small drainage basin and steep-sided valleys.

6 Boscastle is the funnel for three short rivers that quickly flood.

7 Trees became lodged under a bridge creating a dam. The water backed up into the river causing the banks to burst.

8 Walls of water 3 metres high crashed downstream at over 40 mph.

9 Huge boulders, trees and cars were carried by the flood.

10 The river had been made narrower due to the building of tourist facilities.

11 There was no early warning of the flood.

Key
- Area affected by flood
- Built-up area
- Woodland
- Cliffs

Effects of the flood

In just over five hours, Boscastle went from being a pretty Cornish tourist attraction to a disaster zone. As at Lynmouth 52 years earlier, the main cause of the damage was the huge amount of water in the rivers. This moved large boulders and transported vast amounts of material which simply destroyed the village.

1. 36 buildings destroyed or badly damaged
2. 14 bridges in the area severely damaged or destroyed
3. 75 cars and several boats swept away
4. Harbour area badly damaged
5. Cost of the damage estimated at £85 million

C

D

Solutions to the flood problem

The flood has had a serious effect on the people of Boscastle and other nearby villages worried about their own safety. Meetings have been called to discuss safety aspects and advice lines set up for concerned residents. A new flood management plan has also been introduced.

The rebuilding programme has included a number of design features aimed at reducing the effects of future floods.

1. Parts of floodplain left open to take excess water
2. Larger bridges built with wider spans
3. River channel straightened to allow floodwater to flow more freely
4. New culverts built to take away floodwater.

E

Drainage basin mismanagement

For many centuries, rivers have been used for the disposal of unwanted waste. Waste that is put into rivers from farmland, cities and industrial sites, is continually carried away, but there is a limit to how much a river can get rid of. When the limit is reached, there is a serious **pollution problem**.

Rivers are polluted in two different ways. The first is when waste materials are simply dumped directly into the river as a way of getting rid of unwanted materials. The second is when substances from the surrounding area reach the river either by surface runoff or by soaking through the soil and rock below the ground.

In many countries, efforts are being made to reduce river pollution. In Japan, for example, strict pollution laws have successfully cleaned up many rivers and lakes. Lake Biwa was so polluted in the 1970s that it was almost 'dead' to plant and animal life. Now it is clean, fish have returned, and the lake is a major tourist resort.

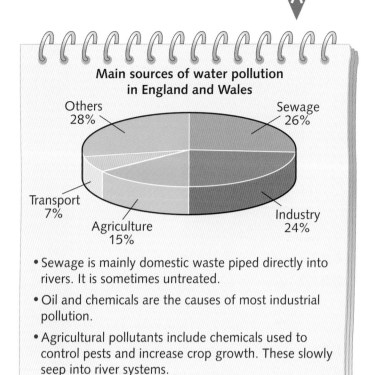

A

Main sources of water pollution in England and Wales

- Others 28%
- Sewage 26%
- Industry 24%
- Agriculture 15%
- Transport 7%

- Sewage is mainly domestic waste piped directly into rivers. It is sometimes untreated.
- Oil and chemicals are the causes of most industrial pollution.
- Agricultural pollutants include chemicals used to control pests and increase crop growth. These slowly seep into river systems.
- 'Others' are from unknown sources.

B Main causes of water pollution

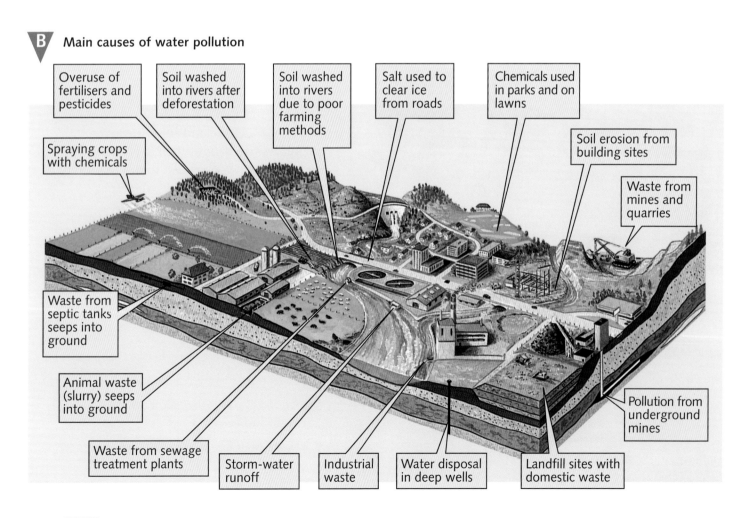

- Overuse of fertilisers and pesticides
- Soil washed into rivers after deforestation
- Soil washed into rivers due to poor farming methods
- Salt used to clear ice from roads
- Chemicals used in parks and on lawns
- Soil erosion from building sites
- Waste from mines and quarries
- Spraying crops with chemicals
- Waste from septic tanks seeps into ground
- Pollution from underground mines
- Animal waste (slurry) seeps into ground
- Waste from sewage treatment plants
- Storm-water runoff
- Industrial waste
- Water disposal in deep wells
- Landfill sites with domestic waste

Drainage basin management

Should rivers be allowed to flood?

Rivers are useful to people, but in times of flood they can cause problems. Efforts have been made in some places to reduce flooding by building dams, overflow channels and embankments.

For most of the time, these methods of flood control are successful. The problem arises when a serious flood occurs. If the embankments have not been built high enough, then large areas of land are flooded and numerous lives put at risk. In these cases, the flood protection schemes can make the problem worse.

Following the serious Mississippi floods of 1993, some scientists began asking whether rivers should be allowed to flood naturally. Others argued for better flood defences and even more control of rivers.

C Advantages of natural flooding

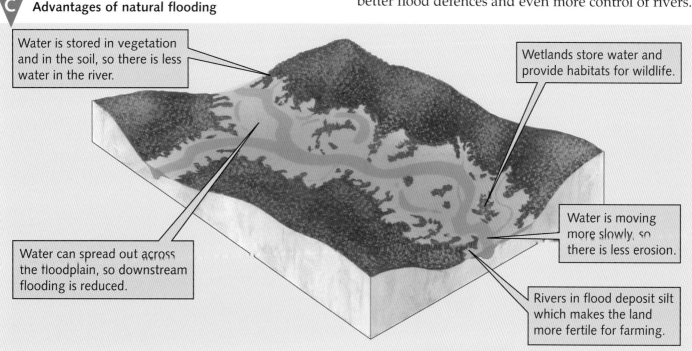

Water is stored in vegetation and in the soil, so there is less water in the river.

Wetlands store water and provide habitats for wildlife.

Water can spread out across the floodplain, so downstream flooding is reduced.

Water is moving more slowly, so there is less erosion.

Rivers in flood deposit silt which makes the land more fertile for farming.

D Disadvantages of flood controls

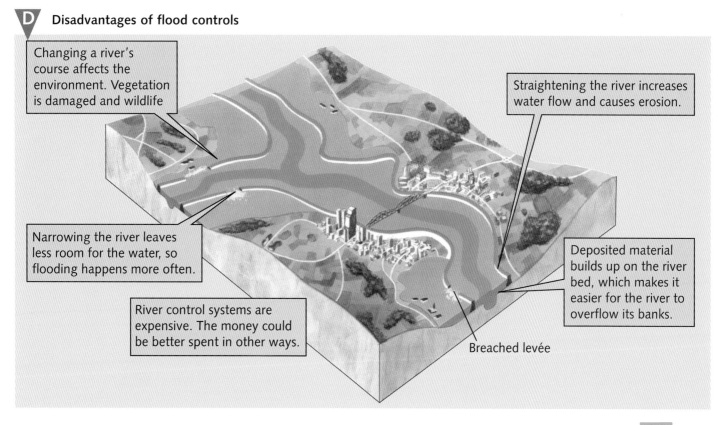

Changing a river's course affects the environment. Vegetation is damaged and wildlife

Straightening the river increases water flow and causes erosion.

Narrowing the river leaves less room for the water, so flooding happens more often.

River control systems are expensive. The money could be better spent in other ways.

Deposited material builds up on the river bed, which makes it easier for the river to overflow its banks.

Breached levée

Drainage basins – management or mismanagement?

The Three Gorges Dam, China

The Yangtze River and the Three Gorges

The Yangtze is China's longest river. It stretches some 5,600 km from its source in Tibet to where it enters the Yellow Sea near Shanghai. Midway down its course, the river flows through a 190 km section known as the Three Gorges. The river valley narrows here, and there are sheer cliffs on either side. The river is fast-flowing, and hidden rocks make it dangerous for ships.

Flooding is also a problem on the Yangtze. Recent damage has been enormous, and over 300,000 people have been drowned in the last 70 years alone. The middle section of the river has some of China's best farmland and is densely populated.

The Three Gorges Project

In the 1990s, work finally started on the Three Gorges Dam. The aim of the project was to control the river and so reduce the danger of flooding. It was also hoped that the dam would improve navigation on the river and provide cheap hydro-electric power for the region.

The dam is the biggest in the world. The whole project will cost at least $20 billion, take 18 years to complete, force 1.2 million people to move home, and will flood vast areas of farmland. Many people are concerned that the project will do more damage than good. The people living here are in constant fear of the river bursting its banks.

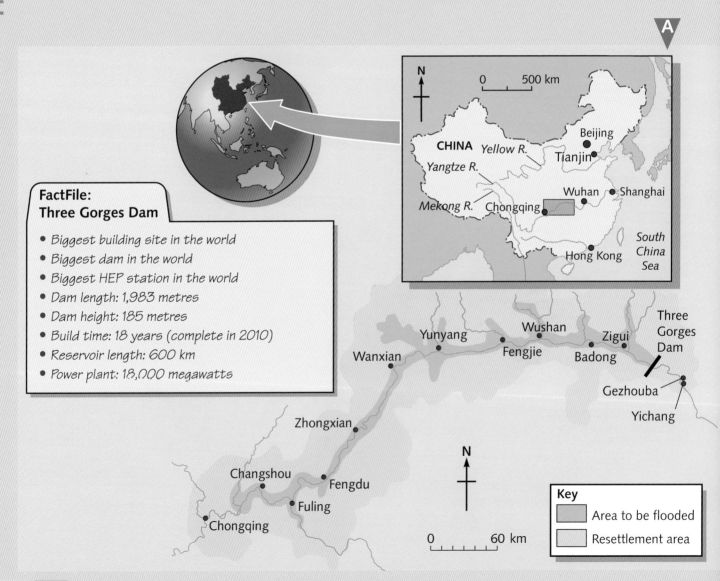

FactFile:
Three Gorges Dam

- Biggest building site in the world
- Biggest dam in the world
- Biggest HEP station in the world
- Dam length: 1,983 metres
- Dam height: 185 metres
- Build time: 18 years (complete in 2010)
- Reservoir length: 600 km
- Power plant: 18,000 megawatts

Key
- Area to be flooded
- Resettlement area

The Three Gorges Dam: For or against?

By summer 2000, more than 180,000 people had been moved from small farms and rivers near the river. The Yangtze had been diverted, and construction of the dam was well under way. By 2004 the dam had been completed and it should be full by 2009.

There has been much opposition to the project. People have been concerned that new villages were being located in unsatisfactory locations, and that new farming areas were troubled with soil erosion as the land was too steep. Some were also worried about safety, and argued that a dam failure could threaten the lives of millions. Foreign countries were also against the project and refused funding.

Those most in favour of the dam lived downstream, where recent summer floods once again caused extensive damage.

For the scheme
- Flooding will be prevented.
- Damage will be reduced and lives saved.
- Will provide 10% of China's electricity.
- Will replace dirty coal-burning power stations.
- Will provide water for 20% of China's people.
- Ships will be able to use the river all year round.
- Will provide several thousand jobs.

B Three Gorges Dam under construction

Against the scheme
- 1.2 million people will have to move home.
- 150 towns and 4,400 villages will be flooded.
- 1,600 industrial sites will be destroyed.
- Farmland and forest will be lost.
- Fertile silt will be lost to farms downstream.
- Wildlife is threatened.
- Archaeological sites and ancient cities will be lost.
- Possible danger because near to earthquake zone.

C One of the Three Gorges before work began on the project

The Nile Valley

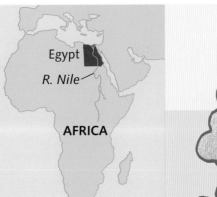

Egypt
R. Nile
AFRICA

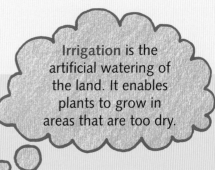

Irrigation is the artificial watering of the land. It enables plants to grow in areas that are too dry.

Ancient writers called Egypt 'the gift of the Nile'. This is because without the Nile, the land would be desert and an impossible place in which to live. For thousands of years the Nile has:
- supplied Egypt's water needs
- at times of flood covered the land in rich, fertile soil
- provided water to irrigate crops.

Irrigation made it possible to farm in an otherwise desert area. Most irrigation happened during the river's autumn flood. Water was allowed to cover the land, where it was trapped by small walls. It then slowly soaked into the ground and deposited its silt. During the rest of the year, water had to be lifted from the river using simple methods. Some of these methods are still used today – they are hard work in the hot sun.

For centuries the Egyptians had wanted to control the flow of the Nile. The problem was how to reduce flooding but at the same time ensure a reliable water supply.

The Aswan High Dam

Eventually, in the late 1950s, Egypt decided to build a large dam across the Nile and create a huge lake behind it. This would control the river's flow and provide a store of water that could be used when needed. The plan also included a large hydro-electric power station.

The dam is 3 km long. It took 11 years to build and was opened in 1971. Lake Nasser, which formed behind the dam, is 550 km in length – about the same as England from north to south. As the waters of the lake rose, many people were force to move home.

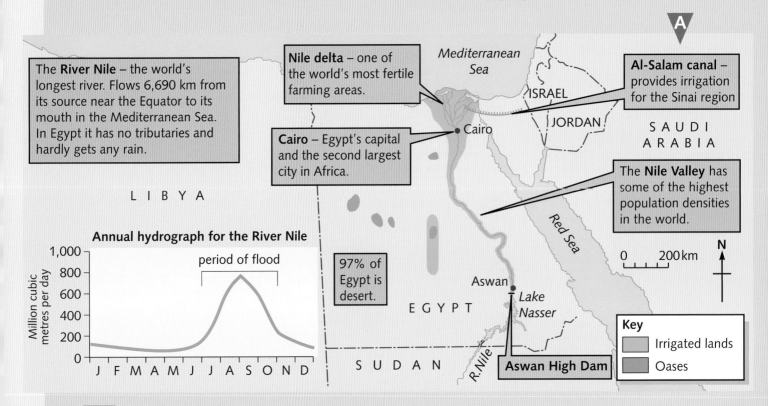

The **River Nile** – the world's longest river. Flows 6,690 km from its source near the Equator to its mouth in the Mediterranean Sea. In Egypt it has no tributaries and hardly gets any rain.

Nile delta – one of the world's most fertile farming areas.

Mediterranean Sea

Al-Salam canal – provides irrigation for the Sinai region

ISRAEL
JORDAN
SAUDI ARABIA

Cairo – Egypt's capital and the second largest city in Africa.

Cairo

The **Nile Valley** has some of the highest population densities in the world.

LIBYA

Red Sea

Annual hydrograph for the River Nile

period of flood

Million cubic metres per day

1,000
800
600
400
200
0
J F M A M J J A S O N D

97% of Egypt is desert.

EGYPT

Aswan
Lake Nasser

0   200 km

N

Key
Irrigated lands
Oases

SUDAN
R. Nile
Aswan High Dam

The present and the future

Egypt's population has grown rapidly since the opening of the dam: it had 33 million people in 1971, 71 million in 1999, and will have an estimated 85 million by 2010.

With an increasing number of mouths to feed, pressure has been put on the country to develop other parts of the desert. In 1997 a canal linking the Nile with the Sinai region was opened. People now live here and, because of irrigation, are able to grow crops on what was previously desert land.

While the Aswan High Dam scheme and other irrigation projects have brought many benefits to Egypt, they have also caused problems. Some of these problems were unforeseen and have been difficult to solve.

Benefits

- The Nile no longer floods, so people and villages are safe.
- Water stored in the lake is available for irrigation all year round.
- More land can be irrigated and more food is produced.
- The dam produces cheap electricity, which improves living standards.
- The river level is kept steady, which helps water travel.
- Lake Nasser is stocked with fish, which help provide a better diet.

B The Aswan High Dam and Lake Nasser

Problems

- Less silt is deposited, so land is becoming less fertile.
- Fertiliser has to be added to the soil, which costs money.
- Fertiliser is polluting the Nile and killing vegetation and wildlife.
- Without a supply of silt, the fertile delta is becoming smaller.
- There are more water snails carrying a disease called bilharzia. Many people die from this disease.
- Water from irrigation evaporates quickly, leaving behind salt in which crops can't grow.

C The River Nile

Desert

Irrigated land

The Nile

1 (Pages 228 and 229)
Write down the meaning of the following terms:
a) drainage basin   b) watershed
c) source   d) tributary
e) confluence   f) mouth.

2 (Pages 228 and 229)
Copy and complete the hydrological cycle diagram using the terms below. Give the meaning of each term.
■ Precipitation   ■ Evaporation
■ Surface runoff   ■ Transpiration
■ Condensation

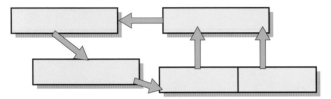

3 (Pages 228 and 229)
a) Copy and complete the diagram using these terms:
■ surface store
■ interception
■ soil storage.
b) Give one example of a surface store.
c) What is interception?
d) Rainfall is one type of precipitation. Give two others.
e) With help from the diagram, describe how rain falling on a drainage basin may reach a river.

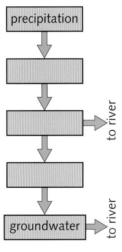

4 (Pages 230 and 231)
a) What is a flood hydrograph?
b) Name and describe the features labelled A, B, C, D and E on the diagram below.
c) Describe four features of a drainage basin that would produce a short lag time.

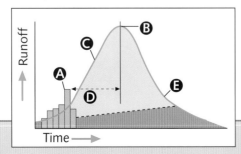

5 (Pages 232 and 233)
a) What is erosion?
b) Describe the four main ways in which a river erodes.
c) What is transportation?
d) Describe the four main ways in which a river transports material.
e) What is deposition?
f) When does a river deposit material?

6 (Page 233)
a) Draw a simple diagram of a river bend, and add the following words and terms:
■ gentle slope   ■ river cliff
■ deposition   ■ erosion
■ slowest current   ■ fastest current
■ floodplain.
b) With the help of another diagram, describe how an ox-bow lake may be formed.

7 (Pages 232, 233 and 235)
a) What is a delta?
b) When do deltas form?
c) Name two rivers that have large deltas.
d) Copy the diagram below and label it to show how a delta forms.

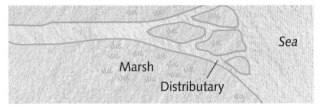

8 (Pages 236 and 237)
a) Name a river that has flooded.
b) Describe its location and main features.
c) Explain why it flooded.
d) Describe the main effects of the flood.
e) Describe what has been done to reduce the flooding problem for that river.

9 (Pages 238 to 241)
a) Describe the main features of the Yangtze River.
b) Describe four aims of the Three Gorges Project.
c) Describe the main features of the project.
d) List the main benefits of the project.
e) Explain why some people have been against the Three Gorges Project.

EXAMINATION QUESTIONS

1

(Pages 228 and 229)

a) Match each letter on diagram **A** with one of the following words:
   ■ interception   ■ watershed
   ■ confluence. (3)
b) Give one example of an input. (1)
c) Give one example of a store. (1)
d) Give one example of a transfer. (1)
e) Explain the meaning of any three of the terms shown on diagram **A**. You may include those you have added from question **a**). (3)

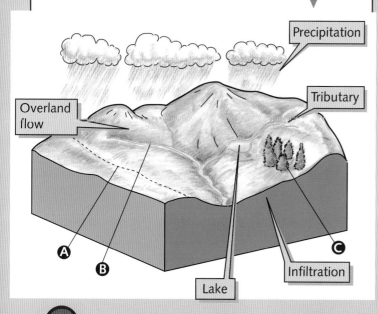

A

Precipitation

Tributary

Overland flow

Infiltration

Lake

Ⓐ

Ⓑ

Ⓒ

2

(Pages 232 and 233)

a) Match each letter on photo **B** with one of the following features:
   ■ waterfall   ■ band of hard rock
   ■ plunge pool   ■ rapids
   ■ gorge. (4)
b) With the help of diagrams, explain how a waterfall moves upstream. (4)
c) What is a gorge? (1)
d) Explain how a gorge is formed. (4)

B **Thornton Force waterfall, Yorkshire**

K

L   N

M

J

3

(Pages 242 and 243)

Look at graph **C**.

a) In which year was the highest flood level? (1)
b) For how many years did the Nile flood? (1)
c) What was the lowest yearly discharge recorded? (1)
d) What has happened to flooding on the Nile since 1967? (2)
e) Explain two **advantages** that the building of the dam may have brought to people living along the Nile. (4)
f) Explain two **disadvantages** that the dam may have brought to people living along the Nile. (4)

C **The impact of the Aswan Dam on the flow of the River Nile in Egypt**

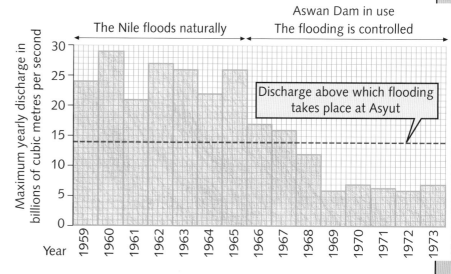

The Nile floods naturally

Aswan Dam in use
The flooding is controlled

Discharge above which flooding takes place at Asyut

Maximum yearly discharge in billions of cubic metres per second

Year   1959 1960 1961 1962 1963 1964 1965 1966 1967 1968 1969 1970 1971 1972 1973

Glacial processes and landforms

Only a few thousand years ago, much of Britain was permanently covered in a thick layer of ice. It would have looked very much like photo **A**, which shows a glacier in Switzerland.

Glaciers form when the climate becomes cold enough for precipitation to fall as snow. The weight of new snowfall turns the underlying snow to ice. When ice moves downhill under the force of gravity, it is called a **glacier**.

Glaciers are like powerful earth-moving machines:
- they dig out rock in the uplands (**erosion**) then
- move the material down the valleys (**transportation**), and then
- dump it in the lowlands (**deposition**).

Much of Britain's scenery is a result of glacial action that happened many thousands of years ago.

Glacial erosion

A glacier can erode much faster than a river. However, like a river it needs a continuous supply of material to help it wear away its valley. The main source of material for a glacier comes from **freeze–thaw weathering** or **frost shattering**.

Freeze–thaw occurs when water gets into cracks in rocks and freezes. As the water turns to ice it expands and widens the cracks. Repeated freezing and thawing causes jagged pieces of rock to break off.

This material, called **moraine**, then freezes into the glacial ice. As it scrapes along the valley floor and sides, it widens and deepens the valley through erosion.

A A glaciated landscape

B Freeze–thaw weathering

Water fills a crack in a rock

The water freezes and the crack is made wider

The rock breaks into several pieces

Two types of glacial erosion

Abrasion is when the pieces of jagged rock and gravel carried by a glacier rub against, and wear away, the sides and floor of a valley.

Plucking is when glacial ice freezes onto solid rock. As the glacier moves, large pieces of rock are pulled away with it.

C

Glacial erosion landforms

Corries

Corries are also known as **cwms** or **cirques**. They are caused by glacial erosion, and are common features of mountainous areas. Corries are deep, rounded hollows with a steep backwall and sides. They are shaped rather like an armchair. Many corries contain a lake or tarn.

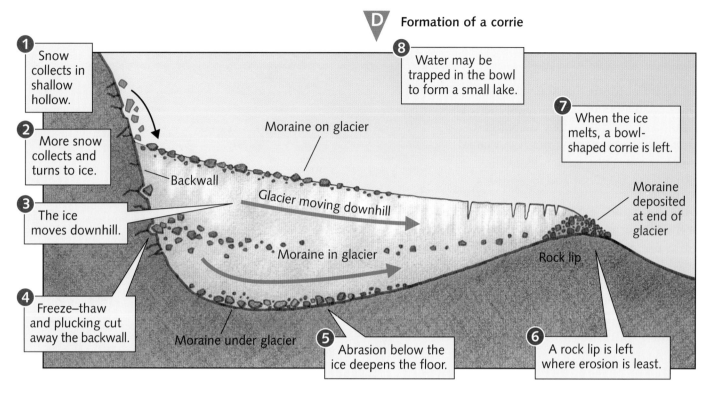

D Formation of a corrie

1 Snow collects in shallow hollow.

2 More snow collects and turns to ice.

3 The ice moves downhill.

4 Freeze–thaw and plucking cut away the backwall.

5 Abrasion below the ice deepens the floor.

6 A rock lip is left where erosion is least.

7 When the ice melts, a bowl-shaped corrie is left.

8 Water may be trapped in the bowl to form a small lake.

Moraine on glacier

Backwall

Glacier moving downhill

Moraine in glacier

Moraine under glacier

Moraine deposited at end of glacier

Rock lip

Arêtes and pyramidal peaks

Corries often develop on more than one side of a mountain. When this happens, the land between them gets narrower until a knife-edged ridge is formed. This is called an **arête**. When three or more corries cut into the same mountain, a **pyramidal peak** is formed.

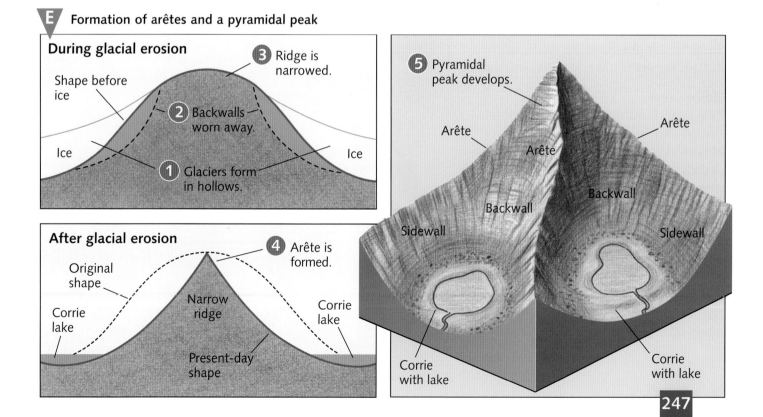

E Formation of arêtes and a pyramidal peak

During glacial erosion

Shape before ice

Ice

Ice

1 Glaciers form in hollows.

2 Backwalls worn away.

3 Ridge is narrowed.

After glacial erosion

Original shape

Corrie lake

Narrow ridge

Present-day shape

Corrie lake

4 Arête is formed.

5 Pyramidal peak develops.

Arête

Arête

Arête

Backwall

Backwall

Sidewall

Sidewall

Corrie with lake

Corrie with lake

Glacial troughs

When glaciers move downhill, they tend to follow the easiest route. In most cases they follow an existing river valley. Unlike a river, however, they fill the entire valley and their power to erode is much greater. This means that instead of having to wind around obstacles like a river, the glacier can follow a more direct route.

The result of this is that the valley is widened, deepened and straightened. The **V-shape** of the river valley is changed into a **U-shaped** glacial trough. A **glacial trough** is a straight, trench-like valley with a wide, flat floor and steep sides.

Truncated spurs

As the glacier moves down the valley it works like a giant bulldozer. It wears away anything in its path and smoothes the valley sides. It removes the ends of **interlocking spurs** or ridges to leave steep, cliff-like **truncated spurs**. Truncated spurs are shortened or cut-off ridges caused by glacial erosion.

Hanging valleys

Hanging valleys are formed as a result of different amounts of erosion in the main and tributary valleys. The floor of the small tributary valley is eroded more slowly than that of the main valley. When the ice melts, the tributary valley is left hanging above the main valley. The stream in the hanging valley will then plunge over the edge as a waterfall.

Ribbon lakes

Many glacial troughs in highland Britain contain long, narrow **ribbon lakes**. Ribbon lakes are partly a result of erosion when a glacier over-deepens part of its valley leaving a hollow. After the glacier melts, the hollow fills with water and a ribbon lake is formed. They may also be formed when a glacier dumps moraine material in an arc-like ridge across the valley, as shown in drawing **C**. After melting, the moraine acts as a dam and traps water behind it, so forming a ribbon lake.

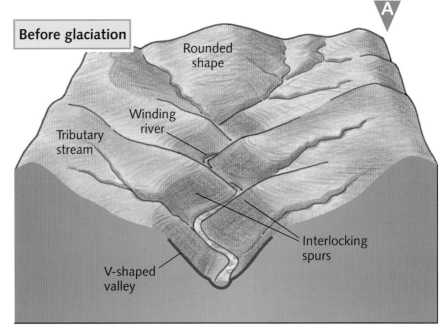

A

Before glaciation

Rounded shape

Winding river

Tributary stream

Interlocking spurs

V-shaped valley

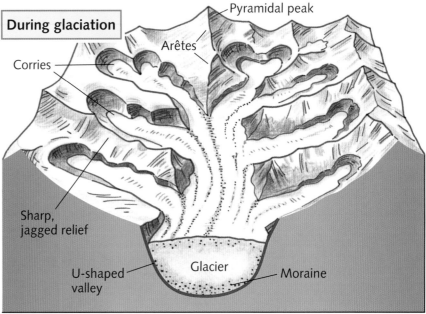

During glaciation

Pyramidal peak

Arêtes

Corries

Sharp, jagged relief

U-shaped valley

Glacier

Moraine

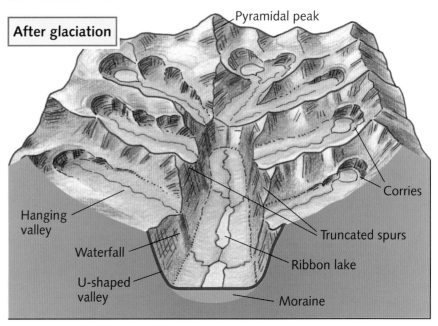

After glaciation

Pyramidal peak

Corries

Hanging valley

Truncated spurs

Waterfall

Ribbon lake

U-shaped valley

Moraine

Glacial deposition landforms

Glaciers **erode** and **transport** huge amounts of material. This material ranges in size from boulders as big as houses to the finest rock particles.

Glaciers eventually dump all the rock debris that they carry. This happens when the ice in the glacier melts. The material that is dumped is called **till**, **boulder clay** or **moraine**. It is easily recognised as an unsorted jumble of jagged and angular rock fragments.

B A terminal moraine in Greenland

Terminal moraine

C

Medial moraine is found in the centre of the glacier. It forms where two glaciers meet. When dumped, it forms a long, low ridge down the middle of the valley.

Lateral moraine is carried on the surface of the glacier. It comes from rockfalls on valley slopes. When the ice melts the material is dumped in a long line along the valley sides.

Glacier

Freeze–thaw on valley sides

Former snout of glacier

Section through glacier

Crevasses

Debris carried at bottom of glacier

Ground moraine is material dragged underneath a glacier. When deposited it forms the flat valley floor.

Erratics are boulders that have been carried long distances by the ice. They are often of a different rock to that found locally.

Drumlins are smooth, rounded mounds of material that usually lie along the direction of ice flow. They are blunt at one end and long and tapered at the other.

Terminal moraine is dumped at the end, or snout, of a glacier. It forms an arc-like ridge across the valley, and may be over 100 metres high.

Glacial landforms on OS maps

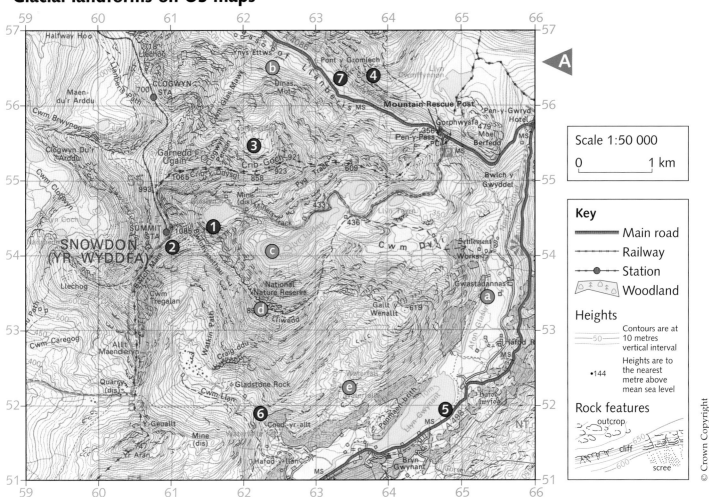

Scale 1:50 000

0   1 km

Key

▬▬▬ Main road

┼┼┼ Railway

┼●┼ Station

⌂ Woodland

Heights

—50— Contours are at 10 metres vertical interval

•144 Heights are to the nearest metre above mean sea level

Rock features

outcrop

cliff

scree

© Crown Copyright

The Ordnance Survey (OS) map **A** shows part of Snowdonia in North Wales. This is a glaciated area and the map shows many landforms caused by glacial erosion. See if you can recognise the ones numbered **1** to **7** in the following list.

Further examples of five of the features may be found at the places marked **a** to **e** on the map. For each one:

- identify the landform
- name the feature
- give the grid reference
- make a simple drawing.

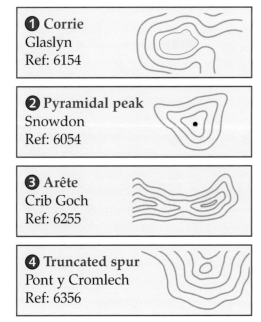

1 Corrie
Glaslyn
Ref: 6154

2 Pyramidal peak
Snowdon
Ref: 6054

3 Arête
Crib Goch
Ref: 6255

4 Truncated spur
Pont y Cromlech
Ref: 6356

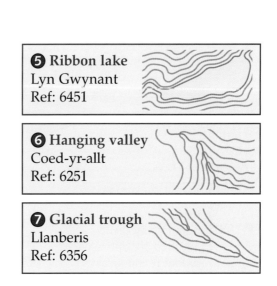

5 Ribbon lake
Lyn Gwynant
Ref: 6451

6 Hanging valley
Coed-yr-allt
Ref: 6251

7 Glacial trough
Llanberis
Ref: 6356

Glacial highlands and human activity

Glacial highlands are areas of attractive scenery with rugged mountains, steep-sided valleys, scattered lakes and fast-flowing streams. Whilst these areas are generally difficult to live in and therefore sparsely populated, there are many features that encourage human activity. There is the danger, however, that development for economic reasons may damage and spoil the natural beauty of these areas. Some examples of this are shown below.

Farming

Advantages

The steep slopes, thin soils and cool, wet climate are ideal for hill sheep farming.

Effects

Apart from modifying the natural vegetation, sheep farming does little damage to the environment. Farms are usually an attractive feature in the landscape.

Forestry

Advantages

Coniferous trees grow well in the poor soil and on all but the steepest slopes.

Effects

Forests of coniferous trees can spoil the look of hillsides. The logging industry often fells trees on a large scale. This can leave huge, ugly scars and if not well managed may damage the environment.

Water supply

Advantages

Ribbon lakes form natural reservoirs. Glacial troughs are ideal sites for artificial reservoirs.

Effects

The drowning of a glacial trough to provide a reservoir means the loss of homes and jobs for people who previously lived and worked there. The new lake can add to the attractiveness of the area.

Tourism

Advantages

The mountain scenery and winter snow attract tourists, walkers, climbers and skiers.

Effects

Winter sports facilities are ugly and can damage the natural vegetation. Walkers can wear away footpaths. New car parks, campsites and other visitor amenities may spoil the scenery and damage the environment.

Coastal processes and erosion landforms

The sea is constantly changing the shape of the land. On stormy days, large waves crash against the shore and wear away the coastline by **erosion**. The sea **transports** the material it has eroded and **deposits** it in places where the water is calm. This ability of the sea to erode, transport and deposit large amounts of material produces a variety of coastal landforms.

Erosion

There are four main processes by which waves erode the land. These are similar to those of a river explained on page 232.

- **Corrasion** or **abrasion** is caused by large waves hurling beach material against a cliff.
- **Attrition** is when waves cause rocks and pebbles to bump into each other and break into smaller pieces.
- **Corrosion** or **solution** is when salts and other acids in sea water slowly dissolve a cliff.
- **Hydraulic pressure** is the explosion of compressed air trapped in cracks of cliffs by advancing waves.

Waves are caused by the wind. The size of a wave depends upon the:

- strength of the wind
- length of time that the wind blows
- distance of sea over which the wind has blown.

Waves are largest when the wind is strong, has blown for a long time and across a great distance of sea.

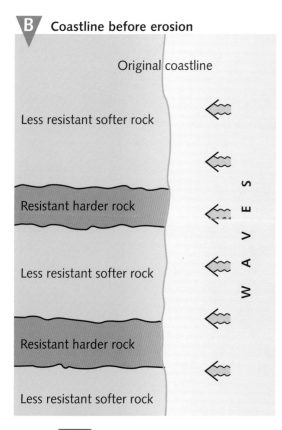

B Coastline before erosion

Original coastline

Less resistant softer rock

Resistant harder rock

Less resistant softer rock

Resistant harder rock

Less resistant softer rock

WAVES

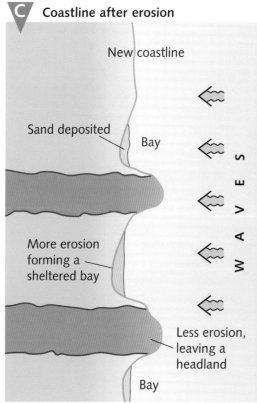

C Coastline after erosion

New coastline

Sand deposited

Bay

More erosion forming a sheltered bay

Less erosion, leaving a headland

Bay

WAVES

Headlands and bays

These features are caused by coastal erosion. They form along coasts that have alternating bands of hard and soft rocks.

The soft rock is easily worn away and forms bays, often with a sandy beach. The harder rock is more difficult to erode and is left jutting out into the sea as a headland.

252

Caves, arches and stacks

Cliffs are more likely to form where the coastline consists of resistant rock which is difficult to erode. Within this resistant rock, however, there will be weaker areas such as cracks and joints which the sea can attack more easily.

Diagram **E** shows how a thin crack in a headland can be opened up to form a cave and then an arch. Eventually the arch will collapse leaving a **stack**. In time, further wave action will result in the stack collapsing to leave a **stump**.

Photo **D** shows the Foreland, a chalk headland near Swanage in Dorset. At one time the two stacks were joined to the mainland.

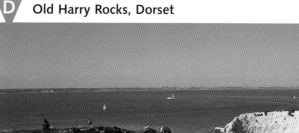

D Old Harry Rocks, Dorset

E Formation of caves, arches and stacks

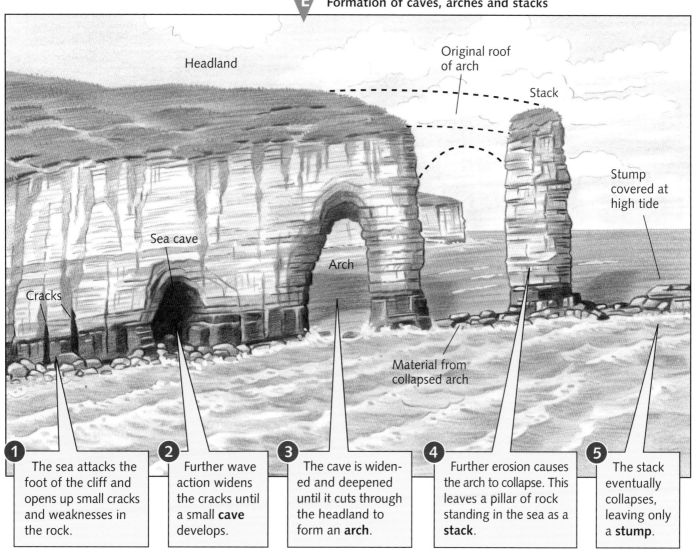

Headland

Original roof of arch

Stack

Stump covered at high tide

Sea cave

Arch

Cracks

Material from collapsed arch

1 The sea attacks the foot of the cliff and opens up small cracks and weaknesses in the rock.

2 Further wave action widens the cracks until a small **cave** develops.

3 The cave is widened and deepened until it cuts through the headland to form an **arch**.

4 Further erosion causes the arch to collapse. This leaves a pillar of rock standing in the sea as a **stack**.

5 The stack eventually collapses, leaving only a **stump**.

The erosion of Barton Cliffs

Coastal erosion can cause severe problems. Agricultural land may be lost, buildings destroyed and leisure amenities put in danger. In some places, attempts have been made to manage coastal erosion. These attempts have met with varied success.

Barton Cliffs are located in Christchurch Bay on the Hampshire coast. The cliffs here are being worn away at a rate of one metre a year, and several buildings situated on top of them have already been destroyed. There are two causes of erosion in this area. The first is the sea, which undercuts the base of the cliffs and quickly removes fallen material. The second is heavy rain, which seeps into the ground and causes landslides.

Over £4 million has been spent on protection measures to reduce erosion at Barton. Despite these measures, the cliffs are still being worn away. In a recent storm, large sections of the cliffs slipped into the sea and parts of the sea defences were also lost.

A Landslip near Barton

Many people are against coastal defence schemes. They argue that protecting one area can cause problems elsewhere. They support schemes which work with nature rather than against it. Schemes like this, they say, do less damage and help retain wildlife and the quality of the natural environment.

B Coastal defence scheme at Barton

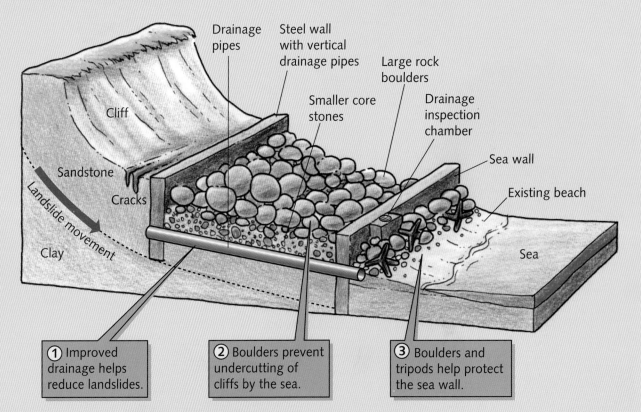

① Improved drainage helps reduce landslides.

② Boulders prevent undercutting of cliffs by the sea.

③ Boulders and tripods help protect the sea wall.

Coastal processes

Transportation

Waves rarely approach a beach at right-angles. They usually approach at an angle that depends upon the direction of the wind. The water that rushes up a beach after a wave breaks is called the **swash**. The swash picks up sand and shingle and carries it up the beach. When the water returns down the beach it is called **backwash**. Due to gravity, the backwash and any material it is carrying tend to move straight down the beach. The result is that material is transported along the beach in a zig-zag movement. This is called **longshore drift**.

Longshore drift is usually in one direction only – that of the prevailing or main wind. For example, the prevailing wind in Britain is from the south-west. This causes material to be moved from west to east along the south coast of England.

Longshore drift can seriously erode beaches. To prevent this, people sometimes erect wooden breakwater fences down the beach. The fences are called **groynes**. They reduce the force of the waves and trap sand on their windward side. This is an advantage to people living in a seaside resort who do not wish to lose their sand. It also helps prevent coastal erosion by protecting the cliffs from the sea.

C Groynes near Barton Cliffs, Dorset

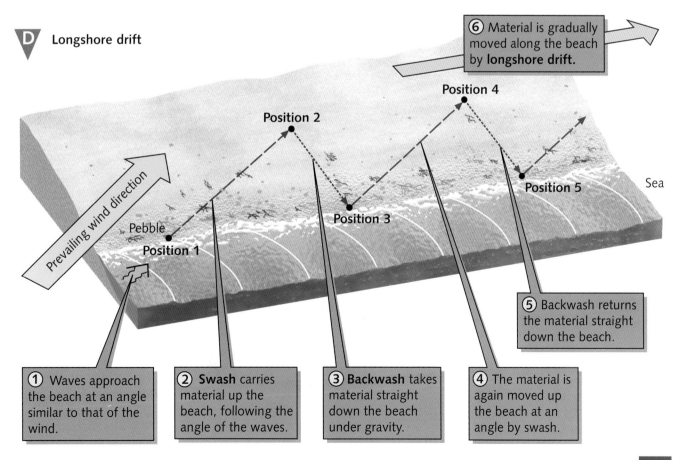

D Longshore drift

⑥ Material is gradually moved along the beach by **longshore drift.**

Position 4

Position 2

Position 3

Position 5

Sea

Pebble

Position 1

Prevailing wind direction

⑤ Backwash returns the material straight down the beach.

① Waves approach the beach at an angle similar to that of the wind.

② **Swash** carries material up the beach, following the angle of the waves.

③ **Backwash** takes material straight down the beach under gravity.

④ The material is again moved up the beach at an angle by swash.

255

Coastal processes and deposition landforms

Deposition

Coastal deposition occurs in sheltered areas where the sea can no longer erode or transport material. This often happens in a bay where wave action is at its most gentle. The most common type of deposition feature is the beach, which may be made up of either sand or shingle. Shingle beaches are steeper than sandy beaches.

Beaches are not permanent features. Their size and shape changes every time the tide comes in and goes out. Storm conditions, when huge waves crash against the shore, can also alter beaches considerably.

Spits

Spits are sand or pebble beaches joined to the land at one end. They are features of coastal deposition and tend to be formed by longshore drift. Most extend at a gentle angle out to sea or grow across a river mouth. Many spits have a curved or hooked end.

Spits only develop in places where:
- longshore drift moves large amounts of material along the beach
- there is a sudden change of direction of the coastline
- the sea is shallow, sheltered and calm.

> Coastal deposition is the laying down or dumping of material by wave action.

> A spit is a narrow tongue of sand and shingle which grows out from the shoreline.

A Dawlish Warren spit, Devon

B Formation of a spit

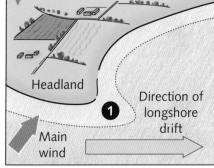

Headland

Direction of longshore drift

1

Main wind

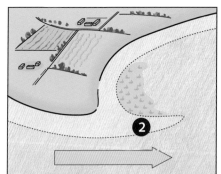

2

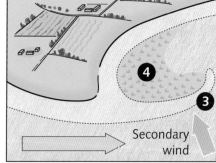

4

3

Secondary wind

1 Sand and shingle are deposited in water which is sheltered by the headland.

2 Material builds up and outwards, forming a spit.

3 A change in wind direction causes the waves to change direction. The end of the spit is made to curve.

4 The shallow, sheltered area behind the spit fills with mud. This is called a **salt marsh**.

256

Sea-level changes

Sea level is always changing. During the last Ice Age, large amounts of water were stored in great **ice fields** and **glaciers**. With less water being available to the oceans, sea level fell. At this time the English Channel, the Irish Sea and most of the North Sea were dry land, and Britain was joined to Europe. At the end of the Ice Age, the melting of glaciers led to a release of water and a rise in sea level, and Britain once again became an island.

The main effect of rising sea level was to drown large stretches of coastline. This led to the development of new coastal landforms such as **fiords** (fjords) and **rias**.

 Geiranger Fiord, Norway

 A ria, Salcombe, Devon

Fiords

Description
Fiords are long, narrow inlets with high, cliff-like sides. They are very deep except at the shallow entrance.

Formation
Fiords are found where glaciers have deepened valleys until they are below sea level. When the ice melted, the sea level rose and flooded the valley that had been formed by the glacier.

Examples
North-west Scotland, Norway, British Columbia in Canada, South island of New Zealand, and Alaska.

Rias

Description
Rias are long, winding inlets with low, gently sloping sides. They are generally shallow, with their depth increasing towards the sea.

Formation
Rias are found in areas that were not glaciated. They result from the drowning of former river valleys and their tributaries.

Examples
Parts of south-west England, Wales and Ireland, also Brittany in France, and north-west Spain.

Coastal flooding in MEDCs

A **storm surge** is when the level of the sea rises rapidly to a height well above the average.

South-east England and the Netherlands

Coastal flooding, when it occurs in densely populated areas, can cause considerable loss of life, damage to property and disruption to everyday life. Such an event affected south-east England and parts of the Netherlands in February 1953.

Causes

Most of the area between the Humber and Thames is low-lying. Indeed some parts surrounding The Wash are actually below sea level. These areas were protected by small sea walls and embankments, many of which were in a state of disrepair after the Second World War. Although even at the time people realised there was a high flood risk, they were totally unprepared for what happened.

On the night of 31 January /1 February 1953, four major factors combined to cause a **storm surge** which flooded large areas of both south-east England and the Netherlands. The causes of the storm surge are shown on map **A** below.

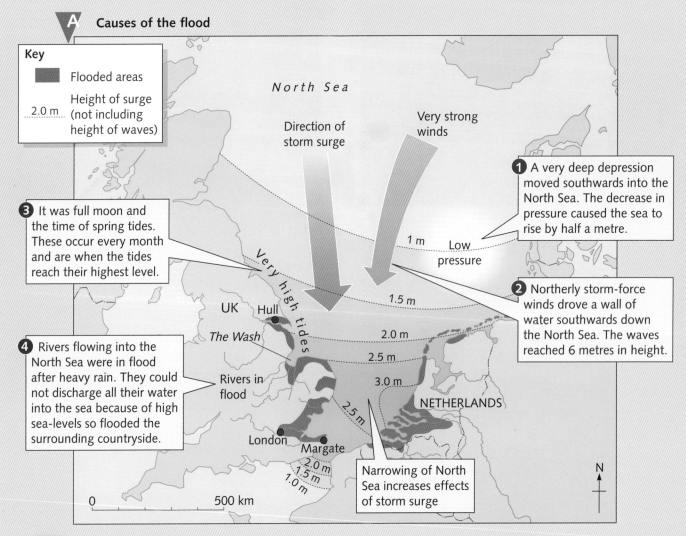

A Causes of the flood

Key

- Flooded areas
- 2.0 m — Height of surge (not including height of waves)

North Sea

Direction of storm surge

Very strong winds

1 A very deep depression moved southwards into the North Sea. The decrease in pressure caused the sea to rise by half a metre.

3 It was full moon and the time of spring tides. These occur every month and are when the tides reach their highest level.

1 m — Low pressure

2 Northerly storm-force winds drove a wall of water southwards down the North Sea. The waves reached 6 metres in height.

Very high tides

1.5 m

UK — Hull

The Wash

2.0 m

4 Rivers flowing into the North Sea were in flood after heavy rain. They could not discharge all their water into the sea because of high sea-levels so flooded the surrounding countryside.

Rivers in flood

2.5 m

3.0 m

2.5 m

NETHERLANDS

London — Margate

2.0 m
1.5 m
1.0 m

Narrowing of North Sea increases effects of storm surge

N

0   500 km

Effects

The storm surge was up to 3 metres higher than the normal spring tide. The surge, coupled with huge storm waves, broke through sea defences both in south-east England and the Netherlands in the early morning of 1 February.

Altogether, the disaster caused the deaths of 2,100 people and made another 330,000 homeless. It also drowned thousands of farm animals and ruined huge areas of farmland. Map **B** and list **C** show details of the effects of the flood on eastern England.

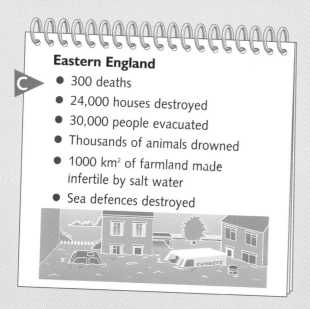

C

Eastern England

- 300 deaths
- 24,000 houses destroyed
- 30,000 people evacuated
- Thousands of animals drowned
- 1000 km² of farmland made infertile by salt water
- Sea defences destroyed

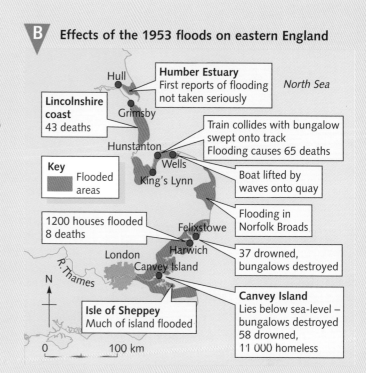

B **Effects of the 1953 floods on eastern England**

North Sea

Hull

Humber Estuary
First reports of flooding not taken seriously

Lincolnshire coast
43 deaths

Grimsby

Hunstanton

Train collides with bungalow swept onto track
Flooding causes 65 deaths

Wells

Key
Flooded areas

King's Lynn

Boat lifted by waves onto quay

Flooding in Norfolk Broads

1200 houses flooded
8 deaths

Felixstowe

37 drowned, bungalows destroyed

London

Harwich

Canvey Island

R. Thames

N

Isle of Sheppey
Much of island flooded

Canvey Island
Lies below sea-level – bungalows destroyed
58 drowned,
11 000 homeless

0   100 km

What can be done to reduce the risk of flooding?

Apart from Towyn in North Wales which flooded in 1990, there have been very few examples of serious, large-scale coastal flooding in the UK since the 1953 disaster. This has been mainly due to the introduction of flood protection schemes and flood action plans during the past 50 years.

Some of the precautions taken include:
- building higher and stronger sea walls
- building tidal barriers across river estuaries, for example the Thames Barrier shown in photo **D**
- stop building on coastal floodplains
- improving weather forecasting and early flood warning systems
- trying to reduce the increase in global warming which threatens to increase the flood risk.

D **The Thames Barrier at Woolwich**

Although these precautions have largely been successful, many people feel that sea defences are unsightly and too difficult and expensive to maintain. These people feel that, as with rivers, nature should be allowed to take its course and that areas prone to flooding by the sea should be allowed to flood. Naturally, people who live and work in these areas disagree and want increased protection.

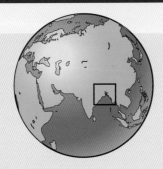

Coastal flooding in an LEDC

Bangladesh

Bangladesh is one of the world's most densely populated countries. Its population of 140 million people live in an area barely half the size of the UK. It is also one of the world's poorest countries. Most people live in small villages and depend on farming for their livelihood.

Bangladesh is located on the **delta** formed by three great rivers: the Ganges, Brahmaputra and Meghna. Most of the country (80%) is less than 1.5 metres above sea level. Every year during the heavy monsoon rains, the rivers flood half the country to a depth of 30 cm. For most people the yearly flood is essential for their survival and way of life. It brings water in which to grow crops, and adds fertile silt to the land.

In recent times flooding has become more severe and has caused great problems for the people of Bangladesh. One of the worst floods was in 1970, when more than 450,000 people were killed and 34 million made homeless.

The Bangladesh government has recorded 14 abnormal floods in the past 30 years, each of which has covered at least 60% of the land and affected over two-thirds of the population. One of the most recent serious floods was in 1998.

A Effects of the 1998 Bangladesh floods

- Three-quarters of the country flooded for almost two months.
- Electricity supply cut off for several weeks.
- Safe drinking water badly polluted.
- Up to half a million cattle and poultry lost.

- Two million tonnes of rice destroyed, and most of the jute, sugar cane and vegetable crops ruined.
- 1,379 reported dead but many more missing.

- Estimated damage put at US$ 1.5 billion.
- Thousands of kilometres of roads and railways flooded. Many bridges destroyed.
- Dhaka International Airport closed.
- Over 7 million homes destroyed and at least 25 million made homeless.

What causes flooding in Bangladesh?

Most of Bangladesh is flat and lies just a few metres above sea level. With very high rainfall and three great rivers flowing across it, it is no surprise that flooding has always been a regular event.

Recent serious floods, however, have been a result of several factors working together. In some cases human activities have added to the problem. Some of these are shown in diagram **C** below.

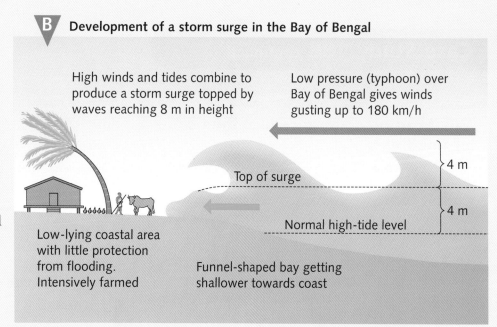

B Development of a storm surge in the Bay of Bengal

High winds and tides combine to produce a storm surge topped by waves reaching 8 m in height

Low pressure (typhoon) over Bay of Bengal gives winds gusting up to 180 km/h

4 m

Top of surge

4 m

Normal high-tide level

Low-lying coastal area with little protection from flooding. Intensively farmed

Funnel-shaped bay getting shallower towards coast

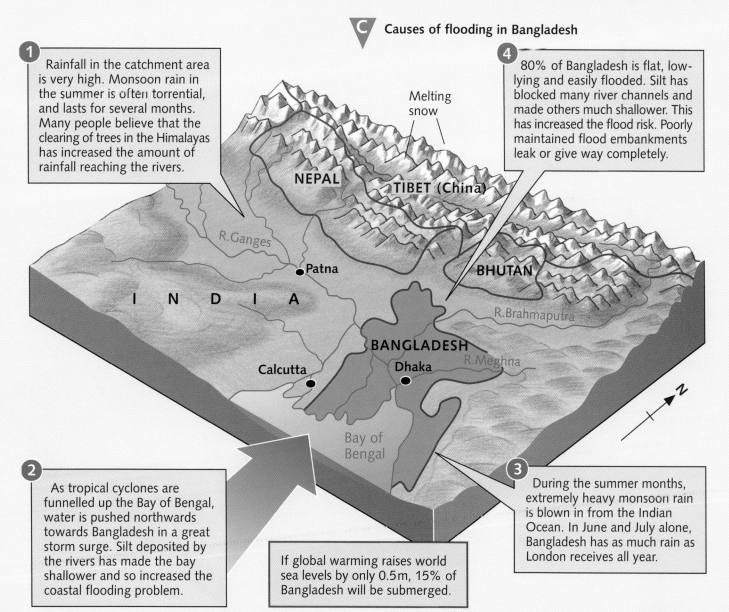

C Causes of flooding in Bangladesh

1 Rainfall in the catchment area is very high. Monsoon rain in the summer is often torrential, and lasts for several months. Many people believe that the clearing of trees in the Himalayas has increased the amount of rainfall reaching the rivers.

4 80% of Bangladesh is flat, low-lying and easily flooded. Silt has blocked many river channels and made others much shallower. This has increased the flood risk. Poorly maintained flood embankments leak or give way completely.

Melting snow

NEPAL

TIBET (China)

R. Ganges

Patna

BHUTAN

I N D I A

R. Brahmaputra

BANGLADESH

R. Meghna

Calcutta

Dhaka

N

Bay of Bengal

2 As tropical cyclones are funnelled up the Bay of Bengal, water is pushed northwards towards Bangladesh in a great storm surge. Silt deposited by the rivers has made the bay shallower and so increased the coastal flooding problem.

If global warming raises world sea levels by only 0.5m, 15% of Bangladesh will be submerged.

3 During the summer months, extremely heavy monsoon rain is blown in from the Indian Ocean. In June and July alone, Bangladesh has as much rain as London receives all year.

What can be done to reduce the risk of flooding?

There is no easy solution to Bangladesh's flooding problem. The enormous size of the problem, the extreme poverty of the country and the difficulty of identifying the exact causes of flooding, make the task almost impossible.

However, in 1989 the Flood Action Plan (FAP) was set up. This was supported by several wealthy countries and many international agencies, including the World Bank. The huge scheme contained 26 action points and cost billions of dollars. Much of the money has been spent on building embankments and dredging major rivers to make them deeper. Dams have also been built to control river flow and hold back the monsoon rainwater in reservoirs. Diagram **A** below explains the main points of the scheme.

Not everyone agrees with the Flood Action Plan. People are concerned that:

- building embankments and deepening rivers could lead to even worse flooding downstream
- half a million people will lose their land to reservoirs and embankments
- embankments will reduce river access to fishing people
- flood control systems may damage the environment
- normal flooding may be reduced and damage farming
- a shortage of money could result in only the urban areas being protected, leaving the very poor rural inhabitants still at risk
- the scheme will take years to construct and require constant maintenance.

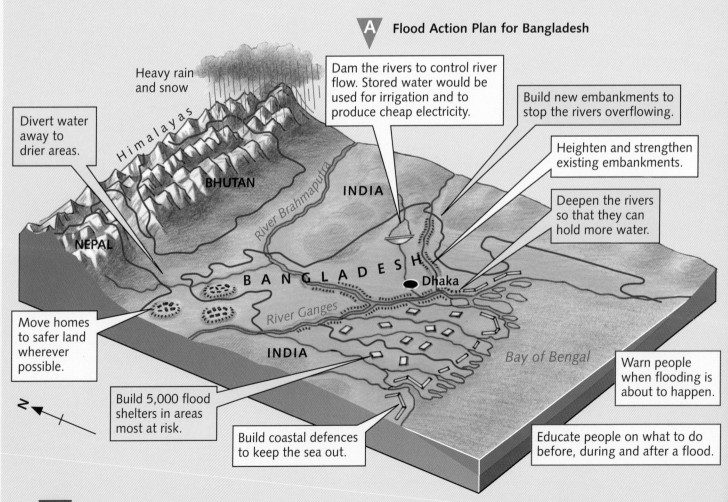

A Flood Action Plan for Bangladesh

Heavy rain and snow

Divert water away to drier areas.

Dam the rivers to control river flow. Stored water would be used for irrigation and to produce cheap electricity.

Build new embankments to stop the rivers overflowing.

Heighten and strengthen existing embankments.

Deepen the rivers so that they can hold more water.

Move homes to safer land wherever possible.

Build 5,000 flood shelters in areas most at risk.

Build coastal defences to keep the sea out.

Warn people when flooding is about to happen.

Educate people on what to do before, during and after a flood.

Himalayas · BHUTAN · INDIA · River Brahmaputra · NEPAL · B A N G L A D E S H · Dhaka · River Ganges · INDIA · Bay of Bengal

B   A cyclone shelter poster

এই আশ্রয়কেন্দ্র ইউরোপীয় ইউনিয়নের আর্থিক সহায়তায় নির্মিত

C   The Dhaka flood embankment

Sustainable development improves the quality of people's lives without wasting resources or harming the environment.

Appropriate technology meets the needs of the local people and the environment in which they live.

What other flood control methods could be used?

Other smaller and less expensive solutions to Bangladesh's flood problems have been proposed. Most of these use **appropriate technology** and provide a more **sustainable** solution to Bangladesh's problems. Examples of these include:

- building flood embankments to protect key urban areas such as Dhaka, the country's capital
- building large numbers of flood shelters for people, their belongings and livestock

- providing better prediction and warnings of floods – improve forecasting using satellite images and early warning systems
- preparing emergency services for quick and effective help during and after a flood.

2005 – signs of success

The Flood Action Plan has enjoyed some success. In May 1994, Bangladesh was hit by one of the strongest cyclones in living memory. Despite this, the death toll was in the hundreds rather than in the thousands as in previous storms. Similarly, in 1998 and 2004, although damage and loss of life was high, it was nothing like as severe as would previously be expected from the storms that hit the country.

The lower death toll and reduction in damage was largely due to:

- a new high-technology meteorological office providing accurate 36-hour warnings
- more flood shelters, with better access, for people most at risk
- improved education – the government printed millions of information leaflets and sent 33,000 volunteers around the country on bicycles to teach people how to prepare for a cyclone.

263

1 (Pages 246 and 247)
a) What is a glacier?
b) How do glaciers form?
c) With the help of a diagram, explain the process of freeze–thaw weathering.
d) Describe two types of glacial erosion.

2 (Pages 246 to 248)
Describe each of the following glacial features:
a) arête   b) corrie
c) pyramidal peak d) glacial trough
e) truncated spur f) hanging valley.

3 (Pages 246 and 247)
a) Make a copy of the drawing below.
b) Label the features marked A, B and C.
c) Draw an arrow to show ice movement.
d) Use the diagram to explain how a corrie is formed.

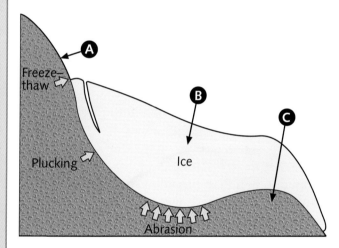

4 (Page 249)
a) What is moraine?
b) Give two other names for moraine.
c) Describe four different types of moraine.
d) What are drumlins?
e) What are erratics?

5 (Pages 252 and 253)
a) What is erosion?
b) Describe the four main ways in which the sea erodes the coastline.
c) What three factors affect the size of a wave?
d) With the help of a diagram, explain how headlands and bays are formed.

6 (Page 253)
Put the following into the correct order to explain how a stack forms.
- Further erosion causes the arch to collapse
- Wave action widens the cracks to form a cave
- The sea attacks small cracks
- The cave is eroded to form an arch
- A pillar of rock called a stack is left.

7 (Page 254)
a) With the help of a diagram, explain how longshore drift moves material along a beach.
b) What is the main problem caused by longshore drift?
c) Explain how longshore drift can be prevented or controlled.

8 (Pages 255 and 256)
a) What is a spit?
b) Copy the diagram below and label it to describe how a spit is formed.

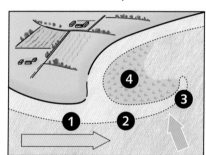

9 (Pages 260 to 263)
Describe the main features of flooding in Bangladesh by answering the following questions:

Flooding in Bangladesh
a) Why is normal flooding important?
b) What were the effects of the 1998 flood?
c) What are the main causes of flooding?
d) Who supported the Flood Action Plan?
e) What were the main points of the Plan?
f) What were the disadvantages of the Plan?
g) How successful has the Flood Action Plan been?

EXAMINATION QUESTIONS

1

(Pages 246 to 249)

a) Name any four of the features
that have been labelled A–E
on diagram **A**. **(4)**

b) Describe **one** process of glacial
erosion which may have helped
form some of these features. **(2)**

c) Choose **one** of the features and
explain how it is formed. **(3)**

d) What sort of material is a
moraine made of? **(1)**

e) Explain how a moraine
is formed. **(3)**

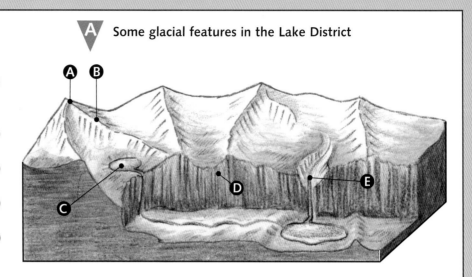

A Some glacial features in the Lake District

2

(Pages 252 to 255)

a) Name the features A, B, C and D
on diagram **B**. **(4)**

b) Which of the following are types of
sea erosion:

- mass movement ■ attrition
- hydraulic action ■ weathering
- corrasion ■ frost action? **(3)**

c) Explain how a stack is formed. **(4)**

d) The beach on diagram **B** was formed
by longshore drift. With the help of a
diagram, explain how longshore drift
moves sand and pebbles. **(4)**

e) What are groynes? **(1)**

f) What effect do groynes have on
a beach? **(2)**

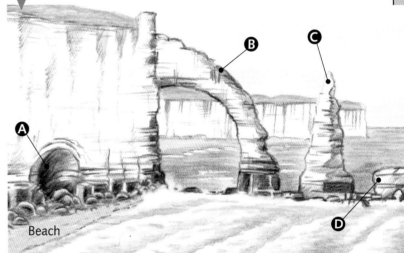

B Part of the Atlantic coast of France

Beach

3

(Pages 252 to 254)

Look at diagram **C**.

a) What happened to the hotel? **(1)**

b) List the two main causes of the
cliff collapse. **(2)**

c) Describe two methods used to
protect coastlines from erosion. **(4)**

d) Suggest one reason why some
coastlines are not protected from
wave action. **(2)**

C The coastline near Scarborough in 1993

Hotel

Soft clay

Sea

Heavy rain
saturates the clay

Slip plane
develops

Wave-
cut
notch

Sea

Cliff collapse
occurs

Slip
plane

Sea

GLOSSARY

Abrasion   Erosion caused by the rubbing and scouring effect of material carried by rivers, glaciers, waves and the wind.

Acid rain   Rainwater containing chemicals that result from the burning of fossil fuels.

Age–sex pyramid   See *Population pyramid/structure*.

Aid   The giving of resources by one country, or an organisation, to another country.

Anticyclone   An area of high pressure usually associated with settled weather.

Appropriate technology Technology suited to the area where it is used.

Arch   A coastal feature formed when waves erode through a small headland.

Arête   A narrow, knife-edged ridge formed by glacial erosion when two adjacent cirques erode towards each other.

Aspect   The direction which a slope or building faces.

Attrition   Erosion caused when rocks and boulders, transported by rivers and waves, bump into each other and break up into smaller pieces.

B

Biological weathering   The breakdown of rock through the actions of plants and animals.

Biomass   The total amount of organic matter contained by plants and animals in a given area.

Birth rate   The number of live births per 1,000 people per year.

Burgess model   An urban land use model showing five concentric zones, based upon age of houses and wealth of their inhabitants.

Bustee   An Indian term for a shanty town.

C

Central Business District (CBD)   The commercial and business centre of a town or city where land values are at their highest.

Chemical weathering   The decomposition of rock caused by a chemical change within that rock.

Climate   The average weather conditions for a place taken over a period of time.

Coastal management   The protection of the coastline and its wildlife, the improvement in the quality of life of local residents and the provision of recreational facilities for visitors.

Collision margin   A boundary between two plates moving together where, as both consist of continental crust, fold mountains form.

Common Agricultural Policy (CAP)   The system of agricultural support adopted by the European Union for member states.

Commuter   A person who travels some distance from their home to their place of work.

Conservative margin   A boundary between two plates that are sliding past each other and where crust is being neither formed nor destroyed.

Constructive margin   A boundary between two plates that are moving apart and where new crust is being formed.

Conurbation   A very large urban area formed when two or more towns merge with each other.

Core–periphery   Economic growth tends to be most rapid in one part of a country (the core), leaving other places less developed and less well-off (the periphery).

Corrasion   Erosion caused by the rubbing and scouring effect of material carried by rivers, glaciers, waves and the wind.

Corrie (cirque)   A deep, steep-sided, rounded or semi-circular hollow, often with a lake, found in glaciated highlands.

Corrosion   Erosion caused by acids in rivers and waves dissolving rocks by chemical action.

Counter-urbanisation   The movement of people and employment away from large cities to smaller settlements within more rural areas.

Crust   The thin outer layer of the Earth.

Death rate   The number of deaths per 1,000 people per year.

Deforestation   The complete clearance of forested land.

Delta   An area of silt deposited by a river where it enters the sea or a lake.

Demographic transition model   A model that tries to show how changes in birth and death rates over a period of time may be related to different stages of economic development.

Densely populated   An area that is crowded.

Dependents   Those people who rely on others of working age.

Deposition   The laying down of material previously transported by mass movement, water, glaciers, waves and the wind.

Depression   An area of low pressure in temperate latitudes usually associated with cloud, rain and strong winds.

Desertification   The turning of land, often through physical processes and human mismanagement, into desert.

Destructive margin   A boundary between two plates that are moving together and where one, consisting of oceanic crust, is forced downwards and destroyed.

Developed country   A country that has a lot of money, many services and a high standard of living.

Developing country   A country that may be quite poor, has few services and a low standard of living.

Development   The level of economic growth of a country or region and the processes of change taking place within it.

Diet   The amount (measured in calories) and quality (the balance between proteins, carbohydrates and vitamins) of food needed to keep a person healthy and active.

Discharge   The amount of water in a river at a given time, usually measured in cumecs (cubic metres per second).

Dispersed settlement   Several farms or buildings spread out over a large area.

Drainage basin   The area of land drained by a main river and its tributaries.

Drought   A prolonged period of dry weather.

Drumlin   A smooth, elongated mound of material deposited by a glacier, and streamlined in the direction of ice movement.

Earthquake   A sudden movement within the Earth's crust, usually close to a plate boundary.

Economically active   Those people who work and receive a wage.

Ecosystem   A natural system in which plants (flora) and animals (fauna) interact with each other and the non-living environment.

Ecotourism   A sustainable form of 'green' tourism aimed at protecting the environment and local cultures.

Employment structure   The division of jobs into, traditionally, primary, secondary and tertiary sectors, together with, more recently, the quaternary sector.

Energy flows   The transfer of energy through an ecosystem by means of a food chain (food web).

Enterprise Zone (EZ)   An area recognised by the UK government in the 1980s as suffering from acute physical and economic decay and in need of urgent regeneration.

Environment   The surroundings in which plants, animals and people live.

Epicentre   The place on the Earth's surface immediately above the focus of an earthquake.

Erosion   The wearing away of the land by material carried by rivers, glaciers, waves and the wind.

Erratic   A large boulder transported by ice and deposited in an area of totally different rock.

Ethnic group   A group of people with common characteristics related to race, nationality, language, religion or culture.

Evapotranspiration   The loss of moisture from water surfaces and the soil (evaporation) and vegetation (transpiration).

Exfoliation   A physical weathering process by which, due to extreme changes in temperature, the surface layers of exposed rock peel away.

Exports   Goods transported by one country for sale in a different country.

Favela   A Brazilian term for an informal, shanty-type settlement.

Fiord   A long, narrow, steep-sided inlet formed by glaciers and later drowned by a rise in sea level.

Flood   A period of either high river discharge (when a river overflows its banks) or, along the coast, an extremely high tide.

Floodplain   The wide, flat valley floor of a river where silt is deposited during times of flood.

Food chain/web   The transfer of energy through an ecosystem from primary producers to consumers and decomposers.

Footloose industry   An industry which, as it is not tied to raw materials, has a free choice of location.

Formal and informal sectors   The difference between employment controlled by large companies and the government, and employment dependent upon the initiative of individuals.

Fossil fuels   Non-renewable forms of energy which, when used, release carbon.

Fragile environment   An environment which, if it is not carefully managed, may be irretrievably damaged.

Freeze–thaw weathering   A process of physical weathering by which rock disintegrates due to water in cracks repeatedly freezing and thawing.

Front   The boundary between two air masses which have different temperature and humidity characteristics.

Function   The main purpose of a town. Functions include markets, and industry, port and resort facilities.

Geothermal energy   A renewable resource of energy using heated rock within the Earth's crust to produce steam and generate energy.

Glacial trough   A steep-sided, flat-floored glaciated valley with a characteristic U-shape.

Global warming   The increase in the world's average temperature, believed to result from the release of carbon dioxide and other gases into the atmosphere by the burning of fossil fuels.

Green belt   An area of land around a large urban area where the development of housing and industry is severely restricted and the countryside is protected for farming and recreation.

Green Revolution   The introduction of high-yielding varieties (HYVs) of cereals (rice and wheat) into economically less developed countries.

Green wedge   A sector of land in a city where the development of housing and industry is severely restricted.

Gross National Product (GNP) per capita   The total value of goods produced and services provided by a country in a year, divided by the total number of people living in that country.

Groundwater   Water stored underground in permeable rocks.

Groyne   An artificial structure running out to sea to limit longshore drift.

Habitat   The natural environment (home) of plants and animals.

Hanging valley   A tributary valley left high above the main valley when its glacier was unable to erode downwards as quickly as the larger glacier in the main valley, and whose river now descends as a waterfall.

Hierarchy   A ranking of settlements or shopping centres according to their size or the services which they provide.

High-order goods   Products that are usually expensive and only bought occasionally.

High-tech industry   An industry using advanced information technology and/or processes involving micro-electronics.

Honeypot   A place of attractive scenery or historic interest which attracts tourists in large numbers.

Hoyt model   An urban land use model showing wedges (sectors), based upon main transport routes and social groupings.

Human Development Index (HDI) A social welfare index, adopted by the United Nations as a measure of development, based upon life expectancy (health), adult literacy (education) and real GNP per capita (economic).

Humus Organic material found in soil derived from the decomposition of vegetation, dead organisms and animal excreta.

Hurricane See *Tropical cyclone*.

Hydraulic action Erosion caused by the sheer force of water breaking off small pieces of rock.

Hydrograph A graph showing changes in the discharge of a river over a period of time.

Hydrological cycle The continuous recycling of water between the sea, air and land.

Hypermarket A very large shop selling a wide range of goods, usually located at the edge of a city.

Igneous rock A rock formed by volcanic activity, either by magma cooling within the Earth's crust or lava at the surface.

Immigrant A person who arrives in a country with the intention of living there.

Impermeable rock A rock that does not let water pass through it.

Imports Goods bought by a country from another country.

Infant mortality The average number of deaths of children under 1 year of age per 1,000 live births.

Inner city The part of an urban area next to the city centre, characterised by older housing and industry.

Interlocking spur One of a series of spurs that project alternately from the sides of a V-shaped river valley.

Karst An area of Carboniferous limestone scenery, characterised by underground drainage.

Lag time The period of time between peak rainfall and peak river discharge.

Lava Molten rock (magma) ejected onto the Earth's surface by volcanic activity.

Levée (dyke) An artificial embankment built to prevent flooding by a river or the sea.

Life expectancy The average number of years a person born in a particular country might be expected to live.

Linear settlement Buildings spread out in a line along a main road, a river or a railway.

Location the position of a place.

Longshore drift The movement of material along a coast by breaking waves.

Low-order goods Products that are usually low cost and bought often.

Magma Molten rock occurring beneath the Earth's crust.

Malnutrition Ill-health caused by a dietary deficiency, either in amount (quantity) or balance (quality).

Mantle That part of the Earth's structure between the crust and the core.

Market A place where raw materials and goods are sold; a group of people who buy raw materials or goods.

Mass movement The downhill movement of weathered material under gravity.

Meander The winding course of a river.

Megacity A city with a population of over 10 million.

Metamorphic rock A rock that has been altered by extremes of heat and pressure.

Migration The movement of people (and animals/birds) either within a country or between countries, either voluntary or forced.

Million city A city with over one million inhabitants.

Model A theoretical representation of the real world in which detail and scale are simplified in order to help explain the reality.

Moraine Material, usually angular, that is transported and later deposited by a glacier.

Mudflow A rapid form of mass movement consisting mainly of mud and water.

Multicultural society A society where people with different beliefs and traditions live and work together.

Multinational company See *Transnational corporation*.

National Park An area set aside for the protection of its scenery, vegetation and wildlife, so that it may be enjoyed by people living and working there at present, by visitors, and by future generations.

Natural increase The growth in population resulting from an excess of births over deaths.

Negative factors Things that discourage people from living in an area.

Newly industrialised country (NIC) A country, mainly in the Pacific Rim of Asia, that has undergone rapid and successful industrialisation since the early 1980s.

New town A well-planned, self-contained settlement complete with housing, employment and services.

Non-renewable resource A finite resource, such as a fossil fuel or a mineral, which, once used, cannot be replaced.

Nucleated settlement Buildings that are grouped closely together.

Nutrient recycling The process by which minerals necessary for plant growth are taken up from the soil, and returned when plants shed their leaves or vegetation dies.

Overcultivation The exhaustion of the soil by growing crops, especially the same crop, on the same piece of land year after year.

Overgrazing The destruction of the protective vegetation cover by having too many animals grazing upon it.

Overpopulation When the number of people living in an area exceeds the amount of resources available to them.

Ox-bow lake A crescent-shaped lake formed after a river cuts through the neck of, and later abandons, a former meander.

Permeable rock   A rock that allows water to pass through it.

Photosynthesis   The process by which green plants (primary producers) take in sunlight, carbon dioxide and water to produce energy and oxygen.

Physical weathering   The disintegration of rock by mechanical processes without any chemical changes within the rock.

Plate margin   The boundary between two plates that may be moving towards, away from or sideways past each other creating volcanoes, fold mountains, island arcs and earthquakes.

Plate tectonics   The theory that the surface of the Earth is divided into a series of plates, consisting of continental and oceanic crust.

Plucking   A process of glacial erosion by which ice freezes onto weathered rock and, as it moves, pulls pieces of rock with it.

Pollution   Noise, dirt and other harmful substances produced by people and machines which spoil an area.

Population density   The number of people living within a given area (usually a square kilometre).

Population distribution   How people are spread out over an area.

Population explosion   A sudden rapid rise in the number of people in an area.

Population growth   The increase in the number of people in an area.

Population growth rate   A measure of how quickly the number of people in an area increases.

Population pyramid/structure   The proportion of males and females within selected age groups, usually shown as a pyramid.

Porous rock   A rock containing tiny pores through which water can either pass or be stored.

Positive factors   Things that encourage people to live in an area.

Precipitation   That part of the hydrological cycle where atmospheric moisture is deposited at the Earth's surface as rain, hail, snow, sleet, dew, frost or fog.

Prevailing wind   The direction from which the wind usually blows.

Primary industry   An industry, such as farming, fishing, forestry and mining, that extracts raw materials directly from the land or sea.

Pull factors   Things that attract people to live in an area.

Push factors   Things that make people want to leave an area.

Pyramidal peak (horn)   A triangular-shaped mountain formed by three or more cirques cutting backwards, and with arêtes radiating from the central peak.

Quality of life   The satisfaction of people with their environment and way of life.

Quaternary industry   An industry, such as micro-electronics, that provides information and expertise.

Racial tension   A mixture of nationalities in an area that is causing problems.

Range of goods   The maximum distance that people are prepared to travel for a specific service.

Redevelopment   Attempts to improve an area.

Refugees   People forced to move from an area where they live, and so made homeless.

Regeneration   Renewing and improving something that has been lost or destroyed.

Renewable resource   A sustainable resource, such as solar energy or water power, which can be used over and over again.

Residential   An area of a city where people live.

Resource   A feature of the environment that is needed and used by people.

Ria   A river valley drowned by a rise in sea level.

Ribbon development   Settlements that have a long, narrow shape.

Richter scale   The scale used to measure the magnitude of earthquakes.

Runoff   The surface discharge of water derived mainly from excessive rainfall or melting snow.

Rural   An area of countryside.

Rural-to-urban migration   The movement of people from the countryside to towns and cities where they wish to live permanently.

Rural–urban fringe   A zone of transition between the built-up area and the countryside, where there is often competition for land use.

Saltation   A process of transportation by rivers in which small particles bounce along the bed in a 'leap-frog' movement.

Science park/city   An estate, often with an edge-of-city location, or a newly planned city, with high-tech industries and a university link.

Secondary industry   An industry that processes or manufactures primary raw materials (such as steelmaking), assembles parts made by other industries (such as cars), or is part of the construction industry.

Sedimentary rock   A rock that has been laid down in layers, often as sediment derived from the erosion and transportation of an older rock.

Self-help scheme   A method of improving shanty town areas by encouraging and helping people to improve the housing themselves.

Service industry   See *Tertiary industry*.

Services   Facilities that help people.

Settlement function   The main activity, usually economic or social, of a place.

Settlement pattern   The shape and spacings of individual settlements, usually dispersed, nucleated or linear.

Shanty town   An area of poor-quality housing, lacking in amenities such as water supply, sewerage and electricity, which often develops spontaneously and illegally (as a squatter settlement) in a city in a developing country.

Site The actual place where a settlement (or farm/factory) is located.

Situation The location of a settlement in relation to places (physical and human) surrounding it.

Smog A mixture of smoke, fumes and fog.

Soil The thin, loose, surface layer of the Earth which provides a habitat for plants and which consists of weathered rock, water, gases (air), living organisms (biota) and decayed plant matter (humus).

Soil creep The slowest type of downhill movement (mass movement) of soil due to gravity.

Soil erosion The wearing away and loss of soil due to the action of rain, running water and strong winds, often accelerated by human activity.

Solar energy The prime source of energy on Earth, taken into the food chain by photosynthesis in plants, or used by people as a source of electricity.

Solution A type of chemical weathering in which water dissolves minerals in rocks.

Sparsely populated An area that has few people living in it.

Sphere of influence The area served by a settlement, shop or service.

Spit A long, narrow accumulation of sand or shingle formed by longshore drift, with one end attached to the land and the other, projecting out to sea, often with a curved (hooked) end.

Squatter settlement See *Shanty town*.

Stack An isolated piece of rock detached from the mainland by wave erosion.

Stalactite and stalagmite Formed by water containing calcium carbonate in solution, evaporating in limestone caverns to leave an icicle-shaped feature hanging from the roof (stalactite) or a more rounded feature on the floor (stalagmite).

Storm surge A rapid rise in sea level caused by storms, especially tropical cyclones, forcing water into a narrowing sea area.

Stream density The total length of all the streams and rivers in a drainage basin divided by the total area of the drainage basin.

Subduction zone Occurs at a destructive plate margin where oceanic crust, moving towards continental crust, is forced downwards into the mantle and destroyed.

Subsistence farming Where all farm produce is needed by the farmer's family or village, and where there is no surplus for sale.

Suburbanised village A village that has increasingly adopted some of the characteristics (new housing estates, more services) of urban areas.

Super city A city with a population of over 10 million.

Suspension A process of transportation by rivers in which material is picked up and carried along within the water itself.

Sustainable development A way of improving people's standard of living and quality of life without wasting resources or harming the environment.

Swallow hole/sink A hole in the surface of a limestone area, usually formed by solution, down which a river may disappear.

Synoptic chart A map showing the state of the weather at a given time.

Tectonic process A movement within the Earth's crust.

Tenure The way in which a house or land is occupied, e.g. rented or privately owned.

Tertiary industry An occupation, such as health, education, transport and retailing, which provides a service for people.

Threshold The minimum number of people needed to ensure that a specific service (shop, school, hospital) will be able to operate economically.

Traction A process of transportation by rivers in which material is rolled along the bed.

Trade The movement and sale of goods from one country (the producer/exporter) to another country (the consumer/importer).

Transnational corporation A company which, by having factories and offices in several countries, is global in that it operates across national boundaries.

Transpiration The loss of moisture from vegetation into the atmosphere.

Transportation The movement of material by rivers, glaciers, waves and the wind.

Tropical cyclone A severe tropical storm, characterised by low pressure, heavy rainfall and winds of extreme strength which are capable of causing widespread damage.

Truncated spur A former interlocking spur in a pre-glacial V-shaped valley which, during a later period of glaciation, had its end removed by a glacier.

Tsunami A huge wave or series of waves, usually caused by an earthquake on the ocean floor.

Urban A built-up area, such as a town or city.

Urban Development Corporation (UDC) Created by the UK government to promote new industrial, housing and community developments in an urban area with large amounts of derelict land and buildings.

Urban growth When towns and cities get larger.

Urbanisation The increase in the proportion of people living in towns and cities.

Urban land use model A simple map to show how land is used in a city.

Urban sprawl The unplanned, uncontrolled growth of urban areas into the surrounding countryside.

Volcano A mountain or hill, often cone-shaped, through which lava, ash and gases may be ejected at irregular intervals.

V-shaped valley A narrow, steep-sided valley formed by the rapid vertical erosion of a river.

Water cycle See *Hydrological cycle*.

Watershed A ridge of high land that forms the boundary between two adjacent drainage basins.

Water table The upper limit of the zone of saturation found in a porous or permeable rock, or soil.

Weather The hour-to-hour, day-to-day state of the atmosphere in relation to temperature, sunshine, precipitation and wind.

Weathering The breakdown of rocks either by mechanical processes (physical weathering) or by chemical changes (chemical weathering).

INDEX

Note: Geographical locations are indicated in **bold type**.

A

abrasion 246–247
acid rain 178–179, 184
ageing population 11
age–sex structures 8–9, 15–17
aid 154–155
air masses 168
air pollution 60, 100, 178–179
Alaska 106–109
altitude 161
Amazon basin 15, 196–197
anticyclones 166–167
appropriate technology 126–127, 150
arches 253
arêtes 247
Aswan Dam 242–243
attrition 232
Australia 4

B

Bangladesh 4, 260–263
biological weathering 202
biomass 105
birth rates 6–9, 16–17, 156–157
Boscastle 236–237
Brasilia 14
Brazil 14–17, 72–73, 102, 129, 196–197
brownfield sites 57
Burgess model 38

C

Cairo 242
California 26–27, 59
Calcutta (Kolkata) 70–71, 74
Carboniferous limestone 204–209
caves/caverns 201, 205, 253
census data 44–45
central business district (CBD) 38–39, 40, 50–51
Chamonix 138–139
chemical weathering 202
China 12–13, 240–241
cirques (corries) 247–248

cliffs 253
climate 160–185
 British 160–167
 drought 182–183, 208–209
 equatorial 170–171
 hot desert 174–175, 242
 Mediterranean 136–137, 172–173
 monsoon 260–261
 precipitation 162–165
 temperature 160–161
 tropical continental 194
coal 100
coasts 252–265
 flooding 177, 181, 260–263
 management 254, 262–263
 processes and landforms 252–257
 tourist resorts 136–137
Colombia (Almero) 203
Common Agricultural Policy (CAP) 83
commuting 42, 56, 58–59
coniferous forest 195, 249
corrasion 232, 252
corrosion 232, 252
Costa del Sol 136–137
counter-urbanisation 22–23, 56
crust 214–215

D

death rates 6–9, 16–17, 156–157
deciduous woodland 249
deforestation 192, 178–179, 206, 208–209
deltas 70, 235, 242, 262
demographic transition model 7, 16–17
dependents 8–9, 13
deposition 232
depressions 164–165
desertification 208–209
development
 measures of 148–149
 sustainable 98, 126–127, 151
 trade and aid 152–157
diet 94–95
discharge 230–231

drainage basins 228–233
drainage density 231
drought 182, 208–209
drumlins 249

E

earthquakes 62, 212–215, 220–223, 224
Earth's structure 214
ecosystems 186–189
edge of cities 45, 42–43, 55
Egypt 242–243
employment structures 76–77, 156–157
energy 98–111
 biomass/biogas 105
 coal 99–100
 and environment 99, 106–107
 fossil fuels 99–100, 106–109, 110–111
 fuelwood 101
 geothermal 103
 hydro-electricity 99, 102, 240–241
 non-renewable 98–101
 nuclear 99, 101
 oil and gas 99–100
 renewable 98–99, 102–105
 solar 105
 waves and tides 105
 wind 104
energy flows 186–187
Enterprise Zones (EZs) 118–119
environment
 energy 106–109
 farming 92–93
 industry 126–127
 mining/quarrying 135
 tourism 134–135, 137, 140–141, 144–145
equatorial climate 170–171
erosion 232–235, 246–247, 252–253
erratics 249
ethnic groups 20–21, 24–25,

41, 71
European Union (EU)
 farming 82–87, 90
evapotranspiration 228–229
Everglades (Florida) 188–189
exfoliation 202

F

farming 80–97
 arable 85
 commercial 81, 86–87
 and environment 92–93
 EU/CAP 82–87
 extensive 81
 food supply 94–95
 Ganges Valley 88
 Green Revolution 89
 intensive 81
 and irrigation 93, 242–243
 Mezzogiorno 86–87
 pastoral 84
 subsistence 86, 88, 196
 system and types 80–81, 88
favelas 68–69, 72–73
fiords 257
flood hydrographs 230–231, 242
floodplains 235, 239, 262
floods
 on coasts 177, 181, 258–263
 flash floods 72
 of rivers 230–231, 235–237, 240–243, 260–263
food chain/web 186
food supply 94–95
footloose industries 113
forestry 196–197
formal and informal sectors 71, 124–125
fossil fuels 99–101, 178–179
fragile environments 106–109, 143
France 138–139
freeze–thaw weathering 202, 246
fronts 163–165
fuelwood 99, 101

G

Ganges 88, 260–263
geothermal energy 103
Germany 24–25
glacial processes and landforms 246–249
glacial trough 248, 250
global warming 180–181, 197, 259
government policies 52–53, 73, 82–83, 112, 118–119, 123
granite 200–201
green belts 43, 54
greenfield sites 57
Green Revolution 89
Gross National Product (GNP) 148, 156–157
groynes 255, 264

H

Hampshire 254
hanging valleys 248, 250
headlands and bays 252, 264
health 71, 94–95, 149
hedgerows 93
hierarchies 34–36, 48–49, 128
high–tech industries 103, 116–117, 128–129
honeypots 145
hot desert climate 174–175, 242
hot desert vegetation 193
Hoyt model 38
Human Development Index (HDI) 149
hurricanes 176–177, 185
hydraulic action 232, 252
hydro-electricity 99, 102, 196, 240–241
hydrographs 230–231, 242
hydrological cycle 228

I

Iceland 213–215
igneous rock 200–201
immigration 18, 20–21, 24–25, 47
impermeable rock 201
India 70–71, 88, 215–216
Indian Ocean earthquake and tsunami 212, 220, 224–225
industry 112–131
  Brazil 129
  cars 121
  developing countries 124–127, 129
  at edge of city 39, 45, 117

employment structures 76–77, 156–157
environment 126, 238–239
footloose 113
foreign workers 24–27
formal and informal 71, 124–125
government policies 118–119, 123, 137
high-tech 116–117, 123, 128
inner cities 39, 40–41, 44, 118–119
intermediate technology (IT) 127
iron and steel 114–115
Japan 60–61, 123, 128
location factors 112–115
newly industrialised countries (NICs) 122–123
science/business parks 61, 116–117
sustainable development 126–127
system 112
transnational corporations 120–121
infant mortality 8–9, 16
inner cities 20, 40–44, 52–53, 118–119
interlocking spurs 233
Intermediate Technology (IT) 127
Itaipù 102

J

Japan 60–61, 123, 128, 156, 220–223

K

karst 204–205
Kenya 9, 127, 142–143, 157
Kobe 60–61, 128, 220–223
Kolkata (Calcutta) 70–71, 74

L

Ladakh (India) 151
lahars/mudflows 72, 203
Lake District 56, 84, 144–145
land use
  edge of cities 42–43, 45
  inner cities 39, 44
  new towns 48–49
  urban models 38–39, 48–49, 68, 74
  values 38–39
latitude (temperatures) 161
levées (dykes) 235, 239

life expectancy 8–9, 13, 16–17
limestone 200–201, 204–205
location factors 30–31
London 23, 52–53
longshore drift 255–256
Los Angeles 26–27
Lynmouth 236

M

M4 Corridor 131
magma 205, 214, 216
Malaysia 122
malnutrition 94–95
management
  coasts 254, 262–263
  drainage basins 228–245
  National Parks 134–135, 144–145
Manchester 119
mass movement 203
meanders 234
Mediterranean areas
  climate 136, 172–173
  tourism 136–137
  vegetation 192
metamorphic rock 200–201
MetroCentre 54
Mezzogiorno 86–87
migration 18–29
  counter-urbanisation 22–23, 56
  guest/migrant workers 24–27
  international 18
  Mexican migrants 26–27
  push–pull 66–67
  refugees 19
  rural depopulation 66
  UK – into/within 20–23
million cities 64–65
models 6–7, 38–39
monsoon climate 88, 260–261
moraines 249
Mount St Helens 218–219
mudflows (lahars) 72, 203
multinational (transnational) corporations 120–121

N

National Parks 134–135, 144–145
natural increase (population) 6–7, 16–17
New Commonwealth immigrants 20–21
newly industrialised countries (NICs) 122

new towns 48, 73
New York 46–47
New Zealand 103
Nile 242–243, 245
non-renewable resources 98–101
nuclear energy 99, 101
nutrients/humus 186–187, 190, 197

O

ocean currents 161
oil and natural gas 99, 100, 106–109
one child policy 12
Osaka–Kobe 60–61, 128, 220–223
OS map 37, 250
overcultivation/overgrazing 206, 208–209
overpopulation 11, 12
ox-bow lakes 234
ozone 179

P

Pacific Rim 122–123
Paris 31
pedestrianised zones 51
permeable/impermeable rock 201
physical weathering 202, 246
plates (crustal) 28, 214–215
  boundaries 214–215
  collision 215, 216
  conservative 215, 217
  constructive 215, 217
  destructive 215–216, 220–223
plucking (ice) 246–247
pollution
  air 47, 61, 72, 178–179
  water 61, 72, 92, 178, 238
population 4–17
  ageing 11, 13
  birth and death rates 6 9, 16–17
  distribution and density 4–5, 14, 16–17
  growth/trends 6–7, 10–11, 15, 16–17
  migration 18–29
  overpopulation/ underpopulation 11
  pyramids/structure 8–9, 12, 16–17
  under 15s 10–11
porous rock 201